TALLAHASSEE
LIBRARY
COMMUNITY COLLEGE

The Pinocchio Effect

The Pinocchio Effect

On Making Italians (1860–1920)

SUZANNE STEWART-STEINBERG

University of Chicago Press   Chicago and London

SUZANNE STEWART-STEINBERG is associate professor of Italian studies and comparative literature at Brown University. She is the author of *Sublime Surrender: Male Masochism at the Fin-de-siècle.*

The University of Chicago Press, Chicago 60637
The University of Chicago Press, Ltd., London

Printed in the United States of America

16 15 14 13 12 11 10 09 08 07   1 2 3 4 5

ISBN-13: 978-0-226-77448-0 (cloth)
ISBN-10: 0-226-77448-1 (cloth)

The publication of this book is supported in part by the Modern Language Association's Aldo and Jeanne Scaglione Publication Award.

Library of Congress Cataloging-in-Publication Data

Stewart-Steinberg, Suzanne.
The Pinocchio effect : on making Italians 1860–1920 / Suzanne Stewart-Steinberg.
p. cm.
Includes bibliographical references and index.
ISBN-13: 978-0-226-77448-0 (cloth : alk. paper)
ISBN-10: 0-226-77448-1 (cloth : alk. paper)
1. National characteristics, Italian. 2. Italy—Civilization. 3. Nationalism—Italy—History. 4. Politics and culture—Italy—History. 5. Collodi, Carlo, 1826–1890. Avventure di Pinocchio. I. Title.
DG442 .S74 2007
945'.084—dc22

2007015192

♾ The paper used in this publication meets the minimum requirements of the American National Standard for Information Sciences—Permanence of Paper for Printed Library Materials, ANSI Z39.48-1992.

For Pina Swenson

Contents

Illustrations

Acknowledgments

Pinocchio's strings constitute a complex weave of relations that together make up an intricate family romance. While Carlo Collodi created his little puppet primarily for children, he also gave him a complicated family life. In a similar manner, *The Pinocchio Effect* derived its original impulse and continued elaboration from family members in its immediate sense, as well as more broadly conceived. My son Ben's passionate attachment many years back to the story demanded a repeated, indeed, repetitive, engagement with Pinocchio in all his incarnations: in print, in film, and in music. Ben may very well have taught me the extent to which Pinocchio—like all children—insists on his existence. The considerable reserve about such attachments demonstrated by his brother Jonah and his stepbrothers Daniel, Andrew, and Jamie were equally instructive. John Stewart—a Montessorian child—generated chapter 7 in his challenge that I consider the relationship between Montessori's method and Catholicism. My daughter Anna—another Montessorian child—allowed me to attend her classes and thereby come to know Montessori's method as a practice. My husband, Michael Steinberg, was always present to participate in an at times Pinocchian family life and transform such an experience into a text. Julia Stewart tracked down all sorts of errors with great diligence. Gregory and Matoula Halkiopoulos—family by adoption—provided warmth and support at all points. I am deeply grateful to all of my family, young and old, who have sustained me throughout the process of thinking and writing.

Family relations always reach, of course, beyond the immediately private. The bulk of this book was written during my many years at Cornell University as a member of the Department of Romance Studies and within an intellectual environment—as for instance in the Italian Studies Colloquium and the European History Colloquium—that has always fostered an intense and high level of intellectual inquiry. In particular, I would like to thank my colleagues Timothy Campbell and William Kennedy and my students Anna Paparcone, Lisa Patti, and Daniel Tonozzi for their generous support in this project. Dominick LaCapra will always remain one of the mainstays of all of my intellectual endeavors. Julie Copenhagen and Caitlin Finlay at the Cornell Interlibrary Loan Services tracked down even the most obscure requests; this book could not have been written without them. Mary Ahl rescued me at crucial moments from all sorts of computer follies, while also making sure that I met deadlines for grants from the Cornell Humanities Council in order to track down documents in Italian archives.

New colleagues and students at Brown University were especially supportive in the final stages of the book. I am particularly grateful to Massimo Riva for a smooth transition to Brown and a shared passion in Pinocchiology and to Ronald Martinez for a decisive reading of this book. Carolyn Dean responded early on to the chapter about the Italian infanticide debate and improved the argument considerably. My students Benedetta Gennaro, Jessica Laser, Stephen Marth, Emily Morash, Erica Moretti, and Lisa Tom gave generously of their time in order to provide visual support for my text. And Mona Delgado provided much sustenance—emotional and technical—in times of transition.

Beyond the province of home institutions, old and new, comes the input of other interlocutors who have given me sustained and critical support throughout. Judith Surkis has always been a special comrade in arms in the matter of nineteenth-century constructions of masculinity; I cannot imagine thinking without her. And very special thanks are due to Karen Pinkus and Barbara Spackman for their attentive readings of the manuscript for the University of Chicago Press. Svetlana Boym, during many long walks in Berlin, engaged Pinocchiology with intelligence and enthusiasm. Francesca Trivellato is undoubtedly the expert on the phenomenon of Catho-communism, and it is from her that I learned to become attuned to this matter. Luisa Villa pressed me on Sighele's significance for the construction of the postliberal subject. Paola Trabalzini and Elena Dompé at the *Opera nazionale Montessori* provided a warm welcome at the Montessori archives in Rome and generously lent their time and interest in my studies of Montessori. I additionally thank the *Opera nazionale Montessori* for generously allowing me to use and reproduce all the archival and visual materials that appear in this book. Paolo Tappero at Lombroso's Criminal Anthropological Museum not only opened the doors to the museum when they were closed to the public, but also allowed me to rummage through the extensive archive and spent hours on a weekend in Turin answering my many questions. Nanette Salomon, a born Pinocchiologist, queried from the very beginning the existence of master narratives in Pinocchio's trajectories.

Susan Bielstein at the University of Chicago Press has become noted as a "dream editor." This is no myth. I feel particularly fortunate to have been one of the beneficiaries of her singular intelligence and wisdom; from its early stages, *The Pinocchio Effect* has been beautifully managed by her able hands.

This book is dedicated to Pina Swenson, senior lecturer and head of the Italian language program at Cornell University. Many years ago, Sigmund Freud's daughter, Anna, spoke of a phenomenon that she called "retiring in favor of others." Pina has made this practice a central part of her existence—in the classroom with her students, in the training of aspiring graduate students and young faculty, and in the generous support of her colleagues. She trained me as a pedagogue of Italian language and Italian culture; her impeccable taste and unerring understanding of all the issues at stake in this book guided me throughout. She read and reread endless drafts of this book and in her quiet and retiring manner has stood behind all that is positive in what follows. I am deeply grateful for those quiet hours of conversation early every morning when thinking about Italians became for me a possibility.

Excerpts or earlier versions of some of this work have been previously published: a shorter version of the final chapter on Montessori appeared in *Forum Italicum* in the spring of 2006, and a slightly shorter and modified version of chapter 2 on Scipio Sighele's "succubal subject" appeared in *diacritics* in the spring of 2005.

Introduction

It is no longer enough to call oneself a liberal. FRANCESCO DE SANCTIS

The history of Italy between the founding of the unifying constitutional monarchy of 1861 and the rise of fascism in 1922 is the history of a state in search of a nation. It is the history of a fragile political structure in search of a national culture that would authenticate and legitimate it. According to an almost mythic cliché, the Risorgimento leader Massimo D'Azeglio stated: "We have made Italy, now we have to make Italians." As many readers will know, in addition to being attributed to D'Azeglio, these words are also dismissed as apocryphal; such is the mark of founding statements. And yet, despite the post-Unification period's status as a mythical moment in Italian history, this remains a moment strangely under-studied and under-theorized. It continues to be a period virtually unknown to English-speaking audiences and is in Italy still caught in a kind of methodological inertia of a tradition that has typically focused on either the Risorgimento period immediately preceding Unification or on the following fascist period. (There are some exceptions, in particular the work of feminist historians and cultural analysts.) Compared to the rich literature on the French Third Republic or the German Bismarckian period, for example, the second half of the Italian nineteenth century remains a lacuna in theories of modernity and nation-formation. Yet it is the Italian case in particular that can sharpen our understanding of the dual processes of modernization and secularization—if for no other reason than because Italy had the Catholic Church as its home base and as a major political and cultural player after Italian independence. This book seeks to begin to fill this gap.

The fact that in Italy a political structure needed to produce a culture does not imply that politics and culture occupy separate spheres. Indeed, this constitutes one of the primary methodological concerns of my study. I therefore distance myself from the position, so widespread in past and present interpretations of the period, that the split between state and nation paralleled a split between politics and culture. According to this view, one associated above all with the important and influential work of the Marxist literary critic Alberto Asor Rosa, Italian intellectuals felt, and in reality were, separated from the state and from the economic world, and this fact impeded the creation of a group of organic intellectuals capable of actively participating in the transformation of Italy into a modern capitalist society. According to Asor Rosa (1975), this meant that Italian intellectuals tended to engage in a kind of *deprecatio temporum,* in a self-deprecatory staging of powerlessness, as also in a reliance on a precapitalist nostalgia that prohibited effective intervention in the much bemoaned gap between the "real" and "legal" Italys. Thus, according to this narrative, in a country where immediately after Unification 75 percent of the population was illiterate and where only eight out of a thousand Italians spoke the national language, not only were Italian intellectuals, state bureaucrats, and administrators divided over how to convert such a population into an organic unity of Italian citizens, but, more importantly, they were incapable of overcoming their fear of the new.

Anxiety does in fact describe the post-1860 moment. While most Italian nation-makers explicitly committed themselves to the construction of liberal bourgeois culture, they remained profoundly anxious about the disruptions to old orders of politics and culture, the latter certainly including religion. This anxiety is at once political and cultural and, within the context of my argument, fundamental to Italian modernity rather than an impediment to it. While this book is, then, an argument for Italy's modernity prior to, for instance, the country's entry into World War I or the fascist regime, I do intend to take seriously the pervasive rhetorical self-deprecatory gestures that traverse so much of the literature.[1] To say that these gestures were and are rhetorical does not mean that they did not have real effects. I argue, essentially, that the formulation of an Italian national self was predicated on a language that posited marginalization and powerlessness as fundamental aspects of what it meant to be modern Italians. Furthermore, these qualities of marginalization and powerlessness were from their inception linked to other qualities of so-called *italianità:* superficiality, rhetoricism, absence of essence, and a childlike nature.

Two aspects of the project of "making Italians" were central from its inception. First, its rhetoric was not about the emancipation of adults, but instead about the education of children. Even when the focus was on the literal education of children, as in the case of Maria Montessori's work, the metonymic referent was in fact a nation composed only of children. It was this aspect that answered to the idea that Italians were essentially children, that Italy—and this particularly when compared to other modern nations—was in a state of perpetual infancy. The childlike Pinocchio as a cultural icon must, therefore, be understood in these terms. Second, and this aspect addresses especially the idea of powerlessness, this project and its language referred to men or future men only and in that sense was directly concerned with masculine performativity.[2] However, the project of making Italians was not predicated on the simple exclusion of women, even if it did necessitate their exclusion from the political realm. In other words, to say that these discourses were gendered does not imply that they were thereby necessarily ordered by a logic of exclusion. It does, however, imply that gender constructions played a constitutive role in how national discourses were to be made effective, not just rhetorically but in their ability to define what in fact constituted a legitimate political realm. In post-Unification society and culture, it would be the Catholic Church, as I will show in my discussion of the Italian infanticide debate and of the work of Maria Montessori, that most understood this difference and—in its embrace of an extraordinarily complicated politics of marginalization—was thus able to make women the vehicle by which the Church itself returned as a major political actor after 1870.

The educational and gendered language by which Italians were to be made circled almost obsessively around three concerns. The first was the notion that the liberal subject, founded in contract and consent, was no longer viable. All of the writers discussed here shared this idea, and all of them therefore worried about the possibility of articulating a subject capable of existing in a postliberal environment. The second concern was founded in the perceived need to *invent* a national tradition, as Eric Hobsbawm has put it, to create a civic religion that was postulated on reintroducing status into the social contract, or superior and inferior into the world of legal equals. Concretely, the specifically Italian invention of tradition showed all the symptomatic signs of the traumatic rift opened up between the state and the Church, because being an Italian now potentially signified the exclusion of a Catholic identity. The third concern pertained to the fact that the project of making Italians relied on, but also produced, discourses about gender and sexuality (and here Italians were no different from other nation-making discourses[3]), whereby the problem of making an Italian subject came to be lived as a crisis of the paternal function and hence as a crisis of male performativity, on the one hand; and on the other hand, as a positive confirmation of feminine values as a key structuring element that, by virtue of its very feminine nature, required transcending.

These three concerns—the crisis of liberalism, the crisis of religious conscience, and the crisis of paternal, masculine performativity—coalesced in an anxiety about the possible lack of interiority that seemingly described the modern Italian. Indeed, the resultant national subject that emerged from these discourses was an anxious ego, an ego of anxiety—as opposed to, say, a national ego of desire. Of necessity, these discourses in turn generated strategies to deal with this anxiety. They comprised, first, strategies designed to ward off such a perceived lack by relying on a nationally and internationally supported language of sentimentality that still today spans from the heart-warming bowl of pasta, the "latte" available at every Starbucks in the United States, or even the endearing "ungovernability" of Italians, to the more ominous corruption, the Mafia, or the continuous collapses of the country's governments—and this despite the remarkable long-term stability of the country's ruling elite. Until quite recently—and probably not to be excluded from the future political scenario—Silvio Berlusconi perhaps most closely embodies the sentimental discourse of and by Italy, for he is both the "*faccia tosta*" who shows arrogant Europe its own stuffy failings and the demonstration to Italy and to the world of how ungovernable Italians really are; not even its head of state can abide by the most basic rules of propriety. In the fall of 2003, not coincidentally, Berlusconi was portrayed with a long Pinocchio-nose on posters all over Berlin. Roberto Benigni, another recent Pinocchio portrayer and new representative of a childlike Italy, constitutes the other side of this sentimental discourse. Like Berlusconi, he is a clown or endearing puppet abroad, and his inevitable elasticity is so extreme that he is unable to sit still in his chair even at the Academy Awards. Benigni and Berlusconi consistently represent themselves as mortal enemies. Perhaps they are, but whatever the meaning of their interaction, it is nonetheless the case that each of them can be understood as a puppet whose strings are held by the other.

Nevertheless and in opposition to this sentimentalized (self-) presentation, Italian national culture produced from its very inception an extremely refined discourse about the anxiety of its own existence, and it did so, to a large extent, by developing from its inception an understanding of the modern subject as postliberal, a subject, in other words, who existed as the result of a crisis in the political order. I argue that such a subject was not one that had not yet reached modern forms of existence. The myth of Italian backwardness, as John Agnew has described it (1997), was and is just that: a myth buttressed by the idea of Italy's comparatively late industrialization, modernization, and national integration, as well as by the country's stubborn adherence to prototraditional or protoirrational political structures.[4] Yet myth is not fiction, and in these continuous stagings of such a crisis identity, one may detect a quality that was and continues to be explicitly performative, that is, self-conscious of the subject's own fictional status. In the chapters to come, I will insist on these rhetorical or fictional strategies and claim that the discourses that pertained to the making of Italians in the nineteenth century were eminently modern. The specificity of the Italian case may very well lie in the articulation of this fictional identity, though here I would like to render unto such a conception something more profound than the stereotypical designation of Italians as superficial, childlike, or devoid of depth.[5] Indeed, such profundity may be confirmed by the fact that it was Italy, after all, that "invented" fascism as a politics that gave new meaning to a subject who is simultaneously devoid of depth and yet "profoundly" national. In addition, and this too is not a coincidence, Italy developed one of the most powerful and enduring legacies of socialism and communism in Europe, both in terms of theoretical developments after Marx's death and of the pivotal cultural and political role the Italian Communist Party would play until the collapse of the Soviet Union. Both fascism and communism provided powerful answers to the problem of Italian postliberalism. Whether coming from the Right or the Left, the very idea of the constructed nature of the subject took place in conjunction with the perceived crisis of finding a coherent and enduring bond of that subject to the nation in its broadest sense. Thus, the construction of the Italian subject, in the period here under discussion, was closely aligned to the need to formulate something close to a theory of ideology, which is another way of saying that Italian intellectuals in the post-Unification period made important contributions to thinking about the nature of the social bond in the context of a modern, postliberal mass society. This is also another way of saying that theories of ideology are relevant here for both cultural and historical studies, as well as for literary analysis, and this despite all the possible deconstruction one may exert on the relationship between "reality" and fictional and rhetorical structures. In other words, the theory of ideology, in its very *historical* emergence, must ask the question of the relationship between history and theory, between national subjects and the discourses that make these subjects possible.

It is the strange combination of anxiety about the potential emptiness of the Italian subject, his fictional and rhetorical quality, his immaturity and even inhuman, puppet nature, and yet also the profundity of Italian interrogations of the social bond in a modern, postliberal society that I have dubbed the Pinocchio Effect. Pinocchio is neither child nor adult; neither human nor inhuman; neither traditional puppet nor autonomous subject. He does not even belong, in a self-evident manner, to a Western Enlightenment tradition concerned with automata or experiments with the idea of a mechanized subject. At least, I do not use Pinocchio in this latter sense in this book. Instead, I place him here into a broader discourse about the postliberal subject, one who comes into being in the context of a meeting point between two other discourses: that concerned with the problem of ideology, on the one hand, and on the other, with the materiality of life, of a form of biopolitics that in Italy found its most articulated expression in positivism. The figure of Pinocchio is my governing metaphor and Italy's. From his invention and explosive success in 1881, Pinocchio has been both boy and man—his age has been furiously debated; secular renegade and modern, popular Jesus; puppet and free agent. Pinocchio—famously—has no strings; this book is about all the strings to which he may in fact be attached.

A Note on the Ideological Apparatus and on Biopolitics

> A web of microscopic, capillary political power had to be established at the level of man's existence, *attaching men to the production apparatus,* while making them into agents of production, into workers. This *binding of man* to labor was synthetic, political; it was a *linkage* brought about by power. There is no hyperprofit without an infrapower.
>
> MICHEL FOUCAULT, "TRUTH AND JURIDICAL FORMS" (MY EMPHASIS)

Michel Foucault wrote these words as a counterargument to "academic Marxism" and its economic determinism, and he thereby sought to render to power its own autonomy. It is not insignificant the extent to which the theoretical terms of the argument replicate the issue at hand: how and to what degree are subjects attached, bound, and linked to something beyond the self? And to what degree is it possible to articulate a *theoretical* model for such an attachment, a model that has determination (in the last instance or otherwise) and autonomy (relative or otherwise) as its most important stakes? The question at issue here is the problem of the body's attachment to an apparatus, a problem that lies at the center of the constitution of the postliberal subject.[6] In fact, Foucault's insistence on the body's synthetic attachment to the production apparatus echoes Louis Althusser's formulation of ideology as the interpellation of individuals as subjects via the so-called Ideological State Apparatuses. And both Foucault's and Althusser's articulations of the nature of the modern social bond find, as I will show, remarkably similar elaborations in the texts that I analyze in the succeeding chapters.

The point that Althusser insists on is that ideology, rather than functioning as "false consciousness," is first and foremost at the service of the reproduction of the conditions of existence of the capitalist mode of production. In other words, capitalism must continuously reproduce labor power and does this "outside the firm" (1994, 102), in what he calls the Ideological State Apparatuses (ISAs). Entailed here is the (re)production of a fundamental competence: the ISAs must transmit both "know-how" *and* submission to the established order. The ISAs both "ensure *subjection to the ruling ideology* or the mastery of its 'practice'" (104). In speaking to the complexity of this "or," Judith Butler has remarked: "Though one might expect submission to consist in yielding to an externally imposed dominant order and to be marked by a loss of control and mastery, paradoxically it is itself marked by mastery. . . . Neither submission or mastery is *performed by a subject;* the lived simultaneity of submission as mastery, and mastery as submission, is the condition of possibility for the emergence of the subject" (1997, 116–17).

Nevertheless, one must interrogate the nature of these bonds to the ISAs, bonds that Althusser describes as "attenuated and concealed, even symbolic" (1994, 112). It is their very invisibility that makes them ideological. From whence, Althusser's famous formulation of his "theses": "Thesis 1: Ideology represents the *imaginary* relationship of individuals to their real conditions of existence" (123; my emphasis). Nonetheless, since he rejects the conception of ideology as "false consciousness," Althusser also posits his second thesis, to wit: "Ideology has a *material* existence" (125; my emphasis). Such materiality is guaranteed because ideology always exists "in an apparatus, and its practice, or practices. This existence is material" (126). Ideology exists beyond mere "ideas;" it comprises a "consciousness" that drives a subject to a freely accepted act. The materiality of ideology is given by the fact that it exists at the level of the subject, that it is constitutive of a conscience that *must* be converted into an act, an act that in turn must be performed "conscientiously." As Butler points out, to perform tasks conscientiously implies repeating these tasks, which in turn guarantees the acquisition of mastery. Labor is not, therefore, a mere behaviorism or mechanical reaction; nor is it a deliberate project or voluntaristic appropriation of the external world (1997, 118–19). The famous scene of interpellation, the hailing of the individual that makes him turn around and thereby constitutes him as subject, is a scene of conversion (Althusser 1994, 131). The question is: what makes the individual turn around in the first place? On the one hand, one may say with Butler that this turning is a turning of the subject toward him- or herself, a self-restriction that must exist prior to the subject. It cannot, therefore, be thought of as an interiorization of the law, because it predates that encounter. Interpellation already depends on the presence of conscience: "Conscience is fundamental to the production and regulation of the citizen-subject, for conscience turns the individual around, makes him/her available to the subjectivating reprimand. The law redoubles that reprimand, however: *the turning back is a turning toward.* How are these turns to be thought together, without reducing one to the other?" (Butler 1997, 115) On the other hand, and in order to avoid such a reduction, Althusser claims that the act of turning is in fact specular: it occurs in a scene of conversion as recognition. The interpellation of individuals as subjects occurs "in the name of a Unique and Absolute Subject." The "mutual recognition of subjects and Subject, the subjects' recognition of each other, and finally the subject's recognition of himself" are proposed within the context of an "example" of the ISAs, namely the "Christian Religious Ideology." Althusser thereby renders Christianity exemplary of all ideology.

Conscience thus produces the subject in the first sense: as free subjectivity, as a responsibility for one's actions, including the act of turning toward the law. God or the Law produces the subject in the second sense: by posing as the site of reciprocal identification, by constituting itself as the Subject, the subject is subjected, *"stripped of all freedom except that of freely accepting his submission"* (136; my emphasis). The rub lies precisely in this latter exception. The free choice of submission is both what binds the subject to the law and yet also is that element that exceeds the law. It constitutes what Žižek has called a short-circuit between internal belief and the external machine of the law (1989, 43). This short-circuit is also, as many critics have noted, a kind of short-circuit in Althusser's theory of ideology, for what he fails to theorize is the ways in which the subject becomes *attached* to the State Ideological Apparatuses. For Butler, for instance, Althusser fails to account for how the scene of interpellation is also a scene of love, of a *passionate* attachment to the law (1997, 128–29). For Mladen Dolar, Althusser's insistence on clean cuts or breaks, epistemological and otherwise, prevents him from thinking the relationship between exteriority and the constitution of interiority. We are here placed before an impossible choice: "either materiality or subjectivity; either the exterior or the interior" (1993, 77). Dolar goes on to insist that the clean cut is in fact never clean, that in order for it to exist, it must produce a remainder that will come to haunt subjectivity. Dolar names this element beyond interpellation love. While "falling into ideology" takes place at the level of the Symbolic, "falling in love" both grounds and exceeds symbolic law and in that fall gives birth to the postliberal subject, or at least to a subject who exists beyond his/her ideological relation to the state. Love makes possible a psychic space for the subject, but, paradoxically, only in the form of this same subject's passionate attachment to society and state. In this sense, one may say that the subject's autonomy and attachment exist in the form of a simultaneity.

Ideology, as Žižek has stated, "is not all." Nevertheless he insists that, even in the face of the difficulties of drawing a clear line of demarcation between "ideology" and "actual reality," that is, in the face of theoretical models that do not assume the subject as a pregiven entity, we must still "maintain the tension that keeps the *critique* of ideology alive" (1994a, 17).[7] Ideology "is not all" because of that passionate attachment to an apparatus that both Butler and Dolar name love. Ideology produces a certain kind of *pleasure,* one that is not reducible to the effects of ideology. This is a perverse pleasure, to the extent that it exceeds ideologically established norms but nevertheless dictates the subject's movements, his turning around in order to face the law. These two forms in which there is more to ideology than ideology itself—the need to keep the critique of ideology alive and ideology's excess as perverse pleasure—are in fact closely related. In a certain sense, they are both psychotic. On the one hand, then, it is no coincidence that for Žižek the modern form of ideology is grounded in a disavowal: we know that the subject is not a preconstituted being, but nevertheless we must *pretend* that he/she is. On the other hand, the acknowledgement of the perverse pleasures that stand at the basis of our attachment to power require us to believe in the possibility of an autonomous psychic space and make us desirous of our own submission to the structures of power. We actively desire power and yet make that desire subject to "ideology critique."

While the theory of ideology and ideology itself produce an excess of pleasure that neither can control but that nevertheless sustain their effects, both also suffer at the moment of their emergence at the middle of the nineteenth century from a sort of displacement and incursion—due in part to the existence of this same excessive pleasure. Ideology as both an effect and a theory is always an operation that pertains to the state, to what Foucault calls sovereign power, and to the state's involvement in the constitution of subjects. And yet, quite paradoxically, the very idea that subjects are bound to the state in an ideological, that is, imaginary and yet material, manner coincides with the birth of another form of bondage, a disciplinary one founded on the production, management, and enhancement of life. Biopolitics, as Foucault terms this other form of power, challenges the juridico-ideological operations of the state, though, despite its incursions, it does not entirely displace them. The nature of the interaction between these two forms of power in some sense constitutes the central historical and theoretical concern of this book. If sovereign power is challenged in the modern era by the disciplinary knowledges that make up biopolitics, then what relevance does an analysis of ideology still hold? The historical and theoretical interest of the Italian case is located here: to the extent that Italy develops a "historic compromise" between these two forms of power, it constitutes a singularly clear case, within the project of making Italians, of an attempt to theorize the relationship between sovereign power and biopolitics, between state and national culture.

The Italian philosopher Roberto Esposito has recently centered his work on just this relationship (2003 and 2004). In particular, he has focused on the modern "community" as one that simultaneously engages and is traversed by practices and relations of "immunity." I cannot here do justice to Esposito's extraordinarily rich history of what he calls the "immunitary paradigm," one that he traces through a fourfold trajectory that encompasses political philosophy, theology, anthropology, and biopolitics (2003). The advantage of Esposito's work over, for instance, that of Giorgio Agamben or recent recuperations of Pauline theology lies in its rigorous historicization of these discourses and its refusal to return political and cultural thought to "political theology," that is, to ontological categories within what is now being called the "postsecular."[8]

Esposito begins with what has become a dominant obsession in a globalized culture: the individual body is besieged by a diffuse and indeterminate invasion of illnesses, and it can no longer defend itself alone against these attacks. Similarly, the political body is assailed by an Other (immigration or terrorism, the latter especially in the form of biological warfare). And the electronic body, too, is threatened by deviant messages in the shape of computer viruses. Borders, in this new and pervasive cultural *Angst,* are thus seen as threatened, and inside and out perceived to be increasingly indistinguishable. The answer to such a generalized threat to and contagion of the proper by the Other is what Esposito terms the logic of immunization, one grounded in a fundamental paradox. Modern biology has taught us that immunization is created by an injection of the very forces that we fear. If the community is seen to require immunity, this requirement—according to Esposito—is in fact *not* founded in an oppositional relationship between community and immunity. Etymologically, the opposite of *immunitas* is *munus*—that is, service, office, function, and duty, even gift. Immunity therefore signifies a dispensation or exception to a general rule, a particularity or propriety that is not common to all, and also an interruption in and of social circulation (as, for example, in the idea of diplomatic immunity). After the rise of modern medicine, *immunitas* also refers to the body's capacity to ward off a contagious disease. Most fundamentally, in modern bacteriology, immunity is provided by an attenuated form of infection able to protect the body from a more virulent form of the disease.

Though he by no means neglects these multiple meanings of *immunitas,* Esposito is most interested in this last use of the term for his analysis of the modern social bond. Within the confines of the immunitary paradigm, evil is opposed not by keeping it beyond life's borders, but instead by including it through a process of an excluding inclusion or of an exclusion by inclusion: evil is thereby displaced, deviated, deferred but not eliminated. Salvation, Esposito states in language reminiscent of Richard Wagner's *Parsifal,* is bound to a wound that cannot heal because it is salvation itself to have produced it.[9] Immunity, states Esposito, "is the internal limit that cuts the community by folding it back on itself in a form that is both constitutive and destitutive" (2003, 12).[10] The immunitary paradigm is therefore founded in a fundamentally aporetic structure that conditions the language of modernity. On the one hand, the individual qua immunized body constitutes the "proper," that is, the not common, and as such is geared to self-preservation (Esposito 2004, 61). On the other hand, the immunitary paradigm makes evident that life is incapable of self-preservation, that it requires the artificial injection of that which is against itself. Only by negating itself, says Esposito, can nature affirm its proper will to life (2004, 56). The history of the immunitary paradigm is therefore *secularizing* (as it cedes hegemony to a biomedical language of the body) and simultaneously *denaturalizing*.

Central to Esposito's work is a genealogy of Foucault's notion of biopolitics and of the latter's proposition that life, bare life in its biological reality, constitutes the immediate content of modern politics. For Esposito, as for Foucault, such a genealogy encompasses most fundamentally a displacement of sovereign power, and it is this displacement that Esposito names the paradigm of immunity, the capacity, that is, for power to exercise itself as a kind of homeopathic operation that has life at its center. But because "life itself" cannot be managed beyond its existence within a body, it is within the history of the body that Esposito places the history of modern biopower. While, then, the body as a political metaphor seemed to have died around the middle of the seventeenth century (to be replaced by Hobbes's mechanistic, individualistic paradigm and later by contract theories), it was instead, according to Esposito, the progressive rearticulation of this organic metaphor that guaranteed the establishment of the immunitary paradigm, indeed, that made possible a change from this metaphor to its eventual literalization.

Three major steps were necessary for such a literalization to occur. The first centered on the localization of disease. Premodern political theory had explained the death of the political body by internal causes, whether these resulted from natural aging or internecine wars. Given these internal causes, a cure was provided either by re-creating internal equilibrium or by exporting the sick part of the organ. With the rise of interstate contacts and conflicts and with transformations in medical knowledge, the diseases that struck political and individual bodies came to be viewed as coming from the outside: the pathogenic element was now foreign and transmitted by a contagious, infiltrating element not generated by the organism itself. Sixteenth-century medical texts on syphilis and the plague challenged the Galenic theory of humors in the same manner that political theory began to focus on prophylactic measures in order to protect the state against infiltration by allogenic elements. Second, a new relationship between disease and cure found its most important medical expression in Paracelsus's discovery that a cure derived not from a disease's opposite but—homeopathically—from what was *like* it. A similar idea emerged in political treatises: already in Machiavelli, but also in the political theory of Tudor and Stuart England, the political body came to be represented as an integrated system of functions, where potentially destructive elements could be put to productive uses in order to strengthen the whole of which they were a part.

Finally, during the nineteenth century, political and medical discourses were unified into a single language. The clearest example of such a merger was, for Esposito, the one developed by the Berlin cellular biologist Rudolf Virchow. Virchow's main thesis was that the organism was not an undivided whole, but a totality composed of elementary particles that he defined as cells. The body was thus made up of a discrete multiplicity of differentiated entities that interacted and conditioned each other. Virchow's cells were not a mere substratum of the activity of blood and nerves; the latter did not exert a hegemonic relation of center over periphery. Cells had their own specific identity, and they set up relations of mutual independence. Indeed, the regulation of the organism gained in efficiency to the extent that its individual components acted autonomously vis-à-vis each other. Countering the old organicist metaphor, one founded in the hierarchy and absolutist power of the brain and the heart, for Virchow "the life of a people is nothing but the sum of the lives of each of its citizens" (cited in Esposito 2003, 158). Virchow's *Zellenstaat* (cell state) constructed a state conceived as an articulated entity of autonomous and interconnected relations that dispensed with a despotic unity made from above. As Georges Canguilhem has put it, Virchow's biological theory was dominated by political theory: "Who can say whether one is a republican because a supporter of cellular biology, or one is a supporter of cellular biology because one is a republican?" (cited in Esposito 2003, 156).

Virchow's *Zellenstaat* was central, according to Esposito, to the making of modern biopolitical discourse, because it inaugurated the idea of a community that was created by the constitutive differences of its members. The political body was neither an absolute kingdom nor a nation unified by a general will, but a community constituted by the equal differences of its members. And this theory also deconstructed the individual, who was now divided into thousands of fragments united only by their own divergence. It is here, then, that Esposito detects the origin of a politics enclosed within but also constitutive of life. Biopolitics cannot in this sense "be found within the pleats of a sovereign power that includes life by excluding it."[11] On the contrary, he continues, biopolitics "must refer to an epochal conjuncture where at its outset the very category of sovereignty cedes space to, or at least interweaves itself with, the category of immunization. This is the general process within which politics and life come to cross one into the other" (2003, 166).

In the School of the Nation

According to Giacomo Leopardi, perhaps the greatest Italian poet of the Risorgimento, modernity is constituted by one important and singular fact: that by way of its rationalism and demystification it undermines all grounds for (ideological) belief and therefore destroys the social bond. Thus, traditional societies cohere to the extent that they are still capable of galvanizing belief. Modernization is thus, for Leopardi, a paradoxical process, because it leads to science and reason but also to the discovery of a great void, to a fundamental insubstantiality of and in the subject. Modern progress is hence essentially destructive. In his extraordinary 1824 *Discorso sopra lo stato presente dei costumi degl'italiani* (Discourse on the Present State of the Customs of the Italians), Leopardi makes an unexpected claim about his fellow Italians. In opposition to many of the tracts on Italianness written by both Risorgimento nationalists and foreign observers, Leopardi claims that the problem with Italians is not that they are premodern but instead—and this quite paradoxically—that they are *post*modern. Ever since the French Revolution, he writes, Italians have been "philosophers, reasoners, geometers as much as the French and any other nation; indeed, . . . the Italian people is perhaps more so than any other nation. . . . Like all other nations, [Italy] lacks any foundation for morality, any real social bond and conservative principle for society" (1998, 55–56). What distinguishes Italians, in comparison to its neighbors on the other side of the Alps, is the absence of a society or a nation: "the other civilized nations . . . have a conservative principle of morality and therefore of society that, though minimal and almost vile compared to the great moral and illusory principles that have been lost, nevertheless has important effects. This principle is society itself" (50). The principle of society is a powerful illusion because it provides—through such ideological elements as ambition, honor, and etiquette—the basis of a new social bond capable of disguising the void that exists at the foundations of modern life. The "vivacity of the Italian character," the love of spectacle and entertainment, the dominance of the Church, and above all the radical cynicism of Italians guarantee that a closely knit civil society cannot come into being in Italy, thus condemning Italians to life in an absolute and constitutive void: the Italian "disposition . . . is that of a full and constant cynicism of soul, of thought, of character, of customs, opinion and actions" (65).

Francesco De Sanctis—literary historian, pedagogue, and repeatedly Minister of Education—was a careful reader of Leopardi. Indeed, his extremely influential *Storia della letteratura italiana* ends with an assessment of the poet's work for the future of culture in a unified Italy. De Sanctis's was a study that single-handedly constructed the idea of a specifically Italian literary tradition, one that nevertheless was poised on the point of a fundamental paradox. While dedicated to proving the existence of an Italian literature, his book nonetheless depends on the basic argument that Italians quite simply do not exist, except as a retroactive *effect* of De Sanctis's book itself. Crucial here is that De Sanctis echoes Leopardi's characterization of Italians as fundamentally cynical, and he traces this characteristic back to the absence of a Reformation in Italy. While the Reformation brought with it freedom of conscience and rational principles of Bible interpretation, the Council of Trent made religion into a political instrument of tyrannical government. With the erosion of religious belief, however, it was difficult to reimpose faith in Italy. The result was hypocrisy, that is, "the observance of form in conflict with conscience. What turned into a rule of wisdom were dissimulation and a falsity in language, in customs, and in private and public life: a profound immorality that divested conscience of all authority and life of all dignity. The cultured classes, incredulous and skeptical, resigned themselves to this life as a mask with the same ease by which they adapted to foreign servitude and domination. As for the people, they vegetated, and it was in the interest and care of their superiors to leave them to their blessed stupidity" (De Sanctis 1996, 546). And speaking of Goldoni, but immediately generalizing his attributes to that of a national trait, De Sanctis writes: "what he lacked was an interior world of conscience, a world that was laborious, expansive, passionate, animated by faith and sentiment. What he lacked was what has been lacking to all Italians for centuries and that has made their decadence incurable: sincerity and the force of conviction" (758).

De Sanctis consistently relates this insincerity as a lack of interiority to a feminized and feminizing sentimentality, to a rhetorical quality of Italians that severs their relationship with the word and catapults them into the melodramatic world of music and opera. The word is extremely powerful, he states, when it comes from the soul, but when interiority is nonexistent or empty, it becomes insipid and boring. In Italy, the word had become a sound; literature had become music and song. Hence, "melodrama and musical drama are the popular genre, where scenery, mimicry, song and music work on the imagination far more powerfully than an insipid word, a vacuous sonority, which has turned into a mere supplement" (615).[12]

The project of making Italians is founded for De Sanctis in two related gestures. The first is constituted as an act of looking inward, as a kind of soul-searching geared to countering rhetorical excess and sentimentality and to undoing an artificial and vacillating consciousness. The Italian's life is "still exterior and superficial. He must search himself, with clear vision, devoid of all veils and all wrappings, and look at the real and effectual thing with the spirit of Galileo and Machiavelli" (814). The Italian must therefore construct for himself an interiority on a scientific, material basis. The second gesture is closely related to this demand for realism and comprises a mediation between high and popular culture, between the state and the body of the people, between direction from above and active consent from below. Italians must produce an effective and enduring social bond. In this latter sense, De Sanctis argues for the need for a cultural elite, a "valuable nucleus of citizens" capable of expressing the unity of Italian culture (1970c, 104). Culture had to *irradiate* (1970c, 103) or insinuate itself into the last untouched spot of the Italian peninsula: "A society is not remade from one day to the next. The work of education [*educazione*] is slow. But having made it possible that a healthy instruction [*istruzione*] and above all an efficient education gradually implant [*insinuare*] their salutary effects into the humblest of social strata, it is good that we now focus on solidifying that part of society that is on top and from which derives the impulse. One must not forget that the impulse for a united and true Italy came from above" (1970g, 188). National health, De Sanctis states in "La maggioranza," can come only from above (1970e, 161), for if left to their own devices, the uneducated lower classes tended only to their personal interests. Because they could not therefore govern themselves, they were easy prey for false prophets, that is, for radical democrats (1970d, 137).

Nevertheless, classical education was no longer sufficient; particularly if it was understood as mere instruction, in other words, as something imported and repeated in parrotlike fashion (1970c, 102). Today, De Sanctis writes, students are too impatient to hear their teacher sing and to clap their hands in approval; they are too steeped in theatrical habits (1972, 310–11). Knowledge and culture must be acquired in the new Italy by the sweat of one's brow in order to be transformed into a national patrimony. It is for this reason that realism must become the great new educator, realism and all the new sciences of the physical and moral orders, such as economics, pedagogy, and sociology (1970f, 165). Realism and the scientific method "remake life for us and remake a unified ideal. The *conformity* of the ideal with life is the measure of the ideal. A *measured* ideal is a realized ideal" (1970f, 165).

In the conformity and measuredness of the ideal lies the entirety of De Sanctis's educational project. It constitutes the basis for a completely new creation: "It is necessary to remake man, to educate him to this measure," he writes in "La misura dell'ideale." Both antiquated and decadent culture exhibited traits of *scioltezza* (looseness), and thus they refused the human ideal (1970b, 156). A positivist education, while vulgarly perceived as egotism, materialism, and rejection of the ideal, as a thought without imagination and sentiment, is, if properly understood, not a negation of but a counterweight to the ideal: "it inspires that sense of the relative or limit that alone is capable of realizing the Idea" (1970a, 170). Not sufficiently weighted to the ground, Italians tend to absolutize the idea; they understand the idea as an absolute freedom, as something that exists *in opposition* to the limit. Hence they view the state as a force that is contradictory to individual liberties. But such beliefs are nothing but traditions and reminiscences of the past: "Last century's motto was liberty, but this is, for better or worse, a moment that we have absorbed and thus surpassed. Our century's motto is the limit. It is no longer enough to call oneself a liberal. Liberty is a means, not an end. It is an empty form if we do not give it a content—that is, our national life and our ideals. And this content is liberty's limit. This limit prevents liberty from becoming an abstraction, and instead turns it into a living thing" (1970a, 173).

As the result of a sterile instruction that relies on pedagogical methods from the past, De Sanctis's students are, in his opinion, eager to learn, but unready for the great collective project of making the Italian nation. While Italians now have a fatherland, today's sons of the nation, "between one ideal that is satisfied and another that is still to come," lack a sense of direction. They are like husband and wife, as De Sanctis describes it in a now famous simile; they are satisfied and bored because they have not yet attained the necessary seriousness for building a family (1972, 307). Italian students had won their fatherland without having to work for it. Today they have to transform liberty into a positive good; they must give liberty a positive content, and thus imbue a geographical entity with moral and intellectual meaning.

The site where geographical Italy is to be transformed into a nation is the school. For De Sanctis, the school must provide a training in nationhood, just as the nation itself must function as a great school. As Alberto Asor Rosa has pointed out in reference to De Sanctis's use of the concept of 'limit,' the circularity of the relationship between limit and duty exposes De Sanctis to a tautology, whereby 'limit' ultimately means that "our duty as Italians is to be Italians" (Asor Rosa 1975,

866–68). One might say the same for the relationship between nation and school. For De Sanctis, the school must create a moral atmosphere insofar as it is to exert a continuous and all-encompassing influence on students. Simultaneously, and in seeming contradiction to this totalized and totalizing role of the school, students are not to receive knowledge from above; they are not to be limited in the exercise of their minds and bodies. Instead, they must look for and find this knowledge within themselves. School has to become a laboratory where students and teacher work together (De Sanctis 1972, 305). In this scenario, all are actors; nobody is allowed to be a mere spectator, and there will be no master. The student will become a man, his mind and body formed through an act of self-limitation. This is nothing short of—*avant la lettre*—Althusser's notion of turning toward the law in an act of mastery and submission. De Sanctis's limit is thus essentially a limit imposed autoreflexively, and this autoreflexivity produces, paradoxically, a double fissure, one, nevertheless, that constitutes a new subjective bond within the self and between the self and hegemonic culture. De Sanctis's limit creates a subject divided within itself as subject and substantial matter, a subject that is thus capable of recognizing its own determination. As Slavoj Žižek has described such a process in tones that also evoke Esposito's immunitary logic: "We could say, paradoxically, that the subject is substance precisely in so far as it experiences itself as substance (as some alien, given, external, positive Entity, existing in itself): 'subject' is nothing but the name for this inner distance of 'substance' towards itself, the name for this empty place from which the substance can perceive itself as something 'alien'" (1989, 226).

The DeSanctian position has enjoyed a long life in Italy. In the mid-1970s Gianni Rodari, at a conference on *Pinocchio* sponsored by the Fondazione Nazionale "Carlo Collodi," reiterated in virtually identical terms the failure of the Italian school system to provide an *education* for its citizens: "the issue is that of imagining and creating a school where children must not simply learn a given (all told, negligible) quantity of information, but of creating for themselves a free and critical attitude towards knowledge, that is, towards human reality in all its aspects. Children must create for themselves a mind that judges. The condition for this is a school of research and along with it . . . a school of creativity" (Rodari 1976, 55). Rodari gives two examples of how such an educational project can be put into place. The first, and this point is reminiscent of Maria Montessori's educational theories, is provided by an experimental project in an elementary school where the class jointly wrote a book geared to "a pedagogical and didactic project that is fairly complete, given life by teacher and children together" (56). Here the children's imagination took its daily nourishment from the real, a fact that dictated how the children encountered the written word. Rodari's second example is *Pinocchio*—and this directly ties the centrality of Collodi's book to a DeSanctian pedagogy. A reading of *Pinocchio* in Italy's schools today serves, according to Rodari, "to set in motion the energies of the mind and of fantasy, to reawaken . . . the spirit after nocturnal sleep, just like an alarm clock or Mom when they wake up the body" (56–57). This would undoubtedly surprise the truant Pinocchio; after all his escapes from the routines of school life, he would become a teacher, the "animator of activity, the suggestor of interesting work" (Rodari 1976, 57).

And here we come upon Pinocchio's strange status. He is both puppet at the mercy of others, a helpless object of an external will and thus perpetually influenced by and acting at the behest of ideology or "suggestion"; he is also immensely influential himself, the biomaterial animator and suggestor of work, a figure capable of educating while being educated. Pinocchio, as a puppet without strings, is the embodiment of the DeSanctian educational project, for he exists by virtue of a self-limitation whose school is the Italian nation and who, in turn and by a self-reflexive turn, defines the contours of a character trait to be henceforth named as "typically" Italian.

Giuseppe Prezzolini once remarked that those who understood Pinocchio, also understood Italy. Pinocchio's material nature in some manner *binds* him to the Italian national character, a character that is grounded in the problem of governmentality raised by the Italian's peculiar mobility, to wit, his penchant for movement and elasticity, by what Pasquale Turiello will call "*scioltezza.*" It is then no coincidence that the nature of Pinocchio's movement is so strange, for he is *both* a puppet who moves at the behest of an other and an autonomous being who has no strings attached. Pinocchio's *scioltezza,* his unboundedness, his perpetual running has peculiar *effects,* because his looseness hinges on the construction of a social subject who is nevertheless conceived in terms of his puppet status. In other words, such a subject is *nothing but an effect,* bespeaking thus an anxiety about what may lie inside the subject beyond a piece of wood.

Pinocchio is a productive sort of fellow. In this book he functions as a *hinge,* a mode of entry into discourses about the making of Italians that revolve around questions pertaining to his own rather broad field of effects. Indeed, Pinocchio produces an entire apparatus, first and foremost, one that is capable of keeping him, in his own mechanical being, going. Additionally, however, Pinocchio is deeply enmeshed in a national and theoretical apparatus—an ideological state apparatus—that has turned him into a "representative" of the nation and made him able to bring into focus those mechanisms that pertain to the making of the modern, postliberal Italian subject.

The Pinocchio Effect: On Autonomy and Influence

Carlo Collodi's immensely influential novel for children *Le avventure di Pinocchio: Storia di un burattino* [The Adventures of Pinocchio: The (Hi)Story of a Puppet] was first serialized in the *Giornale per i bambini* between July 1881 and January 1883 and then published in a volume in Florence in 1883. *Pinocchio* tells the story of a puppet without strings, created by the carpenter Geppetto, of Pinocchio's travels through the Tuscan countryside, his encounters with magical creatures (talking animals and the Blue-Haired Fairy), repeated encounters with death, but then, at the end of the novel, his transformation into a *ragazzino per bene*—a real or proper, but also *upstanding*, boy. An immediate success, by the first years of the twentieth century, *Pinocchio* had become both a national and international bestseller. It was translated into about two hundred languages and became the basis of not only Walt Disney's 1940 classic film—in all probability a reading of the story that is more familiar to American audiences—but also a favorite object of mass reproduction for the Florentine tourist and international toy industries alike. The book has also spawned an industry of criticism, a significant part of which is dedicated to explaining and celebrating its popular success in Italy as well as abroad. From the very beginning, then, an important aspect of *Pinocchio* has been the text's reproducibility—and this whether this reproduction has been faithful or not. Pinocchio, the little wooden puppet, bears within his body a mechanical quality that makes him—and this despite the fairy-tale world that he inhabits—an eminently modern man.

Pinocchio has exerted, therefore, an influence all of its own. Giuseppe Prezzolini stated in 1923 that those who understood the beauty of *Pinocchio* understood Italy. He has not been the only reader to see some connection between Pinocchio, his status as puppet without strings, and the people and the nation that he represents. *Pinocchio* appears representative of a larger entity—Italy, the Italian subject—which is perhaps why the text suffers from a kind of interpretative overload. Marco Bazzocchi has pointed out that *Pinocchio* criticism is apparently fueled by the desire to convert the text into something else (a real boy, perhaps?) and that it therefore comprises a continuous beating of Pinocchio's body, which—given its wooden nature—it is able to resist (1992, 148–50).[1] One might suspect that its author colluded in this almost hyperinterpretability of *Pinocchio,* enabling later readers to render to the text a kind of exemplary status. References to a long-standing literary tradition, religious allegories, as well as opportunities for a psychologico-pedagogical reading of Pinocchio's adventures abound in the text itself, as if they had been put there to lead the reader on a course that replicates Pinocchio's own frantic running.[2] By virtue of its constant reference to Pinocchio's traditional status, Pinocchio criticism has turned itself into a tradition of its own, one that Jennifer Stone has aptly named "Pinocchiology" (1994). The text invites this, for its primary desire perhaps is to invent a *tradition* of the Italian subject. Nevertheless, and given the prominence rendered to Pinocchio's nose, the puppet appears to be a subject that is self-consciously modeled on a lie, one conscious, that is, of its own status as fiction.

In this chapter I wish to explore four hypotheses that may aid in placing *Pinocchio* into a set of historical and theoretical coordinates, and that thereby might explain the text's immense and enduring success. First, the figure of Pinocchio is born at an approximate midpoint of a set of discourses about the modern subject whose privileged metaphor is that of the puppet. Though it existed already as an object of fascination for Enlightenment thought, the puppet becomes a specifically political figure only at the point when it is linked to a *crisis of attachment,* that is, to a moment when the modern subject's bond to the sociopolitical sphere is sensed as highly problematic. The puppet as a metaphor for the subject's attachment to society arises, then, at the point when the nature of the social bond comes to be questioned and given new impetus. At the center of such questioning are placed the human body and the forces that make it move: Does the body move because it so wills, or does it receive its directions from above? Does it act autonomously, and if it does, are its actions always reliable? Or, alternatively, does the body act on a stage, perform its movements because it must do so, out of an imperative and impetus whose provenance or strings may be either known or unknown? Pinocchio, I then argue, is one site where the crisis of the liberal subject comes to be thought and where the contours of what I have called the postliberal subject find one form of expression.[3]

Second, the discourse of the postliberal subject's problematic attachment, of which *Pinocchio* is emblematic, coincides with the birth of a term that in its own discourse will bind the subject to power by ever-more complicated and puzzling strings; I think here of the term *ideology*. Poised between the materiality of the body and the disciplining project of the modern subject on the one hand, and on the other hand, the divine directive of the subject's theatrical performativity at the behest of an Other—whereby obedience is exacted either blindly or in the name of love (but then is not love always blind?)—the puppet as metaphor of the modern subject is soldered both to the discourse and the workings of ideology. It is for this reason that the ideological subject also coincides historically with the birth of the disciplined body, for the "theory of ideology" asks the question of why and how subjects come to attach themselves to power, why, that is, they either willingly or unknowingly turn themselves into puppets.

Third, and this point is linked to the subject's new existence in the discourse of historical materialism *and* the techniques of Foucault's biopower, the figure of the puppet-subject is tied in complex ways to the process of secularization, the displacement, that is, from religious to secular cultural categories. Within the context of my present concerns, *Pinocchio* plays a crucial role in this displacement, insofar as Collodi's text exists within and negotiates both religious and secular domains. And one may recall here Walter Benjamin's famous First Thesis on the Philosophy of History, where the puppet called Historical Materialism wins all chess games because it has enlisted the services of theology as its hidden and thus invisible puppeteer (1969, 253).

Fourth, given that *Pinocchio* addresses the problematics of both ideology and biopower, the text depends for its own narrative consistency on a reliance and an elaboration upon two other terms: *suggestion* and *love*. While suggestion seems to emphasize the puppet's strings, in other words, seems to describe some power of influence—visible or not (and in fact, the powers of suggestion become more invisible as the century progresses)—love appears to be linked to a subject whose space is assumed to be autonomous, independent, and private. *Pinoc-*

chio constructs a compromise figure: while the subject of suggestion is a kind of puppet, the subject of love has been able to cut its strings. Nevertheless, this compromise becomes increasingly problematic and entangled, especially in the last decades of the nineteenth century, and it is this very entanglement that will allow for discourses of the postliberal subject to sustain themselves in the face of mass politics.[4]

By bringing these four hypotheses to bear on the text, I do not wish to provide here simply another reading of Collodi's little puppet. Instead, I propose Pinocchio as one site in and through which questions of the Italian subject came to be worked out in late nineteenth-century Italy, to the extent that he embodies broader social and cultural conflicts centered on the problem of the postliberal subject's increasingly contested autonomy in the face of forces beyond his control. In this sense, I apply the terms *autonomy* or *inside* and *influence* or *outside* not only to reflect this beleaguered subject, but also to indicate the text's place within a wider historical context. I also wish to think of the relationship between "inside" and "outside" at a level that pertains to the methodological problem encompassing the relationship between text and context, but exceeds it insofar as my own text is put into play here, and this not only via its own investments, but more broadly as perhaps the most pressing methodological problem confronting cultural analysts today. I speak here of the demand that theoretical sophistication not occur at the expense of historico-cultural sensitivity, and vice versa, that our theoretical apparatus not give way to cultural relativism and descriptivism and hence give up on its critical edge. The relative autonomy of theory and history having been asserted, however, the goal must still be to move beyond elegance of style or what Dominick LaCapra has called "weak montage," wherein theory is simply made to weave as flawlessly as possible between the ins and outs of history (1989, 193). My explicit aim here, as also throughout this book, is to have text, context, and theory inform each other, remain in dialogue and tension with each other. The goal is to steer through overcontextualized readings of a text that obliterate the text's autonomy, on the one hand, and on the other hand, overly presentist readings that refuse the traces of its influences. In this sense, I attempt to take seriously LaCapra's warning that "extreme contextualization of the past in its own terms and for its own sake may lead to the denial of transference through total objectification of the other and the constitution of the self either as a cipher for emphatic self-effacement or as a transcendental spectator of a scene fixed in amber. By contrast, unmitigated 'presentist' immersion in contemporary discourses, reading strategies, and performative free play may at the limit induce narcissistic obliteration of the other as other and the tendency to act out one's own obsessions and narrow preoccupations" (1994, 34).

Pinocchio's Brothers

When Pinocchio entered the puppet theater, an incident occurred that caused a near revolution. . . . "It's Pinocchio! It's Pinocchio!" shout all the puppets in chorus, leaping out from the wings. "It's Pinocchio! It's our brother Pinocchio! Long live Pinocchio!"
CARLO COLLODI, *THE ADVENTURES OF PINOCCHIO*

In the relative autonomy or relative influence to be established between text and context, Collodi's novel requires us to think about the revolutionary environment evoked by the author himself, an environment that comes into being through Pinocchio's brotherhood and not through any reference to a paternal tradition. Pinocchio's first set of brothers come, as is made clear by his reception in Fire-Eater's theater, from the world of puppets (see fig. 1.1). Indeed, Fire-Eater's theater constitutes a restaging, as Antonio Gagliardi has aptly noted, of Freud's society of the primal horde, that band of brothers at the mercy of but in constant revolt against a ruthless and cruel father (1980, 67, 69). In 1884 Collodi's friend Yorick Figlio di Yorick (the lawyer P. C. Ferrigni) wrote his *Storia dei burattini* (The History of Puppets), and it seems entirely legitimate to read it as a companion piece to Freud's *Totem and Taboo.* Yorick tells the story of Italian puppets as one that is intimately tied to the fortunes of Italian national popular culture, to the history of secularization and—by extension and as a consequence—to the nar-

Figure 1.1 Carlo Chiostri, *Pinocchio's Brothers* (1901).

rative of a family romance of whose vicissitudes through paternal authoritarianism and filial freedom the puppets are emblematic (1884).[5] Indeed, their condition as puppets functions, for Yorick, as an allegory of the Italian spirit through the ages. Until the advent of the Renaissance, puppets, whose birth Yorick had traced back to the creation of religious idols, had been firmly bound to the Catholic Church. Marionettes, he claims, are etymologically related to the "mariettes," that is, to small figurines representing Mary. The puppets performed, in fact enacted, the Church's message in the shape of mystery plays, thus tying themselves, in their wooden being, to Christ's death on the wooden cross in their emulation of worldly suffering. The puppeteer is a god and has a relation of filiation with his puppet sons who daily enact their own deaths and resurrections for their father. The puppets are affixed to their own crosses, and their strings are nailed to their bodies in imitation of the stigmata (see figs. 1.2 and 1.3).

But these strings snap with the arrival of secular culture. This is a break that constitutes a crisis and a turning point for the puppets and their historian alike, and it has the potential of turning the puppets into men: "Once the age-old chains have been broken—chains that had made puppets the ultimate slaves of sacerdotal power—very suddenly the thread of historical memory is broken as well. This thread had guided us along the tracks made by our interesting little wooden figures up until the age of the Renaissance" (Yorick 1884, 104). And with the interruption of the tradition, darkness reigns over the first independent life of the rebellious marionettes. It appears, however, that, like Pinocchio, they take to the squares and the roads of Italy and that they gradually merge with and eventually take over the *commedia dell'arte* tradition. Undoubtedly, these are for Yorick the golden years for Italian puppets (and for Italian masculinity), years in which they will blossom under Goldoni's reform of the theater and when they keep alive popular culture and social satire. It is here that they take on, despite regional differences, the character of *national* subjects: "the marionettes have preserved their place in the national theater. With the poisonous blade of satire, they have wounded all abuse, prejudice, and arrogance; all utopias, all religious, political, literary, social, scientific, and economic tyrannies. They defended Galileo against the Inquisition, Giordano Bruno against the Holy Office. . . . They attacked feudalism, intolerance, priestly celibacy, the starched and inflated Classicism of the Academies, court intrigues, cheating speculators, military conceit, the insolence of friars, and feminine corruption" (105–6).

Figure 1.2 Giotto di Bondone, *St. Francis of Assisi Receives the Stigmata*. Fresco. Upper Church, S. Francesco, Assisi. (Photo © Scala/Art Resource, New York.)

Figure 1.3 Fra Filippo Lippi, *The Virgin Adoring the Child, with Saints John the Baptist and Bernard of Siena* (*The Adoration in the Forest*) (ca. 1459). Oil on poplar. (Photo: Joerg P. Anders. Gemäldegallerie, Staatliche Museen zu Berlin, Berlin, Germany. © Bildarchiv Preussischer Kulturbesitz/Art Resource, New York.)

As a consequence of the puppets' revolutionary acts aspiring to freedom, the Eternal Father, who had in the past always been present on the scene in order to counteract the doings of Satan, took flight; he "indignantly left the scene, and the devil remained . . . as was natural. He really felt at home! . . . Indeed, by the end of the last century and the beginning of our own, when the puppet theater was invaded by romantic literature and fairy tales, the Devil-puppet did good business, for instead of dying, he took a wife and peopled the stage with his bizarre and numerous progeny of both sexes: the magician, the Fairy, the Genie, the Monster" (Yorick 1884, 180). For Yorick, these are the most glorious years for Italian puppets. Having freed themselves from the power of God and Church, they can freely exercise their imagination and become the vehicles for a renewed and imaginative national character. And yet, "being made of wood does not protect them from the influence of progress!" (166), for Yorick's puppets are soon assailed by two forces that undermine their newly gained freedom. For one, the puppets of Yorick's time strive for too much realism. They try too hard to look like real actors and thereby lose their own specificity, that is, their ability to make fun of the real world. Second, one of their greatest talents—their extraordinary capacity for dance[6]—has been converted into choreographic exercises or spectacles that reduce the puppets' feats to mere gymnastics and acrobatics. All of this is leading to a *mechanically produced realism,* whereby puppets are acquiring a new form of dependence, one no longer dictated by the Eternal Father, but by the technological exactness of machines: "If we go on like this, puppets will gradually turn into automata, and the puppet theaters into marvelously and smartly conceived machines. And then, good-bye to originality and inspiration, to the direct and immediate actions of the puppeteer's ingenuity!" (202) Cinema, George Bernard Shaw predicted, would kill puppets (see fig. 1.4).[7]

Figure 1.4 Emile Reynaud, *Theatre Optique* (1889). (New York Public Library.)

Slightly earlier than Yorick's *Storia,* in 1872 Francesco De Sanctis asked each of his students at the University of Naples to produce a verbal portrait of Pulcinella. One of the submissions, from Giorgio Arcoleo, has been preserved, for it was published as part of De Sanctis's response to Arcoleo in *La Nuova Antologia* in August of 1872 as the essay "La Scuola."[8] According to Arcoleo, while for Hamlet, Faust, or Prometheus reality is a struggle to be confronted with the concentration of thought and the profundity of feelings, for Pulcinella reality is but a plaything; he merely floats on the difficulties of life. Pulcinella lacks sensitivity, he is only "mechanically moved by the pain of others, like the telegraph that registers the defeats at Sadowa or Sedan, or like a minister of finance who, by a stroke of the pen, casts a thousand families into misery" (Arcoleo 1972, 499). And yet Pulcinella is a strange compromise formation between the new and the old, for not only is he mechanically moved, he is also one of those popular characters who are the product of an instinct of rebellion against reason. Not imprinted by art, such characters exist in some liminal state between inside and out, they are "half men, half puppets, idols of the people when the people live off milk and honey, but toys that are to be broken when the people enter the intimacy of conscience" (500).

Pulcinella lives under Neapolitan skies and is the product of what Arcoleo views as an essentially theatrical culture. Half animal, half man, Pulcinella has survived in the theater like a *deus ex machina,* denying representation and reigning in person. A mask covers his face but never his soul. His large nose reminds us of the general Neapolitan type. His world, Arcoleo continues in a vein reminiscent of Baudelaire, is the accidental, the fugitive, and the present. His language is made up of paraphrase, equivocation, noise, lies, and nonsense. Pulcinella is marked, above all, by the fact that he is outside himself. His home is on the streets beyond domestic walls. He is beyond religion; his love lies not in the soul but in the senses; his life not in conscience but in form. His tendencies are material, his problems gastronomical. He believes in illusions, appearances, the resurrection of the dead, magic, the lottery, and the devil, but not in himself. Pulcinella is thus everything except himself (Arcoleo 1972, 506).

And the people call him brother (501). They recognize in him the indolence and superstitions of the Neapolitan people, whose good qualities are suffocated under a mountain of prejudices, and who, though now freed from political and religious tyrannies, are still willing to enslave themselves to old privileges and habits. Pulcinella and his brothers lack the required seriousness for life, they have not learned the lessons of 1789. And yet, Arcoleo predicts, Pulcinella will fall because the alphabet will kill him. When the Neapolitan masses start to act like citizens, Pulcinella will have to withdraw completely to the theater, he will be transformed from flesh to wood. Once the people distance themselves from him, his laugh will become mechanical, indeed, pathological. Then reality will be perceived with the necessary seriousness: as difficult and angular, as something to be confronted not with a song but with the iron hammer of will and the joys of labor.

Ten years after Arcoleo's study of Neapolitan popular culture, and while *Pinocchio* was appearing in the *Giornale per i bambini,* the southern writer Pasquale Turiello was busy on a large and widely read study of the Italian national character in a book entitled *Governo e governati in Italia.* Availing himself of historical, ethnological, anthropological, and mythical materials, Turiello attempts here to give a picture of the Italian mentality and collective imaginary as it had come to be shaped during the first two decades of national unification.[9] What he finds is a lack of collective imaginary, or what he also calls organicity. And yet Turiello does, quite paradoxically, detect a *national* character, one whose purest form is to be found in the Neapolitan. What defines the Italian, according to Turiello, is his individualism, his refusal to submit to a collective definition, because such a definition would require that he accept external limits and discipline. While Germans, for instance, are devoted to subordination and thus are "natural subjects," Italians have no sense of external limits. The Italian "I" is too prominent, too superabundant, and this fact leads to diffidence not only in the social and civic spheres, but also to a diffidence toward the self.

The key term that for Turiello describes the Italian national character is what he calls "*scioltezza*"—a looseness or elasticity of both mind and body. *Scioltezza* is simultaneously an excess and a lack of affect or imagination that points to an overdevelopment of individualism *and* to its absence.[10] This paradox leads to a state of perpetual civil war not just between individuals but also within the individuals themselves (Turiello 1994, 39), whereby they both refuse all social limits and engage in a cult of power. The Italian refuses all civic ties and instead produces personalized relations of power. Such personalized relations inform the Italian penchant for clientelism, secret sects, banditry, and the Mafia. *Scioltezza* guarantees the predominance of the personal over the social in all aspects of life: family over civic duties, usury and quick financial gain over industry and the social division of labor. In art, Italians prefer the human form to landscapes; in religion, the Catholic Church could not sustain itself without the cult of images; in music, melody and song predominate over complex harmonies and choruses.[11] While the Italian bourgeois and cultural elite has tended to the care and refinement of its cleverness, to its beautiful prose at the expense of good works, while public entertainment has brought pleasure but not created a brotherhood, the children of the poor have acquired the character traits of puppets in the face of the complete failure on the part of public education to turn them into modern workers and citizens. National public administration has produced only negative results, and what, Turiello asks, are the uses of freedom, taxes, people's delegates, and citizenship if all these things have brought about a worse situation than the one created by tyranny?

It is clear to Turiello that in order to make Italians, one must unmake all forms of clientelism, banditry, sectarianism, and party politics, as well as promote free and honest ties between individuals within the framework of a unified authoritative state. What is needed, then, is a doubly pronged movement that simultaneously ties and unties social relations as they currently exist. "Rousseau, in his *Emile,* imagined the best education of the child as one that most untied [*sciogliere*] him from the moral chains of law and convention" (Turiello 1994, 89). However, while northern and Protestant countries have more faith in individual initiative, Turiello continues, southern countries must create a cohesive social unity via the opposite route, that is, through the authority of the state. And yet, Turiello does not advocate repressing the Italian national character—an effort that would in any case be futile, because its *scioltezza* would resist such an external limit. The Italian cannot be tamed if he is not persuaded. His freedom must be *educated* rather than destroyed. Because the Italian is, in his looseness, elastic, the best result will come from a vigorous push: "As with an elastic body, here the greatest fruit of his natural elasticity will be obtained by a vigorous push [*una spinta vigorosa*] that will then leave him free in all his successive movements" (Turiello 1994, 17).

The Pinocchio Effect

Shortly before his suicide in 1919, Victor Tausk, one of Freud's most promising disciples, published an essay entitled "On the Origin of the 'Influencing Machine' in Schizophrenia" (see fig. 1.5). Encountered as an important phenomenon among a broader symptomatology in schizophrenic patients, the influencing machine is described to Tausk

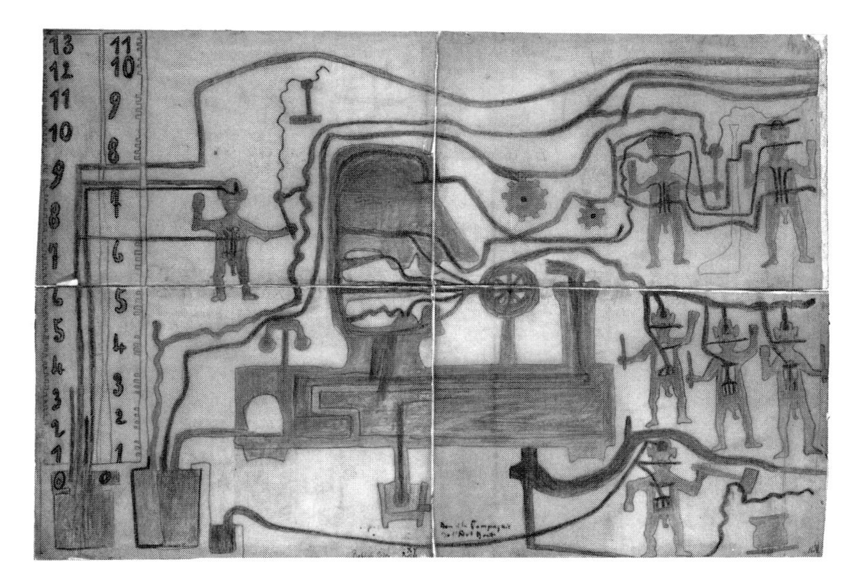

Figure 1.5 An influencing machine. Robert Gie, *Distribution d'effluves avec machine centrale et tableau metrique* (ca. 1916). Pencil and color crayon on paper, 48 × 69 cm. (Photo © Claude Bornard. Collection d'Art Brut, Lausanne, Switzerland.)

by his patients "as a machine of mystical nature. The patients are able to give only vague hints of its construction. It consists of boxes, cranks, levers, wheels, buttons, wires, batteries and the like. Patients endeavor to discover the construction of the apparatus by means of their technical knowledge, and it appears that with the progressive popularization of the sciences, all the forces known to technology are utilized to explain the functioning of the apparatus. All the discoveries of mankind, however, are regarded as inadequate to explain the marvelous powers of this machine, by which the patients feel themselves persecuted" (Tausk 1991, 186). Such a machine, like a magic lantern or a cinematograph, has the power to make patients see pictures. It furthermore has the ability to both produce and remove thoughts and feelings. It is therefore a kind of "suggestion-apparatus" that exerts its power through the use of mysterious rays or forces. It also can produce motor phenomena in the body that deprive patients of their will or even their sexual potency. Here, too, such deeds are accomplished by means of "suggestion or air-currents, electricity, magnetism or X-rays" (187). And last, the influencing machine is more generally capable of generating bodily responses and sensations beyond the patients' control and beyond their ability to describe or explain these responses' provenance. The machine, most frequently connected to the patients via invisible wires, is at the service of enemies, because it persecutes its victims for unknown reasons and by unknown means.

For Tausk, the influencing machine represents the terminal stage in the evolution of psychotic symptoms, symptoms that begin with internally perceived sensations of change and/or estrangement. The influencing machine is thus simultaneously a reaction to and a making sense of the disruption caused by change. Given the "need for causality that is inherent to man" (188), Tausk remarks, the schizophrenic patient *constructs* this apparatus in order to account for what Tausk sees as only internal changes within the patient him- or herself. Such a machine is constructed because these changes cannot adequately be addressed either at the level of the ego or of the holding environment. The influencing machine is, then, for Tausk, the result on the patient's part of an effort at self-cure, a mechanism put in place to furnish an explanation for the subject's very existence in the world. In the absence of better theories, the influencing machine is a figure, a space of negotiation for the articulation of the ways in which *all* human beings at their earliest stage of development take the outside inside them and thus become constituted as subjects. Tausk finds himself here in profound agreement with Freud's own theory of the constitution of the ego: "Freud emphasized that the infant's conception that others knew its thoughts has its source in the process of learning to speak. Having obtained its language from others, the infant also received thoughts from them; and the child's feelings that others know his thoughts as well as that others have 'made' him the language and, along with it, his thoughts, has therefore some basis in reality" (215n5).

What causes, Tausk asks, "the formation of the ego and, as a reaction to the outer world, the ego boundaries, and what arouses the realization of individuality, of self, as a distinct psychical unit?" (199–200). I would like to depart here from Tausk's more narrowly clinical answers to these questions and focus instead on two points that he makes early on in his essay. The first point: "We may say that in the case of an impaired ego organization, the ego finds itself facing the task of mastering an insane outer world, and hence behaves insanely" (201). The second point: "We are familiar with [the] infantile stage of thinking, in which a strong belief exists that others know of the child's thoughts. Until the child has been successful in its first lie—the parents are supposed to know everything, even its most secret thoughts. . . . The striving for the right to have secrets from which the parents are excluded is one of the most powerful factors in the formation of the ego, especially in establishing and carrying out one's own will" (199).

And here we enter the world of Pinocchio, a world conceived as an influencing machine that binds its subjects by invisible wires, a world where the "popularization of sciences" points to the growing influence of technology but where the latter retains some of its marvelous qualities. While there are few references to technology in the story of Pinocchio, its many animals nonetheless prefigure the new means of transportation and the experience of the speed of the modern age (Gasparini 1997, 120–21; see fig. 1.6). Pinocchio's world is one that struggles with its rights to privacy—the Italian language lacks this word, symptomatically, altogether—but also one where the right to have secrets must be established in the form of a lie. This is also a world portrayed by Collodi from the very beginning as an insane world, one where innocence is punished with imprisonment and where only the strongest and cleverest succeed and rule.

Here is a brief overview of Pinocchio's adventures. The carpenter Master Anthony—better known as Master Cherry on account of his red nose—is the first owner of a piece of wood that he plans to make into the leg of a table. Upon carving, however, the wood cries and laughs like a child and, horrified, Master Cherry passes the wood on to Master Geppetto, another carpenter, who wants to carve a beautiful puppet with which to take to the roads of Italy and make some money. Geppetto, too, has his problems with the puppet that he names Pinocchio: no matter how much he carves, Pinocchio's nose grows insistently, and as soon as he has his legs, Pinocchio escapes. Geppetto is arrested and sent to jail, while Pinocchio must immediately fend for himself. His first encounter with a magical creature—the Talking Cricket—ends badly, for rather than heeding the cricket's advice to be good, Pinocchio crushes the bug against the wall. Geppetto returns, feeds the starving puppet, buys him a schoolbook, and sends him off to school. From this point on begin Pinocchio's adventures that take him not to school, but to Fire-Eater's puppet theater, where he is able to earn five gold coins; into the arms of the Cat and the Fox, who want Pinocchio's money; and finally to his encounter with the assassins (the disguised Cat and Fox) and therefore to his execution by hanging on the Great Oak Tree. Dying (with the gold coins hidden in his mouth), Pinocchio cries for his father: "Oh, dear father! . . . if only you were

Figure 1.6 Carlo Chiostri, *Pinocchio's Flight* (1901).

here!" Pinocchio remains hanging from his cross, "as though frozen stiff."

In this manner ends chapter 15 and what, in the serialized version of the story, Collodi planned to be the last installment. However, and true to both Christian doctrine and market demand, Pinocchio is resurrected. He is cut down from his cross and tended to by the Blue-Haired Fairy. When Pinocchio tells his first lie, namely, that he has lost all his gold coins, he grows a long nose. He comes clean, gets his cute nose and money back, and is sent off to his father, once he has promised the Fairy that from now on he will go to school. Pinocchio meets the Cat and the Fox again, who promise him that if he plants his coins in the Field of Miracles, his money will grow on trees. He is robbed of his coins and as a punishment must go to prison in the land of Catchafool. Once released, he meets the Serpent, who laughs herself to death. Then he is turned into a watchdog and finally arrives at the Island of the Busy-Bees. Here he meets the Blue-Haired Fairy again, who, now as a mother figure, teaches Pinocchio the benefits of hard work and school and promises to turn him into a proper boy. But the influence of the bad boy at school, his friend Lampwick, sends Pinocchio off to Funland, where there are no schools and no work, but where boys are transformed into asses. As an ass, Pinocchio is sold to a circus, and when he goes lame, he is sold again for his hide. Pinocchio is saved and then takes to the sea. He meets the Great Fish, is swallowed by him, and in the belly of the fish finally meets up with his father again. Once they make their escape and return home, Pinocchio works at many jobs for little pay, takes care of his father, and finally earns the right to become a *"ragazino per bene."*

With Pinocchio, we move into a new episteme when compared to the older Risorgimento project of national liberation. If, as Antonio Gagliardi has remarked, Manzoni's hero Renzo of *I promessi sposi* had to confront a crisis of reality, Pinocchio's problem is a crisis of the self (1980, 11). Such crisis takes upon itself the massive burden of distinguishing between "subject" and "suggestion."[12] The crisis is thus one of determination, of causality, as Tausk so rightly understands. Pinocchio's crisis—the requirement that he move from a logic of suggestion, or influence, to one pertaining to the autonomous subject—raises the question of origin, though this is an origin predicated, paradoxically, on its loss. A DeSanctian unoriginal originality—an autonomy that inevitably appears as coming from somewhere else—will henceforth describe and prescribe what it means to be an Italian subject. Thus, while

Carlo Collodi may have inherited the Manzonian theme of conversion, Manzoni's conversion had been a religious one, since it originated from above. For Manzoni, Gramsci once remarked, people have no interior life; they lack a deeper moral personality (Gramsci 1977, 87). For Pinocchio, who lives in an age when it is no longer possible to be either a religious subject or a liberal one, the process of conversion is far more complicated: it will remain incomplete and generative of its own peculiar and unpredictable effects.

Carlo Collodi's *Pinocchio* directly engages Yorick's claim that the modern mechanical age would both kill the puppet and give birth to a new man so disciplined and manageable that he would be indistinguishable from his wooden predecessor. While Tausk recognized the psychosis at work in the modern world as it turned subjects into the spectral objects of a cinematic apparatus, while Yorick was bemoaning the end of a long cultural tradition turned now into gymnastic feats and spectacles, Collodi was occupied with giving birth to a creature whose sole purpose was to run and dance, and thus he sought to give new life to a dying tradition. While Arcoleo threatened Pulcinella's death by the alphabet, Pinocchio and his school friends deftly turned the tables on the whole affair and, using copies of Collodi's own pedagogical tracts, engaged in a battle of the books whose content was indigestible even to the fish. And while some proponents of the Italian gymnastics movement promised, as I will discuss, a new man by reattaching him to the strings of a gymnastic apparatus, Collodi cut all strings and turned Pinocchio first into a puppet without strings and then into a proper boy.

Antonio Gagliardi has noted that Pinocchio's body constitutes a remainder, a difference or foreignness capable of generating a disturbance in the economy of capitalist expansion into an agrarian countryside that the critic perceives as still tied to the instinctual cycles of nature. The fundamental problem in *Pinocchio* is, for this critic, therefore, that of the relationship between the bourgeois state and the subaltern masses, of the relations inside and outside of the workplace, of the construction of a social conviviality that is predicated on the construction of a new social subject, to wit, the salaried laborer. Gagliardi thus distinguishes two economies in the text: on the one hand, an older, natural one founded in the laws of violence (as exemplified by Fire-Eater's theater), betrayal (the Fox and the Cat), and mendicant artisanship (Geppetto and Master Cherry); and, on the other hand, a new economy predicated on the autonomy of behavior founded in wage labor. Pinocchio's wooden existence, the fact that his makeup recalls the laws of nature, puts him into conflict with a civil society where the state apparatus functions as the fundamental mediator of existence (Gagliardi 1980, 8–9). As absolute difference, as an antibody, Pinocchio lacks self-sufficient values; his needs are continuously rendered subaltern and self-destructive. Pinocchio is beneath reality because this reality speaks in a language that is foreign to his own code: "From the depths of the process of nullification, from the dark grounds of depersonalization, Pinocchio can speak without naming himself, disappearing as subject from both praxis and language. A foreign image creates for him and confirms a truth within which Pinocchio is only a spoken object: 'How funny I was when I was a puppet! And how glad I am now that I've become a proper boy!'" (Gagliardi 1980, 12).

Gagliardi makes these remarks with reference, of course, to Pinocchio's last and final transformation into a *"ragazzino per bene,"* an ending that Collodi does not remember ever having written! Pinocchio's is not so much a transformation as it is a displacement. The puppet does not turn into a boy but leaves behind his wooden existence, and the latter's remnants are left lifelessly propped up in the corner of the room (see fig. 1.7). The peculiarity of this transformation has been the subject of much debate: Why does the puppet remain, and what is the nature of the hilarity provoked by it?[13] And what is the nature of the final *perbenismo,* the propriety that in its doubling appears so improper? If *perbenismo* can simply be reduced here to normalization, then this still leaves open the question, as Pietro Toesca has pointed out, of what such normalization might mean (1997, 486). In other words, is this a normalization identical in its nature to the self-cure imposed on Tausk's victims of the influencing machine? Is it thus psychotic, or does it propose what Toesca calls "an extraordinary example of self-education" and "a curriculum for the education to freedom"?

For Toesca, to stay for a minute with a good example of a positive reading of the text's final denouement, Pinocchio's story is truly miraculous because it redefines obedience as the possibility of self-definition as a literary event; it is a kind of "writing of the soul," in Ian Hacking's phrase, that counters the deceptions exacted by ideology and the mechanical obedience exacted by a repressive state. Collodi's *Pinocchio* thus constitutes a critique of ideology and state, both of which require subjects to live their lives either as puppets or as asses. The *separation* between puppet and boy allows for an ending whereby past and present are allowed to coexist to the extent that they are not resolved or

Figure 1.7 Enrico Marzanti, *Pinocchio and His Puppet* (1883).

overcome. According to Toesca, the puppet comes to function as Pinocchio's memory of the process wherein he became a subject, a memory made up not only of his father's advice, but one that also functions as the repository of a literary tradition (Don Quixote, Robinson Crusoe, Aeneas, etc.), in such a way as to make possible Pinocchio's (and Italy's) participation in a canonical literary tradition. Folklore is transformed into literature to the extent that it not only becomes unconscious, but creates an unconscious as such. "Pinocchio," Jean-Marie Apostolidès writes, "is situated at the turning point. By transforming the images of folklore into traits of his own unconscious, he achieves individuality; he leaves behind the strings that tied him to tradition" (1988, 84). Pinocchio's unconscious memories allow for a "suspension" of his position by virtue of the split between puppet and boy and thus for a rejection of *perbenismo* understood as mere conformity and renunciation (Toesca 1997, 462). Through a writing of the self, *that* monster can be slain from within: *per bene* for Pinocchio signifies "something else" (Toesca 1997, 463). It now means loving the other and tending to him; it means being a son of the people through critical engagement with the world. Finally, it means going beyond ideology, beyond credulity and appearances, which is where Pinocchio had started from, taken in by everyone and everything.

Pinocchio is born into a world of lies in which he is—famously—its biggest liar, outdone, possibly, only by Collodi himself. His nose, of course, belies the privacy or secrecy of Pinocchio's lies. In fact, two types of lies seem to be at play within the text. On the one hand, the lies of bad people and of the world into which Pinocchio is born, a world connected to or understood as theater where subjects are required to perform roles. These subjects, when they lie, do not grow a nose. Indeed, these theatrical role-players—of which the Fox and the Cat are most emblematic—are condemned to a bad fiction, as Pietro Toesca calls it; they are nothing but fictionality, and Pinocchio will have to learn not to believe their stories. Prior to this lesson, however, Pinocchio always remains *"con un palmo di naso"* (Perella 1986, 29), that is, surprised, confused, and unable to read the signs put before him in his world. The unreadability of this world begins in Pinocchio's bodily demand for food. Pinocchio's is a hunger that grows as fast as his nose, one that can be "cut with a knife." In the throes of his first pangs of bodily need, Pinocchio rushes to the hearth, where a kettle is boiling, but *"la pentola era dipinta sul muro. Immaginatevi come restò. Il suo naso, che era già lungo, gli diventò più lungo almeno quattro dita."* [14]

Pinocchio cannot read the signs of the world around him. His encounters with the Fox and the Cat do not immediately teach him the fact that money does not grow on trees, and his failure to understand this earns him stints in jail and something resembling death by another suspension from the Great Oak Tree (see fig. 1.8). More immediately, of course, Pinocchio's encounter with hunger and bodily need teach him that neither painted pots, nor reliance on the goodwill of others, nor the program of the pleasure principle of wish-fulfillment, nor the theatrical world of make-believe and performance can substi-

Figure 1.8 Carlo Chiostri, *Suspension from the Great Oak Tree* (1901).

tute for subjectivity, that is, for the negotiation between inside and out. For Pinocchio to be, he must first have; he must, as Gagliardi has put it, swallow the gold coins, the medicine, and ultimately the message (1980, 77). That, or be had: "Would you be so kind," Pinocchio asks the Dolphin upon his arrival on the Island of the Busy-Bees, "as to tell me whether there are any villages on this island where one can eat without danger of being eaten?" (Collodi 1986, 271).

Pinocchio's lies, in contrast, give birth to what Gagliardi calls a "new psychic dimension" (1980, 85)—and here the critic echoes Tausk—a psychic space predicated on a rupture between things and words, that is, on new modes of creating reality that take their distance from referentiality and symbolic creation. Once set on his trajectory of lies, Pinocchio will leave the theater and become a spectator of the playacting of others. His own playacting will eventually take the form only of regression—in his transformations into watchdog or ass, for example. Pinocchio's lies create a psychic dimension for himself and thereby a vehicle to combat an insane world wherein the subject is to find his origins, his provenance, but against which he must seek his own autonomy. As Tausk so rightly understood, this autonomy not only takes the form of a lie, but of a construction, of an apparatus; it is a lie but one nevertheless predicated on an accurate reading of signs that pertain, ultimately, to an insane world. As such, one might argue, Pinocchio takes seriously the old accusation that Italy is nothing but a fictional geographical entity.

Thus, Pinocchio's initially passive trust or credulity must be converted into an autonomously conceived signifying chain of substitutions, a chain finally embodied in his last substitution as boy. This is the paradox that lies at the heart of the text: if Pinocchio begins in an illusionary because arbitrary world of mirrors that generate spectral and oneiric images, his last change, too, can only be confirmed by a mirror: "Then he went to look at himself in the mirror, and he thought he was somebody else. He no longer saw the usual image of the wooden marionette reflected there. . . . In the midst of all these wonders . . . not even Pinocchio knew whether he was really awake or whether he was still dreaming with his eyes open" (459).[15] Pinocchio requires the mirror in order to confirm that his transformation is not a dream. And yet the mirror cannot answer the question about the Other, the possibility of a "somebody else." In fact, there is no way of knowing how the idealized identification here is different from an earlier moment in the text of clearly narcissistic and thus misguided identification. Geppetto has just finished carving the puppet a second pair of feet (the first set having been burned in a fire) and made him a set of clothes: "Pinocchio immediately ran to look at himself in a basin full of water and felt so pleased with himself that he said, as proud as a peacock [*pavoneggiandosi*]: 'I look like a real gentleman!' 'Quite so,' replied Geppetto. 'Because, and keep this in mind, it's not fine clothes that make a gentleman, but clean ones'" (133).[16]

While for a reader such as Toesca the difference between the two scenes lies in the falsity of the reduction of subjectivity to clothing, clean or otherwise, as well as in the fact that the later mirror image has been given depth by Pinocchio's unconscious in the corner of the room, for other readers, this final "mirror stage" is the ultimate guarantee of Pinocchio's self-alienation. What Pinocchio sees is not himself but an idealized visualization and hence an external and therefore wrong confirmation of self. His identity necessarily comes into being as a misrecognition. This doubling of the self returns Pinocchio, according to Mino Gabriele, to the opposition between puppet and puppeteer: "If the puppeteer is fixed in the reflected image of the puppet, he runs the risk of confusing his interior place as 'guide' with that which is 'guided,' that is, its exterior form" (1981, 46). Similarly for Gagliardi, the mirror image becomes for Pinocchio a new sovereign, a witness to any possible transgressions that would result in Pinocchio's immediate return to puppet or ass. Pinocchio turns into a prisoner of that image to the extent, precisely, that the image cannot be recognized as image by Pinocchio: "The mirror of bourgeois ideology returns a false and falsifying image that superimposes itself on the concrete reality of the puppet who no longer has any way of distinguishing truth from lie, his being from the image that substitutes for him" (Gagliardi 1980, 161). This is, for Gagliardi, a superimposition akin to the one where the biopsychic quality of the human is superimposed on the materiality of Pinocchio's wood (18).

These two very different, apparently opposed, readings trace, then, two distinct trajectories of Pinocchio's movements. Toesca would describe the passage as one from influence to autonomy, a passage that understands Pinocchio's leap into the symbolic as one that cuts strings. Gagliardi and Gabriele, on the other hand, view such a trajectory in exactly the opposed direction, as one that ends with Pinocchio's final change into the "real" puppet, a transformation that is all the more effective ideologically in that Pinocchio can no longer even recognize himself as such. According to the first reading, *Pinocchio* constitutes a critique of ideology or alienation; it describes a process whereby the subject comes into being in and through the discovery of truth. According to the second, the text describes the very installation of the ideological subject, a subject constituted through a certain misrecognition in a process of "ideological interpellation through which the subject 'recognizes' itself as the addressee" of a command that elicits the response: "I was already there" (Žižek 1989, 2–3). And yet, despite Toesca's adherence to a kind of Habermasian intersubjective community of transparent communication, his understanding of the subject nevertheless depends on its very fissure, its internal split between boy and puppet. On the other hand, Gagliardi's reading of the text as a parable of the subject's insertion into ideological misrecognition relies on a prior existence of the subject as "natural" or nonalienated. What both readings share, in other words, is what Žižek calls a logic of alienation, the notion of a subject who is either conjuncturally or structurally the product of an internal (self-) division.

I would like to propose here an alternative reading and argue that Collodi suspends the logic of alienation by delineating a map of Pinocchio's movements that ends up confounding all oppositions and dichotomies, making this map virtually unreadable. What *Pinocchio* first of all lacks is direction. Pinocchio's double trajectory—his passage both out of and into ideology is the very essence of the Pinocchio effect. The real meaning of Pinocchiology lies in the text's ability to both pin the tale down to a moralizing ethic of either "disobedience punished and obedience rewarded" or "nature refuted and culture obeyed," *and* to generate a kind of hypertext of proliferating meanings that have thereby permitted Collodi's classic to become absorbed into its mass (re)production as commodity. It is this double movement that makes possible an understanding of ideology that is radically new, one that points not to a postideological phase, however, nor to its critique. Rather, a kind of cynicism pervades the text, and this despite all its heartfelt and eminently marketable warmth. Through the course of the tale, Pinocchio does not actually learn anything of himself or of the world. He is, for instance, from the very beginning "good." His biggest sacrifice—that of his life—had already been proposed in Fire-Eater's theater, where he had offered himself as firewood in the place of Harlequin. And he already knows, before Geppetto ever speaks, the lessons and advice given to him by his father. It is not clear how his final transformation is significantly different from his previous ones, because his final embodiment as boy is not necessarily any more stable than his change into an ass. Pinocchio's last transformation is thus not one predicated on having learned his lesson and thus bettered himself. His transformation must for that reason be tied to something or someone else.

Indeed, what the tale lacks, in the absence of moral progress, is a master signifier, or at least a signifier capable of grounding the tale in some ultimate significance. Given this fictionality, the fact that words and things live in an unstable relationship, Pinocchio's lies, as symbolized in his nose, cannot be led back—or at least not in an obvious manner—to the genital apparatus. Pinocchio's influencing machine derives its power not from genital sexuality—which already presupposes an interiority or privacy of the subject, and is thus another, favored form of "Pinocchiology"—but from the fact of its own fictionality. In any case, his nose makes its appearance not only in connection with his lies. Pinocchio's nose is far more duplicitous, an unstable signifier of his desire and of his will. His nose points to the phallus and not genitality, but only if the phallus is understood as the point of coincidence between omnipotence and total impotence. Hence, as Žižek has put the point, the phallus is both: that part of the body not subject to the control of the will and, as the joke goes, the lightest object on earth, because the one object that can be elevated by mere thought. Thus, the phallus "designates the juncture at which the radical externality of the body as independent of our will, as resisting our will, joins the pure interiority of our thought." The "phallic dimension" stands for the "act of formal conversion of reality *as given* into reality *as posited*" (1989, 223).

The story of Pinocchio (and *Pinocchio*) is the story of the postliberal subject, a subject whose contours are indeterminate insofar as his origins are always already profoundly unoriginal, always coming from elsewhere in the form of something posited. Pinocchio is produced by and in turn produces Pinocchiology, that is to say, he is not only the product of an ideological apparatus or machine but himself generates ideology. In this latter sense, Pinocchio is, despite his apparent resistance to the work ethic, a mechanical maker or producer; he is himself an influencing machine. In this double existence of his, Pinocchio might be read as an allegory of the movement and function of ideology per se, insofar as he literalizes in his puppet/boy existence both subjection and subjectivity, influence and autonomy. While Pinocchio enacts the subject's interpellation and submission to the ideological apparatuses, however, he also points to the limits of this process, for Pinocchio also exceeds the subject of ideology. In Pinocchio's becoming a subject, in the process of his interpellation, there is a remainder: he will become a boy but on the condition that the puppet still be there, lifeless and propped up against a chair in the corner. Not coincidentally, in Greek *wood* and *primal matter* derive from the same root. The Pinocchian apparatus will exceed Pinocchiology; it will place itself beyond ideology, producing a kind of materia prima, as Mladen Dolar terms it (1993), a leftover that cannot be either mastered or symbolized. As such, it will produce its own kind of pleasures—pleasures that are deeply implicated in their status as fiction and that reside in an ambiguous space, between day and night, nature and artifice, in and yet beyond the great educational project, in and out of the text: "And during the evening hours [Pinocchio] practiced his reading and writing. . . . For a few cents he had bought a big book from which the title page and table of contents were missing [*al quale mancavano il frontispizio e l'indice*]; and from this he did his reading. As for writing, he used a twig he had sharpened in the manner of a pen; and because he had neither ink nor inkwell, he would dip it into a small vial filled with blackberry-and-cherry juice" (Collodi 1986, 453).

I would therefore propose that Pinocchio is both produced by and itself produces Pinocchiology; that is, it describes the constitution of the modern subject as the contradictory result of a process of simultaneous attachment to and refuse of the ideological state apparatus. Pinocchio is both, only ideology and that which cannot be subsumed into ideological discourse. He is the allegorical brother, in this sense, of Gregor Samsa and other Kafkan characters who confront the ideological state apparatus in the form of a blind, nonsensical bureaucracy but who are not integrated into that apparatus. Kafkan subjects confront the state apparatus, Žižek holds, in a relationship of interpellation without identification or subjectivation (1989, 44). Pinocchio is the product of a narrative strategy "characterized by a radical split, a kind of structural imbalance, as to the possibility of its narrativization: the integration of the subject's position into the field of the Big Other, the narrativization of his fate, becomes possible only when the subject is in a sense already dead, although still alive, when 'the game is already over.'" The subject is placed here into a position where he can only "observe helplessly how the trap set by the investigative—i.e., discursive—machinery, nominally led by himself, tightens around him" (Žižek 1992, 151). Pinocchio is subject to Kafkan transformations that are uncannily similar to the artistic or aesthetic transformation executed by Marcel Duchamp in his 1920 revisioning of Etienne-Jules Marey's apparatus, constructed to observe the revolutions of a string that in their gyrations produce a geometric solid (see fig. 1.9). Duchamp here reconfigures Marey's attempt at representing movement as a "personal mythology of mechanical apparatus" (Davies, 1979, 89; see fig. 1.10). Duchamp's *Rotating Glass Plates* are, like Pinocchio, both subject and apparatus, geared to furnishing the support and coordinates of that subject. Pinocchio and the rotating glass, like Kafka's Odradek in "Die Sorge des Hausvaters"

(1970), are neither human nor inhuman but a kind of human motor capable of producing their own energies. Collodi's own particular narrative strategies rely for this Pinocchian effect on two factors: the nature of Pinocchio's bodily movement and, closely tied to this, the fact that this movement takes place within the context of a crisis of the paternal order.

Figure 1.9 Etienne-Jules Marey, "Stereoscopic Chronophotograph of Volumes Engendered by the Revolution of a String" (1891–92). Chronophotograph on a fixed plate. (Musée E. J. Marey, Beaune. © J. Cl. Couval.)

Figure 1.10 Marcel Duchamp, *Rotary Glass Plates (Precision Optics)* (1920). (Yale University Art Gallery, New Haven, CT. Gift of the Collection Societé Anonyme. © 2006 Artists Rights Society, New York/ADAGP, Paris/Succession Marcel Duchamp.)

Pinocchio's Pleasures

The nature of Pinocchio's movement is nothing if not of a contradictory nature and is most definitely related to the old Italian problem of *scioltezza*. First and foremost, and this is a fact that is strangely neglected in the vast body of criticism of the story, Pinocchio is a pup-

Figure 1.11 Etienne-Jules Marey, "Chute du chat" (1894). Chronophotograph on mobile film. (Musée E. J. Marey, Beaune. © J. D. Lajoux.)

pet without strings. In other words, the very term that defines Pinocchio more than any other—that is, the peculiarity of his movement—is largely ignored in favor of the moralizing message of the text. And yet Pinocchio moves by a force that cannot in any obvious way be determined. On the one hand, because he is a puppet, his movement is heteronomously determined, that is, dictated or influenced from the outside; he is driven by forces that he cannot either know or control. On the other hand, because he is without strings, Pinocchio is self-propelled and autokinetic: he moves because it is in his essence to do so, insofar as he obeys a kind of internal motor.

The existence of such a human internal motor would be proven in 1892 in Etienne-Jules Marey's laboratory, where experiments were afoot to demonstrate the age-old saying that cats always land on their feet. Such wisdom in fact contradicted Newton's law that once an object moves, the object's course can be altered only by an *external* force.[17] With the aid of his camera, Marey provided incontrovertible proof that, if a cat was dropped with its back to the ground, it could use its own body weight to twist around and land on all fours (see fig. 1.11). Such wisdom proven as correct, however, there nevertheless remained two limit conditions to such an experiment. First, of course, was the continued, albeit limited presence of the master puppeteer on the scene, whose hands, after all, dropped the unfortunate cat from heights to which the cat could only make its personal adjustments—hands that, symptomatically, remained all too visible in the scene. Second, both the cat and Pinocchio constituted the very embodiment of *both* laws of thermodynamics, as established at mid-century, that validated the positivist claim that laws were applicable to all science and hence to both human and nonhuman nature. The first law of thermodynamics (formulated by Hermann von Helmholtz in 1847) stipulated that all forces of nature, whether mechanical, chemical, or electrical, formed a single universal energy that could be neither added to nor destroyed. This *conservation* of energy principle was supplemented almost immediately by Rudolf Clausius's second law, stating that the conversion of energy from a warmer to a colder body always entailed a loss of energy and thus the inevitable depletion of force. This theory thus made entropy into a law of nature. As Anson Rabinbach has argued, these two laws turned labor into a universal attribute of nature and made possible a transcendental materialism that founded production as *Kraft* and its attendant dissipation as no longer a function of human will and moral exhortation but of scientific discovery and intervention. Fatigue, the expression of the second law of thermodynamics, came to be not a sign of idleness but rather evidence of the body's physiological reaction to modern industrial production techniques (Rabinbach 1990). The body—and here the Pinocchian body—is a human motor that both produces and conserves energy, while at the same time it is continuously assailed by the dangers of depletion or fatigue. As a human motor, Pinocchio is also—as I will have occasion to discuss—beyond good and evil; that is, beyond the ultimately economic problem of idleness and moralization.

Pinocchio runs. He runs because he must, for running has for him the status of a drive. He runs for a good or a bad reason—he is hungry or caught in a bad situation; or because he wants to avoid school or work—but nevertheless for a reason. In these moments, he is reacting to the world around him and thus obeying or disobeying the reality principle. But he also runs for the pleasure of it and, by virtue of this pleasure, demonstrates all the characteristics of what Lombroso describes as "vagabond madness":[18] what Pinocchio desires most in life is "eating, drinking, sleeping, having fun, and living the life of a vagabond from morning to night" (Collodi 1986, 109). But Pinocchio does not stop running even here. If he did, then the *Adventures* would be nothing but a "psychological journey" that weaves its way between the pleasure principle and the reality principle, whereby, on becoming a boy at the end of the story, Pinocchio finally obeys the dictates of reality.[19] Such a journey, conceived in terms of a *Bildungsroman* or conversion narrative that binds Pinocchio first to the pleasure principle and then to the reality principle, does not, however, account for the fact that Pinocchio's running generates a kind of surplus energy, an energy that has no reason and that is thus radically heteronomous to the economies of need and desire.

Pinocchio's movement is a figure for the essential paradox of modern pedagogy, the desire, that is, to have heteronomously imposed behavior transformed into obedience as an act of free will. As such, his movements go straight to the heart of what will become the project of reforming the bodies of Italian schoolchildren. Because of the nature of his movement, Pinocchio is both a puppet and his own puppeteer and therefore he embodies, and quite literally so, two forms of power that are consonant with two types of law. Pinocchio is a transitional figure, for he represents, on the one hand, the universe of the master puppeteer or the King; and on the other hand, the universe where that King is dead and where power must be exerted in the form of an inner mechanics or of what Michel Foucault has called the disciplinary economy of the body. In this latter sense, Pinocchio has abolished the gap between the puppet and the puppeteer (Givone 1981, 65). The problem is that such a project is marked, as Eric Santner has pointed out in a different but related context, by "an aberrant and 'perverse' productivity": "The conversion of heteronomy into autonomy . . . leaves a residue of heteronomy . . . that not only resists metabolization . . . but returns to haunt and derange the subject whose physical, moral and aesthetic cultivation that system was designed to achieve" (1996, 91). Pinocchio's conversion cannot be reduced, therefore, to the effective setting into place of repression, nor can it be understood as a tale of Christian conversion. Pinocchio is more accurately subject to Kafkan metamorphosis, whereby his transgressions increasingly take on an aspect of perverse pleasure. There is an "odor of sulfur" around Pinocchio (Givone 1981, 63), and this odor perversely produces an energy and pleasure that derange Pinocchio's quest for a stable subject-position, but that nevertheless also make it possible.

Pinocchio's senseless running bespeaks the presence of such a residue of heteronomy, caught as it is within the coordinates of eminently modern measurements of time and space that in the text are calculated in hours and kilometers. Pinocchio is both the product and the refuse resulting from a new body politics, a biotechnics of the body that "*literalizes* the 'performative magic' sustaining the authority of [the] values [of law and freedom] and the institutions built upon them" (Santner 1996, 91). For this reason, Pinocchio is born into a brotherhood and not into a family, because disciplinary power at least partially converts symbolic authority qua Law of the Father into the regulation for the material control and administration of bodies.[20] By no means does this suggest the end of patriarchal power, however. The conversion is indeed partial, and its partiality has the effect of slowing down Pinocchio's running, as he now must take upon himself the burden of the father.

Having engineered his own and his father's escape from the belly of the Great Fish, Pinocchio must shoulder the full weight of his father as they make their way home: "Just lean on my arm, dear Father, and let's go on. We'll go little by little, just as ants do, and when we're tired we'll rest along the way" (Collodi 1986, 443). Tired for the first time, Pinocchio at the end of the story will come to be inserted into an economy of energy that has as its counterweight the fatigued body, thereby becoming the bearer of both the First and the Second Laws of Thermodynamics.

When the primordial father, the King, or master puppeteer dies or is murdered, Freud states in *Totem and Taboo,* his surviving sons have two possible courses of action: either the father's place is reoccupied by one of their group and the cycle of violence continues, or they decide that the dead father's place should be kept vacant, in order for that empty space to become the holder for a new, democratic order. In the latter case, political power is to be now symbolized in the form of permanent institutions in which all brothers participate. Paternal power has here no bodily existence but is nevertheless exacted in the name of the father; it speaks his language, but only because the father is already dead. Such continued attachment to the father after his death, Freud explains in terms of the transformation of guilt into love (1950). Pinocchio is born into a world where there is no primal father or king. "Once upon a time there was . . . 'A king!' my little readers will say right away. No, children, you are wrong. Once upon a time there was a piece of wood." So read the first sentences of the novel, opening onto a space that Gagliardi calls an interregnum but that perhaps more accurately posits a site of transformation, the passage through which changes all things forever. And Pinocchio is, of course, not born from a woman but from a man, conceived from this man's desire or idea: "This morning," Geppetto tells Master Cherry, "an idea popped into my head [*mi è piovuta nel cervello un'idea*]. . . . I thought of making myself a fine wooden puppet; but a wonderful puppet who can dance, and fence, and make daredevil leaps. I intend to travel around the world with this puppet so as to earn my crust of bread and a glass of wine" (Collodi 1986, 89).

Pinocchio is then conceived by Geppetto's desire to make a minimal living by hitting the road and exhibiting one of those miraculous wooden bodies whose existence was already threatened, according to Yorick, in the face of greater technological miracles. Collodi himself also conceives him as the child of a tradition that flourished in Tuscan legends, paintings, and marionette theaters as apocryphal texts and lore. In finding a putative father for Jesus, so the story goes, an angel suggests giving a piece of wood to all unwed men. He whose wood flowered would be his father. Joseph (Geppetto) was that man, and he became the custodian of Mary, who at that time was still a child.[21]

Apocryphal or not, not all is well in the Collodian domain of paternal tradition. While Geppetto may to some extent be capable of symbolizing his needs and desires when he fabricates his puppet, he can in reality only conceive of such symbolization in terms of a regression. The chapters that precede Pinocchio's birth describe the theatrical world of the *commedia dell'arte* where Geppetto and Master Cherry play out the conflicts of an old world through their stagings of mimetic violence in a manner that is wooden, repetitive, and puppetlike. Here Geppetto seeks to transcend his miserable life by himself becoming a puppeteer, a master of his destiny that he can ideally manage by pulling the strings of his creation. And yet this is an old society of men that can no longer reproduce itself because, unbeknownst to Geppetto, the King is already dead, the strings have been already cut. And hence the disruption caused by Pinocchio's birth: "When the eyes were done, just imagine [Geppetto's] astonishment when he realized that those eyes moved and that they were staring him straight in the face. Seeing himself looked at by those two eyes of wood, Geppetto took a little offense and said in an irritated tone: 'Spiteful wooden eyes, why are you looking at me [*Occhiacci di legno, perchè mi guardate*]?'" (Collodi 1986, 97) And after this, of course, comes the nose that grows and grows quite vigorously despite all of Geppetto's carving. As each body part is shaped, it reacts with impertinence until finally Geppetto exclaims: "Scamp of a child, you aren't even finished and you're already beginning to lack respect for your father! That's bad, my boy, bad!" (101) And once Pinocchio has his feet, he will start running and refuse the role assigned to him as the puppet of his father's desire.

Pinocchio, as a puppet without strings, embodies both the fact that the father is already dead (the father, the puppeteer, the King, God) and at the same time, in his capacity as a runner, the act of the father's murder. Pinocchio is the result of a dysfunction in the paternal order. He is faced, in fact, with an impossible command: to obey the father, but not to imitate him—to be both a puppet *and* a son capable of taking upon himself the paternal function in ways of which Geppetto is himself not capable. And if the first sign of a crisis in the patriarchal order is given by Pinocchio's *necessary* lack of respect, then the second appears in the fact that this order is produced phantasmatically, that is, without the intervention of a mother. Pinocchio's first escapes are dictated by the search for that mother who will appease his bodily needs (hunger, cold, and illness).

The Blue-Haired Fairy, who lives in the realm of necessity and death and whose laws must be obeyed unconditionally, is made, as Gagliardi puts it, of the same wood as Pinocchio (1980, 25). The puppet's relation to her preexists culture; it is instinctive and symbiotic. The Fairy's law is founded in the economy of the immediacy of desire and fulfillment, and it therefore lacks mediation and the capacity for deferral. And yet Pinocchio inhabits a world where there is no mother earth capable of instinctively feeding its offspring, and the Fairy is thus already the transmitter of bourgeois pedagogy in the context of the father's uncertain power. This explains the extraordinary cruelty and sadism of her child-rearing practices, as well as her many transformations; her use of psychological violence and the fact that she takes on many appearances (little girl, grown woman, spectator in a circus, goat) may be interpreted as a temporarily necessary usurpation of paternal power. The Fairy, in the absence of the father, the puppeteer, the King, stands in for the father, as Apostolidès has put it, and thus participates in his death. For this reason, if order is to be established, she must be superseded by a new masculine subject. When on the Island of the Busy-Bees she has turned into a bourgeois woman who butters sandwiches for children's birthday parties, Pinocchio must leave her realm and begin his real search for his father. After this point, he will have no more direct encounters with her, and his relationship to his mother will become reversed: at the end of the story, Pinocchio will—from afar—tend to her on the condition that she keep her distance.

Maternal law, the law to be first learned and then refused, finds its fullest representation on the Island of the Busy-Bees. Here, culture has a false ring to it; it is comprised of hard labor, heartlessness, and unnecessary obedience at home, at school, and at work. Gagliardi describes the situation on the island as one of "imposed labor in which no one recognizes himself, a labor imposed by a Queen Bee to whom all submit" (1980, 114).[22] The island world is a world predicated on a slave labor that is feminized and feminizing. Here the Fairy is only intent on her own needs: Pinocchio slides into a kind of stupor in this place, into a near-death state, rendering his obedience only passively. His passage from the Island to Funland is thus a quick one. Funland—where there are no schools, no teachers, no books, but only vacation and play; but where underneath all its fun lurks a tyrant ready to turn boys into asses—is a mirror image of the Island of the Busy-Bees. Both countries mask an undercurrent of violence; to be schooled in these places means learning dependence and senseless labor. The knowledge transmitted here is, as Toesca remarks, purely theoretical, the product of a false utopian desire that leads to an asinine existence. It is of a theatrical quality, one reminiscent of Fire-Eater's theater of puppets on strings. The ass that Pinocchio becomes in Funland also leads him straight to another theater, the circus, where he must perform tricks at the behest of others and where he must live with the threat of his asinine hide being turned into a drum to beat the pace of others' movements.

In order to avoid the traps laid by slave labor and theatrical performance, Pinocchio must make his escape from the maternal symbiotic relationship and go in search of his father, who has been meanwhile swallowed by the Great Fish. As Gagliardi has described it, Pinocchio has had an appointment with the Fish from the very beginning. His and his father's rebirth from the Fish will give rise to a relationship with the paternal order of a fundamentally new kind (see fig. 1.12). Pinocchio must, in fact, resolve the contradiction in which he had been trapped from the start. According to Apostolidès, Pinocchio must exceed his father's lower-class demand to become productive and his mother's bourgeois command to behave like a child, her desire that he "live the life of the modern adolescent" (1988, 78). Pinocchio must do both: provide food and eat, direct his destiny and submit to it. He must take on the responsibilities of a son and exclude the mother from the new family constellation, and in the process he must also manage the various class demands that arise from these new responsibilities: to refute Geppetto's professional poverty and relinquish his desire to be a gentleman. By configuring the father-son relationship as one of ethical responsibility, the class relations that stand behind it are, as Gagliardi states, disguised. And so is, one might add, the gender relationship, for Geppetto and the Fairy cannot cohabit the same space: marriage between Geppetto and the Fairy, and the creation of a bourgeois nuclear family with Pinocchio as their son, is definitely not an option contemplated by anyone.

But what is this new relationship between father and son, founded as it is on the absence of both the King and the mother? And what kind of schooling has Pinocchio submitted to, what has the puppet learned that he can thus become a proper boy? The text certainly betrays an anxiety about an Italian universal public education, and it questions its value for those who are starving. Collodi's doubts, supported by his other journalistic writings (1995), translate into books that not even the fish can digest and turn Pinocchio into an autodidact. Pinocchio's excessive *scioltezza* neither represents the energy necessary for a move up on the social ladder, nor can it be converted or sublimated into a new way of knowing. As I said, Pinocchio's adventures do not constitute any form of *Bildung*. One must wonder, then, whether this

Figure 1.12 Carlo Chiostri, *Pinocchio Leaves His Mother* (1901).

"self-education" has any connection to the DeSanctian project of creating the great nation-school through the act of self-limitation, or whether it instead describes an abandonment by the state that leaves the subject destitute and without parents. Pinocchio must, as Asor Rosa points out, do everything alone. There is no state in Collodi's text, no social assistance, and, also, no appeal to class solidarity, patriotism, or the cult of the bourgeois family. What remains, to continue to paraphrase Asor Rosa, is the need to convert popular restlessness into order and discipline through sacrifice and through the virtues of work as the vehicle for personal transformation. "What was needed was the invention, therefore, of a new pedagogical 'form,' one that was highly indirect and mediated, a kind of fantastic parable, in other words, that was capable of reabsorbing and appropriating for itself certain aspects of the popular spirit, of its ways of being and 'conceptualizing'" (Asor Rosa 1995, 934–37).[23] Collodi is able to recuperate popular inventive energies in such a way as to articulate and map them in the form of a double passage: on the one hand, the passage from popular traditions to the ideology of the dominant classes, and on the other hand, from the naive and primitive stage of infancy to the relative maturity of adolescence. Modernization and growing up become homologous processes.

The question remains as to what actually happens to these Collodian inventive energies. The problem is that the passage described by Asor Rosa constitutes neither a passage nor even a clean break or rupture between nature and culture. It is certainly true that culture is transformed into a "natural" order or propriety that depends on a father no longer understood as genitor but as pater familias. According to Gagliardi, the King's absence will be reconfirmed in the *symbol* of the father, and the mother's absence will be legitimated by the autarchy of the child through his ability to autonomously confront the processes of social valorization. Pinocchio must leap into the *symbolic* order, accept the law of economic value, and relinquish the maternal desire of immediacy: "Natural, unproductive, and incestuous need-desire is replaced by cultural need, that is, a need mediated by exchange and value" (Gagliardi 1980, 26–28). Pinocchio is chained to the symbolic order where the continuous repression of the object of desire and the substitution occasioned by difference and deferral produce his submissiveness as a subject. The very exchangeability of father and mother, of wood and man, of man and beast, frees man from nature and allows for a continuous movement along the symbolic chain. "The subject of history . . . is he who is able to substitute and exchange objects of need without the bearer of need feeling a loss of subjectivity" (47). And yet it is also true that Pinocchio's leap into the symbolic, which Gagliardi sees as taking place in Pinocchio's encounter with the big Serpent, lands him headfirst in the mud and then right away into another transformation: a chained watchdog. Meanwhile, the Serpent dies of laughter. The substitutive chain, its capacity for endless substitution, appears to border on what Hegel described as a bad infinity, a chain that either keeps reproducing itself or that collapses in exhaustion.

And here we arrive at the essence of the puppet in the corner, one that may very well constitute the crux of Pinocchio's modernity and explain his capacity to exert influence still today. The puppet most certainly constitutes a threat to Pinocchio's integrity, but it also serves as a reminder of a pleasure, as an object that exceeds the symbolic order. The puppet functions as a threat of punishment—and thus stands in for the law—but also turns up as the law's underbelly, the sign of the father's perverse enjoyment. The symbolic order in the final scene of *Pinocchio* generates propriety while it also points to a fundamental loss of innocence and consistency. The puppet continues to insist in its presence on the possibility of Freud's other option after the father's death: the return of the primordial master puppeteer. This is an insistence that has been particularly well captured by the illustration of a recent *Pinocchio* edition (see fig. 1.13). In this remainder's insistence, the father is both absent and overly present; the puppet is a primordial father not simply because he represents Pinocchio's past existence as presymbolic force; it is a power that knows enjoyment in all its mobility. The knowledge of enjoyment is one that "is by definition excluded from the Law in its universal-neutral guise: it pertains to the very stature of Law that is 'blind' to this knowledge." For this reason, there is no "nature" in *Pinocchio*. The primordial society that Pinocchio allegedly belongs to is already a thoroughly modern one; the primordial father, the master puppeteer, is here already "the result of the decline of the paternal metaphor" (Žižek 1992, 159). Collodi, with his creation of a puppet without strings, creates a subject who gives up on the possibility of universal law and universal access; by fantasizing the death of the father as his ever-more-pressing return in the form of a hard-core reality beyond symbolization, he literalizes the subject's attachments to that order of which he is both the product and refuse. It is not merely that Pinocchio, through all his sacrifice, becomes an object of exchange on the labor market; his subjective destitution, which is also the condition for his becoming a subject, introduces a breakdown of that exchangeability. The disciplining of Pinocchio's body, his self-

Figure 1.13 Roberto Innocenti, *Pinocchio and His Puppet*. (© Roberto Innocenti 1988 and 2005; first published in 2005 by Creative Editions.)

movement, creates what Foucault has called a counterlaw. Disciplinary powers have the "precise role of introducing insuperable asymmetries and excluding reciprocities." By virtue of such asymmetries, disciplinary power has the effect of suspending the law in such a way that the law thereby is never total but never completely annulled either (Foucault 1977, 222–23). And in this suspension, again literalized by Pinocchio's body, lies the meaning of the Pinocchio effect, for it undoes all before and after, inside and out, nature and culture, law and violence. And the very hilarity that this movement generates—as exemplified by the phallic Serpent, who laughs herself to death—this self-propelling movement creates an influencing machine as a kind of performative magic that may run of its own accord. This influencing machine, as it works over popular "inventive energies," creates its own meanings and pleasures that can never be completely anchored to the symbolic order in ways that would make stable meanings possible: "Because, you see, whereas all other persons who feel sorry for someone either cry or at least pretend to dry their tears, whenever Fire-Eater was really touched, he had the bad habit of sneezing. It was as good a way as another of letting people know he had a heart with feelings" (Collodi 1986, 149).

When in 1920 Freud discovered a force that operated "beyond" the pleasure principle, he located this discovery in the demonic compulsion to repeat past unpleasurable experiences. According to Freud, the compulsion to repeat exhibited a "high degree of instinctual character" and thus seemed almost demonic in its insistence (1961, 41). Freud named this demonic, instinctual force the death drive, the compelling and compulsory force that repeatedly places the subject in and before death. The death drive announced that the aim of all life is death, that everything died for internal reasons, and that the complexity of life was nothing but a detour, a deferral of and defense against life's ultimate goal.

Several aspects of Freud's discovery of such a realm beyond pleasure strike me as relevant to my present concerns, aspects that may well bring into focus Pinocchio's own close relationship with death and with demonic forces and that support my contention that the puppet's paths run outside the coordinates that describe those of pleasure and reality. First, Freud and Collodi share narrative strategies for their respective creations; they both posit as their vehicle a simple, undifferentiated organism that must makes its way through life and reality. Collodi's wooden puppet is not so different from Freud's "simplified" living organism that he describes as "an undifferentiated vesicle of a substance susceptible to stimulation" (28). Second, Freud and Collodi share, as we have already seen with Tausk's influencing machines, the idea that projecting mechanisms are in place in order to guarantee not only the safety but the very consistency of the subject per se: " there is a tendency to treat [internal excitations] as though they were acting, not from the inside, but from the outside, so that it may be possible to bring the shield against stimuli into operation as a means of defense against them" (Freud 1961, 33).[24] Hence, the relationships between inside and outside are negotiated here by the operation of the compulsion to repeat, insofar as instinctual drives are now made to reappear beyond the boundaries of the subject. Third, to the degree that the instinctual urges connected to the death drive are unbound and mobile, precisely because unconscious and unsubordinated to the demands of egoic pleasure and reality, Pinocchio's movements, his essential elasticity, become the very embodiment of the death drive: "an instinct is an urge inherent in organic life to restore an earlier state of things which the living entity has been obliged to abandon under the pressure of external disturbing forces; that is, it is a kind of organic elasticity, or, to put it another way, the expression of the inertia inherent in organic life" (43). Pinocchio is thus both an irresistible, moving urge and the expression of a fundamental inertia. Finally, if Pinocchio is bound in his elasticity, his inevitable *scioltezza,* by the logic of the death drive, by a perpetual and compulsive repetition, then, like Freud's "other" instinctual force, he can provide only a "deceptive appearance" of forces that tend "towards change and progress, whilst in fact they are merely seeking to reach an ancient goal by paths alike old and new" (45). The *likeness* of old and new paths is perhaps the essential point, or what Freud called "the new point now under discussion." In an arresting sentence, within the context of his discussion of the implications of his own *new* discovery, Freud remarks: "But there is no difference in principle between an instinct turning from an object to the ego and its turning from the ego to an object" (66).

It is this lack of difference, in the face of the discovery of the death drive, that ultimately seems the crucial point. Pinocchio in the end does not reach some final destination, because any end would be as good as any other. And indeed, when Pinocchio emerges from the belly of the Great Fish, with his half-dead father on his shoulders, he reencounters the Fox and the Cat, who are now reduced to begging. Pinocchio has no time, food, or money to give them. He may be no longer fooled by their theatrical tricks, but he can nevertheless address them only in the platitudes of his forefathers: "'If you're poor, it serves you right. Remember the proverb that says: 'Stolen money brings no gain.' Farewell, pretty masqueraders [*mascherine*]!'" (Collodi 1986, 443). Pinocchio now sounds like the Talking Cricket, and he spouts the depersonalized wisdoms of the generalized worker-subject in a purely mechanical fashion to which De Sanctis would have had to object. And here the Collodian influencing machine, true to the second law of thermodynamics, simply runs out of steam and submits to fatigue. The absence of steam explains the text's ending, in the same way that its presence had provided its pleasurable energy. Pinocchio's adventures have the structure of a sitcom, and as such they are subject to a kind of sitcom fatigue,[25] to a saturation beyond which the machine will not run because it lacks the necessary ratings. But while the ratings were high—and we must remember that the Pinocchian adventures were produced serially and in tune with market demand—Pinocchio had always been good, made, as Givone remarks, no mistakes, and yet was scamp enough, imperfect enough, to keep the book running. *Pinocchio* does not provide closure—and thus is itself a book without title and index—but instead collapses in exhaustion.

This ending proved to be seasonal and timely, however. Like sitcoms that must take a rest at the beginning of summer in order to return in the new school year with renewed vigor and suspense, *Pinocchio* produced an endless number of sequels well beyond its author's death, belying any suspicion that Collodi had all along been Pinocchio's "real" master puppeteer: "Pinocchio Gets Married," "Pinocchio's Sister," "Pinocchio's Son," even a fascist Pinocchio, an antifascist Pinocchio; endless translations between languages and media: films, cartoon strips, video games; and of course products: puppets, dolls, posters, pencils, restaurant menus and signs, and finally, one must not forget, literary criticism. Pinocchio proved himself to be wonderfully and productively influential: his act of autonomy gave birth to an entire host of Pinocchios, brought about by his multivalent effects via a chiasmic structure where opposites cross back into each other and thereby also provide each other's support.[26] *Pinocchio* delineated a force of gravity whereby the subject was to hold himself up, as it were, by his own bootstraps, and in that act he confirmed his attachment to the apparatus.

TWO

The Secret Power of Suggestion: Scipio Sighele's Succubal Subject

He experiments one by one with about thirty young men. . . . Almost all of them respond immediately to his power of fascination by turning stiff throughout their bodies; their faces become contracted, terrified, sometimes cadaverous; they are at the mercy of the fascinator and follow his movements like a magnet. . . . There is something pitiful, spasmodic in their features, something macabre in their gestures. . . . Donato has them all in his power, he attracts them in threes, in sixes, ten at a time, simply by rapidly staring into their eyes, even against their firm will and their obstinate efforts to resist his suggestion. . . . Donato, in the process, never speaks: he thinks, he wants and points.[1]

Young male bodies that turn stiff despite their efforts to do otherwise—such were the events on the stage of the Teatro Scribe in Turin in 1886, events performed under the direction of the Belgian-born Alfred d'Hont, more commonly known as "Donato," the theatrical magnetizer of crowds. That same year, Enrico Morselli, one of Italy's leading psychiatrists, who himself had assisted and succumbed to the fascination of Donato, drew a rather positive portrait of the man in his important study of animal magnetism and hypnotic states.[2] Donato—in Morselli's opinion—was not a vulgar man. First soldier, then state employee, journalist, novelist, poet, and, finally, student and apostle of animal magnetism, Donato had revolutionized hypnosis through his discovery of a phenomenon called "fascination." Donato, Morselli wrote, was blessed with uncommon physical strength, quick and insistent eyes, a great agility of movement, and much spirit. He had exchanged the magician's cap for the more sober tuxedo—quite appropriately, for he "rejects fluids, rejects the power and transmission of will; nor does he trade in somnambulist lucidity, in sight without eyes, in divination. He does not claim to have special secrets or gifts. Instead he claims that it is his quick and insistent 'gaze' that produces a rapid and sudden shock to the nervous system of sensitive individuals. Where there is no 'orgasm,' he told me—but more accurately he should have said 'predisposition'—his method does not work" (Morselli 1886, 281).

Morselli claims that *these shows come close to producing a political crisis right at the center of Europe* (271). But what was so revolutionary about Donato's method? Why were the spectacles at the Teatro Scribe perceived to be so radically new?

James Braid's discovery in 1842 that hypnotic sleep could be induced by the simple fixation on a luminous object had revolutionized magnetic theory and practice. Braid's was to prove an important discovery, for it made possible the shift from the putative supernatural powers of the hypnotist—based on the theory of the transmission of magnetic fluids or electric currents—to an analysis of characteristics thought to inhere in the hypnotized subject him- or herself. The real cause of hypnosis, its very effectivity, was to be found, as Morselli remarks, not in the magnetizer but in his subject (32). A rethinking, within the late-nineteenth-century literature on hypnotism, of what drives the subject, of what makes him or her act, appears predicated, then, on a peculiar form of interiority, of self-causation within the subject him- or herself, a rethinking that at the end of its historical trajectory would result, first, in the idea of autohypnosis or autosuggestion, and then, by the beginning of the new century, it would also form the foundation of the psychoanalytic subject, one traversed by conflicting desires and topographically split between id, ego, and superego. In both instances, however, obedience is exacted as a result of an internalized command—and here lies the peculiarity and utter novelty of this subject—and *for that reason* the subject ceases to be master of his own house.

In the pages that follow, I will leave aside Freud's own contributions to this new subject and return only briefly to them at the end. The postulation of a subject who obeys orders and follows commands in response to autosuggestion and who because of this generates a political crisis right at the heart of Europe is the concern of this chapter. I wish to trace here a line of thought within Italian positivism, where—quite paradoxically—the modern subject is understood as capable of self-determination in the form of autosuggestion but where, nonetheless, such determination takes place beyond the space of freedom. It is, of course, well known that the Italian positivists insisted that the subject is incapable of free will and that such a subject instead merely obeys social scientific laws of development and cohesion. In other words, the positivist problematization of free will is intimately bound both to the critique of the liberal, democratic subject and, through the articulation of this subject in postliberal terms, to the birth of a new set of disciplinary knowledges; in this case, to an Italian *social science*.

A reminder of how I am using the term *postliberal subject* is in order here. Most fundamentally, discourses that describe the postliberal subject problematize key concepts of modern, democratic political existence, such as the social contract, free will, and consent. Such discourses are furthermore explicitly concerned with what comes to be viewed as the *problem* of masculine sexual desire, that is, the fact that the new political order is lived as an always present threat to that same desire. One example of such a subject is the masochist. The male masochist stages submission to the political, social, and sexual order in the form of a contract and in that move not merely makes evident the repressive or violent foundations of consent but also, in that same move, founds a new form of hegemonic masculinity predicated, paradoxically, on his submission to a fantasized powerful woman.[3]

The masochistic position is, however, not the only place from which to confront the limits and crises of the liberal project. Scipio Sighele, disciple of Cesare Lombroso and arguably the founder of mass psychology, is the author of the 1893 text entitled *The Criminal Couple*. As in masochism, Sighele's subject is explicitly gendered, and, as in masochism, the crisis-nature of his subject appears to hinge on a threat to masculine performativity. But Sighele viewed consent not as contractual, that is, as a result of an act of free will, but as ideological, or what he calls the result of suggestion. Thus, Sighele comes close to theorizing the stiffened bodies of Donato's subjects, their inability to resist suggestion in ways that are remarkably similar to what Slavoj Žižek, following Lacan, calls the paradox of the phallic signifier, the fact, in other words, that the phallic signifier stands for both omnipotence and total impotence. As already recalled in the previous chapter, Žižek describes the basic "phallic experience" in terms of an "everything depends on me, but for all that I can do nothing." He explicates this experience through, on the one side, the Augustinian theory of the phallus as the one object not subject to man's will: "The erection of the phallus escapes *in principle* man's free will. . . . Someone with a strong enough will can starve to death in the middle of a room full of delicious food, but if a naked virgin passes his way, the erection of his phallus is in no way dependent on the strength of his will." On the other side, there is the well-known vulgar riddle or joke: "What is the lightest object on earth?—The phallus, because it is the only one that can be elevated by mere thought" (Žižek 1989, 222–23). Sighele's concept of suggestion brings together this phallic experience with a new understanding of political order, with a specific form, that is, of politics. In the face of the rejection of free will, social existence is here viewed as the product of social-scientific laws whereby obedience is rendered according to principles of scientific rules and hence involuntarily, and thus obedience and its absence come to be subject to disciplinary measures and not repressive legal systems. Not coincidentally, and as I will show, Sighele conceives of these disciplinary measures above all in terms of a politics of sexuality and of the family.

I wish to trace here, then, the connections between more commonly understood political categories and the constructions of gender, on the one hand, and on the other, the complicated, because not reductive, relationship between cultural and political theories and the contexts in which they arise. Even more, I would hold that our modern political concepts rely in significant measures on an elaboration of gender identities and the modes by which they are put into effect. In addition, as a so-called late-comer to the project of nation-making, Italy has traditionally been viewed as less or imperfectly modern compared with its more advanced neighbors on the other side of the Alps. And yet, of course, such envious comparisons are predicated on some notion of a normative path to modernization and a preconceived idea of what it means to be "modern."[4] Nor have Italian critics themselves been immune to an anxiety of influence, as Sighele's own theory of the "succubus" will show. And as Sighele will also show, in such a context of belatedness a theory of the *post*liberal subject becomes all the more interesting, as if to raise the possibility—one already raised by Leopardi—that a crisis of the liberal subject may in fact precede its more normal or normative forms of existence, to the extent that such normativity is predicated on constructions of gender that in turn make these same norms operative.

The Hypnotized Subject

The history of hypnosis's entry into the clinic is well known, dominated throughout the 1880s by the figure of Jean-Martin Charcot, whose theatrical presentations in Paris drew the attention of the medical community, as he proved that hypnosis was especially bound to hysterical phenomena. The theory was immediately contested, of course, and the history of French medical hypnosis was from its beginnings split between the Paris and Nancy schools over the question of whether or not a "normal" person could also be hypnotized.[5] It is possible to view this split between the schools as the result of an even earlier debate within French psychiatry, one that had arisen from the challenge posed by Franz Anton Mesmer's therapeutic practices and between Phillipe Pinel and Jean-Marc-Gaspard Itard over the appearance in 1800 of the so-called Wild Boy of Aveyron.

This child had, during infancy, been abandoned in the woods of Aveyron and had not undergone even a minimum amount of socialization, which included the ability to speak. The debate between Pinel and Itard hinged on the opposition of the roles of nature and culture in psychosocial development and constituted in 1800, in Bianca Iaccarino's opinion, the first such debate in modern psychiatry (1996, 168). Was the child's retardation a function of a malady of his nervous system, as Pinel held, or was it not rather, as Itard argued, the result of a lack of socialization and thus emendable by mechanisms of pedagogical intervention? The centrality that Itard thus claimed for the therapeutic relation, established for him as a pedagogical one,[6] would in the future prove to be of crucial importance in the history of psychiatry, for it would found a line of thought based on the indissoluble link between scientific knowledge and emotional participation. This link would, of course, become the founding stone of Freudian psychoanalysis. Here, in fact, Itard is not far removed from those therapeutic practices advocated by Mesmer, whose stress on the therapeutic relation not only claimed a space for its unconscious workings but also turned the patient into an active participant in his or her cure. As Franklin Rausky has noted, "While Mesmer believes in a psychotherapy in which the therapist is an agent for the patient, Phillipe Pinel proposes a psychiatry where the alienist is an agent for society, for the state, vis-à-vis the patient. . . . While Mesmer . . . wants to shut down all hospitals, Pinel turns the modern asylum into a stronghold for the great internment described by Foucault" (1980, 12–13).

Charcot and the Paris school had only a moderate following in Italy. Italian psychiatrists and criminal anthropologists were profoundly concerned with the therapeutic relation and the possibility that its effects were not always easy to manage.[7] And like Hyppolite Bernheim's school in Nancy, they focused their critical attention on the concept of suggestion and stressed that it was possible to put any individual into a hypnotic trance. What this meant, first and foremost, was that the categorization of individuals according to visible or at least determinable criteria was potentially threatened. In other words, it raised the possibility that the derivation of pathological psychic symptoms from physiological foundations was rendered far more problematic, even within positivist discourse itself. Thus, for example, Morselli begins by claiming that the biological category of woman is particularly prone to hypnotic phenomena, but he then shifts immediately to a sociological or cultural categorization, claiming that it is those social groups most habituated to obedience who can be more easily put into a hypnotic state: women, children, soldiers, domestic servants, sailors, and workers (1886, 38); the hypnotized individual is not simply a pathological subject but more accurately "a grotesque caricature of the normal individual" (203).

And yet, for Morselli, hypnotism also involves the deactivation of the inhibitory function of the brain and the consequent free reign of the automatic reflex activity of the spinal cord. Without this inhibitory function, the subject demonstrates the two most important psychological features of hypnotism: automatism, defined as a lack of spontaneity; and suggestion, or the capacity to receive an infinite number of external stimuli and feelings (92). Automatism would seem to indicate the elimination of will. However, Morselli also tells us that an abstract faculty of willing does not exist in any individual, whether normal or hypnotized. Willing, like all neurological processes, is another biologically grounded brain function. Therefore, faced with so-called conscious wishes, we are simply the brain's spectators, never its actors. We "believe that we act freely and spontaneously only because we are unable to see the intimate link that binds our acts to their causal stimulus" (187). Freedom and willing is not a moral truth but a blindness or psychological error, and it is hypnotism's great merit to have brought to light the mechanical reflex-action that *is* the subject. Suggestion, which Morselli defines as the subject's openness to the outside, simply confirms this blind reflexivity. However, in his argument—and it is worth insisting on this—such suggestive receptivity is fundamentally unstable and opens the way to a mobility of thought that foreshadows

Freudian *free* association. Morselli himself, it appears, is not immune to the powers of this mobility:

> If we hear someone pronounce the word *Garibaldi,* we are immediately and spontaneously presented in our imagination with many other ideas and images about the valorous general, from his kind physique, to his very sweet gaze, his blond beard, his legendary cloak; then behind that image rapidly appear all the memories of his glorious victories, his pains, his wounds. And behind the memory of Aspromonte, step forward the beloved figures of Bertani and Zannetti, busy with the extraction of the bullet from the poor wounded man, and then one thinks of the French surgeon Nélaton, whence of Paris, the "brain of the world," and of Victor Hugo, and then of his *Miserables,* and of the social question, of the masons' strikes, and then of the elegant villas of modern Turin, and of the beautiful Madam X . . . who lives in one of them . . . and so forth, one could go on and on. (151–52)

Such a succession and association of ideas is, for Morselli, both regular and logical, *and* absurd and baroque; they demonstrate how "ideas exercise one on the other a true suggestion, calling each other forth at times, and at others inhibiting one another" (153). In other words, suggestion describes both freedom of movement viewed as the capacity to associate *and* an inhibiting function, a function, in other words, that Morselli had seemingly excluded from the realm of suggestion.

Perhaps the most important metaphor, or, more accurately, the true home of the hypnotic subject, is the theater. This returns us not only to the revolutionary novelty of Donato but also to the hypnotic subject's existence as a "grotesque caricature,"[8] for the hypnotic subject introduces us to a certain kind of pleasure, one predicated on its ability to move between subjects and between states that are neither sleep nor conscious life. Indeed, the pleasure put into play here is that of the world of make-believe. When producing the hypnotic subject, Morselli tells us, we make him act "like a dramatic artist who intends to represent different parts in a comedy or tragedy" (215). Hypnosis produces "dramas, comedies, and farces, without number and without end, that can multiply according to the pleasurable fantasy of the one conducting the experiment and of those undergoing it," plays whose termination must always feel like a curtain falling on a scene that "chills the dramatic sympathy of the spectator" (294–95). And here Donato operates on healthy individuals whom he does not know. As Morselli tells us:

> "Donatism" is a complex phenomenon and a little different from classical hypnotism and Braidism, which, for the most part, bring about unconsciousness, amnesia,

and a more or less profound sleep. Donato up to a certain moment leaves his subjects awake and conscious, even though they appear asleep and like automata (the period of true "fascination"); it is only by pushing his practices or by operating on highly sensitive individuals that he produces somnambulism with unconsciousness or amnesia. . . . "Donatism" . . . leaves the patients awake for a longer period and more aware of themselves, even if he removes from their actions all voluntary control: for this reason it resembles . . . hallucinatory and automatic states of suggestion that are provoked during waking life. (277–79)

While Charcot's subjects were predominantly women, those who climbed the Turin stage were all men (see fig. 2.1). According to contemporary accounts, Donato hypnotized about three hundred subjects during his one-month engagement in Turin. Morselli states that Donato's subjects were generally young students, soldiers, professionals, and dilettantes *"of new emotions"* (273; my emphasis).[9] But who were these men, and what were these new emotions put on display on the stage of a newly created Italy? Clara Gallini, in her superb study of the marvelous in nineteenth-century Italy, asks: "What were they doing, these workers, students, soldiers, and public employees, on Donato's stage, reciting their risible or terrifying dependence, lucidly aware of executing, at that moment, forced actions that did not originate from

Figure 2.1 "Donatizzati." (From *Illustrazione Italiana*, 1886.)

their own will, but were dictated by a stronger force? How and why . . . [do] we witness groups of men climbing to the stage, curious to try out on themselves a new psychological experience, one that becomes almost a collective daring, right at the limit of risk?" (1983, 206).

Gallini proposes to read Donatism as a symptom of a process of what she calls "heterodirection," wherein individuals experienced their insertion into the new social spaces created by urbanization and industrialization as a lack of control over both these new spaces and the modes by which they are inserted into them. The figure most descriptive of this process is, according to Gallini, the automaton. The hypnotized subject is compared to a machine, or more accurately, a human-machine, who imitates a human in looks and functions but is unable to be autonomous because it moves on the basis of a mechanism created by humans. The automaton "refers to a technological universe where the machine is still the instrument of the marvelous and not yet the fundamental support of the economy, where the human body is still entrusted with economic and ideological centrality, making it both an instrument of work and the primary source of the imaginary" (Gallini 1983, 207). The Donatic automaton gains its specificity, its utter novelty, however, from the fact that represented here is a man who mimics a machine who mimics a man. In other words, the scene witnessed is the "drama of the influence of man over man" (199). The imaginary basis of this drama remains anthropocentric, but given its mechanistic, heterodirective effects, a serialized production of social roles points to its source in an external and authoritarian power structure.

I would like to supplement and perhaps modify Gallini's analysis regarding the question of this external, authoritarian power structure, her insistence, that is, on a *hetero*directive mechanism on the Donatic stage. I propose that it is precisely the *externality* of power that is in crisis here and indeed acted out in Donatic phenomena in the form of a new theatrical masculinity. What does it actually mean that the drama of the influence of man over man is presented here on stage and, furthermore, is done consciously, or fully aware, as Morselli and others insist? Morselli speaks of the recitation of social roles as the "objectivization of types" (1886, 213), and he orders this under Donatism's ability to experiment with the transformation of personality:

> His subjects become at his command barbers, photographers, street vendors, acrobats, wrestlers, soldiers, children, etc. Quite delicious is the suggestive experience in which artificial somnambulists are transformed into voters and electoral candidates, improvising an electoral campaign meeting. Everyone, with the great-

est conviction, if not with much talent, identifies with the character assigned to him. On the evening I witnessed this experiment, the candidate (who was a law student) made his speech, but just as slowly and with the same effort we experience in dreams, where we wish but are unable to speak in public. The voters applauded clumsily; the rival candidate, after having scowled at his rival and attempting to contradict him, was finally able to articulate with great difficulty the word "clericalist!" which became the starting-point of a little brawl and of great anger, expressed in the most spontaneous and least parliamentary of forms, that is, with hurtful knocks and punches. (292–93)[10]

It is hardly coincidental that the scenario here is the political arena, pointing not only to an engagement with relations of power, but quite concretely also to the "new emotions" that had been ushered in with Italian unification only two decades earlier. It also points to the need for those new personalities called Italian citizens who were to be both free and secular, and yet also obedient and moral. Furthermore, what must strike the reader here is the *literary* quality of this new male subject, as also his *theatrical* nature and his inability, qua literary character, to stem the threat of violence, so that these plays degenerate into "knocks and punches." Finally, and perhaps most importantly, also at stake here is a *coming together* of heterodirective and autodirective commands. The Italian philosopher Roberto Esposito has named this confluence of forces, as I have already discussed, the immunitary paradigm, whereby violence is not only introjected within the subject, that is, heteroconstrictions are transformed into autoconstrictions, but where also violence comes to be used against itself—in a prophylactic manner—in order to solve the Hobbesian problem of order (2004, 44–45).

The Succubal Subject

Scipio Sighele (1868–1913) was a disciple of Cesare Lombroso and the author of a long list of volumes that centered on the psychology of the crowd. One of the founders of mass psychology, he remains understudied in Italy and ignored entirely in the English-speaking world.[11] Sighele, like so many of his fellow positivists, was trained as a lawyer, and, like Enrico Ferri and Giuseppe Pugliese, he rose to national prominence through defending ordinary citizens who had been caught in mob riots or who had been pushed to desperate actions out of poverty and need. Sighele believed that the individual was profoundly affected by being in a crowd. In particular, and this was the essence of his first major work from 1891, *La folla delinquente,* the presence of a crowd had wide-ranging consequences for the question of responsibility. As he stated: "The idea of criminality and above all of responsibility is not an abstract and purely *moral* idea, but a practical, relative, and *social* idea," an idea that thereby turns the violation of laws into a question of *social* responsibility (Sighele 1923, 131).[12] As Jaap van Ginneken has pointed out, Sighele and other positivist intellectuals defended radical activists in order to facilitate the construction of stable political organizations (the new Socialist Party in particular), to defend the rights of the disenfranchised and the poor, to bring about much needed social and institutional reform (1992, 72), and, as Donzelli has noted, to reorganize consent along lines that rendered the crowd increasingly passive (1995, 10). Reform, in other words, had its limits. Yet these limits were difficult to gauge, because change had to be distinguished from rebellion, political leadership always came perilously close to the suggestive and therefore criminal tendencies of the crowd, and the distinction between stable political organizations and riotous masses ever harder to maintain.

Sighele was obsessed with the drama of the influence of man over man. In his numerous studies of collective psychology, he achieved a transposition of the new political subject along lines similar to those of Braid's hypnotic subject, for what interested Sighele more than the political leader were his followers. In other words, Sighele looked closely at the men who climbed on to Donato's stage; he wondered at their particular morphology. Sighele's interests intersected here with a whole array of obsessions peculiar to post-Unification Italy: the instabilities of the Italian parliamentary system, the lack of regional integration into the nation-state, the restlessness of southern peasant "bandits" and northern workers, and, finally, the unstable gender relations that were treated obsessively in contemporary Italian political and cultural discourses. All these issues are brought together in Sighele's widely read *La coppia criminale: Studio di psicologia morbosa* of 1893. What Sighele achieves in this study is to shift the focus from the hypnotist to the hypnotized within the Donatic couple, from the leader to the led, though now in an explicitly politico-sexual language.

In great part because of its struggle against Catholicism and "atavistic superstition," positivism rejected the concept of free will and, with it, the religious idea of guilt. Instead, it proposed, as I pointed out with Morselli, that human actions were always guided by and subject to the necessity of social-scientific laws. While positivism thus promised liberation from guilt, it nevertheless had trouble defining, let alone managing, these newly determined and determining laws of social action. The discovery of scientific hypnosis and its eventual criminalization were important tools in the creation of a field of study dedicated to the control of social pathology. This was a field whose primary sources were understood to be found in the atavistic throwbacks that pervaded Italian society, both at the ontogenic and phylogenic levels. In a first round of attack, this meant concentrating on bad or dangerous *leaders:* political leaders of "sects" (these could be religious in nature, anarchist, or socialist), corrupt leaders in Parliament, southern bandit leaders, or "great" criminals. All of these leaders were perceived as dangerous because they possessed some inexplicable power that allowed them to dupe the masses; hence, all bad leaders came to be figured as close relatives of the hypnotist or the magnetizer. The hypnotist was dangerous because his power operated secretly and because he was capable of a two-pronged attack on society: first, he was capable of inflicting crimes on unsuspecting victims by paralyzing their resistances (rape was particularly emphasized here); second, and more indirectly, he could turn his victims into automata with his powers of suggestion and thereby coerce the victim him- or herself to commit a crime (and here the crime against private property was of most concern). The proper response to such leaders was repression, and this was in fact the political strategy put into place, especially in the South, by the military policies of the state during the first decades after Unification.

It was the possibility of getting someone else to commit a crime that caused the whole system to unravel, for now the criminal was not only the bad leader but also the victim. Lombroso had articulated the notion of the born criminal, but how was one to categorize the victim of that criminal who him- or herself turned criminal? The "suggested" criminal threatened the very notion of "propriety," both of the subject him- or herself and of the objects that he or she illegally appropriated for him- or herself. And hence crime came to take on a thousand faces, the instigator ever harder to locate, and the distinction between normal and pathological blurred to such an extent that *any* crime could be committed by *any member* of the population on the basis of a perverse suggestive instigation. If hypnosis or suggestion (as hypnosis in its waking state now came to be called) could take its effects when the subject was awake and fully conscious, then how could one tell the difference between normal and suggested actions? Thus, in its very threat to the "proper," suggestion came to be oddly universalized, guaranteeing thereby its role in normal, everyday life. Furthermore, and Sighele insisted on this, the universality of suggestion both derived from and produced actions that were determined noncoercively, that is, consensually, though paradoxically not freely. We find here, with the removal of the hypnotist,[13] a peculiarly acephalous form of power, proper in fact to a democratic polity based on consent. Nonetheless, this was a form of consent that was no longer contractual, but rather ideological and dependent on a displacement of violence downward to the masses. And indeed, the power that resided in suggestion was precisely its imputed ability to transform violence into consent.[14]

Sighele begins here. He considers two facts axiomatic. First, the smallest but most significant social unit is the couple: "In psychology and in sociology there are no simple *admixtures,* or inorganic *rapprochements,* of two or more bodies:—there are only *combinations.* The action that results from the coming-together of two persons is therefore not an *addition* but a *product*" (1893, 87). Second, the social bond within the couple is founded on "the secret power of suggestion" (4). While there may be instances when suggestion appears in such a weak form as to lead one to believe that the individual is actually autonomous, nevertheless it is Sighele's aim "to highlight the efficaciousness of the social factor, that is, suggestion" (23). Two forms of association may be formed from this suggestive relation. Either one partner dominates the other, in which case the stronger partner absorbs the weaker. Or, a mutual fascination may almost equalize their respective importance, and then the two individuals fuse into one. In the case of fusion, Sighele also speaks of suggestion as a form of psychic mimeticism (13). Whether suggestion works as the continuous exertion of power of the one over the other or whether it works reciprocally, the end result is always the same, because this relation *à deux,* this phenomenon of two souls in one body, produces always *one single psychological figure.* Whether absorption (the paradigmatic case of which is the amorous couple) or fusion (such as seen between equals, for example, between brothers), the suggestive relation is central and can be broken down into two *positions:* that of the "incubus" and that of the "succubus," that is, a position that thinks and instigates (the head) and a position that submits and acts (the arm), one that loves and one that is loved. The incubus, in loving, incites; and the succubus, in passively being loved, acts.[15]

The smallest form of criminal association is the one between two people, an association held together not by force or despotically but by one psychological characteristic alone: the *invisible* power of suggestion. Sighele considers the power of suggestion nothing less than a scientific fact, ever since it had been discovered that suggestion could take place while the subject is fully awake. A pervert corrupts a weakling, an evil genius seduces a man of average intelligence and weak morals to a crime, a born criminal makes an occasional criminal into his slave and instrument—this is the criminal couple. And it is only a study of this criminal couple that will allow a full understanding of crime more generally: "I believe that engagement only with the mafia, with the camorra, with banditry, is not sufficient to really know that complex phenomenon that is the association amongst delinquents: . . . it is necessary to go deeper down to the study of its *embryonic forms,* where the criminal bond takes shape in a weak and indistinct manner, and to accompany it through all its successive manifestations as it gains in force and clarity" (16; my emphasis). Sighele thus defines, in his commitment to return to embryonic forms, a spectrum of criminal activity that stretches from the criminal couple to the criminal crowd, a spectrum whose various stages of development comprise an incubatory process giving birth to the nightmarish product of uncontrollable mass movements.

But Sighele wants to make greater claims rather than simply to describe crime in its embryonic form, for the criminal couple functions as proof of the *universality* of the suggestive relationship between incubus and succubus. What the criminal couple teaches us is that "pathology follows the same laws as physiology" (5). Hence, the identical incubatory process may also be observed in "normal" couples and their offspring—normal sects, social movements, and societies: "This form *à deux* of suggestion is not only proper to the world of delinquents; it manifests itself, though obviously in different forms and with different effects, but for the same reason, also in the world of the honest, as well as in the noncriminal forms of degeneration, such as suicide and madness" (17). Here, then, is the normal field. We regularly encounter in everyday life the emergence of a tie between two individuals that arises as a result of fascination or of the domination that one exercises over the other. The normal couple, we could then say, is a Donatic couple. In love, there is always one who loves, one who is psychologically independent and superior (the incubus) and one who is loved, who is dependent and submissive (the succubus). Quite significantly, Sighele believed that the incubus's will is not only imposed on the succubus; rather, the succubus fulfills the partner's wishes because he or she can *anticipate* them. Thereby "the tendencies and habits of the two gradually become the same, not because they were by chance already so beforehand, but because the tendencies and habits of the one *have sweetly won over those of the other*" (18; my emphasis). The incubus and the succubus become one, mimetically, and yet Sighele insists that two people who are identical could not conjoin; they must neutralize each other, as in a chemical reaction. Given this identificatory drive that depends on difference, it is of course difficult to know how desire remains alive, how the moral power of the incubus can be sustained over time, and how "the diversity of function"—the distinction between head and arm—can be kept in place. Why should the arm not begin thinking once absorption or fusion has taken its effects? In fact, Sighele holds quite explicitly to a hierarchization of functions: diversity implies superiority, organization is synonymous to subordination (21), to the extent that suggestion is operative. The glue of society *and* the basis for the division of labor is then constituted and held in place by the power of suggestion.

The prototype of suggestion is to be found in the normal amorous couple, exemplified in particular, Sighele says, by woman's love rendered to "great men." Sighele provides us with few examples of such normal love, but those few are very interesting. One such example is the love between Abélard and Éloise. Sighele cites one of Éloise's letters: " 'I had no thought, you know, of satisfying either my will or my desires, but only yours. While the word bride is holier, I prefer the sweeter one of mistress, that—be not offended—of your concubine or your whore. The more I humiliated myself for you, the more I hoped to win your heart' " (18–19).[16] The advantage of this example, Sighele believes, is that, because suggestion is hard to see in everyday life, where it is weak and indistinct, it is easily visible in strong and impetuous love. In either case, however, the phenomena are identical; they differ only in degree. For example, Sighele immediately continues, and his example is hardly fortuitous, let us imagine one of those dramas that are anything but rare in everyday life, in which a woman turns a man into a slave, making him forget his duties as a husband and son, his dignity as man and citizen, and forcing him to commit all sorts of follies. This is clearly a case of a cold and clever person who binds to herself a weak or enthusiastic man, using all the weapons offered her by art and nature. "Obviously " this man has been suggested, tamed like a domestic animal by his dominatrix and made to forget everything and everybody, just like one hypnotized by a hypnotist (23).

Such, then, are the dynamics of the normal amorous couple, and all other possible couples order themselves along two axes of gradual differentiation: a pathological axis of suicidal couples, insane couples, criminal couples, and degenerate couples; and a sexual-sublimatory axis, if you will, of lovers, married couples, siblings, disciples, friends, and so forth. This dual determination provides an enormous possibility of combinations and configurations:

> In the comparison between the healthy couple and the criminal couple, we have chosen as exemplary of the first the couple of lovers, even though . . . there are couples of brother and sister, teacher and student, male friends, that also exhibit the phenomenon of suggestion *à deux*. The reason for this choice lies in the fact that the amorous couple presents in more pronounced and acute form those traits that are common to the other couples, where they exist in more attenuated form. In criminal couples, too, the psychological bond that unites lovers is always stronger than the one between relatives or two friends. . . . In couples of murderous or infanticidal lovers, the influence on the part of the more energetic character (incubus) over the weak character (succubus) is always stronger than in other couples. This is not because the succubus is more open to suggestion and the incubus superior (these are circumstances that vary from case to case), but only because the sexual bond uniting two people is the most powerful weapon used in persuasion and suggestion. (81)

The graph defined by these two axes is peopled by a potentially infinite number of combinations, giving rise to character types. The point that Sighele makes, and makes repeatedly, is that there are no clear distinctions to be made between born criminals, occasional criminals, criminals of passion, and normal persons. We find only gradations of types, "because each shading of feeling, each minimum difference of character, has an individual who constitutes its representation and living embodiment" (82).

If viewed within traditional gender relations, then the incubus is generally male, a male hypnotist who preys on innocent maidens while they sleep or look the other way, and the succubus is his female, submissive counterpart, dedicated to fulfilling her partner's every wish. But a paradox is built into the heart of this relationship: the Sighelian relation between incubus and succubus is *not* reducible to the performance of the missionary position. Indeed, of the many cases of murderous couples cited, the woman functions as incubus to the male succubus at least half the times. There is gender trouble at the core of the Sighelian couple, not simply because these two positions lack a biologically determined foundation, but more because, at least at a structural level, *the incubus and the succubus do not actually ever meet;* both the incubus and the succubus require an *innocent* partner who, by virtue of this innocence, may be seduced or at least educated into the proper position.[17] Without such gender trouble, Sighele's entire system would in fact collapse; he would simply not be able to explain the existence of crime or violence or account for any other social instability. It is the very indeterminacy of gender relations that is the site or cause for, as well as the symptom of, those broader political problems that Sighele struggles with in his text. The instability, if not impossibility, of the suggestive relation between incubus and succubus is predicated on the fact that what the succubus embodies is a form of being on top to the extent that he is at the bottom—one might even say that this is the essence of Sighele's understanding of revolutionary modernity. Hence, the succubus constitutes a threat to the distinction between incubus and succubus. It is in this threat that political crisis and gender crisis become one within the text, for it is the succubus who bears in his (her?) body, like a germ, the ability to *act:* "The executor of the crime, as for suicide, is almost always he who at first had rebelled against the idea of the crime; the instigator contents himself with planting the seed into the soul of his companion, a seed that slowly grows and then must take possession of him" (25). The succubus is, in other words, an incubator of crime; and the crime is first and foremost the erasure of all distinctions. A succubus is one who takes on—illegitimately—the functions of the incubus, who destroys the couple relation and thereby gives birth to a *social product.* The "pregnancy" of the relationship between the two positions in Sighele's text, the importance rendered to such crimes as infanticide, abortion, and even Malthusian birth control are thus not irrelevant language that can easily be translated back into a more proper "political" discourse. These terms constitute the heart of what Sighele perceives to be the political and social crisis of a modern time and environment where suggestion has become the norm. The indeterminate gender relations between incubus and succubus are not only the prototypes of the actions of the criminal couple, but they furnish the very figural grid by which Sighele is able to make sense of the "invisible power of suggestion" as the essence of modern social and political relations. The succubal position describes a pregnant, a maternal body, an incubatory process that guarantees an albeit uncertain readability of what Sighele calls suggestion in its embryonic form.[18]

In the end, and for these reasons, it is the succubus who truly fascinates Sighele: "the succubus . . . in the criminal couple is the more interesting" (90). Indeed, the succubus acts out for Sighele a whole series of theoretical functions. The succubus is the vehicle by which Sighele rids himself of the category of the Lombrosan born criminal (who is conveniently pushed into the category of the incubus) and by which he focuses on that category of specifically *social* actions that find no evident biological or natural explanation. The formulation of crime as a product of two (a *social product*) also allows him to eliminate the single criminal, whom he in any case considers less dangerous because he invariably acts either from need or from passion. Single criminals are always, for Sighele, a psychological absurdity, or at best a throwback to earlier times. In a later work, Sighele will in fact equate crimes of passion and of need to the crimes of primitive societies. Modern crimes, the crimes of the succubus, are more refined and civilized; they are crimes based on reasoning and logic, exhibiting what he calls "*pazzia ragionante* [reasoning madness]." Ferocity has ceded place in the modern world to fraud, violence to cleverness. The unreadability of this new criminal is fundamental, the fact that he cannot be easily recognized or detected. The man who dresses well does not immediately inspire fear because we unconsciously assume him to be honest. The succubus is fundamentally a bourgeois (Sighele 1913).

Most important of all, the succubus is not simply an automaton, because he is capable of resisting, or at least of distinguishing between, a physical threat and the power of suggestion. Sighele insists that suggestion *always* implies an absence of violence and thus the presence of choice (71–72). Choice appears symptomatically in the presence of moral aversion to the crime, seen most readily in the time it takes the succubus to commit the crime (the period of incubation) and in the guilt felt by him or her, guilt that then leads to spontaneous confession. Perhaps most crucially, the succubus's personality is fundamentally split, whereby an external suggestion, in order to have effect, must be internalized, implanted like a germ. Suggestion is in reality *auto*suggestion, a process wherein the author of the crime believes the deed to have been committed by someone living inside of him or her, someone he or she does not even know. In the end, all premeditation is autosuggestion (77), and the prototype of such autosuggestion is, according to Sighele, abortion. Abortion, which of course is the interruption of another incubatory process, as is infanticide more generally, is usually committed by the mother "alone," a fact that can be explained only by the doubled (here, quite literally, pregnant) nature of the succubal position (55).[19]

I would like to turn now to the fecundity of this interior space as it appears in groups. All life in common is an extremely favorable breeding ground for suggestion, criminal or otherwise; when physical vicinity becomes psychological purpose, then we have a crowd (Sighele 1913, 46). Sighele implicitly distinguishes between traditional social groups that have a powerful incubus and those more modern groups of self-suggesting succubi. Thus, what happens in degenerate couples also takes place at the collective level between a despot and his people. The long habit of submission, as for example in Russia, will organically turn a people into a servile people, leading not only to obedience but also to the love and adoration by the people not only of the leader but also of the structure of obedience itself. This is a Catholic morality, states Sighele, one that turns men into eunuchs, into brutes, into automata; it is a morality where women, who are the victims of their fathers and their lovers, continue to love them hysterically. No social group can avoid this stage of blind obedience, however, just like the young scientist, when attracted to or "suggested by" a theory, must initially accept it in its entirety, like any disciple who accepts all the concepts of the master's teaching. Only gradually will the student be able to distance himself from some of the master's ideas and form his own. "The period of scientific independence follows that of supine obedience, but it cannot do otherwise, it cannot leap over it" (107).[20] Modern society is characterized as a form of communal living that ideally has left behind the position of supine obedience; it no longer has an incubus, or at least not one that is visible. It has, instead, internalized the incubal function, a fact that explains contemporary unhappiness or discontent: "Social life, and therefore also political life, hinges on the phenomenon of suggestion. Happy were the times and the peoples that had a genius on whom to concentrate all their desires, their hopes, and their feelings, a genius who drew blindly behind himself the crowd!" (262).[21]

It is necessary to stress Sighele's own profound ambivalence about such a process of modernization that is characterized by both independence and loss. The belief in free will, he states in *Morale privata e morale politica,* has been destroyed. The human brain, once believed an absolute monarch, has been reduced to a constitutional monarch, whose decrees are nothing but "a crowd of physical, moral, and intellectual factors that leave him with only a semblance of freedom" (Sighele 1913, 67). A single person may *act,* but has he not always been moved, quite unaware of himself, by an invisible crowd composed of his ancestors, his compatriots, his educators, "whose combined and imagined influences in his brain awaken suddenly and by surprise a veritable internal multitude that crawls and ferments inside his brain?" (68). The disappearance of the incubus has given way to another, far more frightening, nightmare, staking out a form of interiorization where power is no longer felt as a weight upon man's chest, but rather as ants crawling inside his brain.[22] What Sighele desires is not a return to happier times—these he in any case equates to superstition and atavism—but to *a consciously desired and visible attachment to power,* which is how he defines legitimate and stable forms of society.

The new succubal ego reduced to nothing but a constitutional monarch cannot fulfill these criteria, for the succubus, like the crowd, is a feminized creature. The crowd bears passively in her hands the fate of the world. The crowd is a woman who arouses in man the love to work for civilization, claims Sighele in series of sliding and mutually sustaining metaphors that return us to the conjugal couple: "It is for her that the hero works, as man for a woman, but just like a woman, the crowd does not know how to be productive alone. Her anonymous glory is to procreate, without knowing it, the genius that will increase a little the catalogue of her riches. Therefore her sole function should be to love and serve the genius, just like the wife who loves and serves her husband" (40–41). The problem is that the crowd is never a wife or a mother, but a mere woman (*femmina*), whose gratitude consists mostly in crucifying her saviors. The lack of conjugal love, the dream, that is, of the ideal missionary-positioned couple, founders on the fact that true partnership has disappeared in favor of a splitting mechanism within the political subject himself. This splitting has the status of a political revolution (one that had also been heralded by Enrico Morselli): to be on top means being—quite strangely—on the bottom, while being on the bottom inevitably is a form of being on top. For this reason Sighele is an antiparliamentarian. Modern politics, in its peculiar confusion of positions, is an immorality, and one has only to study its period of incubation—elections—to realize that the parliamentary process is a new form of brutality and tyranny. The "parliamentary crowd" (parties and mass politics) is itself split, like the succubus, between a majority and a minority, ostensibly for democratic reasons, but in reality because it produces another form of crowd psychology. The parliamentary crowd is ruled by contradiction, cruelty, and the rapid passage from one feeling to the next: "The Chamber . . . is psychologically a woman and often also a hysterical woman" (Sighele 1913, 247). Thus, the male parliamentarian is sucked into the voracious womb of democratic institutions, and Agamben's "homo sacer" is turned, as Žižek has coined the new phrase, into a "homo sucker" (2002, 71).

If the problem of the modern male subject is his loss of power, his feminization, his seemingly inevitable status of "being-under-the-influence-of," then the evidence for this is, paradoxically, not that he must submit to an incubus. On the contrary, it is the growing *ineffectiveness* of the incubus that is ultimately so threatening. The more suggestion is operative, the weaker is the incubus, and this because the succubus is only too obedient and in that obedience gains the capacity to swallow up the incubus, to derail the incubal function and turn it into autosuggestion. Sighele hints here at a totalitarian form of power that is predicated on the *absence* of a leader, which he understands, paradoxically, as a threat to masculinity. It is for this reason that Sighele insists on the *couple,* in particular on the continued theoretical function or, if you will, on the *hypothesis* of the incubus. The incubus bears the weight of both a temporal and a structural function in Sighele's text. The incubus stands in, on the one hand, for a lost form of political power, for a dream, that is, of masculine performativity. On the other hand, he stands in for that which enables the succubus to be himself, to be an agent. The incubus takes effect only as absence, that is, as his own self-effacement: Donato's subjects are able to act out their roles without the hypnotist's actual presence, or more accurately, only when they can autosuggest themselves. The incubus effects the *gap* necessary within the succubal subject, the space where power can operate phantasmatically as the subject's interior other. Morselli points indirectly to this function when he insists on Donato's ability to bring about a deferred action in his subjects, that is, to get them to act in a posthypnotic state. While the succubus may be the product of the incubus, it is nevertheless also the case that the incubus, qua hypothesis, is structurally an aftereffect of the succubus. The incubus and the succubus exist in a relation of an inevitable and even tragic *Nachträglichkeit.* The succubus depends on a complexly defined positionality where he is both part of a whole (the couple) while also standing in for the whole itself. The Sighelian fantasy couple is in this sense always gendered, gendered not simply to maintain traditional relations of power but because it points to and upholds difference as such. The Sighelian couple thus embodies a universality predicated simultaneously on the acknowledgment and the foreclosure of difference. When Donato put his men on stage, he did not only convince them to act like men who imitated machines who imitate men. These subjects were also men who imitated women who imitated men.

It is because of the articulation of this political crisis as a crisis of gender that Sighele's text ends with a seemingly bizarre appendix divided into two parts: an extended discussion of child murder and a reprinting of the 1891/92 proposal before the Italian Parliament to protect abandoned and abused children. Here the management of family relations becomes the foundation for the resolution of all political relations. The relations of love within the family are in fact indistinguishable from the suggestive relations of civil and political society; both are driven by the same passions that make and unmake private and public relations. There are, for Sighele, two aspects to the problem of child abuse: abused and abandoned children are both victims and little succubi who, at their parents' behest, become members of the world of crime and prostitution. "Most of the crimes committed by children are to be attributed to their families' bad examples or indifference, and therefore it is these families who bear . . . the largest responsibility" (Sighele 1893, 122). And this is because the difference between a parent who abandons a child to the "immoral suggestions and economic difficulties of the social environment" and a parent who beats, hurts, or even kills a child is merely one of degree (127).

What Sighele points to here is nothing less than a crisis of the family, one predicated on the fact that love is in reality suggestion and therefore always open to a return to violence in the form of crime. Though he does contemplate the possibility, Sighele does not believe that such domestic violence can be resolved through paternal or domestic repression: "Is it not easy to exceed correction? Who can tell where just severity ends and useless cruelty begins?" (129). Nor does he see repressive state laws as an effective answer. For one, Italians both refuse the state's intrusion into the privacy of the family—along the lines of "every man is master of his own house"—while at the same time overly relying on the state to fix all problems: "We are unable to do anything on our own; we expect everything from the state. Italians are, by virtue of their race, anti-individualists. We expect from Government and from Parliament all the things that we deem useful and necessary" (146). And Sighele rejects a repressive solution as well, because it is always and inevitably a "miserable weapon against crime," since it can only helplessly strike back after the fact and since it is unable to furnish an example, that is, a model to be emulated. Violence and repression can only passively imitate each other; they cannot bring forth change (143).

The solution for Sighele lies in the creation of what he calls a "*juste milieu*" (132), one that takes into account a fundamental instability or injustice at the heart of the family: "Equality is not a law of the human heart, and the proportional distribution of affect is a more insoluble problem than that of the proportional distribution of wealth." While we easily speak of parental love, we rarely confront the problem of parental hate. In reality, "in every family where there is more than one child, there is always a preferred one, a Benjamin, and a neglected one, a Cinderella" (129). And in a footnote, Sighele expands on this "psychological mystery" of gendered injustice: "Generally the father prefers the girl and neglects the boy; while the mother prefers the son and neglects the daughter. This cross-gendered sympathy between parent and child is perhaps nothing but . . . the pale reflection of love as it has prolonged itself across the generations" (129n2). One is reminded here of Freud's own theory of (political) justice that he too sees as originating in the nursery. Freud's mechanism is of course reversed, for while Sighele views injustice as originating from the *real* difference in love proffered to the child, Freud's perspective is that of the child. It is the child who lives with the *suspicion* or *fantasy* that he or she is unequally loved, whence from envy he or she decides to forfeit primacy as long as the siblings do the same. For Freud, it is the child that founds justice; the origins of justice always stem from the child's revolt against parental authority. The Freudian scenario is thus a reenactment of the social contract based in consent (Freud 1959b). Sighele's family romance, on the other hand, is grounded in an inevitable, because "real," violence. Sighele's reversed Oedipal scenario of intergenerational and cross-gendered love has as its underbelly the almost inevitable degeneration into domestic violence, where neglect turns into injustice and beatings and where Cinderella turns into a victim (Sighele 1893, 130).[23]

Given this cross-gendered nature of violence—where by definition Cinderella is the victim and never Benjamin—such violence always originates with the mother: "*libericide* is *usually* committed by the mother" (128). Sighele explains this by reference to the hothouse nature of the family environment, as well as by the fact that the mother is confined to this space by contemporary social structures: "While man commands a much broader field in which to live his feelings and thoughts, woman has in today's society nothing but the restricted field of the family. Man lives, fights, fears, hopes for *ideas* and *things,* as well as for *people;* woman, on the other hand, generally lives and fights only for people" (131). Because her emotional life is less diffused, woman lives her existence in a more intense way. Hence she is both angel and demon, Christian sister of charity and tiger or hyena. This excess of emotion gives her the strength to subdue man; the family is founded in a psychological rapport between a perverse mother and a weak father, between a maternal incubus and a paternal succubus. A woman may be a mother when she delivers a child, but in her later actions and in her will she is inevitably a stepmother to her Cinderella (141).

If the relationship between incubus and succubus produces always a *social fact,* and if the succubus is both part and result of this relationship, then the succubal father might very well provide the port of entry into the management of the family. And indeed such is the tenor of Sighele's proposed legal reform. Given the already proven incapacity of the father to take upon himself the responsibility of his children, the protection of children must revert to society, and to the state in particular, though not through acts of repression (of the father or the children), but instead through agencies capable of *protecting* children. The goal of the state must be to "observe" and "provide," to "inspect" and "free" children from the suggestions that are rampant in the family. Repression and legal measures are to cede place to example and discipline, that is, to an alternative *social* suggestion, and in that move, the newly conceived disciplinary knowledges are to directly confront and also manage the fact that power now resides in and as the "social."[24]

Other Theaters

In 1890, four years before martial law was declared on the island by the Crispi government, the Sicilian village of Mezzojuso was the site of another drama, one that had as its basic plot a family romance gone awry. As with the Teatro Scribe in Turin, this too involved a drama that centered on the problem of fascination, which constituted an integral part of the religious culture of southern Catholicism.[25] Sighele's account of events dates from the same year as the publication of *La coppia criminale* and appears in a sort of criminological atlas of Italy under the title *Il mondo criminale italiano.* "The Drama of Mezzojuso" is placed under the heading of "crimes of superstition" and is divided into two parts: the "facts" and an "expert opinion."[26]

"Did the atrociously savage scene that I am about to narrate really happen in Italy, or is it not perhaps a sad dream brought back from Medieval chronicles?"—so Sighele begins his account of events "whose actors and setting of a drama" do not belong, it seems, to "our century," but to "another age, to the strange phenomenon of collective atavism" (1893–1894, 13). The drama centers on the Carnesi family, composed of the father, Rosario; the mother, Vita La Gattuta; and their seven children. This is a family, according to Sighele, in which *patria potestas* is in place, where all is *"casa e chiesa."* Vita La Gattuta is more nun than wife—though this is somewhat belied by the existence of her seven children—and she exhibits "a strong neurological coloring" and an "excessive and morbid religiosity" (16). These characteristics she has handed down to her children, especially to her first-born, Biagio, and her daughter Lucia. Religious fervor, it appears, solders Biagio and Lucia into a "possible incestuous relation," thereby proving that "mysticism at times may descend into obscenity" (16). On December 8, 1890, on the Feast of the Virgin, Biagio undergoes an intense religious conversion that takes the form of mystic delusions and hallucinations, and he manifests a melancholia that prevents him from getting out of bed in the morning. Thus, "he no longer was a man, but a beast" (18). Biagio's melancholic religiosity, it proves, is contagious, and within a month his brothers Salvatore and Tommaso succumb to identical symptoms. Lucia and the youngest son, Giacomo, soon follow.

Lucia's religious "insanity," however, differs from that of her siblings. Whereas her brothers become melancholic, her insanity is that of a "religious exaltation that left her intellectual faculties intact and multiplied by a hundred her moral energies and physical strength" (21). Above all, Lucia gains healing powers and is able to save her father's life in one incident, as well as improve the condition of her brother Giacomo. Lucia is also held partly responsible for the fact that an oak tree uprooted during a storm does not destroy the parental home.

On the night of the crime, cousins of the Carnesis, the Nuccio family, take in Lucia, Caterina, and Giacomo, while the Carnesi parents remain at home to watch over the brothers Biagio, Tommaso, and Salvatore. It is at this point that Lucia, in a trance, makes the decision to save her beloved brother Biagio from the spell cast upon him, and she sets out to her home with her cousins and a growing crowd of villagers. "The hour of martyrdom had arrived; religious sacrifice had to find its outlet in blood" (28). At the Carnesi home, at Lucia's command, the whole village kneels and prays for Biagio's salvation: "The women implored grace with sighs and sobs and put into their prayers the savage furor that is proper to their sex when it is invaded by mysticism. The men, due to contagion and to that unknown bond that exists between transport to God and to woman, imitated the women, and thereby they formed a confused, clamorous, and diabolic collectivity" (29). Within this crowd, it is only Lucia who thinks and acts; she is a true incubus to succubal others who are "suggested by her; they are the blind instruments of her will" (30). Lucia's object of exorcism is Biagio, and in a rising escalation of violent religious ritual, Lucia, with the sacred wood of Saint Anthony and her fingernails, beats to death and then castrates her brother in front of the entire village. Lucia had passed from mere "savage mysticism" to "sensual mysticism" and in that act torn the veil cast over centuries of civilization: "The human beast revealed itself in all its brutality across the stratification of centuries, a beast no longer contained by modesty and purity. Known to be a most modest virgin, Lucia was transformed by one of those rebellions of the flesh that remind of the intimate connections between the sexual instinct and love for the divinity, between human sacrifices and the religious prostitution of ancient times" (33). The following morning, the members of the Carnesi family are arrested. Lucia, Salvatore, and Tommaso are eventually confined to a mental institution; the rest of the family is released because the presiding judges determine that they had acted as a result of suggestion—in other words, their will and responsibility had been only temporarily derailed. This is a verdict founded in an expert understanding of the event because founded in the distinction between incubus and succubus, and therefore deemed by Sighele an honor to Italian psychiatric science (35).

Sighele—in Mezzojuso—hits a kind of theoretical bedrock as he gazes, fascinated, at that "shred of soft, velvety, and bleeding flesh," at that "dead virility" held in Lucia's left hand (35). He repeats through his own prose the very obscenity that he so deplores, because if there is a true succubus in Sighele's work, then it is the brotherhood that he joins gathered under the leadership of Lucia—and the collectivity's most eloquent bond is the gaping wound of castration around which this group is assembled. Biagio's dead, emasculated body, his destroyed virility, haunts the second part of Sighele's account like a specter, provoking both the best and the worst analysis of which Sighele is capable. And so his explanations of the events in Mezzojuso are divided into three points: the specificity of the village's religious structure, its socioeconomic base, and Lucia's psychic makeup. Together, they found, for Sighele, the very possibility of causal historical narratives, and yet they also signal the (traumatic) collapse of those same narratives.

Mezzojuso is religiously split between the Greek Orthodox and the Roman Catholic Churches. Though this division has not resulted in sectarian conflict—the inhabitants of the village have intermarried, and both religions are frequently practiced within one family—the existence of alternative religious practices has contributed in the village to a heightened awareness of religious rituals. This awareness explains why mysticism is deeply rooted in the culture of Mezzojuso—more, indeed, than in the religiously unified villages nearby, where, therefore, secularization has made greater inroads. And hence, "from religiosity to superstition to a tendency toward the supernatural—religion's carnal sisters—it is but a short step" (38). Aside, then, from this last statement regarding "carnal sisters"—why carnal? why sisters?—Sighele's is, in fact, a rather subtle analysis of the complex roles played by religious factors, an analysis that itself is profoundly secular yet sympathetic in its conception of how subjects are constituted in often contradictory ways. Thus, his analysis of the village's religious culture is anything but reductive. In the split signaled by the presence of two churches, Sighele claims a space of negotiation for the construction of religious culture that can neither be reduced to the Church's hegemonic practices, nor be viewed as simply outside the realm of the Church. For the same reason, also, Sighele does not place the village's religious identity "beyond the state" or "beyond modernization." Instead, he tends to view the construction of religious identity in terms of complex structures of mediation between popular and hegemonic culture.

The same may be said of Sighele's socioeconomic analysis. The economy of Mezzojuso feeds the mysticism and superstition of the peasants because, more even than the rest of the south, the village finds itself in an acute crisis. Its major symptom is emigration, an emigration that regularly takes Mezzojuso's best inhabitants and that has disproportionately hit the Greek Orthodox community. As a result, Roman Catholicism is spreading, and the ancient Albanian customs and the traditional language are disappearing; the village is becoming culturally more homogeneous. The poor leave "as if obeying a fatality . . . and religious belief saves them from moral shipwreck, from despair. . . . It follows that the village is made up of an oscillating, transitory population, and religious mysticism is, so to speak, magnified by that tendency to adventure and the unknown that is proper to those peoples who have not yet achieved the stability of a home and are, more than elsewhere, put to the test by the harsh conditions of life" (40–41). The people of Mezzojuso do not "struggle, they disappear" (41). And therefore, "fed by the misery that transforms all the ancient small landholders into the mere manual laborers of the ungrateful American territories" (42), the drama that takes place in the Carnesi household "has found in the present conditions of the Mezzogiorno its *historical moment*" (42).

There is a break in the page as we pass from the Carnesi family as both the producer and the product of a historical moment to a very different kind of symptomatic analysis, one that is predicated on the medicalization of the Carnesi family and that has as its epicenter the figure of Lucia. Every sick organism, Sighele states, "has one point in which its morbid manifestations become acute and that apparently require the extreme remedy of surgery" (42). For the village of Mezzojuso, this point of acute morbidity is the Carnesi family. And what follows is, predictably, a compendium of the physical blemishes of the individuals of the family, a list of physical traits that are to speak an eloquent language of predestination, a language that reneges on the possibility of a sociohistorical discourse founded in conjunctural and accidental factors. Rosario Carnesi sports a cranial structure replete with "anomalies"; he is nothing but a "grotesque figure of savage man" (43). Vita la Gattuta suffers from hysterico-epilectic convulsions that are located predominantly in her jaw muscles. While she exhibits none of the typical symptoms of hysteria, "it is by now a well-known fact that hysteria reveals itself by the most contradictory scenic apparatuses and that it therefore lends itself equally to pervading the obscenity of prostitution as much as the asceticism of saints" (44). Vita's hysteria is that of the saints, and it shows itself first and foremost through her resignation and lethargy.

After passing through her brothers and her cousins—all prototypes of the succubus—Sighele moves on to the real object of his investigation: Lucia. Everyone is her blind and unconscious instrument; she is "the only one, among this group of morbidly undecided and vague figures, to show contours that are truly sculptural. She is the heroine, the sad heroine, of the drama: compared to her, the others seem mere supernumeraries, needed only to sketch out the background of this tragic scene" (46). Lucia is a monster or an animal: savage, with flashing, slanted eyes *"alla chinese"* and protruding upper teeth. Raised under the shadow of her mother's mysticism, she is exaggeratedly modest, literate, and adored by both her mother and her brother Biagio. Her healing powers in regard both to her father and her brother Giacomo fill her with a sense of divine investiture, and it is thus that she becomes a "theomaniac." This investiture, or her theomaniacal conviction, enables her to gather a crowd: "It was her inspired face that in a flash convinced that group of deluded. . . . Contagion does not spread by logic . . . but by silencing it through the impressiveness of the supernatural" (48).

Having thus delineated his context, Sighele goes on to ask: "How should the fact of January 23 be understood?" (48) What is truly striking in Sighele's answer to his own question is that all historical, cultural, social, and economic factors simply fall by the wayside in the last pages of his text, and his analysis is taken over by the overbearing presence of Lucia. It is as if her existence would undo his own discourse, in the face of her suggestive powers. Consequently his analysis must remain, ultimately, ambiguous, confined as Sighele is to a succubal position that enacts or stages the very theory that he seeks to control. On the one hand, then, Sighele most certainly participates in the construction of the cliché of the femme fatale,[27] of a rhetoric of mono-causality that, for instance, argues that on that fateful night Lucia was—after all—menstruating.

And yet, on the other hand, into this biological reductionism enters an uncertainty, a moral dilemma or undecidability between good and evil, an uncertainty that appears for the first time through a comparison of Lucia with another female figure: Joan of Arc. It is Lucia's similarity to Joan of Arc that leads Sighele to wonder whether Lucia may not in fact be the liberator of her people: "Lucia acquired, by divine orgasm, all the necessary efficacy to convince and draw to herself those minds that found themselves more or less at her level; and if, instead of leading to good like Joan of Arc, she led them to evil, then this depends exclusively on the different conditions and aims that were at the forefront of the desires of these two theomaniacs" (51). This strange comparison between the unknown virgin of Mezzojuso and the historical Joan of Arc, Sighele explains in terms of the "fatal cooling of logic and time" (51): while Lucia may be sociologically less important than Joan of Arc, she is more important psychologically speaking. Their differences can be explained only by the fact that they were born into different conditions and times.

> Joan became a heroine because she turned into a theomaniac during a disastrous period for her fatherland, and she led the faithful into a battle of the deluded who were rendered insensible by their fanaticism. Lucia, on the other hand, for whom the world was confined to her tiny and superstitious village, remained an unknown assassin, even while in her aims she was able to persuade all her followers by blinding them. Both were proud virgins and both were in love with God! Both, in order to suggest the masses, availed themselves of that eternal femininity that . . . becomes irresistible, where all the necessary conditions become one in order to constitute the historical moment of a fact, whether this fact be a murder or the liberation of the fatherland. (52)

It is his own construction of this historical fact that ultimately elides Sighele's analysis, for it turns out that it is the very historicity and facticity of any text that constitutes the true drama that arises as both the possibility of a castration and a murder, as—in other words—a return to primal instincts and as a certain unknowability, unreadability, and indeterminateness: "What ferocious instincts . . . made silent in Lucia all her virtues of affectionate sister and Christian virgin? That moment escapes a sure and objective investigation" (52). And hence the lesson. While the memory of the emasculated Biagio will, by virtue of its existence as historical fact, one constructed by the scientist Sighele himself, keep the poor peasants of Mezzojuso from the aberration of fanaticism in the future, for the investigating scientist, the drama of Mezzojuso furnishes the proof not only that "epidemics are a rapid, intermittent acutization of the ills that sporadically afflict daily life in less intensive ways" (57). More importantly, perhaps, it points to an unconscious that cannot be controlled by even the most astute analyst: "Psychology . . . never finds in phenomena the sum of causes, but only the result; a kind of diagonal in that mysterious parallelogram of psychic forces, into which enter not only those forces that are on the surface and known to us, but also the great part of the unknown life of the unconscious" (54).

Ramifications

The official triumph of a doctrine is slow and difficult to bring about, and furthermore is rather a sign that it is beginning to decline rather than showing its true merit. The day in which the principles of our doctrine have been codified will also be the day when another school of thought, younger and stronger, has appeared on the horizon. In addition, just as soldiers are not victorious by directly facing the enemy, but by slowly surrounding him and thus gaining by circuitous paths the best positions through which to deny him all defenses—so also in the battlefield of science one cannot expect to see our adversaries kneel down to our banner immediately. Instead, it is good tactics to try to breach the closed battlefield of the enemy's absolutist doctrines with partial findings and a few theories that have the appearance of being of minor importance. Once this breach has been made, the final triumph is simply a matter of time.[28]

My final comments are somewhat speculative and address the vicissitudes of positivism's role in Italian post-Unification culture. I would be inclined to agree with Sighele that it did not enjoy "an official triumph," but that it was perhaps successful in its Gramscian tactics of a "war of position" to bring about significant but more subtle changes. And here, there might be a further reason why Sighele insists on the distinction between incubus and succubus, one that is closely bound to his need to uphold difference in the face of its collapse in modern democratic societies. If the return to a past transparency of power is, for Sighele, neither possible nor even desirable, then what could provide the foundations—against the invisible power of suggestion—of a new transparency, one capable of generating a reformed moral and institutional order for Italian subjects? The displacement of the incubus into the succubal subject could, in fact, translate only with difficulty into political and administrative measures and regulations. More generally, in the absence of free will and guilt, it was difficult to conceive of legal measures capable of protecting the succubus from himself. Italian positivism lost its power of appeal by century's end precisely because of its difficulty in providing institutional solutions grounded in its social-scientific findings. Sighele's succubus proposed the radical decriminalization of all subjects and their submission to a new, modern logic of preventive and disciplinary controls. These controls were explicitly and of necessity to be beyond the province of repressive laws. More specifically, in an Italy of "new emotions," such a proposal may have been too new—and indeed would have to await the creation of a new order in 1922.[29] In a climate that was still committed to liberal principles and simultaneously to the traditional "sanctity of the family," Sighele's hypothesis of the incubus may be interpreted as a kind of compromise formation that would allow for a subject still capable of taking upon himself the burdens of legal responsibility. If the succubus is by his very nature an extralegal subject, the incubus is not. The incubus is a willing subject, one capable of decisive action, and as such capable of withstanding the trials that modernity exacts upon him. The incubus stands for the possibility of a consent rendered responsibly, even if he is not free to the extent that he must shoulder the burden of his shadowy other: his succubus.

Scipio Sighele and Gustave Le Bon publicly contested each other's claim of having invented the theory of mass psychology and in that sense replayed the theoretical terms at stake: Who of the two had been the true incubus of the theory of the masses? And of course the debate brought up again the age-old anxiety on the part of Italians about their possibly succubal position vis-à-vis French culture. In the annals of intellectual history, Le Bon appears to have won the debate. Nevertheless, Sighele's peculiar engagement with suggestion as the site of construction of the succubal subject functions as a kind of switching point for future developments in Western subjectivity. It is this switching point that merits further study, for Sighele's awareness of the intimate link between democracy and gender remains paramount for any discussion of or investigation into the crisis of liberalism that played itself out at the fin-de-siècle to a significant extent as a crisis of male performativity. And Sighele is pivotal because he symptomatically uncovered two of the directions in which theories of the subject moved after the demise of classical liberalism. He opened the path, on the one hand, to a conception of self as based in "character" or "personality," a conception that would come to replace the category of subject and remain hegemonic throughout the twentieth century and now into our own.[30] On the other hand, his work also provided the grounds for a psychoanalytic investigation into subjectivity, whereby the subject is constituted by desire and, in the wake of the liberation of that desire, saved by its reclaimed freedom.

In the first instance, character or personality studies have given birth to a succubal literature throughout the world and today support a booming industry that takes the shape of manuals of self-help and self-improvement. In Italy, a literature dedicated to the making and strengthening of character came into its own in the period between the two wars, when fascism was hegemonic. Clara Gallini claims to detect in the construction of character the very foundations of a fascist subject. She has noted that Italy during the 1920s and 1930s witnessed an explosion of books dedicated to the development of "personal magnetism" but that none of the manuals made any reference to Mr. Magnetic Man of the Italian twentieth century, that is, Mussolini. In Gallini's description of such a "magnetic man" as he emerges from these manuals, he is strong, calm, simple, and courteous, and he emanates to those around him ease and relaxation. Hence, those less fortunate multitudes of succubi who make up the rank of Italian citizens must use the utmost caution, for the magnetic personality will deplete them of their strength and steal from them those ideas that they do not have the courage to uphold. The goal of the succubus, then, is to develop with much practice and patience those latent powers that lie within him, powers that the magnetic, incubal man expresses naturally. "The *mimesis* of the magnetic man is presented thus as an ensemble of techniques of the body and rules of behavior, that produce internal security and social success through the introjection of the impossible model of the English gentleman" (Gallini 1983, 310). The function of such a literature is to bring about not necessarily a transformation, but instead a peculiarly new form of exercising the imagination through a relationship with the printed word. It is "no longer a human body that directly produces visible symbolic and materially tangible matter, but a printed page upon which the reader accomplishes his own mental exercise of fantastic evasion" (311). Gallini thereby implicitly raises the possibility that fascist masculinity is founded in the succubal subject to the extent that he comes into being through a phantasmatic relation to the written word and not necessarily or directly as a relation to an incubal leader. Such a Sighelian perspective would require us, I propose, to rethink in more differentiated terms the question of consent under fascism as a form of consent that has perhaps relied too much on a notion of Mussolini as "magnetizer."

In the second instance, in 1921 Sigmund Freud remembered his encounter over thirty years earlier with French hypnotic practices, and he claimed that they had even then elicited in him "a muffled hostility to this tyranny of suggestion" (1959b, 27–28). And he also recalled his reading of Sighele and Le Bon and their insistence on the centrality of suggestion as the foundation of society. For Freud—and here he did not differ from Sighele—suggestion was always an act of violence and injustice. Where Freud distanced himself from Sighele was in his claim that suggestion was a violence both in praxis and in theory. Not only did suggestion subdue the subject and thereby render him impotent; it did so illegitimately because such a subject was the product of a theoretical concept that claimed to explain all forms of social existence but "was itself to be exempt from explanation." What Freud pointed to was the concept's *phantasmatic* nature, its ultimate grounding in ideology. Freud proposed, then, to counter this violence by means of an act of liberation: that is, to substitute love or libido in place of suggestion. Love not only provided a better foundation for the understanding of "group psychology," it also constituted for Freud an act of liberation, because it posited consent in the form of *free association* as the foundation of modern democratic society.

THREE

The Queen and the Deputy: The Representative Politics of Matilde Serao's *La Conquista di Roma*

I propose to capture . . . living society in movement, just as the photographer surprises nature and forces her to be reflected in his apparatus. . . . May then arise a man of state of broad vision and iron will . . . with the fixed idea of turning Italy at all costs into an industrial nation.

LEONE CARPI, *L'ITALIA VIVENTE*

The conquest of Rome for the national territory in 1870 transformed the city into the third and permanent capital of a finally unified Italy. However, the integration of the city into the nation was at once traumatic and a project of renewal and self-generation. The seemingly irreparable rift between the new secular state and the Catholic Church, on the one hand, and, on the other hand, the possibility of a capital city insurgent against the nation (as the Paris Commune had made evident in all its nightmarish qualities) constituted the sources of the trauma. As to the project of renewal, in the wake of the annexation of Rome and the creation of the new capital, constructing a new image for Rome that could live up to the city's past glory became a primary focus of the new ideological agenda. At the same time, the project of "making Italians" became a pressing reality, particularly the making of a political class—the political deputies in the Parliament—capable of representing the new nation. And a not insignificant contribution to the cultural construction of the deputy was provided by a genre of literature generally referred to as the parliamentary novel.

In this chapter I will analyze one example of this genre, Matilde Serao's 1885 *La conquista di Roma*. The novel addresses itself to the "Roman question," that is, to the problem of the relationship between the Vatican and the Italian state, though it does so indirectly and in mediated form. The text is also a particularly illuminating engagement with two interrelated problems faced by the new national culture: the first relates to the construction, retroactively, of a national political tradition; the second, to the creation of a male subject capable of fulfilling the mandate of that new tradition. Regarding this second necessity, I will argue that Serao's literary engagement with such masculinity is to posit it as both the product and producer of a subject in crisis, to wit, as a masochistic subject. I will claim more broadly that the project here of "inventing a tradition" entailed for Italy a particular gender politics, one predicated, first, on a complex interrelationship between success and failure, that is, on an investiture of power as marginalization; and, second, on a gendered *vision* of political power organized around an ideological nucleus that had as its two main supports the masochistic male politician and the Madonna- or fairylike queen. I will also argue that in the Italian case the male masochistic subject was linked in crucial ways to the traumatic rift opened up by the separation of state and church. The male masochist thus came into being in the interstices of a historical trauma and as such constituted, through the crisis that it bespoke, a traumatic subject.[1]

The term "invented tradition" derives from Eric Hobsbawm, who defines it as "a set of practices, normally governed by overtly or tacitly accepted rules and of a ritual or symbolic nature, which seek to inculcate certain values and norms of behavior by repetition, which automatically implies continuity with the past" (Hobsbawm and Ranger 1992, 1). Hobsbawm argues that it is crucial that the creation of ritual symbolic practices took place at that historical juncture when liberalism failed, that is, when "new methods of ruling or establishing bonds of loyalty" (263) were required. My usage of the somewhat overworked trope thus seeks to restore some of the historical specificity that Hobsbawm initially attached to the idea of "invented tradition." At stake, then, was the nature of the social bond, the element that bound the subject both to the state and to society. In the face of the rise of the masses during the second half of the nineteenth century and the discovery of "irrational elements" in human nature, a new civic religion was required that "reintroduced . . . status into a world of contract, superior and inferior into a world of legal equals" (10). One might add that such a civic religion—and this was particularly important in the Italian case—had also to absorb and work over in displaced form cultural discourses that had hitherto been dominated by Catholicism. One final aspect of invented traditions should be mentioned here: their ritualistic nature not only blurred the distinction between civil society and the state; they also relied on a notion of politics as spectacle, and here, in the confluence of political and aesthetic problems of representation, rendered to culture a new role in the making of subjects.

Serao's *La conquista di Roma* follows the standard, repetitive plot of the vast number of parliamentary novels written during the forty years after Italian Unification. In the opening pages, the hero, Francesco Sangiorgio, the newly elected deputy from the southern region of Basilicata, arrives by train in Rome. An unknown quantity at first, he rapidly rises to prominence in the parliamentary world. His passionate attachment to politics is converted, however, to a passionate attachment to the married Angelica Vargas, and this conversion will become his undoing. Sangiorgio settles into his solitary love nest and spends the last third of the novel waiting for the "woman who cannot love" and wrecking his political career, until Angelica's husband, a government minister, ends the entire melodrama by sending the unfortunate Francesco back to where he came from. The novel ends with his ignoble return by train to his native Basilicata. Sangiorgio—and this despite his name—has not conquered Rome; she has conquered him.

The parliamentary novel depended entirely on a fixed and irreversible plot—the virgin deputy is burned by politics/woman—and on a set of predetermined elements—the inner struggle of the hero between moral strength and weakness, the spatial opposition between center (Rome) and periphery (the, usually southern, provinces), and the temporal conflict between past and present. Nevertheless, it is also the case, as Giovanna Caltagirone (1993) has persuasively argued, that the genre was able to create what she calls a "topos of the new."[2] Thus, the parliamentary novel not only produced a tradition of its own, one with fixed rules and expectations and with its own ritualistic practices, but it was also capable of working back to reality in such a way as to participate in the discursive construction of a new political reality replete with its own elements of invented tradition.[3] According to Caltagirone, the parliamentary novel, by virtue of its ritualistic, repetitive representation of politics, nonetheless contributed in crucial ways to a broadening of the political sphere into the domain of culture, to the extent that textual strategies increasingly came to reflect political strategies (21). Serao's own textual strategies here rely not only on an interweaving of representation as both politics and aesthetics (and for that reason, her references to representation must always be read in this double sense), but also on an appositional style of writing, an obsessive heaping of phrases upon phrases which enacts the very repetitive and ritual nature of the politics she explicitly engages.

Visions of Rome

The selection of Rome as the third and final capital of the Kingdom of Italy and the attendant consequences dominated Italian internal and foreign affairs both before and after the city was invaded by Victor Emanuel II's troops on September 20, 1870. While this invasion represented the final step toward national unification and hence the completion of a long desired process for Risorgimento thinkers, it also created new divisions and put stress on older ones. Thus, while the move of the capital to Rome promised an end to Piedmontese hegemony in the civil service through the recruitment of growing numbers of southerners[4]—and indeed within only a few decades such a shift had been accomplished—the northern middle classes withdrew, in response, to more lucrative employment in industry and commerce, thereby widening the already existing gap between a northern "productive" or "real" Italy and a southern "unproductive" or "legal" Italy. As Federico Chabod has noted, such a split was additionally strengthened by a northern tendency to focus on its relations with northern Europe, while the south—and this would become especially pronounced under the government of the Sicilian Francesco Crispi—concentrated its foreign policy on the rest of the Mediterranean and in particular on northern Africa, with the prospect of future colonial ventures for the Italian state (Chabod 1996, 149).

Immediately after September 20, however, the "Roman question" would constitute a rude awakening from a dream of unification and turn out to be far more intractable than any of the Risorgimento leaders had anticipated. For one, Romans tended to feel more that they had been invaded and conquered, rather than liberated, by the Italian troops; they resented, on the whole, the far-reaching infrastructural changes necessary to turn Rome into a modern capital, and they objected to shouldering a growing tax burden to pay for these changes. Above all, Romans, for many contemporary observers, appeared stub-

Figure 3.1 Giuseppe Primoli, "Women and Priests under the Sun" (ca. 1888).

bornly to remain not just Catholic, but papist. The so-called black aristocracy ruling the city had solid ties to the Vatican, and it remained loyal to the Pope even after the move of the King to Rome. Its presence confirmed that there were essentially two courts in Rome, whose individual members for years would refuse to step foot in the homes of their opponents and, indeed, were often prohibited from doing so. The population as a whole remained committed to its customs and habits, to a way of life that Chabod describes as that of "sunshine, feasts, and processions against the backdrop of priests, women and foreigners" (151; see fig. 3.1). Paradoxically, however, the resilience of local customs and commitments was directly supported by the new government's policy to keep Rome an economic backwater of the nation, not only in order to appease northern industrial interests but also to avoid creating a national capital with a large working class capable of mounting barricades right at the heart of the nation. It is possible, in fact, that the mounted siege of the French capital by the Communards was understood as an uncanny repetition of the Italian state's own actions on September 20 at Porta Pia, actions that were in themselves never denied but whose traumatic consequences were disavowed after 1870 in the state's handling of the Roman question (see figs. 3.2 and 3.3).

I am here interested in exploring the city's symbolic capital, that is, those particular ideological elements brought together in and around Rome as a national symbolic unifier, a unifier predicated on the need to heal the split between Rome as idea and Rome as merely another Italian city. Here Chabod's comments are arresting. He states: "Having Rome as their capital city influenced the very manner of being and thinking of the Italians and signified the birth not of a problem with well-defined historical and political contours, but the advent of a new mental world in which individual problems were seen in a different light. . . . With Rome as the capital, large strata of the population were led in the long term to evaluate moral and political situations differently" (1996, 150). It is this "different light" and these different evaluations of moral and

Figure 3.2 Paris Commune, Montmartre, March 18, 1871.

Figure 3.3 Porta Pia, September 1870.

political problems that require investigation, differences that Chabod sees as hinging on the superimposition of this idea "upon the contingent, the poor and miserable, aspects of the life of the city and its inhabitants, which thereby disappeared, leaving the moral, religious, political, and cultural significance of the millennial tradition standing alone" (156).

Rome was conjoined to the nation with the semantic overload of a universal ideal—rather than a particular and national one—in that in the world's eyes it was the seat of a universal mission, that is, of the Catholic Church. If Italy was to be a political power in Rome, then it had to find some kind of mission for itself, lest it remain "tiny and trivial in foreign eyes compared to the Vatican" (156). In other words, the new government required some form of self-justification if it wanted to free itself from the nightmarish feeling of not being equal to the Vatican.

Such self-justifications were indeed put forward, both before and after September 20. Giuseppe Mazzini's idea of a Third Rome—republican and secular but nonetheless capable of building a new ethical state, a

Rome that would succeed to and sublate the earlier Imperial and Papal Romes—Mazzini's Rome was to embody the Romantic ideal of national particularism as universal mission. Vincenzo Gioberti's neo-Guelph solution of a return and continuation of "Italic primacy" was grounded in the idea of a reformed and modern Catholicism. And Quintino Sella's proposal to turn Rome into a center of modern science was founded in the belief that only a frontal attack on the Vatican and on Catholic culture would allow Rome to stand up for itself. Anti-Roman voices were not absent, either. Cesare Balbo, Giacomo Durando, and even Cavour himself protested against the symbolic overburdening of a city where there was not enough reality and common sense, but too much antiquity, primacy, and dreaming: "The artistic heritage is killing us, Durando had exclaimed. Balbo had discerned the decadence of Italy in the prevalence of culture and pure form over virtue, of literature over the moral life, of art over social conscience. Cavour was habitually of the same opinion, but when he confronted Rome he leaped over the bounds of reason so important to the Piedmontese moderates into the world of passion and poetry" (Chabod 1996, 165).

In the event, Cavour's approach, one that found its fullest expression in the Law of Guarantees (1871), was the policy pursued by the *Destra Storica*. Cavour's postulation of religious liberty—a free church in a free state—was predicated on the separation of state and church, on the freedom of religious expression, and on a politics of waiting and seeing, all in an effort to alleviate the sense of guilt placed on Catholic consciences since September 20. Cavour's moderates thus refused the construction of an alternative ethical state, as well as any concordats of reconciliation with the Vatican, in the hopes that liberty and a laissez-faire approach would strengthen religion qua moral conscience without interfering with the secular state. Cavour's liberal approach failed, ultimately, for two reasons. First, Pius IX adopted an intransigent position vis-à-vis the state, as he made clear in his 1864 Syllabus of Errors and his 1870 declaration of papal infallibility. Second, religious liberalism did not provide a counterweight to the Vatican's overbearing symbolic presence in the city:

> it gave no satisfaction to those, whether Catholic or non-Catholic, who dreamed of a new mission for Rome. For after all, what was the best possible outcome of present policy? Welcome harmony between the Italian state and the church; the healing of an internal split; the consolidation of the state; the triumph in Italy of the spirit of liberty as both means and end—in other words, a purely national solution, Italian,

honorable, but modest. And which of the two would be the real winner under that state of affairs? As before it would be the church and the papacy that would tower over the city. Rome as the capital of Italy would not add one whit to the stature of old pontifical Rome. Italy would have no mission to the world. (Chabod 1996, 180)

It is in this context of a search for symbolic weight that Italy's long-standing and enduring commitment to its monarchy must be understood, a commitment that, as Alberto Banti has noted, was already inscribed in the language of the plebiscites that annexed Italy to the Piedmontese House of Savoy (2000, 166–67). Domenico Zanichelli, in his 1889 *Monarchia e papato in Italia,* states the matter rather bluntly: "Italy, if it had become a republic, may have been able . . . to drive out the foreigners and tyrants among us. But on the other hand, we are convinced that in the struggle against the papacy a republican Italy would certainly have been the loser. . . . Italy will have a solid hope of winning the battle against the papacy only if it remains monarchical" (1889, 213). And Chabod, echoing this position, asserts that on the "fatal day" when Italy got rid of its monarchy, "the papal tiara shone forth even more splendidly" (1996, 282).[5]

Zanichelli sets forth two reasons that a monarchy was needed in Italy. First, both the papacy and the monarchy depend for the exercise of their power on occupying the first place in the political structure; that is, both must occupy a position of absolute hegemony. Thus, the absolute power of the pope can only be counteracted with that of the king (see fig. 3.4). It is these mutual claims to supremacy that must compel the king to combat any rival on his own territory. "Let us suppose that a clerical-Catholic reaction prevailed in Italy. . . . Let us suppose that this force gained control of the electorate and filled the Chamber of Deputies with a majority ready to make an accord with the Vatican and desirous of giving it what it asks. Anyone can see that on this hypothesis there would be no authority or legal force able to save the secular and national state except the monarchy which, being naturally opposed to the political claims of the church for the reasons given, would summon from within itself sufficient energy to withstand the clerical current" (Zanichelli 1889, 218).[6]

The second argument Zanichelli brings for the necessity of an Italian monarchy is its ability to cast a spell on the popular imagination. What kind of figure would a president or prime minister cut, he asks, when compared with the glamour and pomp of a pope? A president is always a man like any other, "a simple delegate of the nation, with-

Figure 3.4 *Pope and King Arm in Arm.* Famous satirical photomontage of King Victor Emmanuel II arm in arm with Pope Pius IX (ca. 1873). (© Alinari/Art Resource, New York.)

out *intrinsic* force, without traditions, destined to return to the anonymity from which he emerged." A president would be a poor match for an authority that "dominates the earth, claiming heaven's investiture, that surpasses the limits of mere states and relies on the force of a two-thousand-year tradition and of the dominant religion of Italy" (Zanichelli 1889, 220–21). A republican president, next to a pope, lacks *aura:* "Imagine them side by side: the pope arrayed in white with the triple tiara on his head and sitting on the gestatorial chair, surrounded by his court, the most magnificent in the world; and a president dressed in the dark suit of a bourgeois surrounded by ministers and senior functionaries. Imagine this spectacle and you will see at once that, whatever the reality of the situation, the president will appear inferior to the pope" (221). Spectacle and poetry, on the one hand, and the drab prose of bourgeois life, on the other, then; an opposition that, as I will show, will support the coordinates of Giosuè Carducci's own conversion to the monarchical cause, if for no other reason but to give substance to his own poetic enterprise. And here we encounter a specific visual politics, one that is profoundly ambiguous in regard to the possibility of a representative politics in Italy, for can a politics of representation effectively mediate the relationship between inner nature and outward symbolization?

> Nor in the matter of display alone, but also in the inner nature of the institutions, would the pontiff always seem to dwarf the head of the government of Italy, and so win the obedience of the people by winning their reverence. What does the president of a republic *represent*? Nothing except the will of those who . . . have elected him. His power has no other basis than consensus; when that fails him, either in appearance or in reality, he is left with nothing. Thus, in Italy he would be not an *authority* in himself, but simply the holder of a mandate, whose office would depend . . . on the will of the mandater. He might have effective power, but would lack any moral power. (Zanichelli 1889, 221; first emphasis mine)

It is the abstraction subtending representation and the consensual delegation of power that eludes the Italian people; the Italian people would have to "forget its entire history, change its nature utterly, if it wanted to understand sovereignty as anything but *incarnated,* as existent first and foremost in its external attributes. For Italians, if there were no king, no sovereign dynasty of Italy, respected and revered as such, there would be nothing left but the pope" (221; my emphasis).

This insistence on an Italian national inability to conceive of political power in abstract terms and to require instead a power that is incarnated, as Catholicism demands, and that is thus made visible—this insistence has had a remarkably enduring hold on the Italian imagination ever since the traumatic conquest of Rome. Whether this national trait has been understood critically or uncritically, whether it has even been conceived as a strategic necessity, has mattered less than the fact that it nevertheless has the effectiveness of a stereotype. It informs the analyses of the Italian national problem vis-à-vis the papacy of both Zanichelli and Chabod, and it explains as well the mass conversions to the monarchical cause of Italian politicians and intellectuals—even of such die-hard republicans as Crispi and Carducci. It also dominates the analyses of contemporary critics who seek in the Italian propensity to visual, spectacular forms of power an explanation for Italy's failed modernization, failed political revolution, and collapse into authoritarian, fascist solutions.[7]

Among more recent analyses of this phenomenon, Giulio Bollati's *L'italiano. Il carattere nazionale come storia e come invenzione* makes these connections explicit. Bollati not only links the Italian penchant for visualization to its monarchical solution and thereby makes these the causes of Italy's failed modernization. He also insists that Italy proved itself incapable of embracing specifically modernist forms of visualization, as embodied, for example, in the modernist reception of photography as understood by Walter Benjamin.[8] Given Italy's late development and its stubborn adherence to traditional classical culture, the nation's encounter with visual culture in the modernist sense is from the very outset limited at best: "Our relationship to photography is cruder and drowns in the indistinctiveness of experience; it tends to privilege content as its value, and more, it tends to confuse the object and its representation, thus inadvertently slipping into the magical mentality of the Paleolithic hunter. Photography makes us regress to a stage when the image removes itself from the control by rational thought."[9]

Because photography in Italy confuses the object and its representation and thus brings back magic, because it has essentially a regressive function, it can thereby ally itself only to a static past, to a tradition of *vedutismo* that pictures Italy as the site of ruins and as an archeological repository of past glories, or as a catalogue of national artistic beauties such as captured by the Alinari brothers' reproductions of the Italian artistic patrimony or by Count Giuseppe Primoli's photographs of Italian antiquity. Nevertheless, Bollati also insists that such photographic reproductions of the past dominate the very objects they represent. In other words, photography usurps the place of the art objects themselves and turns them into objects of mass media. Consequently, and this despite Bollati's argument about a failed Italian modernization, photography in Italy constructs a "magical object" but does so in the modern sense of commodity fetishes. Thus, and as Bollati himself points out, photography after Unification comes to be closely aligned not only to the mass reproduction of the cultural patrimony, one that replaces, furthermore, the art objects themselves, but also and immediately with positivism and the latter's need to catalogue, classify, make known and common, and, indeed, to exalt. Thus, the positivist application of photography is closely linked to its use by the military and the police in their wars against brigands and criminals (see fig. 3.5), as well as to the realist and *verismo* movements in literature and the arts. Positivism as well as *verismo* constitute the founding stones of a national and celebratory rhetoric that contributes to a broader didactic rhetoric geared to the creation of a visual dictionary of what it means to be Italian.

It remains unclear why such applications of photography should be understood as antimodern, if—and this is the implication of Bollati's argument—they are geared to an application that constructs Italian identity as a media effect. Not coincidentally, and crucial to my own argument here, the centerpiece of Bollati's essay is his discussion of the Italian monarchy, a monarchy that certainly harks back to tradition, but to a tradition that Bollati himself views as constructed or "invented." Bollati places monarchical ideology in a tradition of paternalism, that is, in an Italian refusal of a liberal solution for its new state. Thus, ultimately, the state rejected the argument that the weak could be abandoned to the merciless game of the market or to the terror of a social revolution, as had evidently happened under the Paris Commune. Post-Unification Italy required unity and compactness, and it searched for this unity in the congenial unanimity of a victorious dynasty in order to guarantee both military strength and internal harmony. Nevertheless, Bollati also insists that such a monarchy was constructed in a stylized political-aesthetic image that expressed itself in terms of a feudal, knightly revival, wherein are stressed the values of virtue, grace, goodness, and justice. Bollati's fundamental point is that this is a construction, one that does not simply look back to the past nostalgically, but that reconstructs the past as a modern media phenomenon. For this reason, Bollati's engagement with the Italian monarchy centers on the (re)construction of a medieval castle and village that provided the main focus of attraction of the Fourth National

Figure 3.5 "The War on Brigands." Photograph. (Criminal Anthropological Museum, Turin.)

Exposition held in Turin in 1884 on the occasion of the celebration of the nation's twenty-fifth anniversary.

Margherita

The reconstruction of the castle and village at the exposition was the work of Alfredo D'Andrade, the Portuguese-born painter and architect who would later become the first head of the Delegation for the Conservation of Monuments in Piedmont and Liguria, the predecessor to the later extension of the office to all the regions of Italy in 1891. D'Andrade's project was not a reconstruction or copy of an actual, previously existing castle or village, but rather the presentation of what he thought to be the *essence* of a place and time (see fig. 3.6). Furthermore, his project was conceived not as an inert museum, but instead as a living inventory and dictionary of the Middle Ages. In this sense, it heralded a new era for museum science, not only because it constructed a Disney World–like presentation of the past, but also because it reconfigured the relationship between spectator and art object as a kind of "hands-on" approach.[10] As Rosanna Maggio Serra has noted, D'Andrade's project was not to constitute simply a nostalgic and romantic revival of the Middle Ages, so much as a position statement vis-à-vis very specific problems concerned with productivist and technological developments faced by Italian culture (1982, ix). Here

Figure 3.6 Alfredo D'Andrade, *Medieval Castle and Village* (1884). (National Exhibition, Turin.)

D'Andrade's project must both be placed within the broader European context that includes Augustus Pugin, John Ruskin, and William Morris and their search for an architectural and design aesthetic capable of filling the gap between new industrial production and formal aesthetic imperatives, as also related to a specifically Italian need to bridge the opposition between industrial development and the decline and destruction of older architectonic forms and persistent but threatened artisan production and crafts. Thus, in his exact reproduction of the medieval village replete with artisan shops and workplaces, D'Andrade not only sought to provide a history lesson of a society and style specific to the region, but he also wanted to educate the public in a precious patrimony of manual crafts now threatened by serial industrial production. It was no coincidence that such a project should have been placed in Turin, the industrial capital of Italy, nor that in its drive to provide an inventory of Italian medieval art, it came remarkably close to the positivist construction of visual dictionaries of Italian society.

According to Bollati, all the necessary ideological elements that support Italian regressive seeing were put into play here, in the hyperreality of this fake medieval castle. Present at the opening were the political and intellectual elite of Italy: Carducci, D'Annunzio, Arrigo and Camillo Boito, Giuseppe Giacosa, Serao and her husband Edoardo Scarfoglio, among many others. The center of attraction, in this scene of Romantic chivalry and feudal social structures, was provided by the royal couple: Umberto and Margherita. Bollati is not wrong to insist on the intense symbolic weight provided by politics, literature, art, and religion in this visual re-creation of the Middle Ages, a symbolism geared to presenting the national community as an organic, harmonious village under the guidance of a benevolent Queen, who rather resembled a cross between the Madonna and Collodi's Blue-Haired Fairy (Bollati 1983, 155).[11]

"Margheritsm" denotes a nexus of phantasmatic-ideological elements that were extremely effective, between Unification and World War I, in organizing a family romance of the Italian nation. The term "family romance" derives from Freud, who used the term to denote the either infantile or neurotic fantasy of upgrading one's parents, in the face of post-Oedipal loss, from individuals of low social standing into all-powerful royalty. The family romance thus describes the ways in which individuals may come to insert themselves into the social order at the level of fantasy (Freud 1959a).[12] Like the medieval castle in Turin, Margherita can herself be understood as a kind of fake, to the extent that she was singularly able to seize the moment and build a public persona of herself that denoted elegance, beauty, culture, and the ethereal kindness of the Madonna or the stuff of fables. A typical anecdote will suffice to make this point, one that is supposed to have taken place, according to legend, even before Margherita became queen. According to one observer, "A flock of little birds hover in the sky as a greeting. One of the birds lands at Margherita's feet. She picks it up, caresses it, and returns it to freedom. The people applaud. And the word is out that the princess has begged her father-in-law [Victor Emanuel] for an amnesty that would free all those many who are 'more unfortunate than guilty.' Italy begins to fall in love with Margherita. And so begins 'Margheritsm'" (Gigliozzi 1997, 32).

While Margherita herself laid great emphasis on her culture and her support of the arts—her consumption of books and her Latin lessons were widely publicized and an essential aspect of her legend—she nevertheless remained a dilettante, and her fantasy was crowded by dreams of armored knights and chivalrous lovers. And while she was famous for her beauty and elegance, many commentators have rather dryly commented that she was singularly able to *appear* as such, despite her physical defects and a taste in clothes and jewels that fell short of European standards.[13] Margherita's biggest accomplishment was her talent in effectively marketing herself as a "legend" during her own lifetime on the basis of her skills in transforming kitsch into "royalty." Indeed, her populism was grounded in her ability to bridge the gap that had opened up between the lost aura of the throne and the "Italian people." While her own political convictions were deeply conservative and clerical, antidemocratic, nationalist, and militarist, she had massive popular support even from republican democrats, a support that frequently took on a fetishistic quality.

Margherita's stature as a legend, one that always depended on the public exhibition of her body and of her piety and religiosity, was successful in creating a functioning court society in Rome after 1870 and in mediating the split between the black and white aristocracy of the capital. Margherita produced a devotion to herself and to her rather insipid husband that relied on personal devotion rather than on any institutional-political commitment to the monarchy. The greatest contributors to this devotion were the outpourings of writers. Carlo Casalegno estimates that between two hundred and fifty and three hundred writers produced a literature dedicated to the building of Margheritsm. Giovanni Prati, Giuseppe Giocosa, Giovanni Pascoli, and Antonio

Fogazzaro all dedicated poetry and prose to the Queen at one point or another. D'Annunzio would write in 1884 that seeing the Queen at the premier of *Lohengrin* made him feel the fascination of the "royal eternal feminine"; and Margherita would play a central role in the opening pages of his Wagnerian novel *Il fuoco,* though here she appears only in order to be eventually superseded by the poet-politician.

The central text of Margheritist ideology, however, is Carducci's 1882 "Eterno femminino regale." Two factors are brought together in this text: the people's and the poet's (or the "people's poet's") conversion to the monarchy as an experience of transferential desire for the "ideal woman" and the fact that this conversion takes place as an act of seeing. In other words, conversion is here experienced as the creation of a sublime object of desire, closely modeled on the troubadour poetry of the Middle Ages but given new impetus insofar as it can take place only within the context of the modern crowd. Carducci thus finds himself mingling with the crowd as it awaits the arrival of the royal couple upon its first visit to Bologna since their ascension to the throne. The poet is on the scene because drawn by curiosity: "I, who have so often searched for, observed and studied queens in history, epic poetry and drama, was rather curious to see a real living queen, one, furthermore, who herself took pleasure in poetry and art" (Carducci 1935, 327). And so, as Carducci rubs shoulders with the people, the figure of the Queen passes before him, a white and blond figure "like a romantic image in the midst of a verist description, powerful if you will, but monotonous and boring" (328). Unmoved as yet, it will only be that evening, when the King and the Queen appear on the balcony in the Piazza di San Petronio upon popular demand, that

> those two young persons, returning with an effusion of kindness the salute of the people, from the same place where pontifical legates had appeared in order to disperse benedictions of death, maledictions, hangings, bounties, and all the damages and dishonors brought by servitude and cowardice upon life and upon Italy—they must have, I feel it, touched the hearts of the faithful believers in the fate of the monarchy, now united to the fate of the fatherland. I looked at the Queen.

Margherita appears to Carducci—white, blond, bejeweled in the moving crowd—and the poet is assailed by a fantasy:

> Could perchance she not be one of the Horae that surround the chariot of triumphant Phoebus, who, drawn by a Nordic magician in the night of the Middle Ages and imprisoned in that priestly prison, has come to the window in order to see

whether the moment had not come to throw herself—in flight—behind the chariot of the resurging god? (329)

The coming together of classical visions of Apollo, medieval damsels put in distress by clerical darkness, the play of light and dark produced by the artifice of the fireworks, and finally the enthusiasm of the workers, porters, women, and children get the better of Carducci as he succumbs to tears. And why these tears? Because a naturally skeptical mass of people spontaneously loves, believes in, and enjoys something beyond itself, something that has absolutely no instrumental value. The people gain nothing material from the monarchy; they encounter it purely as an ideal: "The Monarchy was and is a great historical fact, and for many it remains a realized ideal: the people acclaim in those two young persons precisely this ideal made real" (331). If the Italian people incarnate a unified fatherland in the House of Savoy, then this is to be led back to the human need to personally realize its ideals in plastic form; "the head of the Savoy family represents Italy and the State" (333).

While all this may explain the people's adherence to Margheritism, based in its need for plasticity in order to conceive and appreciate the ideal, Carducci's own desires are more cultured and refined, grounded as they are in manners and personal or physical attractions. The Queen, Carducci notes, is a beautiful and kind woman, one who speaks well and dresses even better. No Greek poet or Girondist would ever pass before beauty and grace without saluting them (1935, 343). Great art and revolutionary fervor forbid an engagement with the humdrum tedium of bourgeois equality, a fact made evident and indeed represented by the Queen herself: "Meanwhile the Queen, devoid of all airs and without there being even a trace of a throne in the room, was enthroned for real in the middle of the room. Among those black-tailed suits . . . and those white ties, those ridiculous emblems of equality by which the cynical envy of the Third Estate has united the hero and the waiter, she rose in a rare purity of lines and poses and with a simple elegance that was truly superior to the jewels and a dress (dove-grey, I believe) that fell in broad strokes about her" (335). And so, while Margherita may be necessary food for the people in order for it to get beyond itself and thus be catapulted into the world of the ideal, of the totality of wholesome feeling for the fatherland, Carducci himself is not immune to this construction of kitschy pseudoclassicism draped in simple elegance and dove-grey dressing. Among all the black-tailed waiters of bourgeois life-as-prose, Carducci thus seeks to carve out his own poetic niche in a nation that is now incarnated in the eternal feminine of Queen Margherita.

Representative Politics

As a genre, Italian parliamentary novels came to betray, through the years of their greatest flourishing, an increasingly antiparliamentary tone and growing pessimism regarding the Italian parliament's ability to effectively lead the country. They also exhibited a certain fluidity of positions between, on the one hand, a call for greater democratization and public involvement in the political process and, on the other hand, the claim that the nation required saving from parliament itself by a restricted political elite or a charismatic leader.[14] However, and apart from any specific political solutions proposed, parliamentary novels also functioned as pedagogical tools, as instructional manuals of citizenship for those Italians too distant from the political process to witness it personally. Qua written object, the parliamentary novel provided an instruction in politics for private use, perhaps even private fantasy. As such, these novels functioned much like the self-help manuals I mentioned in the last chapter. The solitary act of reading permitted a peek, from behind the stage as it were, at the making of the Italian political system for those without a ticket of entry. A dialectic of inclusion and exclusion marks these texts; an opening and a closure, of seeing and not seeing, circumscribe the political subject and bring him into being.

"By half-past nine the military cordon had blocked off all the side streets and, ascending toward Montecitorio [the seat of the Parliament], rounded the obelisk all the way to the Uffici del Vicario [the papal offices]. At every entry to the square there was a continuous discussion [*parlamentare*] between the officers and those who wanted to pass without a ticket. Each one of them was looking for a deputy: there he is, he saw him under the atrium of the Parliament, he signaled to him, but no! that deputy was not turning around!"[15] So begins Serao's description of the opening of Parliament whose fourteenth legislative session will swear in Sangiorgio as freshman deputy empowered to represent the remote, poverty-stricken, and neglected Basilicata. The "parlamentare" that takes place between the officers of the military cordon and those without tickets, the futile hope that exclusion can be circumvented by the political representation provided by a glance from a deputy, is avoided by the bird's-eye view of the scene furnished by Serao herself (see fig. 3.7). She also introduces here a possible porosity of the boundaries of the political sphere, to the extent that the act of "parlamentare" takes place *outside* the Parliament, right at the limits of legitimate representation.

Figure 3.7 Giuseppe Primoli, *Umberto I and Queen Margherita Enter the Quirinale* (Rome, April 26, 1893).

What the reader sees is a crowd that "like the movement of the sea, ebbed and flowed and crashed against the wall of the military cordon" (Serao 1997, 30). And as this oceanic mass awaits the arrival of the king and queen and of the elected government, Serao introduces one of the first of her many photographic metaphors that stand at the basis of both her politics of visuality and her own aesthetic practices. "The crowd in the streets, in the alleys, on the balconies, at the windows seemed at times as if struck by a sudden immobility, almost as if it had been petrified by a spell, as if an immense invisible photographic machine were photographing it. . . . Then the spell seemed to break, and the crowd exhibited the restlessness of those who move but always stay in the same place, a circular movement similar to the expansion of the rings of a worm" (31). Movement and stasis become one in a crowd that is fundamentally feminized. Once we have gained access to Montecitorio, "it seemed an irony" but women have invaded every last space and, burning with an "indomitable womanly curiosity," they are there to see and to be seen. And so the magical spell of the giant photographic machine returns inside the parliamentary hall whose "vulgar hue" has the power to absorb all color and all difference:

Thus was produced, when bending over one of the galleries, that optic phenomenon which is the first delusion for those who visit the Italian Parliament: all the faces had the same color; they looked alike and it was impossible to recognize anyone; it was a monotonous whole, without design, without variation, one that tired the eye and because of which one withdrew nauseated.

But this place, which united so many faces, so many people of different ages, conditions and dress, this sort of leveling to which even the most rebellious must submit, this common imprint that no one, once in the hall, can escape, all this produced an immense impression; the hall seemed to be a huge sacred place that reduced the individual to nothingness, a sacred precinct that subdued mind, will, and character and where, in order to rise again, to be *someone,* one required a profound and fervid mystical faith or the sacrilegious audacity of him who upturns altars. (34)

Sangiorgio will pronounce his *"giuro"* unheard by all and in a space where vision is always imperfect and partial:

on the right aisle, the ladies were upset because they were sitting under the gallery of the diplomatic corps and therefore could not see the queen; those in the speaker's gallery were happy, they could not see the king, true, unfortunately, but they had the queen at two meters distance; the women on the left aisle were missing half of the show, the entire diplomatic corps, most of the gallery of the senators, along with the wives of the ambassadors and Italian cabinet ministers; and the galleries in the center, those of the press, the public, the military personnel, and public employees, saw everything but they were too far away. (35)

Serao constructs here a vision of partiality, a blindness that relegates actors and spectators alike to an inevitable marginalization. In the amorphous and blurry hue of the parliamentary environment, an environment that calls for the destruction of the individual and that can only be escaped by those with a "fervid mystical faith" or by an iconoclasm that destroys altars and possibly even thrones, it becomes unclear who is representing whom, who the actor is in this scenario and who the spectator. When, as readers of the text, we witness the *"muliebre"* masses furnish the primary actresses in Serao's spectacle of the opening of the Parliament, the politicians themselves are displaced to the position of feminized objects of the crowd. "The primacy of the gaze," Ann Caesar comments in relation to this scene, "is not only a male prerogative" (1992, xxi). And so Sangiorgio, inaudible in this oceanic mass and elected only by the chance death of his opponent and not because of any intrinsic or acquired personal worth, is confined to the same marginal position within the Parliament, as are his neglected constituents of his native Basilicata. He thus becomes, as Caltagirone remarks about all the heroes of the parliamentary novels, entirely dependent on the genre itself. For Serao, this dependency is gendered and *therefore* reliant on a politics conceived as spectacle. In the later ballroom scene, Serao will describe man's marginalization before a feminine mass in terms of an optical reversal whereby trees cannot be seen for the forest:

Everything was a vivid flux of sparks, a brilliant flash of lightning. The women were bound one to the other, one dress absorbed and confused with the dress of the next, in order for the latter in turn to be absorbed and confused. . . . What dominated everything was the varied and infinite plasticity of the nude arms and shoulders. . . . This plasticity, repeated in different skin tones three hundred times, ended by taking on a different character, of togetherness, like the beauty of a great forest: the individual disappeared here, personality was absorbed. . . . A united chorus where all those voices . . . turned into one sole voice. In vain . . . the thick black and white hedge that made up the men sought to recognize a face, a countenance, a person, the person, that woman. (Serao 1997, 172–73)[16]

While men succumb to this feminized politics and to the latter's representative forms, nevertheless, all aspects of the parliamentary novel converge, so also Caltagirone tells us, on the representation of the young deputy. There is, however, a fundamental paradox that resides within the representation of this representative, for the hero of these novels is a consistently negative one. He cannot, therefore, provide a worthy model of emulation, and this despite the didactic goals of these texts. Sangiorgio, like the rest of his cohorts, is essentially a weak man and the victim of forces that elude him. Furthermore—and this will be his ultimate tragedy—he is called upon to occupy a kind of negative space, one describing the gap opened up by a traumatic rift at the very foundation of the Italian state. If the entire genre circles around missed opportunities—failed speeches in parliament, failed political careers, failed engagements with concrete political agendas and empirical realities, a failure, in other words, to respond to the call of duty, then it is possible to read such failure as a symptomatic filling of a void created by the greatest trauma of Italian unification: the radical and violent separation between state and church. One way by which to understand the negativity that surrounds Sangiorgio and constitutes the essence of his being is as his inability to engage political reality at the level of the concrete, so that he is confined to a perpetual discovery of this traumatic rift.

I would like to introduce here a distinction that Dominick LaCapra has developed in a recent article entitled "Trauma, Absence, Loss" (2001). LaCapra stresses the need for a distinction—*not* an opposition—between the analytic categories of "absence" and "loss." LaCapra defines the category "absence" as the conceptual tool geared to the critique of ultimate foundations, as such absence is understood to be constitutive, transhistorical, and foundational for philosophical, ontological, or theoretical analysis. In fact, he also aligns absence to structural trauma, as a category, therefore, capable of theorizing the psychological subject as constructed and inevitably split. Absence entails the crucial recognition that one cannot lose what one never had, so that living with absence must always be inherently ambivalent, both producing anxiety and yet also empowering, possibly even ecstatic. The affirmation of absence thus allows for a complex and mediated relationship with presence, a term that hence posits a being without totality or fullness. Loss, on the other hand, is always—as LaCapra states—historical, specific, and subject to change and transformation. The concept is historical to the extent that it refers, contrary to absence, to historical traumas, be they individual or social. Loss entails a specified object that is lost (the death of an individual or even the passage from one social order to another). While everyone is subject to absence or structural trauma, the category of loss or historical trauma must insist on careful distinctions between victims, perpetrators, and bystanders; the "victim" is not, as LaCapra puts it tersely, "a psychological category" (2001, 79), because it cannot be confused with the constitutive processes that bring into being all subjects.

It is the confusion between, or conflation of, absence and loss that is LaCapra's object of criticism. What he posits at the door of much recent poststructural, postmodern criticism is a tendency to collapse loss into categories that would make all historical traumas exemplary of constitutive absence, with the result of an insistence within such formulations on endless melancholia, impossible mourning, and interminable aporia (46). One might even hazard that the collapse of loss into absence gives rise to a quasi-celebratory, ecstatic discourse linking loss and suffering to the sublime. In the opposing direction, the conversion or collapse of constitutive absence into loss may give rise to a misplaced nostalgia and a utopian politics in quest of a lost but to be regained wholeness or totality, to the desire for a unified community or self. While the first conflation may condemn us to a kind of impotent politics, the second exposes us to the dangers of a totalitarian, fundamentalist solution to political and social problems, and thus to an inability to live with a partial, fragmented, and diverse reality.

According to La Capra, the act of distinguishing between absence and loss already bespeaks an engagement with the process of mourning and hence points to possibilities of transformation at the constitutive, transhistorical, or psychological level, as well as at the historical level. The capacity to distinguish is in this sense already a "working through." By the same token, then, the reverse also holds true: the conflation of absence and loss "may itself bear striking witness to the impact of trauma and the post-traumatic" (LaCapra 2001, 46–47). The question remains, however, whether such traumatic conflation can be explained without hesitation in terms of an experience of absence or, alternatively, of loss. Thus, I wonder whether the act of conflation qua symptom of trauma guarantees the possibility of teasing out distinctions in such ways that LaCapra rightfully deems to be so crucial.

It might very well be a certain unreadability in this regard that is at stake in Serao's text and, indeed, is put into play by her engagement with the problem of representation. Hence, LaCapra's invitation to be attentive to the act of blurring the distinction between absence and loss certainly provides a productive initial approach to Serao's novel. For instance, the writer's desire for plenitude through constructing a unified community or political institutions can certainly be traced back to a slippage from the constitutive lack that inheres in all constructions of subjects as they are subject to the representative, figural operations of language, to that of a substitutive desire for an undivided national identity.[17] Conversely, Serao equally posits the conflicts and differences as they inhered in the newly established nation as emblematically embodied in her fictional deputy Sangiorgio, whereby he becomes an allegory or instantiation of a kind of impossible or, in Jean-Luc Nancy's phrase, inoperative community.[18] Serao banks on the difficulty of ever clearly distinguishing between absence and loss in her text, to the extent that, for her, the nature of the relationship between constitutive absence and historical loss is precisely what may be at stake. For Serao, the Italian subject is the product of a dawning awareness that the subject comes into being as a function of both types of lack, thereby condemning such a subject to a fetishistic search for an ultimately false plenitude. That Serao's subject is a gendered subject is not fortuitous and constitutes a guiding thread throughout her work. The very genderedness of Serao's Italian subject constitutes the grounds upon which she will both collapse the distinction between absence and loss (wherein the "feminine" comes to occupy the space of plenitude) and also its rigorous separation (the masculine search for utopian plenitude as a fetishistic, false desire that invests the "sublime" woman with the capacity to heal all wounds, whether they are constitutive or historical).

Rome

Impronta Italia domandava Roma,
Bisanzio essi le han dato.
GIOSUÈ CARDUCCI

It is not insignificant perhaps that Serao—and this despite her conservative Catholicism—will never herself allude directly to the "Roman question" in her novel. Nevertheless, she does center all of Sangiorgio's actions and desires at the heart of this trauma—to wit, the city of Rome. Rome for Sangiorgio is a space of fantasy, a blank screen, in itself impenetrable, upon which he projects his desires in the form of his political ambitions. Sangiorgio lives his relationship to the city in "a growing disequilibrium [*squilibrio*] between desire and reality" (Serao 1997, 7), in a fissure that bears the marks of an already radical split within his personality between his "glacial mask" (6) and his burning desire for conquest and self-affirmation. Rome thus represents for Sangiorgio a mission or idea; it constitutes that symbolic weight, as delineated by Chabod, that makes Italians see the city in a "different light." On the train that will carry him to his destination and realize his fantasies, and thus before ever having seen the city, the four letters of her name have written themselves into his fantasy and taken on the obsessive quality of an idée fixe: "He was unable to make a picture for himself of what those four letters, etched as it were in granite, represented. The sense that it was the name of a city, of a large agglomeration of houses and people escaped him. Rome was unknown to him" (6). Sangiorgio cannot give shape to Rome as a concrete entity; instead, Rome herself shapes his desires and appears to him as a "feminine but ideal apparition, as an immense figure of indistinct shape." Rome is experienced as a feminine voice whose call fills Sangiorgio with a shudder of pleasure. She is the mother's voice who calls her son back into her "powerful embrace" (7) and who magnetizes and casts a spell upon him. As priestess, mother, and lover (8), Rome demands atonement and sacrifice; she requires both a pure heart and an iron will.

Rome's double demand for sacrifice and an iron will founds Sangiorgio's personality and defines his attitude toward the city. A will that is iron and simultaneously utterly obedient to her call describes the essence of his masochism, the mastery of his own submission to a call to perform his (political) duties, to represent and thus conquer that which cannot be conquered. Sangiorgio thus lives in his perpetual *squilibrio* between desire and reality, between Rome as fantasy and Rome as real object, between Rome as a mission and Rome as a concrete Italian city. As long as he can view the city from the train or from the panoramic heights of the Gianicolo, as long as Rome keeps her distance and gives herself to no one, Sangiorgio's fantasy life can remain intact. Tullio Giustini, the cynical deputy viewing Rome with Sangiorgio from the Gianicolo, states, " 'This city, neither awaits nor fears you. . . . Her strength, her power, her loftiness is almost a divine virtue: *indifference*. . . . An indifference, an imperturbable serenity, a deaf soul, *a woman who does not love*. . . . And yet there must be some person or some thing capable of disturbing that serenity, of vanquishing that indifference. . . . Oh, that man must have a heart of bronze, an inflexible and rigid will; he must be young, healthy, robust and daring, without ties and without weaknesses. . . . Someone must conquer her, this proud Rome.' 'I will,' said Francesco Sangiorgio" (69).

These same demands made by conquest disturb Sangiorgio's panoramic vision, however. His fantasy is threatened when the city becomes a reality and begins to exude the bodily smells of nights of love. Upon his arrival in Rome and still unknown to all, he is engulfed in the crowds at the train station, crowds that push and jostle him and oppress him with an indifference that now takes on "a heavy and soft atmosphere, a penetrating mist, a rather disagreeable odor, the nauseated and nauseating sight of a city barely awake, in the flaccid heaviness of autumn mornings, with that fever-tainted breath which seems to exude from the houses" (11–12). Sangiorgio's walks through the city elicit in him an aversion to crowds where classes and regions mingle, to muddy streets, and to the damp and heavy air that blurs all distinctions and turns the city into an appendage of the barren and malaria-infested Roman countryside. A "dripping humidity" (160), the "acute stench" of the Roman Campagna "invades his brain, and from the brain invades his blood, like a subtle miasma" (159). And every time he directly encounters Rome, "the sudden vision of the city and the drone and that entirely foreign world would impose themselves on him and ruin his dreams" (189). Sangiorgio has no eye for beauty, but experiences the monumentality of Rome as an oppressive past. In his initial encounter with the Eternal City, Sangiorgio echoes the voices of those anti-Romans who feel oppressed by the city's past, by its antiquities and its overbearing heritage. Thus, on his sightseeing trip of the capital soon after his arrival, a trip undertaken mechanically and guided seemingly by some external command, the Castel Sant'Angelo is merely hemmed in by the filthy waters of the Tiber, by housing tenements marked by the green stains that remind him of leprosy. The façade of Saint Peter's appears to him as "very small and very flat" (19), its square "much like the Roman Campagna, a vast and naked countryside" (20). Sangiorgio is indifferent to religion and immune to mystical experiences; he has only "vague and narrow ideas about art" (20). The Colosseum may be majestic, but under the rain shows only its dirtiness and the ruination exacted by time; it appears to Sangiorgio an immense and useless thing, built by a proud and ultimately mad people.[19] But at the Caracalla Baths the young deputy's distraction is assaulted by a sense of oppression: "He felt small and insignificant, and everything that mortified or humiliated him made him suffer. . . . In that twilight that rose to the cloud-covered sky, he felt belittled, lost in the dangerous and enervating contemplation of the past; a profound oppression sank upon his breast, his soul" (23). Sangiorgio refuses an engagement with the burdensome past and instead aligns himself with the present and the modern. He is a man in love with his times, in love with that "life that he must attain, and not with the one that had passed" (23); he is reanimated by the first gas lights of the evening and by the reappearance of the Piazza Montecitorio, in whose shadows rises the building of the Parliament.

And yet if the past has disconcerting effects on Sangiorgio, no less so does the present, bringing with it the concreteness of the real. Here Rome turns into what Giustini calls an "infernal machine" (68), a machine that produces and consumes, that is alive and yet immobile and that engulfs everything in her "steely springs" (68). Rome is a massive necropolis; a city deprived of its monumentality, a stratification of ruins where even the present is always already a ruin. The city, as it undergoes the rapid transformation into a capital, is one massive construction site; it was impossible to see the Campidoglio, the Arch of Septimus Severus, or the Roman Forum, explains Sangiorgio's guide, because "continuous demolition work was going on in those parts" (21). The present is but a simulacrum of the past, embodied in the fake, marbleized wooden columns that adorn the inside of Montecitorio. The parliament building, the very center of the Third Rome and the site where Sangiorgio seeks self-affirmation, is itself subject to corrupting forces that have the power to attract and absorb man's efforts at self-making. "You cannot see that cauldron of Montecitorio," Giustini tells Sangiorgio on the Gianicolo, "it is drowned among the houses; and we are drowning in it. A furnace of waste paper, in which one cooks slowly by a desiccating heat. . . . Oh, you frightful furnace that shrivels man like a dried bean, man who burns by a furious desire and is consumed by the emptiness of that desire" (67).

Other sites, other attractions that undermine its centrality, also threaten the Parliament: the Vatican ("The Pope is strong. He has on his side the unhappy, the stupid, the humble, the young, and the women, the women who transmit from mother to daughter not a religion but a cult"; 66); the Quirinale, the site of the royal court with its balls, its public pomp and circumstance, and its own will and desires; the salons, the cafes, and the love nests where alliances are forged and plots hatched; and last, the public squares and streets, with their ability to embrace large uncontrollable crowds. Serao describes these centrifugal forces in largely feminized and feminizing terms; the chapter on the opening of Parliament begins in its antechamber, a glove store packed with government officials and their wives and daughters, all preening themselves for the great event. Similarly, the deputies depend for their housing on an overwhelming mass of rapacious women who rent out rooms, apartments, and love nests at astronomical prices.

In his own search for lodgings, Sangiorgio responds to this feminized space with a mixture of fascination and panic, from which he must escape to preserve his integrity. Nevertheless, upon his visit to one of such spaces, "he re-presented [*ripresentava*] in his fantasy the gray and pink parlor, so sweet in its simplicity, the blue room all veiled in white and the floating and billowing double curtains, that gave it an intimate character, of a nest built on high, far away from the world. . . . This feminine interior space he re-presented to himself; but more than any other thing, what most interested him was that red frame that contained no portrait, as if it had been carried away in a hurry by a distressed woman traveler" (51). The void of Sangiorgio's existence and the emptiness of his personality hover around this empty picture frame that inspires in him such a fascination and that he is compelled to continually represent to himself. His fetishistic efforts at filling this photographic frame, of giving body to his desires as representation, as sublime object, are the driving forces behind all that Sangiorgio will do in the future. They will also constitute his undoing.

For the moment, however, Sangiorgio flees the attractions produced by his feminizing fantasies, a flight accomplished with the help of his masculine powers of observation: "Francesco Sangiorgio, once again put back into contact with his world, and taken again by the more serious need for observation, suddenly felt reinvigorated. . . . All those women he had seen . . . had debilitated his mind . . . and reduced his imagination to ridiculous and useless dreams" (53). Relying on his powers of observation, Sangiorgio can now understand that all those rented rooms that "crowd all of Rome and make up a vegetation so broad and powerful so as to almost suffocate the city" (53) are sustained by a "feminine domination" eager for quick gains and determined to invade all aspects of man's privacy and integrity. Sangiorgio's capacity as a reader of coded, double, and even duplicitous messages unlocks for him, but also firmly closes the door on, the dangers of "that entire system of free entries, of apartments with two doors, of buildings with two exits, of locks with double springs, of all this doubling, of this phantasmagoria of closed doors, of clashing bolts, bells that did not ring, female shoes that did not creak, thick female veils and fur cloaks that were hermetically sealed. And the great equivocacy of Roman life, so proper and impassive in appearance, and yet so restless, passionate and burning in reality, was revealed to him in one of its aspects" (53). And so Sangiorgio takes the cheapest and most squalid of apartments in Via Angelo Custode, the street of the guardian angel that is to ensure that no women will ever live there.

The empty picture frame that inspires Sangiorgio both to a projective and phantasmatic filling of the void, and to rally his powers of observation in the service of a textual, readerly practice capable of phallically unlocking for him the mysterious underbelly of feminine domination—this unrepresented and unrepresentable void functions as a metaphor for Rome itself and constitutes the very center of Serao's text. Sangiorgio, whose mandate it is precisely to represent, in his negotiation of this metaphoric relation between woman and Rome, founders on the impenetrability of this blank space. Nevertheless, and at the same time, he also constructs an open semantic space capable of absorbing the projections and fantasies that the deputy has brought with him from the provinces. In this sense, Caltagirone is absolutely correct in insisting that a new Rome is thereby created. Serao, through Sangiorgio's fantasies, creates a modern Rome, a city that may be infernal but that is nonetheless a machine and as such subject to a mechanical operation and to destabilizing forces that unhinge signs from older meanings. Rome, conceived as a new imaginative space, makes possible a freedom of reading, even if only in order to reanchor these signs to a new form of representation. Sangiorgio constructs for himself a phantasmagoric, fetishistic relation to the city that depends not on a basis in reality, but on the strategic success of a performance. "Rhetoric is a form of power" (62), Sangiorgio insists, and thereby reorganizes the politics of meaning into structures of signification that produce the past as a media effect of the present.

Sangiorgio

Francesco Sangiorgio was, as he says of himself (3), born too late to participate in the making of Italy. His job is that of representing and thereby making Italians. He had been elected to this position because Death had been his "considerate ally" and secured him "a sweeping and easy victory," thanks to which he had paid his homage to his dead, patriotic opponent (3). He thus belongs to that generation of Italian intellectuals, so eloquently described by Alberto Asor Rosa (1975), locked out of the glorious heroic and poetic period of Italian unification and condemned to the prosaic period of daily life as an Italian citizen. He therefore also embodies the drab politician deprived of intrinsic worth, as described by Zanichelli's argument for the monarchical principle, and Carducci's waiter-bourgeois aspiring to a glance from the sublime woman. The prosaic product of the parliamentary novel, Sangiorgio quite paradoxically inhabits a world where words have been emptied of their meaning but have nevertheless gained force by virtue of their rhetorical power. Political words no longer seem to carry the weight of the promise articulated in the social contract. They have turned instead into an aesthetic practice whose representative capacities increasingly sever the contractual relation between "*paese reale*" and "*paese legale*" in favor of a politics that sutures this rift through the ritualistic "presentation" of a community that one year before the publication of Serao's novel had found its spectacular embodiment in D'Andrade's fake medieval castle, at the opening of which Serao was present. Within this space of "free" signs that no longer have obligations toward those they represent, Sangiorgio is but a puppet, an automaton at the mercy of forces and passions that describe the Other. However, and by virtue of being a representative of the nation, he is also the puppet's puppeteer. Sangiorgio is the subject of a postliberal law that relies solely on its enunciation, on its performative impact. As Slavoj Žižek has described this condition, "The externality of the symbolic machine ('automaton') is therefore not simply external: it is at the same time the place where the fate of our internal, most 'sincere' and 'intimate' beliefs is in advance staged and decided. . . . Our belief is already materialized in the external ritual; . . . Belief is an affair of obedience to the dead, uncomprehended letter" (1989, 43). Sangiorgio resembles the train that is to transport him to the fulfillment of his desires, that great sleeping house rushing through the night "as if moved by a burning iron will in order to bear along all those wills rendered inert by sleep. 'Let's sleep,' thought the Honorable Sangiorgio" (Serao 1997, 3). Sangiorgio strives for both the iron will of the train and the sleep of those without will; he seeks to be both the vehicle and the content of his desires. He lives in the liminal state of the sleepwalker who moves and is moved and who dreams with his eyes open, for Sangiorgio is not blind; his "Southern mask" allows him at all points to observe himself "just like a disinterested spectator" (4).

Sangiorgio is not alone as a dreamer with his eyes wide open and puppeteer of his own puppet status. Serao's character is born into a world actively engaged in exploring the nature of hypnosis and its immediate predecessors, animal magnetism and somnambulism. Remember that the psychiatrist Enrico Morselli's influential *Il magnetismo animale* was published one year after Serao's novel and was explicitly dedicated to an investigation of the phenomenon of "Donatism," that is, to a phenomenon that put great doubt on the possibility of a freely constituted and acting subject. The problem with Sangiorgio, as with the rest of his Donatic comrades, is that his heterodirected nature is always in doubt. The principal characteristic of Sangiorgio, Caltagirone has pointed out, is his mimetic capacity of installing himself into the symbols of his successive passions: modern life, politics, and ultimately woman (1993, 180).

Such mimetic capacities, his ability to observe, gauge, and then seize the moment, become prominent in the two parliamentary speeches that are responsible for Sangiorgio's rapid accession to fame. That these speeches are only vaguely connected to an actual political program is already evident in the fact that Serao only reports these performances as indirect speech. Sangiorgio's first speech immediately follows that of the Minister of Finance: "The Chamber listened with interest, one that was less ironic and rather benevolent. This was a natural reaction to the effort, the difficulty of comprehension presented by the Minister's previous speech; after the painful tension of following for two and a half hours the fantastic dance of numbers, [Sangiorgio's] rather simple eloquence raised the oppressed spirits" (Serao 1997, 76). What Serao calls Sangiorgio's verist narrative and a mere act of literature is received with great satisfaction by all: the old Right has had its political ego stroked; the extreme Left believes to have found a socialist in the Center group, and so on. "This speech, which on any other occasion would have passed as an *indifferent literary effusion,* today took on a great importance. . . . The Chamber, in other words, at certain moments of kindness, and in the grips of an amorous and almost feminine abandon, took pleasure in these rites full of haughtiness and sweetness" (78; my emphasis). Here, like Donato's subjects, Sangiorgio gives the audience what it wants.

And yet Sangiorgio's mimesis is not a mechanical one, for what he exposes is a fundamental contradiction in the process of adopting any social role. What Sangiorgio's story shows is a process wherein the better one becomes at playacting, the more one will fail at it. Because Sangiorgio's personality entirely depends on the tension or the *squilibrio* between fantasy and reality, on a suspension of any resolution, he must fail at the moment he experiences his greatest success. And here Sangiorgio joins his slightly younger predecessor Severin von Kusiemski, Leopold von Sacher-Masoch's 1870 literary hero and template of a phenomenon that Richard von Krafft-Ebing in 1886 would call masochism (Sacher-Masoch 1991). Both open-eyed dreamers, Sangiorgio and Severin are embroiled in stories of love whose pleasures stem from their desire to submit to a cruel woman incapable of loving. Indeed, the fantasy life of both heroes freezes a plurality of historical, cultural, and political references into a semantic space entirely dominated by the Cruel Woman. The Cruel Woman is turned into a sublime aesthetic object by virtue of her insistence on man's renunciation, which the heroes nevertheless experience as self-fulfillment. Sangiorgio transforms his act of self-making into an act of self-sacrifice as the primary mode of his existence. Serao's hero is

> not blind, not blinded, but waking and desirous of sacrifice. Not a victim murmuring words of despair, a rebel reviling a tyrant, but a happy, contented martyr who blissfully watches his best blood flow from his veins. Indeed, the more blood his love took from him, the more grew his desire, the greater his sacrifice, the greater his desire for sacrifice. Thus a sort of somber, painful pleasure would overcome him when on sunny mornings he would abandon the crowded streets and his work and all movement and life, in order to go lock himself up in a little room in order to wait. Like the fanatical worshipper of Buddha, he climbed and descended all circles of annihilation, down as far as the complete and bitter abstraction, the Nirvana of pain. (Serao 1997, 213)

Sangiorgio is both maker and victim of his own suffering, the subject of his own submission to laws that have the force of a cosmic determination, as they transform historical problems into a universal predicament. And hence he comes to know his own subjectivity in terms of his own marginalization. The concrete historical determinations of his existence, the trauma that creates and disrupts his subjectivity, are not determinations that have to be worked through but constitute instead his salvation.

Angelica

Sangiorgio experiences his last and final mimesis as a salvific act of conversion. The ensuing martyrizing pleasures free him from the internal fever that devours him and make him the consenting victim of Angelica Vargas, a character who should be read in this novel as a sort of Margherita figure. The scene of conversion is appropriately the Pantheon—the site of a triple Rome: pagan, papal, and national—during the memorial services held for King Victor Emanuel II, father of the new nation. The scene opens the third and final part of the novel and immediately succeeds the fall of the government at the hands of Sangiorgio and the latter's refusal to participate in the new Cabinet. Tellingly, then, his conversion occurs in the shadow of a refusal to take a position of power. The "divine figure" of Angelica causes in Sangiorgio a "wondrous transformation" that he experiences as "a penetration of feeling, slow but sure and infallible" (151). Though explicitly compared to "*la celeste Beatrice*" (176), as if her given name did not already vouch enough for her chastity ("Everything in her was chaste"; 175) and for her "spiritual essence of beauty and grace" (185), Angelica Vargas has all the features of the Cruel Woman who "dominates" the masochistic narratives of the late nineteenth century. Her cruelty resides at the center of her "innocence": "And Donn'Angelica remained in that place to which Sangiorgio's love had raised her, the place where she knew to stay by virtue of the full force of her temperament and character, an elevated and solitary niche, unattainable, unassailable, a tabernacle of virtue and purity, from which she would perhaps deign to look down upon him who loved her, smile at him, stretch out a hand, allow him to kiss the hem of her dress. A pitying deity, without however any of those favors that in the least would cloud her aura and without a pity that would ever humanize or feminize her. Everything that came from her was an act of mercy" (223). As the *belle dame sans merci,* Angelica bears all the features of narcissistic self-involvement—"*la femmina è egoista, caro Sangiorgio,*" she tells her lover (165), a narcissism that renders her oblivious to Sangiorgio's desires, needs, and personality. "Angelica was unconcerned with what he thought, felt, or suffered in her absence;

she . . . had no interest in knowing him. . . . Sangiorgio knew her, but she did not know Sangiorgio" (224–25). And yet, despite all her glacial qualities that, like with all other Cruel Women, require her to wear furs (183) and turn her into a statue or a deep lake of steel (185), Angelica is remarkably a product of her petit-bourgeois background, of a prosaic culture that takes on a fake aura through Sangiorgio's love. Sangiorgio, like Carducci before him, translates prose into poetry. He is her "best interpreter, the man all women want, the man who wants to know everything, whose curiosity is insatiable; who understands everything, who indulges all her small failings, who transforms and glorifies her smallest virtues, who turns a word into poetry, a phrase into an emotion, and a kindness into an act of heroism. He is the man who loves" (224).

As he avidly collects the minutest details of her domestic and domesticated existence, all atremble and vibrating with each of her emotions, Sangiorgio "loses his individuality" (225). The loss of self that apparently founds his conversion experience, however, is more complicated than it would at first appear. Sangiorgio's vision of Angelica at the Pantheon occurs, first of all, under the sign of the death of the Father/King and is permeated by a "subtle Christian odor" (151), as well as by a voice that allows Sangiorgio's ultimate mimetic gesture, his annihilation experienced as the annihilation of Angelica. The "silver cross to which the dying Christ the Redeemer was affixed stood immobile in front of the casket. And a voice departed from the music, strident, excruciating, a voice that did not sing but screamed, that did not pray but begged: *libera, libera, libera me, Domine*" (152). Here all the incurable evils of the spirit and the tears that pour forth from all things come to be concentrated in Angelica, the figure of woman as the "magnetic abyss of pain" (150), and she elicits in Sangiorgio a feeling of "amorous pity." And this pity is different and radically new: "This was not the great *natural* pity a man feels for a suffering woman; such pity is still a personal feeling, an egoism and the cry of an individual. It was *he* who now suffered, as if the torture of that womanly heart were his own torture" (15; my emphases). Sangiorgio, in the throes of "altruism" and voluptuous bitterness, makes Angelica his own and hence cries of love.

Sangiorgio's new form of pity redefines the boundaries of his individuality, which is not thereby obliterated but remade according to new laws. He asks nothing of Angelica save her acceptance of this novelty:

"I demand nothing of you, I want nothing from you except your permission to dedicate my devotion to you . . ."

"Today that may be so, but tomorrow love will demand love . . ."
"Who says so?"
"Alas! Experience, my friend."
"Experience lies," exclaimed Sangiorgio violently, "my love is unlike any other." (193)

The pity of Sangiorgio's new love that eschews either experience or the laws of reciprocity forms the foundation of their relationship and becomes the basis of a contractual union that discards, as Hobsbawm says, a world of legal equals and reintroduces relations of inferior and superior. In other words, Sangiorgio's love is that of the parliamentary deputy for the monarchical principle as incarnated in the queen. And here, Margherita/Angelica holds good on her own antidemocratic, antiparliamentary principles. Angelica "never told him that she loved him, nor had he ever requested it. . . . He feared her answer, that serene but cruel answer of a woman who does not love. . . . And so, quite naturally . . . Donn'Angelica had to concede nothing of her heart . . . ; tacitly, for sure, it was understood that she would accept and bear his love, without any obligation of returning it. She was the blessed image that deigned to lower her eyes full of mercy to her devoted lover, while he blessed her ever more, adored her, and spoke to her of his love" (197).

We encounter here the contract that is fundamental to the masochistic scenario, the consensual relation that installs the male subject into relations of power, whereby he may come to experience his subjectivity in terms of his own marginalization. The masochistic contract guarantees not only that the masochist will be physically or morally beaten through his alliance with the Cruel Woman; it also guarantees that for him to become a man, the masochist does not take the father's place nor assume his symbolic mandate. Instead, as Gilles Deleuze has stated, the contract consists in "obliterating [the father's] role and his likeness in order to generate the new man" (1991, 99). It is thus no coincidence that Sangiorgio's conversion experience takes place in the shadow of the King's funeral, nor that this experience is lived as the traumatic dissolution of his individuality. In the face of the King's death and his symbolic replacement by Margheritism, Serao's novel bears witness to what contemporary observers described as the "feminization" of Italian culture.[20] In other words, the masochistic contract effectively captures a political structure that is indeterminate in its gendered qualities and therefore "mixed"; the masochistic contract describes here a constitutional monarchy (see figs. 3.8 and 3.9). The contract provides Sangiorgio with a language by which to make sense of this trauma of

Figure 3.8 The papal court. "Pope Pius IX and His Collaborators" (ca. 1865). Photograph. (© Alinari/Art Resource, New York.)

Figure 3.9 The constitutional monarchy.

dissolution and blurring. As contract, it stages his trauma as rhetorical to the extent that the new man must not be held by real chains but be bound only by his words; it is not by "the absolute power of the other but by the fictitious power that he himself has bestowed on the executioner" that the contract is set into motion and sustained (Smirnoff 1995, 69). The willed enslavement between the deputy and the Queen that the contract initiates remains a verbal agreement only, and the masochist's participation in it requires his presence in a double role: he must be its victim or sacrifice and yet also the contract's originator as fully autonomous subject. Thus, he must always retain the position of witness to his own victimization.

This double position constitutes the constitutional monarchy's, as also the masochist's, undoing. Sangiorgio can experience his own promise of suffering only as a breaking of the constitutional promise. "The sweet woman smiled at him, cruel and innocent; he was suffocating, he shut his eyes, as if lost. He had promised, but why did she not *understand*? So was she not a woman? . . . He had promised, but he was a man, he would not be able to hold up in this battle. . . . How long would he have to bear this cross? . . . He could not rescind his promise, but . . . she should spare him, leave him, never return" (Serao 1997, 231). Sangiorgio's acting takes place only as absence, in a suspense entirely circumscribed by his interminable waiting, a waiting and seeing that had been at the basis of Cavour's liberal waiting-and-seeing in relation to the mutual claims of Pope and King. And thus, at first, Sangiorgio "had been waiting for her for an hour, not yet impatient, still ignorant of the torments of those who wait with the lack of certainty, still trusting in the word of a woman" (189). In the face of Angelica's habitual tardiness, Sangiorgio can experience the pleasures of this waiting only as "that miniscule acute joy of all past suffering" (196).

The site for this eternal waiting is the love nest that he creates at Piazza di Spagna, an apartment that, because of its sensual, Oriental furnishings, may perhaps be too sensual for the chaste fantasy of his object of desire. Its parlor is pervaded by "a deep softness" and is outfitted entirely with cushions from which one "could form a chair, a bed, a throne" (206). In the bedroom, on the other hand, there is no bed; instead, there is a low and broad sofa over which is thrown a large cover of blue velvet embroidered in silver "with one letter [*cifra*] in the middle . . . a long and slender *A*" (206). And here Sangiorgio sits and waits, no longer reading a book or writing reports, and certainly no longer going to Montecitorio. He drops out of the political scene completely and becomes immersed in the "Buddhist contemplation of love" (209).

Frustrated, ultimately, by this contemplation, he attempts to pressure Angelica into the service of the concrete.

"Could you not tell me the day, the hour when you will come?"
"For what reason? Do you mind waiting for me? Are you not at home anyway?"
"Yes, yes, but at least give me the day . . ."
"Don't you like waiting for me? Is there anything you like more?"
"Nothing, Angelica, nothing."
"So?"
"So if you only knew . . . the bitterness of not knowing the day or the hour when you will arrive! This unknown is a torment, a nightmare . . . If you knew, you would have pity." (218–19)

As Sangiorgio is caught in the contradictions of his own agreed-upon waiting, so he is also caught in his desire to see more than he has contracted for. As Angelica dresses for the ball behind shut doors and Sangiorgio must discuss politics with her husband, Silvio Vargas, and while Don Silvio is engaged in the manly deciphering of diplomatic telegrams, Sangiorgio indulges in fantasies about women's underwear and stockings, about womanly disorders that mark a singular reversal of his own earlier manly decipherings of feminine domination. "An evermore consuming desire to know, to hear, assailed Sangiorgio in the warmth of the dining room among all that political talk and that smell of ink. . . . He felt in him a new fascination, completely human, and it dominated him in a different way. . . . He felt . . . the poetic softness of a woman's clothes down there and the great tender and sensual agitation exuded by all those things that have touched a woman's body" (169–70).

And here Sangiorgio's double desire for the concrete and the sublime, his desire to fill the empty picture frame with the fetishism of "*biancheria* [underwear]," a blank, white space, founders on the rock of an ultimate impossibility of representation. "For us women," Angelica tells him, with the full support of Zanichelli, Carducci, and Chabod, "certain ideas, indeed abstract ideas, represent nothing. We need more concrete realities: religion in a church, in the figure of the Virgin, in Christ; the fatherland in the sweet homeland, in the sea, in the hills, among the people we love; who can represent politics or the idea?" (166). Sangiorgio may well assent to such an immediacy, as he does in the name of love, but he cannot make sense of the vulgarity that seems its inevitable result. Angelica will always address him as Sangiorgio, "for the name of Francesco was too vulgar, too unpleasant, and he felt this vulgarity, this unpleasantness and suffered by it, but did not ask her to call him by his name" (224).

And it will be a name that will constitute Sangiorgio's final undoing, a name, however, that is marked only as a cipher, a representation, for all that may have been possible: the *A,* so subtle and so long, inscribed in the cover of a bed that is not even a bed. This feminine *A* signals simultaneously the collapse of all representation and announces a symptomatic excess already presaged and spelled out earlier in the four letters that make up Sangiorgio's fantasy, the conquest not of Rome but by Rome. The written word has lost here its mediating capacities; it can neither fill the frame with a representation nor leave it entirely blank. Serao's prognosis for new representations, for a new tradition founded in the constructive potentialities of the written word in order to mend the world, remains thus equally blank. Sangiorgio can neither submit to the older divine images provided by Catholic culture nor actively shape a new transparent language that is open to his own act of deciphering and interpretation. His conflict, however, heralds the return of the Father, here in the figure of Don Silvio Vargas and later in the form of other strong men who will put an end to the miseries of feminine conundrums. Thus, woman "opts" to exit the scene. And so Angelica entered that bedroom for which "she has never shown any curiosity" (231) and, upon seeing that letter and recognizing its dangers, "let out a subdued scream of anxiety; she looked into Sangiorgio's eyes and the truth became evident to her. Silently she gathered up her hair around her nape, left the room, put on her hat, took her gloves, and left without turning back" (232).

A Woman's Photograph

If woman puts on her clothes and exits the scene, she will nevertheless return in Serao's final chapter, entitled "Leave-taking," to a contemporaneous text, *Il ventre di Napoli* (The Bowels, but also The Womb, of Naples). She returns as a photograph, but for Serao this return is also that of a leave-taking. Woman's return may be thus understood as Serao's own refusal of a fetishistic filling of a blank, white space. The departure of Woman: Angelica's departure toward the end of the novel repeats the other, the unknown woman's departure, when she left, perhaps, on her travels in a hurry and left behind the empty picture frame that gives shape to Sangiorgio's fantasy life.

In what way, Cathy Caruth has recently asked, "is the history of a culture, and its relation to politics, bound up with the notion of departure?" (1996, 13). Departure, for Caruth, describes the latency that inheres in the experience of trauma, the belatedness or *Nachträglichkeit* of Freud's traumatized victims of train rides, like those of Sangiorgio, that leave these victims only apparently unharmed. "If return is displaced by trauma," Caruth writes, "then, this is significant insofar as its leaving—the space of the unconscious—is, paradoxically, precisely what preserves the event in its literality. For history to be a history of trauma means that it is referential to the extent that it is not fully perceived as it occurs, that a history can be grasped only in the very inaccessibility of its occurrence" (17–18).

In a 1904 supplement to her *Il ventre di Napoli,* a text written between 1884 and 1904 as a series of journalistic essays, Serao ends her book on the traumatic destruction of her native city with an essay entitled "Una donna." *Il ventre di Napoli* had been written as a response to a governmental proposal of disemboweling the choleric slums of Naples, of performing a kind of hysterectomy on the city—what the Depretis government had proposed as a *"sventrare"* of the city's poor neighborhoods. In opposition to this policy, Serao places her own photographic prose, a prose that refuses the poetry of a Neapolitan picturesque, the idealized scene presented to the tourists as a mise-en-scène of illusion but that in reality exhibits, by a glance through its torn curtain, all the misery, poverty, and disease of a city from which the government itself had departed (Serao 2002, 104–5). Serao's prose, in its multiple references to an act of seeing that goes beyond fetishistic hallucination, proposes another kind of look at the city, a look that is Serao's own, but that takes place from a certain distance, displaced as the writer is, in Rome and thus not from Naples itself. Serao demands a seeing that she calls *"sogguardare,"* both a looking beneath the surface of illusion and a looking that comes, so to speak, from the side. This is a look made possible by Serao's own departure and by the distancing mechanisms of her prose. Serao's seeing is constructed along what Benjamin called a dialectical image, the capturing of the past as an allegorical simultaneity of and with the present. Thus, behind the screen of Naples's luxury lies "what my eyes have seen" (Serao 2002, 112), a *via crucis* of misery and an imperative to see what Serao had seen as a knowledge of the present: "Look! You have only to look!" (114)

The past returns in the present as a dialectical image, as a photograph, and it returns bearing all the traces of loss, and indeed of melancholy pleasure, punctuated, as it is, by an "as if" quality, by the repeated invocation of a "perhaps":

> Have you ever experienced the subtle and melancholy pleasure, full of secret surprises and intimate leaps, of shuffling through the old portraits of an antiquated album, one that has not been opened for years . . . ? Have you ever fixed your eyes on the pale portrait of those who have died, for—quite mysteriously—all portraits of the dead seem faded? The faces of the dead, the faces of persons who have disappeared, whom you will never see again, the faces of creatures who, perhaps, loved you and that you loved badly, perhaps, and who did not love you at the time, perhaps, the faces already consumed by a sadness or a florid beauty that is almost intangible, the faces of such old portraits, of persons who bore away a part of your heart, that took from you a light in your soul, perhaps, or that, perhaps, left behind with you a profound and indelible memory. . . . And when, dismayed by the ghosts that you yourself have evoked, you drop the album and close the case, waves of bitterness continue to flutter in your blood. Oh past, only you are true! (181)

Serao gazes upon a portrait of a woman, now departed, a young woman of Neapolitan high society, a true Christian who had worked for the improvement of the poor and of the neglected in the slums of Naples. She is Teresa Ravaschieri, Serao's mother. And yet this motherly specter is much different from the ghost that will appear to Lombroso shortly before his own death, a ghost that he had so desperately sought to capture in the frame of a photograph. Nor is she the projection of Sangiorgio's imagination. The image of Teresa Ravaschieri is that of a woman who is both absent and lost, the trace always already of a departure from a masculine desire to decipher her meaning.

FOUR

Love's Gravity: The Perverse Gymnastics of Edmondo De Amicis

The study of gravitation is the physical science concerned with the attraction of bodies for one another. ENCYCLOPEDIA BRITANNICA

Italians are not sufficiently weighted to the ground—so stated Francesco De Sanctis in his important 1878 essay entitled "Il limite"—and for that reason they are overly committed to an absolute idea of individual freedom, one that is in conflict with the limits required by the state. De Sanctis did not view Italian ungroundedness as a flaw in the national character; instead, he sought to furnish it with a historical, dialectical explanation. The belief in absolute freedom was founded in the traditions and reminiscences of the period of European state-formation that, in the late nineteenth century, belonged to the past: "Last century's motto was liberty, but this is, for better or worse, a moment that we have absorbed and thus surpassed. Our century's motto is the limit. It is no longer enough to call oneself a liberal. Liberty is a means, not an end. It is an empty form if we do not give it a content—that is, our national life and our ideals. And this content is liberty's limit. This limit prevents liberty from becoming an abstraction and instead turns it into a living thing" (De Sanctis 1970a, 173). For his own century, therefore, De Sanctis rejected universalist claims and he did so in the name of content, of a substantiality of the body, or what he called "an intellectual and moral *gymnastics* that stimulates and sets into motion all the latent forces of the spirit" (1972, 305; my emphasis). A gymnastics of soul and body had to supplement each other and provide a firm ground under Italian feet. Otherwise, De Sanctis claimed, the youth of the new Italy would indulge in generalizations, in fantasy, vagueness, and abstractions. Italy was perhaps dedicated to instruction—and here De Sanctis echoed a favored opposition of the period—but had no understanding of education: while the state's schools filled young heads with information, they did not educate the whole child; they did not purify its heart, guide its imagination, or harmonize all those forces given to us by nature (1970h, 261–62). Good to his word, in 1878 De Sanctis, in his capacity of Minister of Education, presented to the government the outlines of a law that would make physical education in all schools of the new state compulsory for both boys and girls. The goal of such an education was to be more than the development of mere muscle tone. It was, instead, to aim at something higher, at what De Sanctis thought of as a spiritual unity capable—via the management of the body's gravity—of constructing a new form of gravity. What De Sanctis aimed at was character building, or what he liked to call a "virile education." His proposal was written into law that same year, and this despite the vociferous opposition of Catholic pedagogues alarmed at the idea of an institutionally mandated flexing of young muscles and of gravitational movements that could only lead to the attraction of bodies to one another.

In an Italy where concern about national disaggregation was paramount, the existence of investigations into the characteristics of man's center of gravity is not surprising. Disaggregation was detected at a series of different levels: at the level of the nation, that is, in the continued regionalism of its component parts; at the level of the economy, as Italy shifted from rural, agrarian modes of existence to industrialization and urbanization with all the features of anomie that such new lifestyles entailed; and last, at the level of the individual, who with all his *scioltezza* threatened to become unraveled from the very center of his being, that is, increasingly swayed by passions whose origins were difficult to determine. The landscape was a confoundedly enigmatic and paradoxical one, poised between forces that appeared simultaneously as centrifugal and entropic. People seemed to be in constant movement and yet statically caught in a much-lamented inertia that prevented a break with tradition and the creation of a modern work ethic. Italy, it seemed, required both a vigorous push *and* repose.

In an effort to flesh out the structure and content of a pedagogy adequate to the creation of Italian citizens, the cultural and political elite of the newly created state came up continuously against the problem of how exactly to conceive of De Sanctis's virile education: Would it have to be imposed from the *outside,* or would it instead present itself as the true expression of an already existent quality *inside* the subject, a quality that found its proper translation in the term *italianità?* In an age when it was no longer possible to be a liberal, how could a national pedagogy come into being that was democratic and modern, but nevertheless had the capacity to effectively bind the subject to the state?

The opposition between external determination and internal compulsion was posited with particular clarity in the discussions conducted around the institution of a national gymnastics as a project of bodily reform and subject formation. The investigations into the subject's gravity tracked here a kind of shuttle movement between the physics of the body and the attractions exerted by love. On the one hand, theorists of gymnastics debated whether the body required attachment to a gymnastic apparatus in order to achieve the necessary gravity or whether instead a subject was formed when he moved freely. Beyond the question of mere technique, this problem was viewed to have profound political effects, because it proposed radically different perspectives on how subjects come to be attached, even cathected to a social system. Yet theorists and critics of a national gymnastics repeatedly raised the possibility that gymnastic training was capable of unleashing forces and passions that were not always easily controlled. The fear that there was something inherently perverse to a national gymnastics was voiced both by the essentially Catholic Right—who viewed the exhibition of male and female bodies as a threat to traditional morality—and by leading observers of the Left. The latter too expressed anxiety over a politics of spectacle that was entirely too "German" for Italian bodies and carried antidemocratic implications that potentially betrayed specifically Italian ideals of freedom and modernity. More fundamentally perhaps, and this will be the import of Edmondo De Amicis's contribution to the debate, a national gymnastics appeared predicated on a perverse libidinal attachment to and involvement in relations of power that not only produced new forms of power but also relied on a reconfiguration of gender definitions.

While the Italian debate about the advantages and disadvantages of a national gymnastics may appear a minor point in the history of making Italians during the post-Unification period, this debate in fact aids our understanding of Italian citizenship formation in significant ways. First, it tracks the vicissitudes of a specifically Italian history of what Foucault has called the disciplinary knowledges in the project of creating modern, postliberal subjects. Second, it also explicitly engages the function and performance of ideology as it (consensually) binds subjects to the state. Indeed, one may argue that the debate about the *gymnastic apparatus* constitutes a theory of the *ideological state apparatus*—and this to the extent that the debate engages the function of ideology in its most literal form. The discourses produced around Italian gymnastics generated a theory of ideology and in that sense may fruitfully advance our understanding of the working of ideology. It is as if, Slavoj Žižek has argued in an essay on the logico-narrative reconstruction of the theory of ideology, "at every stage, the same opposition, the same *undecidable* alternative Inside/Outside, repeats itself under a different exponent" (1994a, 17). Finally, the Italian gymnastics movement made use of and also expanded on an important paradigm shift occurring largely in the sciences but that would prove to have a profound impact on the arts and their attempt to represent the modern subject. I am referring to those advances made in the mechanics of knowing the body, which shifted from linguistic and, hence, also nationally bound descriptions of the body to the body's graphic *inscription*. This transformation brought with it not just new ways of seeing but an important reorganization of the body's movements in time and space. In this sense, we find evidence in the gymnastics debate of a move away from the mythic or fetishistic seeing described in the previous chapter, one bound to a kind of Catholic power over the body in the form of spectacle. Here, instead, a new, modernist mode of making the body visible was articulated, where the body was made to speak for itself in the form of a graphism that both relied on but also dispensed with an apparatus that produced a subject that was bound and yet free, a subject whose energies fell, like Pinocchio, always on its feet in its obedience to the laws of gravity, but in that same move produced its own pleasures. Furthermore, this shift would make possible Maria Montessori's pedagogical project.

Graphing Machines

The work of the French physiologist Etienne-Jules Marey (1830–1904) was widely known and circulated in Italy, partially, no doubt, because he spent his adult life divided between Paris and Naples. His connections to the Italian scientific establishment were thus direct and extensive. The inventor of a broad panoply of machines and gadgets designed to register the visible and, more importantly, the invisible movements of the body, Marey created machines that were to have a lasting impact in medicine, and in particular physiology, as well as in aeronautics, military training, gymnastics, ballistics, photography, cinematography, the science of work and industrial organization, and modernist art. Marey was, in the true Lévi-Straussian sense, a *bricoleur;* he found mechanical solutions in a trial-and-error manner that was subservient to the scientific problems he was concerned with at any given time. For this reason, the fact that he constructed one of the first airplanes and made significant advances in photography and cinematography, or "moving pictures," has often gone unnoticed in the history of technology. Marey's own ego was, in the apt words of Marta Braun, "so unobtrusive as to be invisible" (1992, 349).[1]

These words are particularly applicable because what interested Marey more than anything was the world of the invisible, that is, those forces hidden in the body that moved and determined the body's functioning but that were either too big or too small to be registered by the human senses. Modern science encountered here, according to Marey, its two most fundamental obstacles: on their own, our senses were incapable of discovering scientific truth, and language was inadequate to transmit those truths that could be discovered. The French physiologist thus sought the proper means for making representable those invisible agents that were at work in the secret recesses of the body, for *movement* was the central fact of life. In this, he was true to the thermodynamic model of the body as a source and repository of energy. As such, the body had to become subject to economic laws of conservation and dissipation, laws that could be made known only if they were rendered visible through space and time.[2]

Marey thus invented a new language to describe this body in motion, a language that was conceived as an *inscription* and that made possible an analytics of the body, as it was decomposed into its component parts as its representation in time and space. To this end, in 1860 and going straight to the heart of things, Marey invented the sphygmograph, or pulse writer. This machine graphed pressure changes by first registering the movements of the arterial wall and then transferring those movements to an attached stylus, thus rendering those same movements as a fluid transcription. Mary Ann Doane, in connection to this event, has pointed to two fundamental aspects of Marey's method. First, indexicality had a major stake in his representational practices to the extent that the body's movement had to be measured by a direct source; and second, such measuring required a complex apparatus—made up of wires, rubber tubing, and other paraphernalia to bind the subject to the recording machine (Doane 2002, 47–48). And yet despite the presence of the apparatus, Marey considered such tracing of the body's movement to be automatic, in other words, self-generating. The resultant *graphic method,* as Marey called it, produced a permanent record, one oblivious to "the prejudices of the observer or the rhetoric of the expositor" (Frank 1988, 218). The graphic method, because it described and transcribed a "telltale heart," spoke beyond national languages and translated its messages directly into the international language of the body. The rising and falling lines of the graph effectively translated national descriptors into a form of international representation. In a direct attack on the nationalism of statistics, Marey wrote, graphs, by virtue of their capacity to curve through space and time, demonstrated "what has really taken place much more clearly than a column of figures, which is tedious and fatiguing to read down. . . . The sum of every kind of observation can thus be expressed by graphs; changes, pressure, weight, or bulk, or variations of intensity of any kind of force. . . . How is it possible not to anticipate with impatience the day when long and obscure descriptions will give place to satisfactory representations?" (1876, 66).

Marey believed his graphic method to be revolutionary for two reasons. On the one hand, and this claim is perhaps more utopian in its desire for a transcendental scientific language, it was to eliminate the rhetorical excesses and the prejudices of the observer. On the other hand, it conceived of mechanical objectivity as a means to access the primordial, preverbal idiom of images at the origin of civilization. In this sense, it is fair to say that Marey's foremost goal was to locate and then control excess *per se.* His instruments produced a direct writing or transcription, in his opinion, of a fundamental, because originary, truth. They made recordings, according to François Dagognet, "without recourse to the human hand or eye. Nature had to testify to itself, to translate itself through the inflection of curves and subtle trajectories that were truly representative." For Marey, science constituted an act of writing and reading, the act of an archaeologist who deciphered inscriptions in an unknown language. He "thus refused to go down the sloping twists and turns of the visceral. His science brought to the surface what was thought inaccessible, eliminated the superfluous (interference) and kept only the essential (the message from the lines themselves). He directly questioned not only our senses, which deceive us, but also languages that lead us astray. . . . [The graphic sign], in contrast, was to be considered nature's own expression, without screen, echo or interference: it was faithful, clear and, above all, universal" (Dagognet 1992, 30, 62–63). Therefore, Marey, in his drive to control excess, did not view his instruments as prosthetic devices. If his instruments tracked down those phenomena that lay buried deep within the body, then this was because *l'expression graphique* harked back to the origins of civilization in pictographs: Marey was, as Robert Frank has noted, more than just a salesman for a new apparatus (1988, 218). The medium of transmission was thus also its message. For this reason, when in his 1873 *La machine animale: Locomotion terrestre et aérienne* Marey opposed the use of vivisection, this was because it ultimately destroyed the body to be analyzed. Instead, Marey sought to record human movements by nonintrusive instruments, not only to learn the body's messages but also to then reconstruct that body through mechanical models capable of *simulating* the human body's functioning. Marey's was thus also a synthetic method, predicated on the construction of models designed to reproduce nature through the machine. It was this cybernetic replication of the human motor that ultimately permitted him a vision of the body as a self-governing, self-knowing, and self-mending machine.

Nevertheless, Marey soon found that his graphic method had its limits. While his early instruments may have been telltale hearts, they nevertheless rendered the body's movement in a state of repose and thus betrayed its essential nature. Therefore, when Marey saw Eadweard Muybridge's photographs of horses in motion in 1878, he devised a new method of representation that he named chronophotography: the photography in and of time. The advantages of such photography were obvious, for it could both portray movement and render movement's outward form at the same time. In addition, photography also obviated the need for a transmitter that was directly attached to the subject under investigation. True to his desire for an unmediated writing of the body's language, Marey's chronophotographic method detached the subject from its investigating apparatus. But there were also disadvantages to this new method. While graphic transcription could trace movement "with a fluid visual expression for time and motion" (Braun 1992, 61), the camera lost precisely that aspect of continuity. Camera technology at that time could not emulate the graphic method's ability to represent the passage of time in space. While Marey countered this problem by developing cameras that were able to reproduce increasing numbers of images on one plate (see fig. 4.1), he soon found that his photographic method rendered to representation *too much visibility* and thus clouded or obscured his very object of analysis. Marey hit here more than simply a technological complication. As Mary Ann

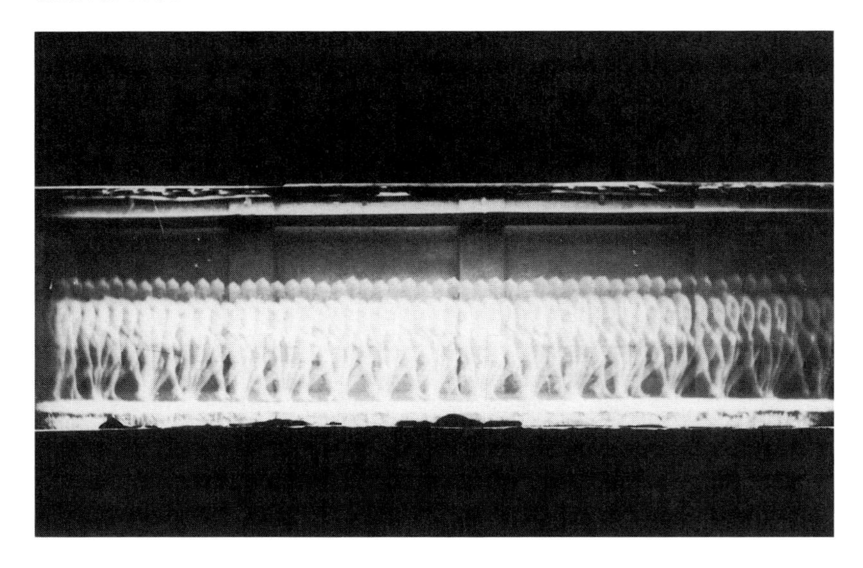

Figure 4.1 Etienne-Jules Marey, "Demeney Walking" (1883). (© College de France.)

Doane has claimed, something was invariably lost (2002, 59). Beyond the *temps perdu* between the body's movement and its registration (in other words, the lapse of time between the body's reaction to a stimulus and the registration of this reaction in the apparatus), Marey was deeply concerned with the time lost between the series of photographic registrations. Photographic accuracy, it appeared, produced illegibility and thus returned the body to invisibility as a kind of blurring of the object. For its part, the graphic method in its original form was readable, while it betrayed time. "If, in his photographic work, Marey respected the integrity of time and attempted to register the smallest displacements, he produced an unreadable record (as a result of excessive overlapping and superimposition). If he strove for legibility in his documents, he betrayed his object (time) and compromised his attempt to represent it adequately" (Doane 2002, 60). On its own, the camera was, in a sense, too representational or realist; it could show what the eye could see on its own, but it could not show that which was invisible to the eye, that which was the object of Marey's analysis.

In order to gain access to the invisible through the camera, Marey combined it with his graphic method by transforming "photographic modes of representation into graphic ones" (Doane 2002, 57). That is, he moved from the graphic method to the photographic method, but only "to defamiliarize, derealize, even de-iconize the photographic image" (54). In a sense, his particular adoption of photography constituted a direct attack on the reality principle. To this end, Marey developed what Marta Braun describes as a "moving skeleton," a body to be photographed that was dressed in black and marked in its joints by bright buttons, which in turn were connected by metal bands (see fig. 4.2). By paradoxically *suppressing* the body's visibility, the resultant images could be returned to their graphic representation in the form of geometric photographs (see figs. 4.3 and 4.4). Like Geppetto, Marey constructed, in other words, a puppet without strings, or—to be more precise—he created a kind of Pinocchio effect.

Marey was a positivist scientist, yet he never had the desire to reproduce what the naked eye could see for itself. While his chronophotography would prove crucial to the future developments of the cinema, he was neither a realist nor interested in the potential of cinema as spectacle.[3] As Marta Braun has insisted, this rejection is grounded ultimately in Marey's desire for a scientific discourse beyond the aesthetic pleasures produced by illusion. Such a desire is evidenced, for Braun, by a contrast to what she ultimately sees as the perverse images produced by Eadweard Muybridge. The latter, she claims, desires to tell a story, to develop a plot by which the viewer is guided to view his photographs. What Muybridge presents us with is the perverse, voyeuristic pleasure

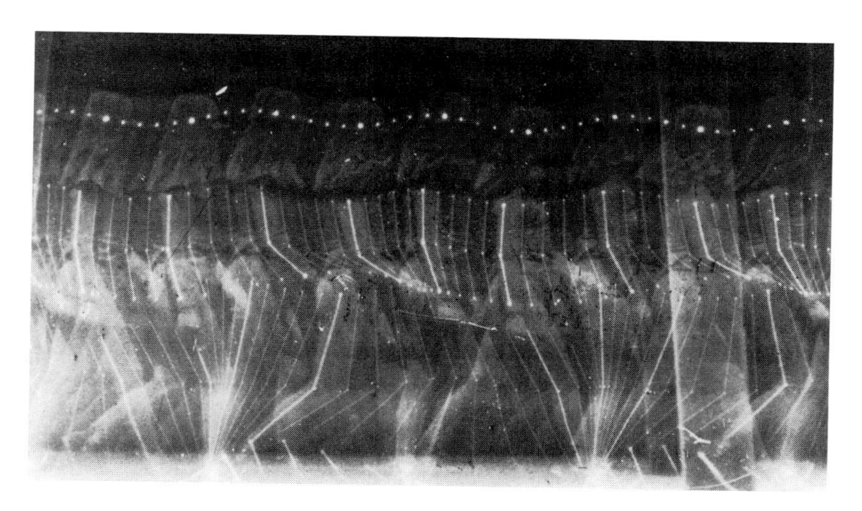

Figure 4.2 Etienne-Jules Marey, "Walk with Bent Knees" (1884). (© College de France.)

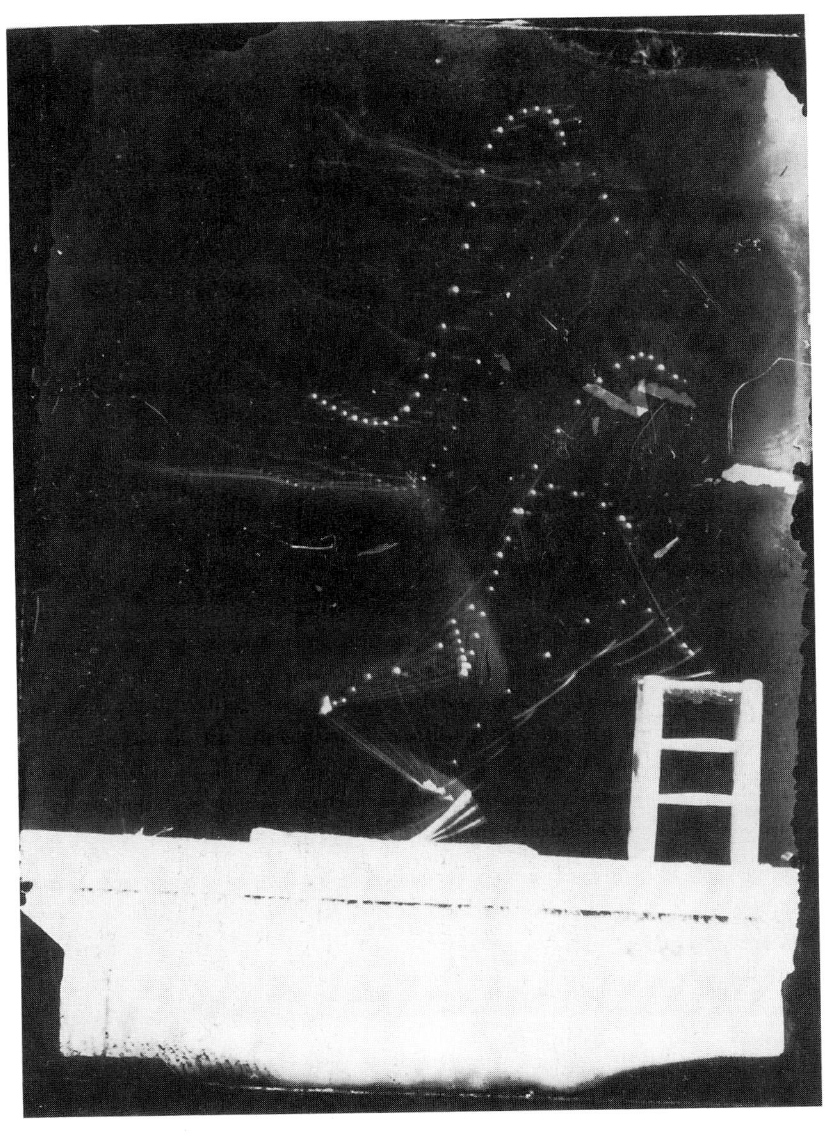

Figure 4.3 Etienne-Jules Marey, "Jump from a Height with Bent Knees" (1884). (© College de France.)

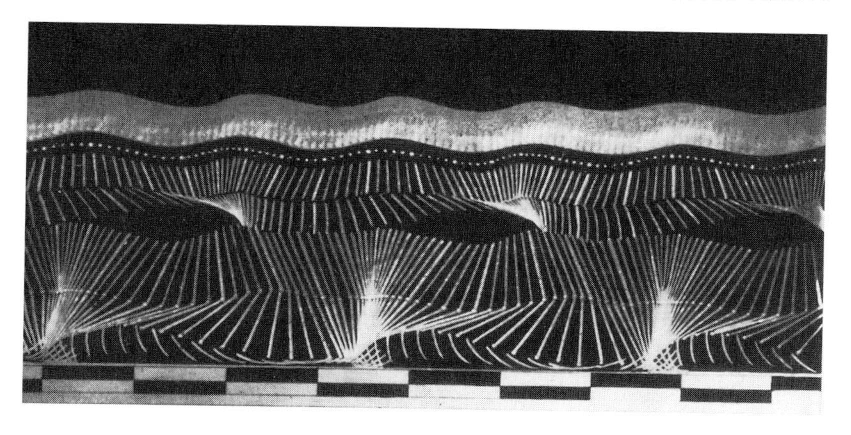

Figure 4.4 Etienne-Jules Marey, "Joinville Soldier Walking" (1883). (© College de France.)

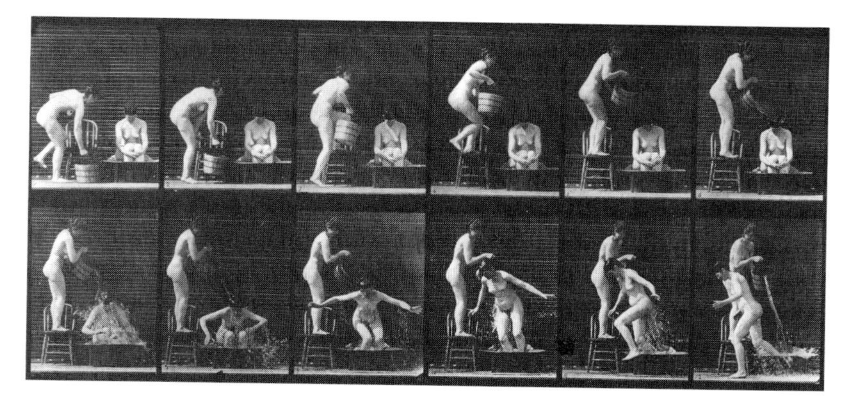

Figure 4.5 Eadweard Muybridge, "Animal Locomotion, Plate 406" (1887). Photograph. (Victoria & Albert Museum, London. © Victoria & Albert Museum, London/Art Resource, New York.)

of looking at women dressing and undressing or splashing in water (see fig. 4.5), of watching men do menial tasks or performing acrobatic feats. In all these cases, "the cosmetic, aesthetic, and narrative requirements of the photographs have triumphed over the need for analytically verifiable data. . . . [Muybridge's] photographs objectify erotic impulses and extend voyeuristic curiosity in a language we now recognize as taken from the standard pornographic vocabulary. . . . Muybridge's concern, then, is with narration, not with movement" (Braun 1992, 247–49).[4]

Figure 4.6 Giacomo Balla, *Study for "Girl Running on a Balcony"* (1912). (Galleria d'Arte Moderna, Milan. © 2006 Artists Rights Society (ARS), New York/SIE, Rome.)

And yet Marey's graphism would have profound effects on modernist art. At a more general level, as Braun acknowledges, Marey's chronophotography shattered Renaissance linear perspective, where the frame of an image was understood to enclose a temporal and spatial unity. His refusal of illusionary realism in the name of a movement or dynamism in time was, according to Braun, to become the dominant pictorial convention in the twentieth century, especially in Italian futurism (see fig. 4.6). But in Italy, Marey's transcriptions of the body's invisible movements were absorbed not just in futurist and other aesthetic forms and practices, but also in the project of creating a *social orthopedics*. As Foucault has written, social orthopedics was a fundamental aspect of the new disciplinary society that depended on examination, surveillance, and correction as its principal methods for exerting political power, but that also produced its own perverse pleasures (2000c, 57). The point is that these two translations of Marey's method cannot be separated; the relationship between aesthetic pleasure and social orthopedics constitutes the core of the Italian gymnastics debate.

Social Orthopedics

Many contemporary observers detected *scioltezza* throughout the social body, even if it was not always called by that name. Positivist scientists, in particular, set out to discover the parameters of this ubiquitous national trait and to provide it with a scientific, indeed, medical explanation. Between 1887 and 1909, as Ian Hacking tells part of this story (1996), the French discovered a new mental malady, one that seemed to affect working-class men above all. It went under the name of ambulatory automatism, by which was understood, in the words of Albert Pitres, "a pathological syndrome appearing in the form of intermittent attacks during which the patient, carried away by an irresistible impulse, leaves his home and makes an excursion or a journey justified by no reasonable motive. The attack ended, the subject unexpectedly finds himself on an unknown road or in a strange town. Swearing by all the gods never again to quit his penates, he returns home but sooner or later a new attack provokes a new escapade" (cited in Hacking 1996, 31).

According to Hacking, ambulatory automatism (*Wandertrieb, determinismo ambulatorio*) constituted a parody of a different, middle-class, and fully legitimate occupation in the new age: modern tourism, whose destinations were more likely than not the Italian skies and shores. In Italy itself, however, where ambulatory automatism had seemingly greater capacities to cross gender and class lines, the malady of compulsive movement was identified a decade earlier. One Antigono Raggi discovered in 1877 an illness that he called clitrophobia, whose special characteristic consisted in a horror of rest and in the compulsive need for movement. In 1880—in other words, right around the time that Pinocchio was to take to the streets and roads of Italy—Cesare Lombroso confirmed the existence of such a syndrome but renamed it claustrophobia, which should be understood, I believe, as a sort of panic about domesticity and domestication. Like Raggi, Lombroso insisted on the illness's novelty, on its modernity (Lombroso 2000a). Citing cases of such compulsive movement in both men and women, rich and poor, Lombroso explained the phenomenon as a natural reaction to either physically or psychically induced muscular pain: "the forced exercise of the muscles decreases the intensity of pain," just as in those people who have had an upsetting experience and thus "feel the need to go outside and move, without which, they say, they would feel suffocated by their pain" (209).

Such claustrophobia is related but not identical to what Lombroso calls the madness of vagabonds (*pazzia dei vagabondi*), which he takes to be largely a hereditary disease but also at times caused by traumatic experiences, a disease that presents itself as an absence of good sense, honor, morality, and love for the family, as well as the tendency toward alcoholism, an excessive libido, the love of intrigue, and, above all, the need to "wander from one town to the next without pause" (210). Vagabonds suffer from common moral madness. They are a group of individuals who constitute the first link in a chain that binds economic necessity to the world of crime: "While a small number of these men are the product of social and political necessity, of unemployment, strikes, and ill health, the largest number, on the contrary, is made up of men who are anything but sick. They are even incapable of real crimes, indeed, have a horror of blood and great thefts, but not necessarily of pimping and prostitution. Above all, they are incapable of steady work. They feel their arms to be weak and therefore they cannot adapt themselves to normal society, which requires stable employment. Hence, they are insensibly pushed toward criminals who constitute their natural friends" (211). And if weak arms are not the sole problem, then it is an irresistible need for continuous locomotion that prevents such individuals from staying in one place for any length of time. Compulsive movers feel the "inverse emotion of nostalgia, because of which any given place, any given set of people and activities become uncomfortable. An office, if it does not allow them to move about and change places, becomes unbearable" (211).

Claustrophobia, for Lombroso, constitutes a singular point of passage, then, between the criminal, the insane, and the normal man struck down by a painful experience. It demonstrates how certain psychic phenomena can be the result of both normality and pathology. Indeed, claustrophobia as a modern phenomenon has a history of normality whose origins are located, he holds, in the nomadic life of primitive humanity. Lombroso thus traces a continuous movement through the history of compulsive movement, beginning with nomadism and continuing through mass migrations, the crusades, pilgrimages, traveling flagellant sects, and roaming monks, all of which lead one to believe that "religion, crime, and madness were fused" by men who "ran here and there without stopping in one place, and who under the pretext of searching for the perfect life, in obeying the Gospels, let themselves be kept in idleness and luxury and mingled with the saddest characters under the pretext of converting them" (212).

In 1872 Luigi Pagliani, professor of experimental physiology at the University of Turin, was put in charge of the sanitary supervision of the agricultural colony of Bonafous. It was the colony's mission to gather up and send to work orphans and foundlings, thus transforming them into productive citizens. In the years to come, Pagliani would spearhead the Italian hygiene movement, which would advocate an alliance between science and charity against the brutal laws of the market and the naked forces of nature. It is noteworthy that the hygiene movement straddled a position that encompassed both a reliance on natural scientific laws and the belief that nature, when left alone, was not only brutal but perverse. This idea, you will recall, is fundamental to Roberto Esposito's idea of the modern immunitary paradigm: biopolitics took on its specifically modern forms once nature was denaturalized and thus rendered subject to a necessary "artificial" intervention.[5] The young inhabitants of Bonafous thus merited intense hygieno-anthropological interest, for, under laboratory conditions, one could through them not only study their passage from precarious existence to healthy living, but also determine the biotechnical possibilities of making nature more regulated and hence more productive. The transition from vagabondage to stable collective life, like the reclamation of land that accompanied it, was predicated on the control of nature through hard but measured work. For Pagliani, the exhaustion and fatigue of mind and body had to be measured and regulated by the proportionately calculated physical strength and constitutions of the members of the colony, along with their innate abilities and talents. A good diet, the proper amount of work, hygiene, and education were able, Pagliani insists, to resurrect and transform those young bodies, and this despite the negative hereditary and birth factors exhibited by the children (1876).

The hygiene movement's birth in Italy coincided with the more general European and American rise of the bacteriological paradigm, in other words and as Claudio Pogliano has noted, with a shift away from the study of symptomatology to that of etiology; with a shift from external signs to internal, invisible causes. Robert Koch's discovery of the tubercular microbe sparked what Pogliano calls a bacteriological passion that provoked an epistemological rupture that affected the natural as well as the social sciences: "Hygiene as a discipline maintained a relationship with the unexplored region of germs similar to the one that metaphysics established with the unconscious or the paranormal. In both cases it was a question of explaining the visible world by invisible forces" (Pogliano 1984, 628). This epistemological break had two important consequences. First, it had the effect of dismantling the virtual hegemony of the theory that disease was socially created, dependent, that is, on lifestyle and morals. If the germ theory was correct, so many of its opponents agonized, then what happened to the role of morality? One Bologna professor of hygiene, Francesco Roncati, for instance, warned against the possibility of moral bankruptcy and was adamant that the gravest danger to society was posed not by microbes but by moral contagion, in other words, by those corrupting and exciting influences that spread by imitation and suggestion. Second, the long-standing explanation of disease as due to inherent, that is, congenital or dispositional factors was also threatened. As Giulio Bizzozero pointed out, "Physical robustness is a coefficient of secondary value when it is a question of preventing a contagious material from entering our body and there producing a disease." Resistance against an infectious disease could not be determined by external signs, and therefore, weakness of the body and resistance against infection were not to be viewed as mutually exclusive (Bizzozero 1898, 619–20).

A new reading practice, then, and a depersonalization of the workings of disease required new battle lines against an invisible enemy that seemingly floated through the air and was imagined to "penetrate the epithelial textures and orifices of man in order to devastate his functioning." In this context, it made little sense to assign responsibility to the patient or to determine some originary transgression; it appeared more appropriate to observe under a microscope the invading agent's morphological and biological properties (Pogliano 1984, 611).[6]

The first adoption of Marey's mechanical discoveries took place in the Italian hygiene movement, which strove, under the leadership of Luigi Pagliani, to become a universal science, encompassing the entire medical field, as well as professionals in sociology, economics, pharmacology, engineering, urban planning, law, pedagogy, and state administration. Crucial to this universalizing project was the organization and rationalization of space, particularly urban space. Pagliani's massive two-volume *Trattato di igiene e di sanità pubblica colle applicazioni alla ingegneria e alla vigilanza sanitaria* covered thus a broad spectrum of problems, from climactic and meteorological phenomena to the proper construction and installation of water fountains. In all cases, the issue was that of providing the correct movements of air, water, light, and bodies through a space that thus guaranteed both health and visibility. An indoor gymnasium, for example, had to provide a "great wealth of light and air, because during bodily exertion the students' muscles have a greater need for air that is clean and well circulated" (Pagliani 1913, 2:867). Schools, where climate permitted, should be constructed as pavilions, open to the outdoors and perhaps even mobile. Pagliani dedicated an entire chapter to the correct construction and installation of the school desk. He stressed the "capital importance of the physiological precept that . . . what must rule in the hygieno-sanitary vigilance of schools is the certainty that students are kept fixed in one spot as little as possible" (878). Repeated "free" movement through frequent recesses and through "rational" gymnastics was to encourage students to sit in an act of normal repose and to write while keeping their spinal column straight, and to prevent them thus from tiring and becoming deformed. Without desks and chairs constructed in the proper proportion to the students' bodies, the act of sitting, paradoxically, became too strenuous and thus led to fatigue and bodily perversion.

Pagliani's proposed "free movement" was, therefore, a highly regimented one. He considered the two-seat school desk a definite advantage over the older, multiple-seated desk, for it prevented the transmission of diseases, while also making it easier to control and discipline students through their separation. In addition, the entrance and exit from the desks could be better observed by the teacher, thereby making the whole process "more orderly and speedy" (889). Once constructed to the right specifications and according to the proportion of the students' bodies, then, and once made adaptable to the growth rate of young bodies, the school desk would provide for good body posture, flexibility of movement, lower rates of contagion, and a disciplinary gaze that, like the freely circulating air, would be able to target each student without any exertion on the part of the teacher. Pagliani's schoolroom would thus be a perfect instantiation of what, already in 1830, Nicolaus Heinrich Julius termed the major problem of modern, functional architecture. Thus, while in the premodern age the problem had been to make a spectacle of an event or of the action of a single individual in such a way as to make that event or action accessible to the greatest possible number of people, now "the fundamental problem confronting modern architecture is the opposite. What is wanted is to arrange that the greatest possible number of persons is offered as a spectacle to a single individual charged with their surveillance" (cited in Foucault 2000c, 71–72).

Theater was thus rejected in favor of a new social arrangement, whose coordinates depended on an economy of the controlling gaze that moved through a constructed space in which bodies were to move in a highly choreographed but nevertheless "free" fashion. The paradox, perhaps, is that such freedom was viewed as guaranteed by its necessity, its determination. The body's movements were free, because rational and self-imposed, and yet also reliant on prosthetic devices—buildings and furniture, for instance, or school desks—that molded the body into its natural shape and hence gave it repose. Correlative of the construction of such objects in space, then, was the engineering of bodily movement, of a corporeality that had as its goal the production of equilibrium and balance between constrained idleness and excessive *scioltezza* or irrational running. This constituted a significant shift away from the older belief that society made people sick. Though such a position was never abandoned, it nevertheless became subsumed to a discourse predicated on the notion of a relationship of internality or immanence between body and society. This constituted the essence of what Foucault calls biopolitics, the fact, that is, that modern medicine is always first a social medicine, a hygiene politics, whereby the biological, the somatic, the corporeal turns the body into a social reality and medicine into a biological strategy (2000b, 137).

I would like to return to the paradox, in my view fundamental, of a bodily movement that is both free and necessary, willed and determined. This paradox is in fact related to what Foucault posits as the battle that would play itself out throughout the nineteenth century up until our day between the legal power of the state and the disciplinary knowledges of the human sciences: "the legal freedom of the subject is proven by the fact that his act is seen to be necessary, determined [i.e., rational]; his lack of responsibility proven by the fact that his act is seen to be unnecessary" (2000a, 190).[7] The problem is also fundamentally connected to De Sanctis's limit in the face of the now impossible liberal subject. In fact, it is also, as I already discussed, the essence of Pinocchio's dilemma or paradox, his reality of being a puppet without strings. At stake, then, is the *mode of attachment* of the postliberal subject to the state and to the ideological state apparatus.

The Gymnastics Movement

By the time physical education became a nationally mandated project in 1878, the leading theorists of the Italian gymnastics movement believed they were standing on firm scientific ground.[8] Nevertheless, a scientific approach to bodybuilding did not guarantee agreement on principles and method. At the heart of the debate was the *supplement:* the question of whether nature alone could make Italians or whether such a project would require external intervention.[9] For Francesco De Sanctis, the great advocate both of education of body and mind and of the "impulse from above," it was clear that nature could not constitute subjects on its own. A lack of intervention would lead, he believed, to a return to primitivism; because civilization did not automatically repress the body and its instincts, the body had to be actively shaped in order for it to become a man (De Sanctis 1970h, 253). But what an Italian virile gymnastics would actually look like no one could agree on, a fact that made a consistent application of De Sanctis's 1878 law on mandatory physical education in public schools virtually impossible. The Italian gymnastics movement was divided between the proponents of the military and so-called German method that advocated a regimented training of the body through mass formations and careful muscular enhancement through the use of the gymnastic apparatus; and the proponents of a civilian gymnastics, the so-called Swedish method, that emphasized the need for "natural" movement freed from all attachments and thus to take place individually, even alone, and outdoors. The main supporters of the German method were Rudolf Obermann and Emilio Baumann, while Angelo Mosso and Luigi Pagliani were ardent critics of the "perversions" of the body exacted by the German method that threatened to take over Italy.

The aptly named Emilio Baumann (Build-Man) was an elementary schoolteacher turned doctor and from 1884 director of the Rome Gymnastics Institute that trained physical education teachers for public schools. After Obermann's death in 1869, he was the most influential theorist of Italian gymnastics. Baumann saw a clear link between gymnastic exercise, new urban and industrial structures, free time, and the psychophysical development of the population. He firmly believed that his own particular method was more attuned to the fast pace of modern life, because half an hour in one of his gymnasia was equivalent in its effects to four or five hours of "Swedish" walking. His overall aim was to bend his gymnastic didactics toward what he called a "psycho-kinesthesia" or the art of forming character (Baumann 1900). Baumann repeated thus the frequent appeal to a national education, in opposition to mere instruction of the mind or mere training of the body; while bodily force alone made only acrobats and clowns, a focus only on spiritual force produced "people full of *'italianità'* and liberalism, but also people who tomorrow would be incapable of withstanding the weight of a rifle or the ordeals of a march" (27).

Modern civilization and all its growing comforts were, accordingly, responsible for a growing lack of movement. Increased mechanization (where, according to Baumann and contrary to all empirical evidence, workers merely idly stood around to guard machines), sedentary living, modern transportation, decreasing levels of immunity to disease (due to the slow movement of blood), the increase of automatic or reflex movement (due to the modern invention of such prosthetic devices as the telescope and the microscope)—all these factors had brought about neurasthenia (weakness of the nerves), mioasthenia (weakness of the muscles), hemoasthenia (weakness of the blood and thus of health), and psychoasthenia (weakness of character). Modern conditions therefore demanded outside intervention, a supplement, or what he calls *"un compenso."* [10] And because cinematics was the science of movement, that is, of the forces that produce movement, Baumann proposed himself as its major cinematographer in the shape of his program of psycho-kinesthesia.[11]

Baumann as cinematographer should alert us immediately to the inherent elitism of his method, to the fact, in other words, that it was geared to building itself as a kind of master art, or an art of the master. Baumann's 1882 *Meccanica umana,* a work designed to interpret man's movements scientifically, was, as he himself states, written only for the few. Nevertheless, the lengthy and virtually unreadable tome begins quite jovially with a pseudo-Platonic dialogue: "It was a summer morning and thirty students . . . were experimenting in the presence of their teacher at the bar with an exercise of tensing and flexing their arms" (Baumann 1882, 1). If gravity entails the attraction of bodies, Baumann begins with the singularly unattractive problem of fat. For enter the fatso: "It is the turn of the third student, a young and corpulent man, fatter than gymnastics may be capable of managing." And hence our first encounter with gymnastics, where gymnastics makes us cognizant of the mortifying impression made upon us by our own flesh: "The gymnast receives from the weight of his own body a first distasteful and mortifying impression in the sense that this weight represents for him a not insignificant difficulty that must be overcome." And yet, even if our own bodies weigh us down, we are fortunately not dead weight. For one, our weight makes us stronger by the very fact that carrying it through the world gives us muscles. And in fact gymnastics, by virtue of its use of the apparatus, adds even more weight to our bodies. Nevertheless, Baumann warns, one should not exaggerate the obsession with weight(s), because weight does not automatically convert into power. The vicious circle that exists between weight-gain and sloth merely proves this fact, because obesity is incurable.

The body's weight is, in fact, relative because it obeys the laws of gravity. It weighs less when the body's center of gravity is lowered, and increases when that center is raised. When the body obeys such laws, it is at rest and thus stable. The body no longer obeys the law of gravity, it loses its center and its stability, when it is given a push from the outside that is stronger than the weight exerted by the body. Baumann distinguishes three types of stability: a body is stable when, in order to move it, it must raise its center of gravity; it is unstable when it must lower it; and indifferent when movement does not affect the center of gravity. The crucial point according to Baumann is that because man is animate, he can create his own equilibrium; he can manipulate his body in such a way as to shift his center of gravity—for instance, he can crouch down and thus lower his center of gravity—and thus regain his composure. Thus, with man his equilibrium is essentially corrigible. Man's center of gravity is variable and subject to manipulation through movement, and therefore his body does not necessarily weigh him down. Gymnastics is thus an essentially experimental art (Baumann 1882, 35), to the extent that it can calculate, manage, and correct man's center of gravity through the (re)creation of equilibrium (see figs. 4.7 and 4.8).

The question immediately raises itself, of course, as to why man is then not autocorrigible, why he needs gymnastics and an apparatus; why, in fact, he needs Baumann. A first answer is that, according to Baumann, habitual movements are in themselves damaging—as both modern life and the problem of obesity have shown. Thus, left to its own devices, the body tends to entropy; it would, essentially, never get out of bed. Second, and this is related to the first point, the body is infinitely malleable. Function makes the organ, and even the hardness of our skeletal structure is subject to the actions of the body's softer tissues (59). Muscles make the man, and gymnastics can act as a true correction only if it is allowed to micromanage each muscle separately. To get from a muscular section its maximum product, one has to put it into action

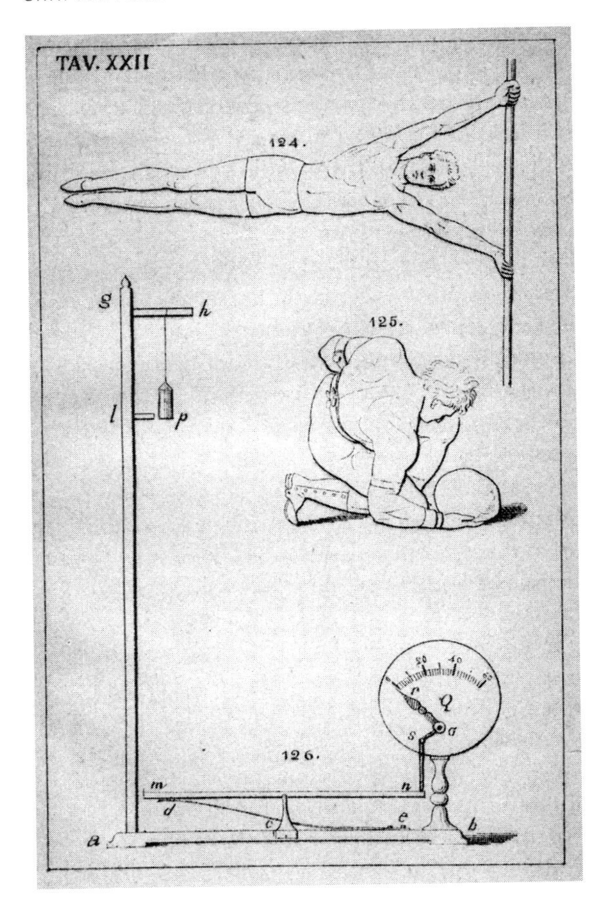

Figure 4.7 Emilio Baumann, illustration from *Meccanica umana* (1882).

in isolation from all other muscles (79). There are two ways by which to isolate and hence educate the muscles, both of which depend on the manipulation of man's center of gravity, that is, on the interplay between movement and repose. The dynamic method depends on man's attachment to a series of contraptions—bars, rings, and horses—the very unnaturalness of which guarantees the production of strength. The second method, which Baumann calls the static method, consists most fundamentally of the act of standing attention, an exercise that he considers a basic aspect of military gymnastics (see fig. 4.9).

Baumann's corrigibility of the body thus depends on micromanaging muscles through experimentation with gravity. The problem of the body's connection to the world is thus *literalized* through its attachment to a gymnastic apparatus the need of which is theorized as founded in the inadequacies of nature. This apparatus is of a paradoxical structure, because it is both prosthesis and yet also a mechanism to which man must, in his more or less helpless flailing, submit as he subjects himself to laws of gravity that are to center him but that continuously allude him as he is hurled through the air (see fig. 4.10). Does he master his body, or does that to which he is attached master him? What kind of relations of power are put into play when a man, in order to be a man, must necessarily master and attach himself to a force that controls and eludes him? Indeed, such were the questions posed by the critics of the

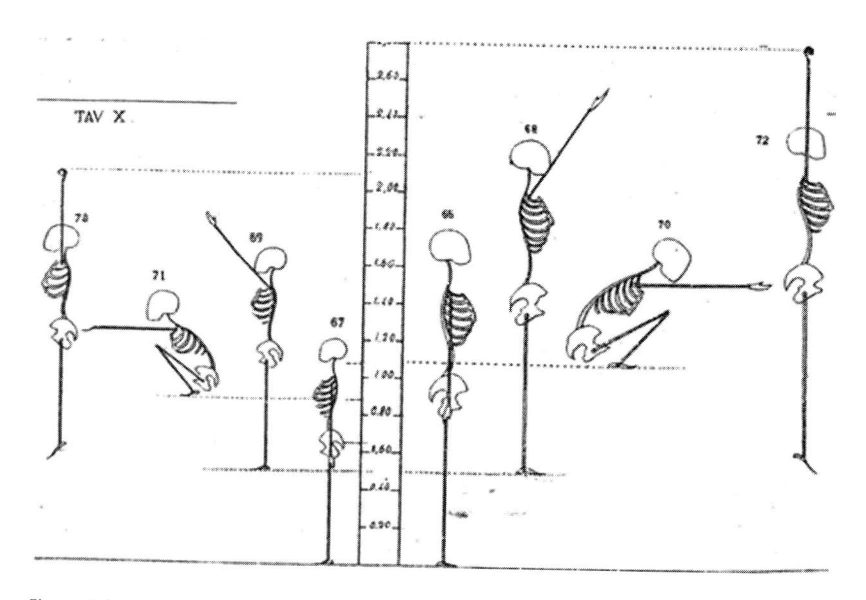

Figure 4.8 Emilio Baumann, illustration from *Meccanica umana* (1882).

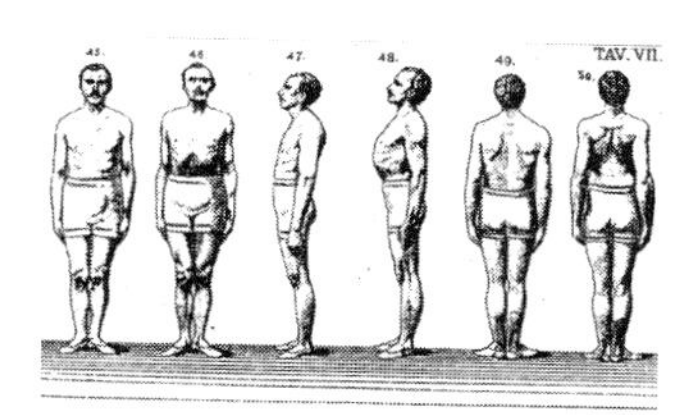

Figure 4.9 Emilio Baumann, illustration from *Meccanica umana* (1882).

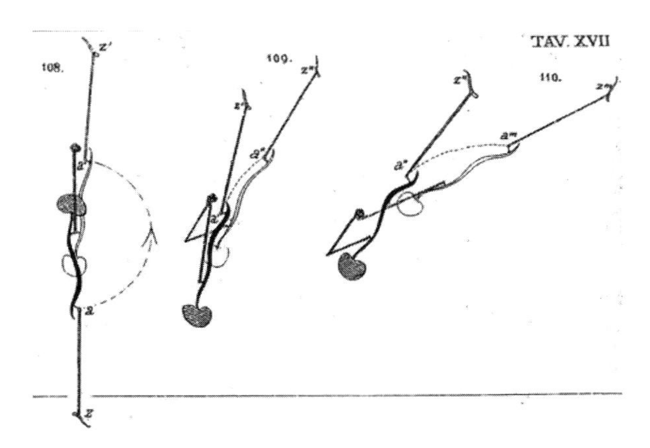

Figure 4.10 Emilio Baumann, illustration from *Meccanica umana* (1882).

German Baumann method from the beginning. Angelo Mosso would call this method not just unnatural, but primitive, for it was not merely a gymnastics of monkeys, but also antimodern, indeed *antidemocratic,* because it brought back the gymnastics teacher as a new tyrant (see fig. 4.11).

Angelo Mosso, the prolific, indefatigable, and fearless author of widely read and translated books such as *Fatigue* and *Fear,* as well as numerous tracts on breathing, mountain-climbing, and comparative analyses of Western pedagogy, was certainly the most ardent critic of the apparatus and the German method dominant in Italy. Mosso was a close friend of Marey's, with whom he collaborated on a series of projects, especially on the ways Marey's instruments could be applied to the study of work and fatigue.[12] And it was apparently Marey who got Mosso interested in the theoretical and practical problems of Italian gymnastics.

Both Mosso and Marey shared an aversion to the so-called German method of gymnastics. To begin with, Mosso believed it was entirely too excessive and partook in and contributed to the creation of people who practiced sports neurotically. As he states in "L'esaurimento nervoso," a neurotic attachment to sports was to be classified as a kind of automatism where the "many cogs in the apparatus [i.e., the body] function completely independently of will. The independence of their function is such that not even will can modify the course of these movements" (1897b, 215). The obsession with sports is thus a disease akin to the one already discovered by Lombroso; it is a variant of "vagabond madness," even though Baumannian gymnastics eschews the outdoors in favor of sweaty and smelly gyms. Above all, German gymnastics is excessive because it is unnatural, invented as a remedy against the sedentary qualities of modern life. German gymnastics is a medicine; it wants to develop the body as quickly as possible—not an unnatural desire, given Italy's anxiety about being a latecomer to Europe's nation building. Yet, while one may be healed by a medicine, one certainly cannot be nourished by it over any length of time (Mosso 1894, 110).

Mosso concedes that there had been a place for German gymnastics prior to Unification. In fact, he states, it had been brought to Italy on the trail of Risorgimento ardor, during the early revolutionary days when fighting and war had been paramount. However, as a civilian exercise it was entirely too violent, especially when practiced on an apparatus. Mosso also admits that military training in Italy remains a problem: Italians have, to their great disadvantage, been cursed not only with the desire for quick results but also with short legs, and thus their training through marches remains essential. The German victory at Sedan was the triumph of German legs; therefore, running will continue to be a

Figure 4.11 Luigi Lamarra, "A Gymnastics of Monkeys: Italian gymnasium in Naples" (1868). Photograph.

fundamental part of the training of Italian bodies.[13] But Mosso envisions this as taking place outdoors, in conjunction with games, massages, light stretching, and aerobic exercises, with the simplicity, naturalness, and hygiene all advocated by the Swedish method (1892, 248ff).

But Mosso is above all interested in a democratic gymnastics, one that should be democratic in three senses. First, it had to allow access for all Italians, rich and poor as well as strong and weak. Indeed, an Italian national gymnastics should not only be universally accessible, that is, easy enough for everyone to be able to participate, but it should also focus especially on the weak, being that they are in the majority, so that they may gain strength and participate in the national project of bodily reform. Second, a democratic gymnastics had to respect difference; the quantity and quality of exercises should be tailored to individual bodies. Third, it should be democratic insofar as it trained the whole body, and not only selected parts of it, as advocated by the German method. Exercise should exhaust all of the body, and in this total exhaustion, Mosso claimed, all would become brothers, because everyone had tired for the same reason and in that move had overcome bodily differences. Universally accessible, easy but complete exercise is what Mosso thinks should be supported, because this kind of support will create workers who want to support themselves. In a passage that tellingly relies on the use of reflexive verbs and thus unties the modern, democratic worker from all forms of apparatus, Mosso writes: "We must help the worker who wants to *educate himself,* who aspires to *raise himself,* who wants to leave behind the humiliating work conditions that reduce him to an animal" (1903, 252; my emphasis).

German gymnastics has put the relationship between physical exercise and democracy into crisis. By its very unnaturalness and in its confusion between robustness and force, it has forsaken its ideal of making citizens, because it has returned gymnastics to spectacle as it celebrates athleticism, acrobatics, and brute force. It has also turned gymnastics into a paid profession for the amusement of the people. Gymnastics competitions have turned into "savage feasts" where children are made to complete utterly senseless exercises in a militarized fashion to the applause of the masses, learning nothing but to blindly imitate each other—not to mention a culture (the German one) that is not even their own:

> When one watches thousands of children who have been patiently lined up in a row, who then start to bow, while contorting themselves to the right and the left with strange gestures that are repeated to the sound of a horn, the spectacle

becomes puerile. Everyone at a sign bows his head, lifts and extends first one arm then another, steps forward then back, hunches down on his heels or stomps his feet, following the sign of the gymnastiarch who dominates everyone while clinging to a ladder. This is a completely useless choreography, because the synchronism of a thousand people's movement is something that never happens in real life. And then what kind of movements? The most banal, those that everyone completes all the time, and it is incomprehensible why they have to be executed with so much solemnity on that precise day. It seems that the only aim is that of imitating a colossal mechanism in order to amuse children. The crowd applauds, but precisely because the crowd desires such spectacles, we are convinced that they are bad. (Mosso 1903, 134–35)

These are revealing words where all the anxieties of modernity come into play: the fear of the masses as the destructive dissolution of individuals, and yet also the anxiety that these masses may be helplessly duped by a new authoritarian leader, the specter of mass politics returning in the form of primitive, puerile, but savage feasts, and the senselessness, perhaps, of bodily mechanization that, paradoxically, has returned man to his former puppet status. Rather than respecting the different energies of individuals, such a gymnastics reduces them to sameness in imitation of a colossal machine.[14] These words are foreboding, as well, for despite the fact that still in 1917 (at the height of World War I) Luigi Pagliani would be adamantly supporting Mosso's demand for a civilian gymnastics, only five years later the entire nation would be engaged in such senseless exercises, though this time not for a public, because the public itself would have been absorbed into the spectacle.

Mosso could make sense of this whole business only through his critique of the apparatus. It was its use that provided him with an adequate vocabulary to aim at the authoritarian nature of the current gymnastics movement. This was a vocabulary that Mosso had acquired from Marey, who, you will recall, not only strove for a noninvasive measurement of bodily movement, but who sought, above all, a scientific method that left the body *free and unattached*. Both Marey's and Mosso's body was asked to speak for itself in its own language. Baumann's gymnastics was artificial to the extent that it sought to supplement the spontaneity of Swedish hygiene and outdoor life. His was a fake or inauthentic language, essentially, a kind of ventriloquism of the gymnastic master. While Marey's ego had been subservient to his scientific enterprise and hence remained invisible, Baumann's apparatus was a symptom of his all-too-visible presence. The apparatus was, in fact, both the condition and result of what Mosso calls the "psychological origin" of German gymnastics (1894, 111). Such a psychology was founded entirely in the *amour propre* of its teachers, the symptoms of which could be detected in the satisfaction of seeing the muscles of the human body activated separately, in the need to give all these movements a technical name, in the formulation of rules, in the ultimate cruelty of gradually escalating the complexity of exercises, which left the body no respite, and in the development of a ridiculous jargon that these autocrats dared call "theory." Furthermore, they actually believed to have made all these military exercises more poetic because children performed them. What Mosso detects is a perverse desire for power and command expressed as symmetry, a desire only truly satisfied when a flaw could be detected that forced the entire group to wait in silence and immobility until everyone got cramps. The apparatus and the militarization of bodily posture in fact required the *professor* of gymnastics, a professor who did not himself exercise or dangle like a monkey from some apparatus, but who multiplied exercises and technical terms, who contributed his "mind" by inventing machines for others that included not only the gymnastic apparatus but also a scientific apparatus to monitor the body. In this sense, Baumann had misunderstood the proper use of Marey's graphic method. In its proponents' desire to make gymnastics an autonomous institution and knowledge, they bloated Baumannian gymnastics with theoretical verbiage and an escalation of exercises: between 1819 and 1875, Mosso claims, the number of exercises had increased from 207 to 1642!

Not only was the gymnasium a prison, not only was the apparatus byzantine or baroque, and not only did such a gymnastics uselessly stress the brain, however. What seems to disturb Mosso most is the fact that "German" gymnastics turned itself into an ideology, whose privileged site of attachment was the monkey bars. Thus, gymnastics as ideology was predicated on there being a leader or professor, one who theorized but did not himself move. By virtue of this fact, however, others had to move, and their movement could be neither real nor natural; it was ideological or phantasmatic. Ideological gymnastics created puppets, it repeated their mode of existence because they were moved by a master puppeteer, attached as they were to an ideological and gymnastic apparatus that functioned as the modern version of strings. And yet, and my sense is that Mosso perceives this, these puppets were also a radically new phenomenon—despite his references to their byzantine or baroque nature. What Mosso detects at the heart of such exercise is an element of perversion, an excessiveness that he names supplemental and neurotic and that he conceives as an elemental passion both prior to and beyond the requirements of civilization.

Love and Gymnastics

Edmondo De Amicis is remembered in the canon of Italian nineteenth-century literature as the author of *Cuore* (Heart). Rather than focusing on this sentimental but sadistic tale of submission to family, work, and fatherland, I would like to recall here De Amicis's far more interesting, raucous, and masochistic *Amore e ginnastica,* first published in *La Nuova Antologia* in serialized form in 1891. By virtue of its telltale garrulousness, heart has here turned into love, into a tale of perversion that finds its brotherhood more comfortably in Leopold von Sacher-Masoch's *Venus in Furs* or in Kafka's perverse characters spat out by a monolithic bureaucratic apparatus. Indeed, it is on the staircase that most of the action takes place in *Amore e ginnastica,* just as in Kafka's story "Die Sorge des Hausvaters," where Odradek, a character neither human nor inhuman, arrives and leaves according to mysterious rules. "The house lent itself to the maneuvers and to the secrets of an amorous passion"—so Italo Calvino condenses the stakes of what he calls De Amicis's most beautiful work (Calvino 1996, vii). Set in fin-de-siècle Turin, the gymnastics capital of Italy, the novel tells the story of the exseminarist accountant Celzani's amorous passion for the gorgeous and foot-free, but nevertheless somewhat pedantic, Miss Pedani, who is a gymnastics teacher and passionate advocate of the "celebrated Baumann." She, of course, has no time for the unfortunate Celzani, because he has not attached even one of his muscles to the gymnastic apparatus, too busy as he is with clinging to staircase banisters and windowsills in an effort to spy on her comings and goings. "La Pedani," on the other hand, has "after the new impulse given to gymnastics by Minister De Sanctis and Baumann's powerful propaganda" been catapulted by her athletic leaps into the limelight of Turinese society. Not only is she capable of executing "the most virile exercises on the fixed and parallel bars; she had, through study, been able to become an insuperable teacher of theory." Because she has taken courses in anatomy, at a first glance "she recognized whether a girl had an aptitude or not for gymnastics, she examined ill-formed bodies, she searched for asymmetrical shoulders, lumpy chests, extended abdomens, crooked knees, and she sought to correct all these defects with a specific order of exercises. She dedicated herself to this with maternal zeal. . . . She would have wished that they invent contraptions to measure the beauty of carriage, of agility, the faculty of equilibrium, of everything" (De Amicis 1996, 14–16; see fig. 4.12). Marriage is out of the question for La Pedani: "A true gymnastics teacher must not take a husband, she must conserve herself as a soldier, she must be free in spirit and body. [She] must completely consecrate herself to her mission. And her mission is not to make children, but to straighten those of others" (24; see fig. 4.13).

Through the remainder of the novella, as La Pedani makes her way to ever greater heights in her deepening knowledge of the texts of Baumann and Schreber,[15] ending with her acclaimed speech on the role of gymnastics in Italian schools at a major gymnastics congress held at the Palazzo Carignano, Celzani, in an effort to get the attention of his goddess, joins not only a gym but begins to subscribe to and read all the most important journals of the European gymnastics movement. He becomes an ardent, theoretical supporter of the apparatus and doggedly pursues Pedani with his new knowledge, hoping thereby to become her humble and bowed down servant in the project of straightening Italian bodies: "Don Celzani read everything in order to prepare certain questions and certain answers, and in that way he was able to keep up with the conversation. He had finally found the hook" (75). Needless to say, by the end of the novella, La Pedani accedes to this desire; she is in essence "hooked." Having come to bid her farewell in his last gesture of complete self-sacrifice, Celzani "had not yet finished saying it, when he felt a strong hand upon his neck and two fiery lips upon his mouth, and in the delirious joy that invaded him in that dark paradise wherein he felt himself raised as if by a whirlwind, he could get nothing out except a strangled cry: 'Oh! . . . Great God!'" (117)—which is, by the way, not a lot more than he has been able to put out for most of the rest of the tale.

Italo Calvino has proposed that the title of the book be not "Love and Gymnastics" but "Eros and Ideology," both because the story addresses the conflict between idealist surges of the civilizing mission and the morbid tangles of secret personal passions and because, throughout the narrative, gymnastics is much discussed but never actually seen or practiced before the reader (Calvino 1996, viii). Stylistically, this latter point is already supported by De Amicis's use of free indirect discourse. Calvino hits on the very nerve of the text, for gymnastics is here an entirely theoretical affair, one that seems to exist only by virtue of its contact with words. It is in this sense truly an ideological

Figure 4.12 The beauty of equilibrium. (From Maria Montessori, *Antropologia pedagogica*, 1910.)

Figure 4.13 Straightening Italian bodies. (From Maria Montessori, *Antropologia pedagogica*, 1910.)

state apparatus. Calvino also goes on to remark that real living and experience happen solely on the side of Eros. And this Eros is essentially "perverse." Celzani is a voyeur, a masturbator, a fetishist, and a masochist. La Pedani is a lesbian and a narcissist: "She walked in strides that were too long, she let slip the intonations of a masculine voice that made people turn around surprised. . . . If someone had heard her without seeing her, he would have thought her a husband and not a friend" (De Amicis 1996, 17, 25). Gymnastics is only ever experienced through the sexual fantasies of Celzani's uncle. As La Pedani tells him about the successes of the Baumannian method, Uncle Celzani, who in any case "was almost always enraptured by the delights of a fantasy world" (47), sits and imagines with closed eyes those "raised legs," "flushed cheeks," "rounded arms," all those *"donnine fatte"* by the miracles of gymnastic training (79–80). The entire text exudes a perverse sexuality that creates a phantasmatic community founded in a feminine energy generated by a "harem without sultan, by a warrior-like phalange of women that moves to the assault and spreads from classrooms and gymnasia" to conquer and entrap men for their cause (Calvino 1996, xi).[16]

We must be cautious with such a reading of the text, however, as it is predicated on an *opposition* between a transgressive because "perverse" Eros on the one hand and, on the other, an ideological state apparatus that has as its goal the production and disciplining of the body. For what does it mean to say that "real life" resides with perverse Eros? Does Eros in fact guarantee, by virtue of its perverse existence, that it is neither occupied by nor supportive of the ideological project? Furthermore, and leaving aside the possible Orientalist fantasies in play here, does a harem without sultan guarantee, through its gender inversions, a space of freedom from the colonizing incursions of the modern state? Is it not possible that in the absence of a master—but then is he really absent?—the subject subjects himself—in love—to an apparatus that binds and unbinds, that subjects and frees, because this apparatus "takes its own failure into account in advance"? (Žižek 1989, 126). Conversely, however, if the perverse, real-life desires of the novella's protagonists are somehow implicated in the success of the ideological apparatuses, does this allow for a reading of the story as one that converts a sexual threat into the reassuring final subordination of woman to the institution of marriage?[17]

De Amicis's writings require a new reading in order to move them away from the monolithic hegemony exacted upon them by his bestseller *Cuore* as the emblem of the petit-bourgeois adaptation to the stuffy, narrow, and insipid Italy of Umberto I. Beyond, if not below, *Cuore,* De Amicis's extensive corpus of fiction, travelogue, and journalism is unfortunately unknown to English readers. But some Italian critics, among them first and foremost Italo Calvino, have called for an engagement with the "other" De Amicis. In the words of the critic Biagio Prezioso, "A narrative that has been unproblematically catalogued as an expression of the ideals of Umbertian Italy . . . has revealed an unsuspected openness toward taking on different cues, of frequently following more than one direction at the same time, including those directions that lead to the rejection and overturning of those values celebrated in *Cuore,* or to the entry into the territories of an Eros which does not reject its piquant elements, such as . . . voyeurism and fetishism" (1995, 7). Like *Amore e ginnastica,* many of De Amicis's stories track down a perverse Eros with often contradictory or unsuspected results. For instance, in his 1899 *Nel giardino della follia* (In the Garden of Madness), De Amicis deconstructs the opposition between reason and madness by having one of the inhabitants of an insane asylum refer to the psychic apparatus as a fundamentally fragile machine, as a "mechanism of nothing [*un meccanismo da nulla*]": "Just cut out that proud self-assuredness of yours, you who believe yourselves to be crossing a bridge of granite but instead are walking a tightrope and teetering at each step, keeping yourself up only through caution and effort, by not risking to look down into that abyss hovering below: be careful, be careful, for the mind is a 'mechanism of nothing'" (De Amicis 1990, 66–68).

In a similar manner, in a story significantly entitled *Cinematografo celebrale,* the "Cavaliere" of the tale, in order to kill a few hours, decides to simply think thoughts, but in the process finds himself in his imagination—not unlike Celzani's uncle—replaying forgotten memories, with the result that in his fantasy he turns himself into an adulterer, a thief, and even a murderer. The cerebral cinematographer, similar to Tausk's psychotic patients, evokes and calls into being another self, one who is out of control and who thus seems to move of his own accord: "Thus, he had not chosen. Thus, he was not thinking of those things of which he wanted to think. Instead he was thinking those things he was forced to think of. What then was spontaneity, what was freedom of thought? What was will? And what was he if not a thinking machine that moved according to its own mechanisms and to which he was nothing but a spectator? And while he reflected upon this, within his mind that was getting more and more confused, he distinctly heard the name: 'Alcibiades!' Marveling, he repeated: 'Alcibiades!'" (De Amicis 1995, 32–33). These cinematographic adventures come, of course, to a close, but they leave the Cavaliere with their memories, and these memories too are hard to manage: "But he never again fell into that sin of meditation; yet it remained in his memory as an orgy of the spirit, fortunately unique, and of which he was a little ashamed" (46).

I propose to read *Amore e ginnastica* as an allegory of the mechanism of ideology per se, a mechanism that De Amicis does not reduce either to a simple understanding of power as repression, nor to ideology's inability to account for those factors and desires that apparently escape its field of operation. It is here that we encounter most clearly the twofold nature of the Italian theory of gymnastics, because, on the one hand, as theory, what De Amicis's text describes is Žižek's point that ideological fantasy, far from functioning as an alienation from reality, serves precisely as a support for reality. On the other hand, De Amicis is also acutely aware of and participates in what Michel Foucault calls the "sensualization of power" and "gain of pleasure" through "perpetual spirals of power and pleasure" (1978, 44–45). It is the deployment of sexuality, rather than its repression, that founds the exercise of power through what Foucault again calls the implantation of perversion: "Power . . . thus took charge of bodies, caressing them with its eyes, intensifying areas, electrifying surfaces, dramatizing troubled moments. . . . Power operated as a mechanism of attraction; it drew out those peculiarities over which it kept watch. Pleasure spread to the power that harried it; power anchored the pleasure it uncovered. . . . Modern society is perverse, not in spite of its Puritanism or as if from a backlash provoked by its hypocrisy; it is in actual fact, and directly, perverse" (44–46).

In the novella, De Amicis overturns, as Pino Boero has noted, his own sentimental socialism into an ironic repertory of private vices and public virtues in order to unmask the arbitrariness and deformations of all textual operations, including the tendency to convert the readers of such texts to "proper feelings" (1984, 35–36). Indeed, De Amicis narrates in the novella nothing less than the story of the subject; how he is called into being through submission and mastery and through what Žižek calls a short-circuit between external machine and internal belief. Celzani falls both into love and into ideology, and it is the intimate connection and interdependence between these two falls, the gravity that they imply, that De Amicis interrogates in the text. What De Amicis shows is that ideological interpellation both presupposes and produces perversion (political, sexual, and gender perversion, as well as the perversions produced by the operations of language); ideology requires and yet suppresses the body, and in that act creates—as I will show—a body of meaning. De Amicis directly and explicitly takes on three critical issues: the foundations of gymnastic fantasies in gymnastics as *theory;* the question of the obligatory or *compulsory* nature of Italian national gymnastics; and the dangers produced by a *women's* gymnastics, the possibility, that is, that gymnastics, especially in its female versions, is always in danger of turning into spectacle.

In 1891, the same year he wrote *Amore e ginnastica,* De Amicis gave a lecture to a largely female audience in the vacation resort of Campiglio Cervo entitled "Ladies, Be Not Alarmed" (*Non si sgomentino le signore*).[18] The alarm in question may have been caused not just by the topic at hand (the attractions and failures of the national gymnastics movement), but perhaps more importantly by the fact that the spectacle provided by female bodies seemed inevitably to produce a kind of mischievously (*malizioso*) voyeuristic tone in both speaker and audience alike. The question of a female gymnastics had, De Amicis asserts, given rise to "innumerable discussions about feminine dignity and modesty, as well as to certain inconveniences and dangers of a very delicate nature. These discussions have for a while now delighted a curious and mischievous public and frightened many mothers" (1984, 16–17). And despite De Amicis's claim that he himself was speaking without "a shadow of malice [*malizia*]" (15), the tone of the lecture is the same as that of *Amore e ginnastica.* Both texts communicate an ironic insistence that alarm is always already deeply implicated in some interest or fascinated engagement with a topic: "Ladies, be not alarmed," so De Amicis opens the lecture, "for the topic can, indeed must be, of interest to you too" (7).

As the school year has finally drawn to a close, De Amicis continues, everyone has been talking about the excesses of intellectual strain imposed on Italian schoolchildren. But this is not a concern just in Italy. All over Europe there have been uncountable conferences, commissions, and books dedicated to proving that immoderate studies coupled with excessive physical immobility have led to the ruination of children's health, thus predisposing them to physical and mental illnesses. In Italy, most boys are unfit for military service, and almost half of the nation's girls are anemic, nervous, hysterical, and have bad eyesight. And what has been done to counteract these negative effects of education? The government has introduced "educational gymnastics." De Amicis goes on to narrate the history of this reform, a history that "is quite interesting and does not lack in its comical aspects" (8–9). The coordinates of this history are already familiar. They begin with De Sanctis's 1878 law and encompass the debates between Obermann and Baumann, as well as the critique of overtheorization already encountered with Mosso. Thus De Amicis can say that Italian gymnastics "still suffers too much from methodism [*metododismo*]; its theory is too minute and verbose; children are not allowed sufficient physical liberty. . . . They are bored" (18). Physical education has, in other words, simply turned into another school subject.

But De Amicis has his own take on this history. Italian gymnastics suffered, in his opinion, from a fundamental transgressive excess, one that he variously named enthusiasm or exaggeration.[19] Indeed, the lecture itself is punctuated by a kind of escalation of this enthusiasm that has its own seductive rhetorical effects on his audience. And so he explains that an ultimately indefinable enthusiasm has had the effect of an almost *spontaneous combustion:* "A large number of gymnasia arose almost as if by magic. Courses were created from which emerged some excellent teachers. From everywhere technical journals were born; in every city passionate propagandists popped up; a legion of doctors dedicated itself to the study of the relationship between gymnastics and science; the German, English, and Swedish methods were widely studied; a vast literature flourished in the field. It is hard to describe the philo-gymnastic enthusiasm that caught fire for some years. . . . Gymnastics became, according to public opinion, the secure means by which to regenerate the world" (9).

De Amicis detects three separate but interrelated dangers of "enthusiasm." Enthusiasm may lead to the perversion of language, the perversion of compulsion, and the perversion of sex. I have already discussed the perversion of language in Mosso's critique of the Italian gymnastics movement.[20] *Theorists* of gymnastics "pushed exaggeration to such a point that in their writings and conferences . . . they appealed to philosophy, ethnology, anthropology. They ran through the history of all times and places and spoke in a language that was so abstruse and pretentiously scientific that they led you to wonder whether they were speaking only of the simple and material act of strengthening bodies and not of some mysterious argument pertaining to metaphysics or higher sociology" (10–11). Such theoretical enthusiasm had eventually to produce its own undoing. In its very incomprehensibility, it had to produce among children a yawn, while in adults like De Amicis's Celzani, it produced a kind of fake substitute: a mere textual engagement with gymnastics seemed to have taken the place of the materiality of the body.

The second problem with Italian gymnastics was its obligatory, its compulsory nature. General enthusiasm for the benefits of bodily exercise had given free reign to those who advocated a compulsory gymnastics for all citizens, independent of sex and age. There were even those fanatics, De Amicis remarks, that envisioned the erection of gymnastic apparatuses in the public squares and intersections of all Italian cities, and they envisioned "the whole population jumping and climbing at specified hours to the command of thousands of gymnastics teachers who would constitute the new aristocracy of the state" (11). Such visionary ardor is compulsory and therefore compulsive and does away with "sentiments of charity and kindness" (13), because it disregards the concrete reality of the reform's recipients.[21] In the wake of compulsory physical education in all schools, public and private, and including as well the religious ones, anyone could become the victim of gymnastic enthusiasm. Nuns, even cloistered nuns; priests; all teachers, male and female and of any age; in fact, anyone who wanted to keep his or her teaching license, had to undergo gymnastic training and the consequent government inspections. "You cannot imagine. . . . One could write a most original book on the topic" (12).[22] As the cloistered nuns lifted their habits to prove to government inspectors that they had learned the proper movements, they were convinced that gymnastics was an immorality and the work of the devil: "it was a spectacle that was more sad than comic" (12). Meanwhile, those "martyrs to gymnastics" less worried about the afterlife, must have thought that the authorities had lost their minds. The older teaching corps could not understand this "forced alliance between the alphabet and acrobatics, between school and circus" (13). And then, of course, there were those "specialists" who had much to lose from the aristocratization of the gymnastics teachers: fencing, music, art, and dance teachers who detected bodies no longer willing or able to perform their tasks; builders of orthopedic apparatuses, pharmacists and surgeons, displaced by the diagnostic efforts of gymnastic enthusiasm, all moved to the attack and accused the gymnastics movement of acrobatism, charlatanism, and pseudoscience (9–10).

The gymnastics movement reached its peak of enthusiasm, however, when it came to the topic of female gymnastics. De Amicis wholeheartedly supports physical exercise for girls and women, and he concedes that, as a result of Baumann's methods, feminine health had improved. It is not legitimate, therefore, to simply understand De Amicis's position as one that reads a newly created horde of Pedanis as a threat to men. For De Amicis the threat lies elsewhere: Pedani does not so much *invade* the social sphere; more importantly, she is *exposed* to it by the perverse, because compulsive, passions unleashed by bodies that have become the objects of an inspecting gaze. "To be fair," De Amicis writes,

> the sympathy for female gymnastics also derived in part from the originality and seductive loveliness of the spectacles that it offered. . . . All those beautiful arms and those little hands in the air, those thick braids bouncing on pink necks and slim torsos, those three hundred arched and subtle feet, and the indefinable grace of those movements—between dance and leaping—and those long dresses that gave them the semblance of a coy corps de ballet—yes, this is a truly new and pleasant thing. And how many government Authorities, both communal and scholastic, how many white-haired and grave men took a liking to it. Many liked it so much that they didn't miss even one of these shows—which consequently became more frequent than necessary. (13–14)

In other words, enthusiasm lay with the wrong people. Baumann certainly had a right to national gratitude to the extent that the ideas and passions that he had generated had much contributed to the love of and necessity for gymnastics well beyond their immediate pedagogical application (17).[23] Nevertheless, Baumann's enthusiasm and personal charisma, which he planned to convert into building an Italian nation of heroes (16), had in fact translated into a lack of fun for children and a perversely pleasurable spectacle for those men who occupied positions of power.

On a first encounter, then, the body as spectacle appears inherently dangerous because it generates a lack of enthusiasm for those who are its objects and too much (passionate) enthusiasm for those who are its privileged spectators. Anita Gramigna has remarked that the proliferation of economic and juridical opportunities for the exercise of human freedom was, in post-Unification Italy, accompanied "by a quasi-mystical and essentially conservative pan-pedagogism, designed to control and dampen any libertarian awakening of personality" (1996, 244). In other words, the pedagogical project shut down human passions. And yet De Amicis's understanding of the economy of passions may be more complicated than the simple recognition that pedagogical requirements dampen impulses that come from below. Alberto Brambilla has pointed out that De Amicis, through the figure of Celzani, pokes fun at the militarization of Italian gymnastics by counterposing "the efforts of Mars to the pleasures of Venus" (1992, 115). Though on the surface this may be the case, it does not account for the gender reversal at play in *Amore e ginnastica,* for the fact, that is, that pleasure seems to lie with the Martial powerlessness of Celzani and effort all with the powerful Venus Pedani. It would seem, in fact, that De Amicis's conception of ideology and of the latter's "quasi-mystical" operations is intimately tied to a masochistic ordering of Eros and gender relations.

De Amicis, I contend, rewrites ideology as masochism; the question is, how is this achieved? Pino Boero, an extremely astute reader of De Amicis, may furnish a first answer. According to Boero, "The writer structures a great deal of his literary products by grafting discourses on to discourses that surround a current social issue, from school to gymnastics to socialism. The narrative outcomes are unquestionably so successful because they are entrusted to what Calvino, speaking of Celzani, defines as the 'perverse potentialities' of Eros" (1984, 36). In the process of translating "serious issues" into a narrative fictional structure, in other words, De Amicis delegates this process to the perversions of Eros and to the body. The body thereby becomes, Boero holds, the rhetorical machine that produces enunciations with persuasive ends (37). For De Amicis, then, narrativization, or the creation of the body of a text, depends on the textualization of the body, on the latter's capacity to create meaning.

The advantage of Boero's analysis is that he implicitly refuses Calvino's opposition between "real life" and ideology because in his own reading Eros exists by virtue of its capacity to generate meaning, to translate, as he puts it, serious arguments into fictional terms. However, he therefore concludes that the actual protagonist of *Amore e ginnastica* is not gymnastics but the erotic and eroticized body. And yet, I would hold, it is this very "seriousness" of gymnastics that cannot be lost, for it is precisely the gravity at stake in these social issues that engenders gymnastics' erotic effects. Gymnastics exists by virtue of the enthusiasm it creates; it produces and is produced by a passion that, by its obligatory nature, turns passion into a compulsion. It is for this reason that gymnastics qua ideology is for De Amicis essentially masochistic.

Ideology and masochism bear some striking resemblances but also some important differences. Both provide answers to the question as to why power is obeyed. And both, to the extent that they are implicated in relations of power, negotiate the relationship between internal and external determinations of that power. Both are concerned with the stakes involved in the subject's simultaneous mastery and submission and therefore of necessity engage the problem of the subject's pleasures and pains. The differences pertain, first, to the obvious inversion of the economy of pain and pleasure: while the subject of ideology submits to power in order to avoid pain, the subject of masochism submits to power in order to gain it. The end result for both, however, and quite paradoxically for the masochist, is pleasure. While the subject of ideology submits to power in response to an external compulsion (the ideological state apparatuses), the masochist submits due to an internal compulsion, that is, in response to a "perverse" drive. Whereas the ideological relation is unconscious and predicated on a fundamental misrecognition, the masochist freely chooses his submission and this paradoxically despite his internal compulsion to obey an external power. For this reason, one may say that the masochistic relationship is both contractual in the liberal sense of the term and a staging of the ideological structuring of relations of power. Masochism is, then, the consensual *representation* of relations of force and not, like ideology, the *conversion* of force into consent.

Given this quality of masochism as staging and representation, we may now make sense of De Amicis's textualization or narrativization of the body. Masochism is fundamentally a textual or discursive operation that has the erotic body as a body permeated by relations of power as its main protagonist. It is important to stress that such eroticization depends on narrativization; Eros does not exist before the body is inserted into discourse. Masochism, according to Gaylyn Studlar, "tells its story through very precisely delimited means: fantasy, disavowal, fetishism, and suspense are its formal and psychoanalytic foundations" (1980, 18). In masochism, narrative suspense is not only displaced from the dramatic to the aesthetic (120), it is also *literalized* by virtue of its stagings in the form of the body's attachment to rings, bars, chains, and strings. In masochism, the body is *inserted* into discourse by the pleasurable pain of an apparatus. In this sense, I think one can argue, the masochistic body belongs in Marey's universe of *expression graphique,* in other words, a self-narrativized but also literalized submission to power. To these aspects of the masochist phenomenon belong its critical capacities, to the extent that masochism lays bare the erotic stakes involved in all ideological structurings of power, the outcome of which is the eroticized subject. Such stakes are especially apparent in a passage from De Amicis's "red" novel *Primo maggio,* the entirety of which is worth reproducing here because it could come straight from any novel written by the inventor of masochism, Leopold von Sacher-Masoch. As in Sacher-Masoch's works, all political bonds are here an entirely gendered and erotic *affair:*

[Signora Luzzi] found [in socialism] nothing but a superficial and bizarre effervescence of whims and revolutionary sympathies, a kind of red eroticism of the little lady who rebels against all laws and that filled her with amazement. At the bottom of socialism and below any subversive theory of the world, it seemed that for her lay a secret ideal of sensuality. It seemed that the objects of her passion were not ideas but people, and amongst the latter only lovers. Oddly enough, she appeared to have read many books on the subject, but had absorbed only that material that, in one way or another, referred to relations between the sexes. And here she possessed singular erudition. The tempestuous passion of Ferdinand Lassalle for Miss De Doenniger, the marriage in extremis between August Spees, condemned to death, and the wealthy Mina Van Zandt, the tender feelings of the soon to be hung Sophia Perowskaia for the young, also to be hung Shelybov, the conquests of the beautiful Valerian Osinski who died on the scaffold—all those adventurous loves of nihilists and anarchists, loves born in intrigues and cemented through escapes, disconcerted by the police, interrupted by imprisonment, retied in exile, followed in every detail by the silent steps of spies and by the black phantasm of the executioner—she knew them all in every detail and she grazed her imagination on them with the avidity of a sick woman. . . . Her imagination was seduced by that ideal of a society where women enjoyed absolute freedom and where love, as she understood it, was released from all fetters and brakes. . . . She knew only of the most ardent and of the strangest ideas with regard to the most stimulating topics: the nude gymnastics of men and women in *City of the Sun,* Saint-Simon's rehabilitation of the flesh, the beautiful women of Morris's utopian society, who on the banks of the Thames offered themselves to all men as a social bonus, and other similar things. (cited in Boero 1984, 37)

Giovanni Ricci has pointed out that De Amicis's famous "didactics of tears," that is, the author's penchant for producing sentimental reactions in his readers in order to convert them to the cause of Italian citizen formation, should not be interpreted as a literature of "effeminacy" (1984, 73). He is certainly right, both insofar as the main targets of De Amicis's literary output were boys and men, the projected supporters of a future manly Italy, and because masochism may not be simply understood as a pathological "exaggeration" of feminine traits. And yet De Amicis's socialist and socially sensitive new man was to have all the features of the bourgeois housewife: he was to be nurturing, caring, and attentive to the needs of the fatherland.[24] Gender reversal is pushed even further in Celzani's fantasy of what it would be like to be the husband of the famous Pedani—she who is *"fredda di cor vulneratrice"* (De Amicis 1996, 88):

her growing celebrity became a new hook for his love, a new biting and exquisite stimulus for his desires. He felt a more refined voluptuousness in imagining himself the sure owner of a known and admired woman. He thought he would be twice as happy in his own obscurity, to have her when she returned from a much applauded conference, to take possession of those bodily forms that others only caressed with their eyes and desired. In fact it seemed to him that his happiness would be all the more sweet and profound to the extent that he remained small and nothing next to her; nothing but a husband and frequently forgotten about during the day, kept like a servant, an instrument, an amusement, a domestic beast. Ah! Great God! And the following inflamed his heart even more: because he possessed the thick skull of a meditative man and did not entirely lack a certain priestly finesse, he had been able to fathom the very depths of her nature and had understood that, once she had taken the step, she would be a woman to remain absolutely faithful to him, if for no other reason than because of her sense of dignity and her force of reason—even if she would keep him under her in all other things. (57–58)

It is unclear from this fantasy the extent to which Pedani, once married to Celzani, would bow, as Daria Valentini claims, to the laws of marriage, except perhaps as dictated by her masculine traits of dignity and reason. The denouement of the story does not immediately promise that Pedani will relinquish her masculine traits. Nevertheless, this passage does raise two other aspects of masochism that belie its transgressive or critical qualities. The first pertains to the obvious gender reversal at play in the text; the second to what De Amicis calls Celzani's "hook," that is, the protagonist's mode of attachment to his desires and the means by which these desires are organized. The two issues are in fact not separate ones, bound as they are by a vision of power that is certainly modern but that hinges on the impossibility of "being a liberal," as De Sanctis would say.

Masochism functions at two levels. *Historically,* it responds to a situation where it is no longer possible to be a liberal, and it expresses this historical crisis through a language that belongs to the relations between men and women. The crisis of liberalism is thus articulated fundamentally as a crisis of masculinity, and masochism *stages* the dual nature of this crisis: as man's painfully pleasurable submission to a feminine Law—in the wake of the supposed collapse of the Law of the Father—and in the form of a renewed passionate attachment to the Law (Deleuze 1991). In this sense, and as I have argued elsewhere, marginalization and submission become a new form of dominance (Stewart 1998). The masochistic gaze, its conscious and freely chosen staging of man's pleasurable investment in power, becomes the vehicle by which power is both exercised and submitted to. The masochist, in this scenario, always remains the stage director of his own powerlessness. Studlar has pointed to the essential affinity between masochism and cinematic practices, whereby masochism not only bears a fundamental cinematic, voyeuristic aspect, but where in turn cinema always contains a certain masochistic element. In our own texts, this point is supported by not only the intimate connection between gymnastics and spectacle, but also—as in the case of Baumann—between gymnastics and cinematics.

Theoretically, masochism responds to and complements the "problem" of ideology: the problem, in other words, of ideology's creation of the subject via both mastery and submission. Masochism seeks to provide an answer to the question of how, in Louis Althusser's theory of ideology, the subject can at the moment of his or her constitution be "stripped of all freedom except that of freely accepting his submission" (Althusser 1994). Masochism addresses this short-circuit of ideology as it founders on the conflict between internal belief and the externality of the machine of the law. In masochism, we encounter, in the form of a reversal of gender relations, another reversal whereby belief is externalized and the machine of the law becomes an internal mechanism. Or, as Žižek puts it, an "'external' ritual performatively generates its own ideological foundations" (1994a, 13). Ideology—masochistically—takes the form of the fetishistic disavowal: I know, but nevertheless . . .

De Amicis formulates this dual historical and theoretical crisis of ideology in terms of Celzani's "hook," which itself functions metaphorically for the masochistic suspension in the apparatus. Celzani in fact comes to be hooked at two critical moments of the text. The first moment pertains to Celzani's fantasy of becoming the submissive husband to the famous and domineering Pedani: "her growing celebrity became a new hook [*esca*] for his love, a new biting and exquisite stimulus for his desires" (De Amicis 1996, 57). The second instance belongs both to Celzani's insertion into the project of national bodily reform and *therefore* to his own seduction of Pedani: "Don Celzani read everything in order to prepare certain questions and certain answers, and in that way he was able to keep up with the conversation. He had finally found the hook [*gancio*]" (75).

What then is the meaning of this hook? Why does Celzani in his trajectory of becoming a subject need it? In its doubled nature, as both bait and point of attachment, it binds Celzani to both desire and a certain knowledge, one acquired through the reading of texts.[25] The hook is most fundamentally Celzani's eroticized attachment to the possibility of providing questions and answers. In this sense, De Amicis creates in the figure of Celzani a Kafkan subject: Kafka develops, so Žižek tells us, "a kind of criticism of Althusser *avant la lettre,* in letting us see that which is constitutive of the gap between 'machine' and its 'internalization.' Is not Kafka's 'irrational' bureaucracy, this blind, gigantic, nonsensical apparatus, precisely the Ideological State Apparatus with which a subject is confronted *before* any identification, any recognition—any *subjectivation*—takes place?" (1989, 44) The point is that the Kafkan subject, who is also the DeAmician subject, succumbs to interpellation prior to subjectivation; it is a subject that "does not offer us a Cause with which to identify" (Žižek 1989, 44). Celzani becomes a subject at the moment that he finds his Cause (the gymnastics movement) in the form of a hook that attaches him to the ideological system. But the hook is precisely doubled because it depends on the perverse existence of the supplement: Celzani's excessive, erotic submission to Pedani (see fig. 4.14). Celzani's excessive enjoyment "is not a surplus, which simply *attaches* itself to some 'normal,' fundamental enjoyment, because *enjoyment as such emerges only in this surplus,* because it is constitutively an 'excess'" (Žižek 1989, 52; first emphasis my own). Masochism marks this excess of ideology; it designates that moment of the "beyond of ideology" that makes the ideological apparatus functional. It marks that point, as Marey would have it, at which that excess comes to be made visible but that also encounters a theoretical and mechanical bedrock that leaves unresolved the demands of visibility and the pleasures such visibility may produce. In the moment of its overtheorization, this is what the debate in the Italian gymnastics movement makes literal; at the very place where the body is attached to the apparatus, De Amicis teaches us, a surplus pleasure is produced that makes such an attachment possible and yet excessive.

One final question needs to be addressed, and it pertains to Celzani's marriage, to the question, in other words, of why Pedani gives in to his desires. In the final analysis, this is a question about a double submission: that of woman to the system of heteronormativity, and that of universally posited juridical structures to disciplinary power or what Foucault calls biopower. Foucault himself refers to the universalist claims of juridical structures as "the deployment of alliance"—by which he means marriage structures for the stable social organization of the sexes and of reproduction—and he claims that "historically it was around and on the basis of the deployment of alliance that the deployment of sexuality was constructed" (1978, 107). Nevertheless, Foucault also notes the gradual displacement or colonization of juridical structures in favor of what he calls an "interstatist" institutional organization of power that ultimately favors the dominance of disciplinar-

Figure 4.14 Don Celzani gets his hook (*Self-Suspension,* from Lewis A. Sayre, *Spinal Disease and Spinal Curvature: Their Treatment by Suspension and the Use of the Plaster Paris Bandage,* 1877. Courtesy of Brown University.)

ity (2000c). Can these two submissions be thought together? Is there a way in which Pedani's ceding on her desires may not in fact be read as itself an allegory for the ceding of a universalist discourse to disciplinary knowledges, to the extent that such a concession rescinds on the possibility of a universal, abstract subject that is empty or devoid of all empirical determination? If this is the case, then the "embodiment" of power and the disciplinary knowledges that accompany and constitute them must claim woman as its first and foremost victim. The problem of such a "feminine embodiment" of disciplinary power constitutes the subject of the next chapter.

An Unwritable Law of Maternal Love: The Infanticide Debate

In the years that spanned the creation of the Italian nation-state in 1861 and the collapse of the liberal government after 1922, Italian legal theorists and cultural critics produced an inordinate number of texts dedicated to the problem of infanticide. Not only that, even those critics who may not have dedicated entire volumes to infanticide nevertheless found the issue to be emblematic of political, social, and cultural problems more generally. This fact is surprising for several reasons. First, while discourses treating the infanticidal mother reached high levels of urgency and expressed a sense of profound crisis in the institution of motherhood, they did not appear to be responding to a sudden epidemic rise in actual infanticides. On the contrary, quite the opposite trend seems to have been the case (Di Bello and Meringolo 1997, 110). Second, Italian theorists were largely unconcerned with the deaths of infants, generally agreeing, in fact, that these products of nonnormative sexual relations were best off dead. The well-being of infants would become a political and social issue only as a consequence of the pronatalist policies of the fascist regime. Third, and this is certainly the most surprising characteristic of these texts, many of their theorists—and this would prove the distinctive trait of the Italian debate—appeared to be *celebrating* the woman who kills her newborn but illegitimately conceived infant as a national hero or as a martyr to the new nation. The infanticidal mother had all the features of a *mater dolorosa,* of a suffering mother who took upon herself the negative effects produced by the ills of modernization and the imperfections of national integration. Analogous to the figure of the suffering mother, the discourse of infanticide seemed to itself carry multiple symbolic charges in the making of Italian modernity.

The discursive, indeed literary, aspects of social and political theories by no means belie the social reality of the problems they engage. In this chapter I trace the history of the discourse of the infanticidal mother to determine its impact on more general notions of Italian motherhood in the years between Unification and fascism. Such a discourse was produced by the self-described melancholy sons of the recently born Italian state, who saw themselves as the writers—however paradoxically—of an unwritable law of maternal love. Infanticide came to be figured during this period as the female crime par excellence and as an immensely productive model for establishing connections between subjectivity, legal responsibility, and sexuality. The power of these connections proved instrumental both in removing the discourse of infanticide from earlier theories that rendered it a crime against nature and in proving that *all* maternity, when left to its own devices, tended to exhibit dangerous antisocial behavior that therefore required expert intervention.

I want to emphasize the *discursive,* if not outright literary, qualities of these theories for two reasons. On the one hand, through their articulation of maternity as a social fact, they highlighted the social construction of subjectivity *against* laws of nature. On the other hand, they pointed not simply to a discussion about legal reform—though such a discussion did have important effects in the domain of law—but, and perhaps more crucially, to the possibility of something "beyond the law" that could be confronted only at a discursive, indeed literary, level. Ultimately, it is this discursive construction of the infanticidal mother that would make possible an engagement with Catholic culture, the decriminalization of failed maternity, and the construction of the Italian welfare mother. Such a construction would terminate, during the first decades of the twentieth century, in a notion of maternity as one dedicated to the propagation of the national body, and one that thereby rescinded on the idea of the dignity and honor of the individual subject.

By the end of the nineteenth century, most modern industrialized nations had largely reformed their laws regarding infanticide and depenalized it to such an extent that infanticidal women more often than not "walked" out of the courtroom. Given that infanticide had prior to these reforms been considered one of the most heinous crimes against nature, such a reversal requires explanation. The new understanding of infanticide depended on a broader set of interrelated shifts by which control was exerted on deviant behavior. First and foremost, in the wake of the great legal reforms at the end of the eighteenth and the beginning of the nineteenth centuries, legal theorists, criminal sociologists, and anthropologists shifted their attention away from an analysis of crime to that of the criminal. While Cesare Beccaria had sought to devise a systematization of criminal acts and the appropriately measured punishment for their repression, in Italy both the so-called Classical School of legal theory and the positivist criminal anthropologists made the criminal agent their basic unit of analysis. Rather than formulate an abstract notion of criminal acts, these new theorists sought to *embody* these acts in the life histories of concrete individuals. It was the potentialities that lay within the individual, his or her motivations and sociobiological determinations that became important in the assessment of the criminal's impact on social life. The Italian theorists referred to this as "*temibilità*," which became the criterion by which to gauge the individual's dangerousness to society. The motives and potentialities of social subjects came to be written into the legal codes as "extenuating circumstances," or indeed "states of exception," allowing thereby not only for a shift from the abstract legal subject to one fully embedded in the specificities of biosocial life, but also requiring expert, extralegal evaluations of the individual criminal's lifestyle and history.[1] The investigation of crime was linked to the material necessity or facticity of the body and thus separated from the realm of law and free choice. Giorgio Agamben has related the legal state of exception to the construction of a *space of necessity,* whereby "de facto proceedings, which are themselves extra- or antijuridical, pass over into law, and juridical norms blur with mere fact. . . . A threshold of undecidability is produced at which *factum* and *ius* fade into each other" (2005, 29).

As a consequence, crime was no longer perceived as an act against nature but as one against society. For the theorists of post-Unification Italy, this shift was of particular importance, because it signified an assault on the Catholic formulation of crime as an act against nature and against God. This shift furthermore had the effect of undermining natural law, and the consequences for this were profound and far-reaching, as nature was now viewed as incapable of self-regulation. A natural given, as Agamben has put it, was transformed into a political task (1998, 148). Again, such a transformation—as exemplified by the infanticide debate—speaks in a direct manner to Roberto Esposito's argument that the biopolitical immunitary paradigm denaturalizes nature itself. For the theorists of infanticide, it was maternity—that hitherto most "natural" of loves—that pointed to an untamed force that could not be known with precision but that nevertheless operated at the very foundations of society. It raised the possibility that an anti-natural force or drive lodged within the condition of maternity itself, a drive whose outcome was anything but certain. Maternity appeared to contemporary observers as something too complex to be left to the chances of instinctual destiny. It required time to develop, and it required education in order to be transformed into a social sentiment. Thus, as Raffaele Perone-Capano would assert at the end of the century, the physiological datum of birth was never sufficient in itself; a second stage, that of an active social intervention, was also required. A biological mother had to be trained to become a cultural mother (1889, 37–38). As Joshua Cole has remarked in relation to contemporary French reactions to refused maternity—and these observations would also hold good for Italian theorists—"Identifying motherhood as the natural destination of all women could only increase the level of anxiety," because it revealed "a 'natural' state that could not take care of itself. And if 'nature' was not self-regulating, how useful was the concept as a foundation of social policy?" (2000, 210–11).

The definition of punishment underwent a dramatic transformation, one intimately connected to the requirements to regulate nature and respond to the greater or lesser dangerousness of the criminal. Italian positivism took the most radical position in this regard, because it in effect eliminated the very idea of punishment in favor of reform or elimination of the criminal (depending on whether the criminal's recuperation was deemed possible) and prophylactic measures aimed at those sectors of the population that research had targeted as likely to commit a crime. The infanticidal woman "walked" out of the courts and escaped punishment, but only to enter an extensive network of surveillance and disciplining in institutions created for that purpose. Michel Foucault has argued that it was this new mechanics of discipline that permitted the insertion of medical experts into courtrooms and that allowed for the penetration of the legal system "from below" without necessarily changing the system of legal adjudication (2000a, 187).

The notion of individual responsibility was radically undermined by the entry of the social and biological sciences into legal thought and practice. If the criminal acted in response to a network of determinations that had their origins in the extenuating circumstances of social and biological factors, then it became questionable the extent to which he or she could be held responsible for any acts against society. Indeed, the positivists eliminated free will altogether as both a philosophical and sociobiological category. Foucault speaks of a "general and diffuse causality" (1978, 65) and claims that, while legal responsibility was upheld in the criminal codes, the positivists successfully imposed their reconceptualization of responsibility in the civil codes. The articulation of the legal codes and the science of criminology were thus made possible by the idea of a calculability of risk factors and their inscription into civil codes through the concept of no-fault responsibility in cases of accidental injuries and harms. Responsibility was thus detached from the subject and reconfigured as the calculation of a predictable quantity of malfunctions within sociologically observable social laws (Foucault 2000a, 195–96). It was, as Esposito has remarked, the tear that opened itself within a more primitive immunitary paradigm that "determined the need for a different defensive apparatus of an artificial type dedicated to safeguarding a world that was now constitutively exposed to risk" (2004, 52).

A diffuse or capillary system of social causality is also what describes the working of sexuality in its polymorphous or perverse nonnormative forms. During the second half of the nineteenth century, Italian legal theorists, penal sociologists, and a wide array of cultural producers actively engaged in creating the specifically female criminal.[2] The gendering of crime became a primary means by which to lend crime a sexual component, a component that could then retroactively and by a form of associative logic also be applied to men. The association between crime and sexuality or drive would hence never be lost. The introduction of sexuality and gender as fundamental aspects of crime made two transitions possible. On the one hand, sexual or gendered infractions against the law could be understood as deviations from both heterosexual and conjugal *norms,* without this transition necessarily being made explicit at the level of the law. On the other hand, the specificity of a woman's crime, as it came to be figured in the debates leading up to the passing of Italy's first unified criminal code in 1889, raised the question of woman's equality before penal law, in other words, the question whether the new code should not reflect the already established gender inequality of the 1865 Civil Code. While the 1889 Codice Zanardelli reaffirmed woman's *de jure* equality as a criminal subject, the idea of a specifically female criminal permitted differential treatment at the moment of the law's application and administration. Women were generally perceived to be more corrigible, and thus the punishment advocated for them shorter and "sweeter." Though not formally removed from the legal domain, through the *cultural* construction of the female criminal, women became the bearers and supports of the instantiation not of a new legal system, but of a new regime of norms, and thereby they embodied the transition described by Foucault from legal rationality to disciplinary logic. In a recent essay on infanticide, Tony Ward has argued that the question of infanticide's lesser criminal nature ultimately reflected a tension between two modes of subjectivation. Thus, while juridical doctrine presupposed an autonomous subject who was rationally calculating and unswayed by passions beyond the subject's control, the discursively constituted subject of the disciplinary knowledges was the victim of influences, whether they came from without or within the subject. Ward's point is that such a contradiction was frequently resolved according to the gender of the defendant: "courts are more likely to accept portrayals of women offenders as 'sad' or 'mad' rather than 'bad,' and less inclined to treat them as rational, autonomous subjects" (2002, 269).

While the Italian debate shared many of its features with other national debates on how to address the problem of criminal maternity—a general trend toward the liberalization of infanticide laws and the eventual medicalization of the infanticidal mother—there are nevertheless a series of characteristics of this Italian history that are distinctive. These differences must be attributed to the hegemonic role of the Catholic Church in Italian culture. Most important of all, "the persistent and widespread preoccupation with the evidential weight of concealment by unmarried mothers, and with the social and legal implications of secrecy" that Mark Jackson considers the most consistent feature of all formulations of regulatory measures against infanticide across time and space (Jackson 2002, 5), played itself out quite differently in the Italian case. Unlike the situation in countries where concealment of an illegitimate pregnancy or birth was itself considered a crime, in Italy under Church law such secrecy was in fact mandated. An Italian Catholic woman who conceived out of wedlock was required both to conceal her pregnancy and, at the birth of her child, to deposit the infant at one of the turnstiles, or "wheels," of the many Church-run foundling institutions. A woman was therefore *required* to conceal her illegitimate child and rescind on her maternal duties. This would guarantee, in the Church's view, the honor of the woman and of her family, as well as the child's baptism in those cases where the woman would otherwise be tempted to have an abortion or commit infanticide. The wheels thus protected family honor and Christian souls and acted as a safety valve against criminal impulses. They also guaranteed the Church's sole control over reproduction and sexuality, a control founded in a series of key principles: "that all babies be baptized, and, along with this, that abortion and infanticide be stopped; that family honor be preserved; and that only couples duly married by the Church be permitted to raise children. Not only was the honor of women—and thus the social honor of their families—to be protected, but men were to be protected from the product of their own unlawful sexuality, shielded from responsibility for the children they sired out of wedlock" (Kertzer 1993, 78–79).

The attempt on the part of the new Italian state at seizing control over sexuality and reproduction necessarily had to take this situation into account. This meant that the state had to secularize the understanding and management of sexual relations. Both the relatively liberal penal code finally passed in 1889 and the earlier 1865 Civil Code were geared to wresting control from the Church over Italian bodies and souls, and particularly over those new citizens who had slipped through the net of economic and social success. And here late-nineteenth-century Italy witnessed important shifts in the perception and management of poverty, due in large part to the secular state's direct confrontation with the Catholic Church. While pre-Unification Italy had relied to a large extent on charity institutions run by the Church to absorb the needs of the poor, by century's end, poverty came to be viewed—and this was closely tied to the government's anticlerical politics—as a result of movements and shifts in the national economy. No longer an individual affliction, poverty was borne by social classes and had to be addressed by the state through programs of social administration and legislation.

What remains striking, nevertheless, in the state's confrontation with the Church was its willingness and need to fall back on norms of Catholic morality and to use them toward novel ends. Ironically, the new theorists of infanticide thus rearticulated traditional Catholic normativity for their own secularizing and modernizing purposes. The secularizing theorists of infanticide—themselves deeply grounded in Catholic culture—upheld womanly honor and, indeed, celebrated it. Even more dramatically, they claimed that *infanticide furnished the proof that a woman had honor,* thereby turning her into a modern version of the *mater dolorosa*. A religious figure of purity was thus translated into a figure of transgression—but one who, by virtue of that same transgres-

Figure 5.1 Domenico Induno, *Abandoned at the Wheel* (1865). (Private collection.)

sion, regained her purity (see fig. 5.1). Both the Classical School of legal theory and the positivist criminal anthropologists—and this despite their differing views on how to transpose this new subject into an object of effective social policy—supported this contention.

Such celebration had a series of consequences, not all of which could be effectively controlled. First, because legal discourses celebrated the honor of the infanticidal mother and promised her minor or no sentencing in the courts, she was lured out of hiding. The woman's anonymity was undermined, as her honor now found, in the very spectacularity of her crimes, unrelenting representation in the courts, in the newspapers, in novels, and in the growing number of treatises dedicated to infanticidal mothers. Of the texts analyzed here, Lino Ferriani's is exemplary of this process, because he not only converts infanticide trials into theatrical stagings wherein the failed mother plays the role of tragic heroine, but he also insists that this is the only proper and just representation of infanticide. Second, as a consequence, the infanticidal mother turned into a kind of cultural heroine, a true Italian who, as a victim of repressive social and religious practices, committed a crime even against her own flesh and blood in order to uphold the age-old Italian commitment to honor. In such a representation of the infanticidal mother, she was nothing less than an exemplary martyr to the new nation. Honor became coupled here, paradoxically, not to the buttressing of traditional sexual relations but to the passionate transgression of norms, in other words, to the critique of traditional sexual relations. Indeed, transgressive subjects, at least as embodied in the infanticidal mother, produced in the theorists a fascinated engagement, a kind of libidinal investment in transgression. Such an investment in subjects who placed themselves, in Cesare Lombroso's words, "beyond marriage and prejudices" took the form of a strange identification—across gender lines—between the infanticidal mother and what was fantasized as the ideal middle-class male. This identification was perceived largely as an aesthetic and aestheticizing operation, that is, as a conscious cultural construction of social subjects. Through this process, identification became the vehicle for distinguishing between so-called egoistic women and honorable women, whereby the latter took on decidedly virile traits, traits that were then interpreted as desirable, indeed, worthy of emulation. The honor attached to the infanticidal mother was viewed as one that parted with its "selfish" counterpart to become a social attribute to be shared by all good citizens. Such will be the import of Lombroso's contribution to the question of infanticide. For Lombroso, honor becomes the signifier of a social passion or, rather, a passion for the social that this critic perceives as constituting the very foundation of all societies.

The image of the infanticidal woman as modernizer of sexual relations and as martyr to the nation was on its own unsustainable, both as a cultural icon and in practice. First and foremost, of course, such an image provided a rather inadequate model for a new motherhood; in other words, it did not bind women to a commitment to raising children. And while the Church upheld a policy of forced separation between mother and illegitimate child, the new state was dedicated to constructing new institutions and practices for the proper organization of sexuality and reproduction. As a result, a new image or construction of the infanticidal mother was rather quickly imposed on the first, a construction in many ways in opposition to the heroic one. She became in this new version the very embodiment of the dangers of modernity, of those forces and passions that are unleashed when traditional structures lessen their grip on social subjects. The infanticidal mother's passion for honor was translated into an uncontrolled passion, into what Silvia Schafer has suggestively called a "dangerous unhappiness" (1997, 3). This construction of the infanticidal mother not only allowed but also required regulation and management, though not necessarily in the courts—the site of her heroic representation—but rather in the hospital under the scrutinizing gaze of the gynecologist. As passion became an illness, honor was subsumed into the mother's psychobiological destiny, and the stress now fell on the psychological makeup of the failed mother, that is, on the social fantasy of a murderous woman who was psychologically incapable of doing otherwise. Here, a woman was seen as prone to turning her aggressive instincts toward herself, to interiorize her conflicts. Female criminality was almost always a form of insanity, lived privately and controlled more effectively by its medicalization rather than its repression. More radically perhaps, and this would become the leading chord in a symphony of voices describing and analyzing female sexuality, it was woman's innate predisposition to instability that made her more available to "forced ideas," hypnotic deliria, and suggestive impressionability. The very facts of woman's menstruation, pregnancy, and birth made her, as the gynecologist Muzio Pazzi claimed, an easy, indeed inevitable, target of "puerperal mania," a condition that led straight to infanticide. All mothers, infanticidal or not, were now viewed as potentially dangerous to social relations, because maternity itself came to be seen as a possible deviation from normative behavior. Infanticide merely furnished the proof of this understanding of maternity. It signaled that maternity could not be left to its own devices. Thus, the figure of the infanticidal mother became one of many other figures (such as the prostitute or the wet nurse) that furnished the grounds for a disciplinary-administrative logic whose privileged subjects were all women. Nevertheless, these later formulations relied crucially on the earlier formulations of the infanticidal mother, to the extent that they depended on her removal from the repressive practices of the Catholic Church and from "outdated" conceptions of the rule of law. By the early twentieth century, the infanticidal mother had ceased to have the "protection" of her earlier anonymity; she had become thoroughly secularized and largely decriminalized. No longer a subject of repression and secrecy, she now became one of open regulation.

Though the first representation of the infanticidal mother predated the second, the heroic version was never entirely displaced by the medicalized one. Both images coexisted and both mutually supported and contradicted each other, as I will show in the work of Vincenzo Mellusi, the last great Italian theorist of infanticide, who wrote his most important texts on infanticide under fascism. Mellusi is perhaps the theorist of infanticide who most effectively translated the Catholic mysteries of motherhood, its sublime qualities, into its scientific management. Indeed, he transposed the Christian unwritable law of love into the extralegal *savoir* of the social sciences in his figure of the *"madre dolorante"* who was saved by her theorist in order to dedicate herself to the heroic reproduction of the Italian nation. Mellusi's infanticidal mother functioned in this sense as a true compromise formation of conflicting and contradictory forces, whereby she may be understood as a condensation of a series of social anxieties that were produced by the conflict between modernity and tradition, on the one hand, and on the other, between the liberalizing tendencies of the law and the regulatory requirements of disciplining the sexualized body.

Social Honor

In the years leading up to the passing of the Zanardelli Code, legal scholars were actively involved in debating the function and content of this code in Italian post-Unification society. This debate found itself split between the Classical School of legal theory, a school that saw its origins in the work of Cesare Beccaria, and the positivist school, founded by Cesare Lombroso. Of particular pertinence were the question of the relationship between juridical discourse and other knowledges, disciplines, and institutions and how these two different sets of discourses would organize and promote both the constitution of Italian subjects and the building of social unity. While, in the end, the legal debate was formally won by the Classical School, a victory reflected in the Zanardelli Code, positivist thought became not only a hegemonic cultural force but was also able to dictate social policy at state and regional levels well into the fascist era. The infanticide debate constituted here an important instance of a compromise between the two schools—on the one hand, the new articulation of infanticide in the criminal code and, on the other hand, a substantial invasion into the legal arena by nonlegal discourses through the construction of what Foucault has called "the dangerous individual" who is no longer subject to the concept of responsibility. Such a compromise allowed for considerable fluidity and elasticity in the definition of subjectivity, while it also generated what Silvia Schafer in a different context has called a "curious relationship between power and uncertainty" (1997, 4)—to wit, the porosity of the two domains and the ultimate difficulty on the part of legislators and social engineers to delimit their respective fields of operation.

The central mechanism by which this compromise took place was through an engagement with a woman's honor. The concept of female honor possessed the necessary elasticity to negotiate the relations and conflicts between the legal and extralegal domains. While classical penal doctrine made infanticide a primary object of analysis in order to bring about systematic legal reform, the newly founded positivist criminal anthropology focused on the agent of the crime in order to develop a full-blooded model of the infanticidal woman. However, one should not exaggerate the conflicts between the two schools, for both actively engaged in creating the figure of the infanticidal woman and her particular characteristics. In its reform of infanticide laws, Italy followed a trajectory not dissimilar to other European countries during the course of the nineteenth century.[3] Most legal theorists agreed that the older laws against infanticide were overly harsh and in conflict with the strictures imposed on poor, unmarried, and defenseless women who killed their offspring in order to hide their shame and save themselves and perhaps their children from destitution. And it was here that infanticide as a legal entity came up against extralegal considerations. As early as 1764, Cesare Beccaria had articulated this meeting of domains as an "inevitable contradiction": "Infanticide is . . . the effect of an inevitable contradiction, one in which a woman is placed when she has either submitted out of weakness or been overpowered by violence. Faced with a choice between disgrace and the death of a creature incapable of feeling pain, who would not prefer the latter to the unavoidable misery to which the woman and her unfortunate offspring would be exposed? The best way to prevent this crime would be to protect weakness with effective laws against tyranny, which exaggerates those vices that cannot be covered with the cloak of virtue" (1986, 60). Beccaria, aware of the existing conflict between social norms and the legal system, saw the only effective means of preventing infanticide in the fight against tyranny, that is, in legal reform. Similar to trends in the rest of Europe, the reform of infanticide laws depended on the idea of *"causa honoris,"* that is, the possibility that a woman committed infanticide in order to protect her honor. It depended, in other words, on the introduction of an "extenuating circumstance," on the existence, that is, of extralegal or "exceptional" considerations, while nevertheless upholding a liberal notion of law and state.

The *causa honoris* stipulation, and thus the tendency to distinguish the crime from other forms of homicide, had already existed in pre-Unification Italy's multiplicity of legal codes. In the post-Unification period, most legal scholars supported such a stipulation and thus the specification of infanticide as a crime *sui generis*. Infanticide was to become a crime of extenuating circumstances, and those same factors that had been earlier viewed as signs of its gravity (for example, the child's lack of registration in the local registers), now became arguments for its substantial decriminalization. The 1889 Criminal Code followed classical legal doctrine and hence the liberal approach advocated by Beccaria: the abolition of capital punishment, the redefinition of infanticide as attributable to the desire for honor, and the view that the loss of the child's life did not constitute a social danger. The final law as laid out in Article 369 reads: "When the crime provided for by Article 364 [voluntary homicide] is committed on the person of an infant not yet registered in the registers of the Civil Code and during the first five days of its life, in order to save one's own honor, or that of the wife, of the sister, of the descendant or adoptive daughter, the punishment is imprisonment from three to ten years." The Zanardelli Code did away with all references to illegitimacy and emphasized the woman's honor as central to the definition of the crime. And while infanticide technically remained a form of homicide under the Code, many judges largely ignored this fact and treated the crime as if under a special title.[4]

If the reform of infanticide legislation followed a pattern similar to the rest of Europe, what was distinctive about the Italian use of a woman's honor was its connection to the problem of her anonymity. In England, for instance, concealment of either an illegitimate pregnancy or birth was illegal, but in Italy, as I have already mentioned, it was not only legitimate but mandated by Church law. Interestingly, the 1865 Civil Code upheld this anonymity, in that it prohibited not only paternity searches but also those against maternity claims.[5] A woman, then, had not only a legal right to protect her honor; she had a legal duty to do so. And yet a woman's right and duty to anonymity constituted an enormous problem for secular policy makers and for the new theorists of criminal mothers. With continued Church control over sexual relations and, in the wake of the confiscation of Church properties, the rising fiscal burden of the foundling institutions, policy makers campaigned for the closure of the wheels and for some form of incursion into the law prohibiting the search for maternity. However, in order not to alienate a nation of Catholics, secular theorists felt compelled to fall back on traditional Catholic family values, though now in a displaced, secularized form. In their battle against the "Catholic" secrecy of a woman's sexual relationships, secularizing theorists sought to bring a woman's secrets into the open by redefining the meaning of her honor. Indeed, and in a complete reversal of the traditional meaning of the term, a woman's honor came to be seen as confirmed by the public display of her sins. In addition, honor was conceived no longer as the attribute of a presocial, natural subject but as a social function that was alienable and exchangeable according to modern rules of social exchange.

Female honor became in the process an essential criterion for the definition of infanticide and distinguished the infanticidal woman as well. Only "honest" or honorable women committed infanticide, while the category of common homicide was to be reserved for dishonorable women. Thus, the great legal theorist of the Classical School, Francesco Carrara, mounted an all-out attack on the old conception of infanticide in his important study *Programma del corso di diritto criminale*. Carrara insisted that the maternal role could be realized only within the conjugal bond and the family, and that beyond the confines of marriage and family the weakening of maternal sentiment was not only comprehensible but also justified. Carrara distinguished between infanticidal mothers who acted "egoistically" and those whose actions could only be understood in terms of their desire to protect their honor. For Carrara, it was precisely this desire behind the crime that argued for its mitigation and its specificity (1912, 331). Illegitimacy in itself could not be viewed as part of the cause. In other words, the fact that the woman had earlier sinned, Carrara considered irrelevant, because what really counted was *motive* (342). In effect, the material existence of the infant was less significant; it was, rather, the child's function as public evidence, its ability to generate dishonor, that mattered. The child's function as witness to dishonor turned it from a material into a *social* problem; with infanticide, a woman "has sought not only to destroy the material existence of the creature; but above all, [she] has wanted to destroy its name and the knowledge of its birth in the eyes of the world. In this *end* rests all the specificity of the crime" (329).

Motive, or the "subjective factor of crime," was, for Carrara, directly linked to the social and political nature of the crime's impact. Infanticide did not affect society; indeed, it derived from a *positive* feeling toward society, one geared to protecting society's fundamental structures and institutions. Carrara added to this positive social feeling, furthermore, an important extenuating circumstance that could drive a woman to infanticide. A woman's subjective moral force was weakened because of the additional burden imposed on her by her psychological state while and immediately after giving birth (341). Along lines that would become crucial in later debates, classical legal theorists viewed the psychological and somatic results of delivery as in themselves enough to cause and define this specific form of murder. The damage provoked by the crime, then, was reduced to what various theorists referred to as *"allarme sociale."* Carrara distinguished between theorists committed to an ascetic principle that insisted that a sin could never excuse a crime and theorists, modern like himself, who argued that actions had to be evaluated on the basis of political principle. Thus, according to such a political argumentation, the "spectacle" presented by the infanticidal woman "could excite aversion, indignation, pity for the victim, but not fear in the hearts of citizens: hence the negative impact [of infanticide] is minor" (330). Infanticide did not threaten social institutions and structures, and no real social value could be attached to a child who, by virtue of its illegitimate status, was in any case destined to become a criminal later in life.

The positivist school shared in the classical commitment to a legal reform capable of drawing the contours of concrete, specific subjects of the law. The positivists initially attributed infanticide to social factors: the infanticidal mother was forced to her criminal act by virtue of her poverty, seduction, and ignorance. Hence, the problem of infanticide was to be placed within a wider narrative about civilization and modernization. Infanticide had become secularized, Rafaello Ballestrini argued, and it could therefore no longer be simply viewed as a sin (1888, 10). In making such a sociological argument, positivism itself contributed in no small measure to this process of secularization, to the creation and promotion, that is, of modern social values. The force of the positivist argument stemmed from its peculiar mixture of a commitment to modern, scientific arguments and its continued adherence to traditional moral values. The call to honor evoked traditional norms, but it did so in and from a new voice, that of the positivist scientist. Honor became the linchpin of a new system of values of which Italians had largely to be convinced, because they were still bound by antiquated understandings of such honor.

Scipio Sighele's 1889 essay "Sull'infanticidio" exemplifies such a positivist double narrative. According to Sighele, the contribution by the Classical School was that of having made motive and social conditions fundamental to the definition of the infanticidal act. It had already proposed that infanticide was nothing but a painful fact (*"un fatto doloroso"*) rather than a social evil. Loyal to the biopolitical translation of law into fact, it is on the articulation of the specificity of this *"fatto doloroso"* that Sighele focuses in his essay. How, Sighele asks, should this crime be defined today for modern life? Like Carrara, Sighele turns to the question of motive. A mother "not only wants to kill the child, but above all to destroy all traces of its existence. With infanticide, *the intention is to hide [the child's] birth*" (1889, 186). Two considerations, he claims, are of particular importance: the effects the infanticidal mother has on society and, conversely, the effects society has on the infanticidal or potentially infanticidal mother. But because infanticide in the modern era is a *social* act, positivists must interrogate the concrete social danger of the infanticidal woman. Though Carrara, too, had recognized that the infanticidal woman could not inspire fear, Sighele adds: "While for the classical school the recognition of the criterion of the delinquent's danger had existed only in an embryonic state, as a recognition of all the imperfections of a truth only divined, and all the uncertainties of a truth not yet avowed, for the positivist school, the delinquent's danger was placed at the forefront, it was considered the surest sign capable of determining the quality and degree of social reaction to antisocial acts" (194). The evergrowing and progressive understanding of the law's function in civilization is thus viewed by Sighele in terms of a metaphor that itself borrows from the theme of pregnancy, birth, and the placement of its product in society at large. While the Classical School understood the nature of crime and its agents only in embryonic fashion, it is positivism that will give birth to the body of a criminal whose social function will be not only properly understood but well-managed in the future. The child's life, on the other hand, has only a relative existence, one that acquires value, in Maria Pelaja's words, "only under limited conditions: that it be legitimate and thus protected from marginalization and the inevitable sufferings of an 'irregular person'" (1981, 50).

But infanticide is also an effect of modern society. Thus, "of the unwed mother . . . society demands, in the form of a brutal dilemma, either her dishonor or the sacrifice of her child's life. Therefore, she does not struggle between morality and a common and vulgar desire that, in order to be appeased, requires the committing of a crime. Instead, she struggles between the feeling of pity and the sense of honor, the first mitigated by the knowledge that the creature would suffer little in dying and perhaps suffer much in living; the second rendered more acute by the knowledge that, once her honor had been lost, one could say that the moral life of a woman has been killed" (Sighele 1889, 199). Sighele thus rejects a purely physiological definition of the infanticidal mother's condition. Infanticide proves that a lessened legal responsibility cannot and should not always be traced back to either physical or mental illness. It is the socially rejected mother who is of real interest, for she evinces only a temporary cruelty; her cruelty is "like a flash of lightning that in a sinister manner interrupts the normality of her life" (197). Infanticide is not necessarily a sign of a mother's perversity, but in more cases than not may be traced back to her social environment. Indeed, infanticide is the crime par excellence that has its roots in the social: "infanticide is a symptom of a given moral environment" (198). Indeed, one might say that infanticide is the most social of crimes, for it places the mother before the "brutal dilemma" of having to choose between two values: pity and honor, her (private) love for her child and her (public) love for society. It is important to note here that, for Sighele, both loves are to be understood as "civilized" forms of love and *not* as naturally grounded. The relative value, as Pelaja calls it, of the child's life is the means by which Sighele constructs a notion of maternal love that understands the child's life in terms of social value, one subject to the determination of the quality of life. Pity does not exist in the form of a presocial bond between mother and child. The positivist mother and child relation—contrary to the classical "embryonic" one—is always already constituted by social subjects. This explains, according to Sighele, why infanticide is most prevalent in those forms of social living where honor is most prized, while it abates in those societies where a woman's honor has lost all its value. And this explains also why Sighele's understanding of modern infanticide is so seemingly contradictory. Honor as a social value—in particular, woman's sexual honor—refers to a value in conflict with modern society, where honor has lost all its value, and to a new set of family relations, whose vectors are now subject to interventions by society at large. Honor is here both a private and a public relation: private because it is founded in the need for a material secrecy, and public because it is concerned with the demand for public acceptance. Honor is configured as both traditional, because it protects the autonomy of the family, and modern, because it necessitates the state's intervention into and management of the family in order to protect its continued viability. Sighele therefore concludes that infanticide is caused by both tyrannical social prejudice and by the ever-growing immorality of modern society, which places all emphasis on the immediate pleasures of life and forsakes its concomitant pains, such as childbirth and the duties of maternity.

Both classical and positivist theorists agreed, then, that honor was the only motive relevant to a definition of infanticide. It was a crime committed by an honest, albeit strayed, woman who through her act sought to avoid dishonor in a situation where, if the child were detected, she would cover herself and her family with shame. Nevertheless, the distinction between the honest woman and the woman of shame proved hard to maintain, given the slippery and mobile characteristics of honor itself. One fundamental aspect of honor, as understood by these theorists of infanticide, was that it had regenerative capacities. Honor was understood not simply as an individual attribute but as an agency that could redeem social agents, indeed, a force that could constitute subjects as social subjects. Honor had a kind of interpellative power. It functioned, in the words of Alessandro Stoppato, as an *incitement* to become a valuable member of society: "Society is not wrong to establish a difference between women who let themselves go and women who respect themselves, between those who disparage and those who preserve one of society's most precious goods: the honor of the woman, the sacred law of matrimony. But such socially necessary severity is not for the fallen woman an incitement to aggravate her fault. Instead, such incitement has over her all the more power to the extent that she has been made more sensitive to her modesty and her suffered affront" (1887, 26). Stoppato does not view the absence of honor as necessarily a stigmatization of those who transgressed the norm, as a way by which to signify the "other," but rather as an instrument of recuperation for social agency. As he states, "Even the public prostitute, in the misfortune that has struck her and against which modern society is no help, is a woman. She too undergoes physio-psychological changes . . . ; through the act of giving birth, she succumbs to the laws of female nature and she cannot even be comforted by the idea of legitimate maternity. Yet, sooner or later, even in the prostitute remorse may come into being, advice and reproaches may exercise a positive effect, and it is not impossible that, because of the innumerable resources of moral activity, a sense of shame takes charge of her soul and she thus becomes a better person" (156).

The category of infanticide performed, then, an important but perhaps destabilizing function. By virtue of its connection to honor, it enabled a reconfiguration of honor from a "private" attribute to a social function. Honor thereby became a constitutive moment of social subjectivity, of which the infanticidal mother was exemplary. It could do this by using a traditional norm applied to women and modernizing it for radically new usages. Not only was infanticide given a social explanation (i.e., seen as caused by the poverty, despair, or legal status of a woman) and therefore severed from a naturalist explanation, but it came to be viewed, quite paradoxically, as a reconfirmation and a defense of social existence. Women killed their children not merely to save their honor as an aspect of their personal dignity as subjects; more importantly, infanticide was seen to *generate* honor, in particular, public or social honor, retroactively. There was something in the act of infanticide that had redemptive capacities. The honor that pertained to infanticide was one that could be publicly enjoyed; it was viewed "as a good capable of being exchanged and reintegrated. The woman who loses her honor can see it given back to her either through marriage or, paradoxically, through a criminal gesture that cancels the obvious proof of her lost honor" (Selmini 1987, 35). And thus honor was severed from anonymity and coupled to a public act, dependent in turn on a peculiar logic: a dishonorable woman killed her child, an act that by definition was not infanticide because the crime was understood as an act that protected a woman's honor. Nevertheless, precisely by killing her child, she *became* honorable, and thus she did commit infanticide, because honor had the ability—via infanticide—to generate itself retroactively.

If, however, honor did not naturally adhere to specific subjects, then who could rightfully participate in infanticide? Who, other than the woman herself, had the right to take an active role in the protection of a woman's honor? Legal theorists largely regarded the woman's family as the rightful depositor and guardian of her honor, a fact that was written into law by the Zanardelli Code. The one noteworthy exclusion from the law was the woman's seducer; he, when an accomplice to the act, was to be tried for complicity in murder. The problem of complicity thus created a tension between individual and social honor, for as individual honor, the act of infanticide by another interested party had of necessity to be considered murder; but as a social honor, conceivably *anyone* could participate in and benefit from the creation of an honorable woman. Legally, the problem was not satisfactorily solved, and judges were inconsistent in how they treated accomplices to infanticide. And yet, as a *cultural* construction, the discourse of infanticide *causa honoris* made social intervention and regulation possible even when the laws dictated otherwise, to the extent that infanticide was understood as socially caused. Social intervention found its mode of entry through the socialization of honor, expressed in the form of a generalization of and participation in guilt. In particular, the claim that society and its mores were at fault when it pushed women to acts of despair, when it placed women in an impossible conflict because of its double standard, shifted the locus of responsibility from women to society itself. As Laura Berry has argued, the publicity that surrounded infanticide in the nineteenth century had less to do with the murderous woman than with the possibility of generalizing shame and culpability (1999, 134–35). Through infanticide, a "mutual affinity" or identification was created between the criminal mother and society represented by the benevolent middle-class male, an identification created by a slippage between the guilty perpetrator and society more generally. On the one hand, the identificatory relation between the fallen woman and the middle-class male permitted societal intervention because infanticide became a social problem that affected all. On the other hand, class entirely circumscribed who would be included in this collective, though the operative notion of class had borrowed its terms from gender metaphors through an elective affinity between the poor infanticidal mother and the middle-class male. This social honor was a class honor, geared to protecting middle-class, heteronormative values, and it was radically distinct from a subjective or individual notion of honor or human dignity. It could thereby exclude the "egoistic" honor of, for example, the "seducer," the profligate male who was incapable of controlling his desires. That the bourgeois male or social-cultural theorist elected the poor and destitute single mother as his double explains why middle- or upper-class infanticidal women were treated with such extraordinary harshness in the courts (Selmini 1987, 134). Quite paradoxically, honor could be applied only to the unwed, working-class, and *disreputable* woman, an application nevertheless designed to invoke middle-class, conjugal norms.

Lino Ferriani: Infanticide as Literature

Lino Ferriani was not only a lawyer and legal theorist, but also a prolific author of children's books. He placed great value on the redemptive capacities of literature, seeing in literary creation an effective instrument for the diffusion of morals and for the formation of character.[6] In his most important text dedicated to the problem of infanticide—a work composed with much effort toward poetic description—he called for a collaboration between writers and lawyers to actively intervene in the education of Italy's citizens of all social backgrounds. Ferriani opens his 1886 *La infanticida nel codice penale e nella vita sociale* with an invocation of Luigi Capuana's comment on verismo literature, that the most impossible novels are those that occur every day before our very eyes. The true site for such daily human dramas is, for Ferriani, the court of law. Here the real triumphs without rhetoric; here human documents are written (or write themselves) and become the sons of truth (Ferriani 1889, 18). Just as the modern novel mirrors all facets of social life without hypocrisy, so also the courts represent the true life of the people. Indeed, the honest form of theater that the courts of law are, in a version of an early "reality TV show," should ideally provide the literary model for novels and newspapers. Nonetheless, there are forces at work that undermine all such honest passion and true human drama: misguided legal theorists, such as the positivists, who seek to destroy the very existence of the legal codes with their critique of free will; members of the jury who do not know enough about the problems of modern society and thus return verdicts that are either too strict or too lenient; and finally the spectators present in court who come to observe the trials not in order to come away from them with an education in the public duties of citizenship, but rather for their private delectation and entertainment. In this last category of misguided social citizens, Ferriani singles out the overwhelming presence of female spectators as particularly pernicious to citizenship formation through literature, seeing in the female riffraff of the court galleries concrete examples of modern, egoistic women who are mere consumers but not producers of the national project.

In Ferriani's universe, women do not belong in the gallery but on stage.[7] The courtroom provides the theatrical platform on which appears the infanticidal mother in her true and real form, but where she is nevertheless expected to obey specific literary guidelines. Her genre is tragedy, Ferriani claims, and her author is the cultural elite of Italy, as he exhorts at the end of his book: "Philosophers, moralists, journalists, novelists, playwrights, all of you who have a heart and an educated pen, go, go to the courts, and preferably go there when in the dock of the accused sits an *infanticidal woman:* note her, study her, then write the *truth* and, united, begin a glorious war capable of bringing about the rebirth of modesty through education, and give back to woman that aura of purity that alone will make her deserving of the name *angel of the family*" (182–83). Ferriani thus seeks a bond of affinity between judges and writers, on the one hand, and the infanticidal mother, on the other, in a move that privileges the latter against the more "modern" female spectators. It is the infanticidal mother who, it appears, has the most potential to become transformed into an "angel of the family."

The bulk of Ferriani's text consists of fleshing-out his cast of characters, stereotyped to such a degree that his analysis can hardly be read as a sociological explanation of the phenomenon. Indeed, his list of social types betrays, rather, his own anxieties about population shifts brought on by urbanization. Ferriani describes schoolteachers, who are "well-dressed" and speak relatively "good Italian," but who have become a social scourge since they have recently been forced from their rural familial homes and have arrived in the cities alone, defenseless, innocent, and the easy prey of seducers. They are followed by domestic servants who have been seduced by their masters or their masters' sons; by seamstresses who are trying to make ends meet and who, desperate for marriage, have fallen for the promises of men who abandoned them when they became pregnant. And they, in turn, are followed by prostitutes—certainly sinners, but who, nevertheless, also deserve pity and compassion. Ferriani even produces a young upper-class woman of considerable beauty (though infanticidal women, in his opinion, are never attractive): she is, however, a girl ruined by modern upbringing, that is, by her mother's continual absence and by an education that has taught her a little about everything but nothing about her domestic and conjugal duties.[8]

Once his actresses have been properly presented, Ferriani moves on to a definition of their acts. The script is by now a familiar one, with a discussion of the history of infanticide as the history of an ever-growing leniency, a history that Ferriani wholly supports. While adhering to the general concept of the more volatile female nervous system, Ferriani still places great emphasis on two, and for him interrelated, factors: women's social position and the feminine, but always threatened, instinct for honor amongst the poor and traditional classes. A shamed woman "wants *à tout prix* to reconquer the place that has been robbed of her by the seducer, because *sa pudeur n'est pas morte*" (109).

Infanticidal women are divided into two groups: the honest and the fallen. Ferriani proposes to leave the latter to their fate and to focus instead on those women who "though having committed a grave crime, can pronounce the word 'honor,' that very honor that is the most important patrimony of the family and whose integrity is especially entrusted to woman" (113). A family's honor is a woman's virtue and duty. In an *honest* woman, who values the social role of the family, the shame of an illegitimate pregnancy gives birth to horror, a horror that in turn gives birth to a reborn honor. Such newly awakened honor places before the honest woman three choices: suicide, abortion, or infanticide. The true culprits in this tragedy are the woman's family (to the extent that the family has succumbed to the trends of modern society) and the seducer. Both have failed to uphold the individual honor of the woman herself, as well as the social honor of the family and the nation. A good family, Ferriani asserts, leads to a good society, which in turn leads to a good nation. Infanticidal women understand this series of relations; it is they who best comprehend and guard the interests of family, society, and nation. Infanticidal women alone embody the honor of the nation; they are its true representatives. Consequently, Ferriani declares himself in favor of acquittal in the courts of law of those women who show true signs of honorability.[9]

Not to be acquitted, however, are modern society and its first and foremost representative, the seducer. Both are responsible for the existence of the infanticidal mother. She is nothing but the effect of modern life: "It is absurd that there should be a strict law for [infanticide], because such a punishment would be striking down an effect, whose cause was neglected by the legislator" (124–25). Infanticide is the inevitable result of the incursions made by modern life into the family, and no law can change this fact. Nevertheless, Ferriani does not therefore argue for nonintervention by the state; on the contrary, he argues that the state must protect the family against the vicissitudes of civil society. The state must function as an educator in morality: "To prevent the evil, it is necessary to improve the family, to surround it with respect, to strictly defend it against seducers, and teach parents . . . the holy duties involved in the education of their children, to start a war against artificial education, to inculcate in everyone the fact that education is . . . a damaging thing when not accompanied by moral education" (136–37). The fact that women are killing their children is a symptom of the much more important fact that modern society is killing the family. Matrimony has become confused with patrimony; marriage has been reduced to a social contract, one geared to increase the riches and income of the family unit. Infanticide is the result of a corrupt society, and it is hence no wonder, Ferriani adds, that the crime is so predominantly committed by literate women who cast their newborns down the urban latrines. Infanticidal women prove that personal egotism has triumphed over the feeling of justice.

Egotism or a sense of honor? Ferriani's text is circumscribed by this contradictory reaction to the infanticidal mother. On the one hand, Ferriani is sure that what the murderous mother really wants is the respect that she deserves. On the other hand, as the product of modern society, she is also perceived as nothing but an effect of forces that lie beyond her control and have the power to turn the weak woman into an egotist. Valeria Babini, in her reading of Ferriani's treatise, privileges this latter aspect of his text. Thus, for her, Ferriani's infanticidal woman is essentially a minor player in a play that casts the seducer and his environment as its major protagonists. She is neither heroic nor passionate, but the dupe of others; she is the privileged victim of contemporary society, a privilege that comes to her by virtue of her feminine nature. For Babini, Ferriani has constructed an image of a sick society that does not respect the values on which it is nevertheless founded (1986, 469). Such a conclusion is also supported by Rossella Selmini's analysis of the infanticide cases tried in the Bologna courts between 1880 and 1913. According to Selmini, the aim of infanticide trials was twofold. On the one hand, they transformed a social wound into an arbitrary or involuntary gesture, into what Ferriani dubs a societal effect. Infanticide trials functioned conservatively to allay public fears, to reaffirm the universality and naturalness of maternal feeling, and to prove that the latter could be undone only temporarily and as a result of some malfunction, be it individual or social. On the other hand, the trials also evidenced a drive to "diffuse in a capillary manner into the countryside and to the more 'unruly' social classes a model of regulated life that is orderly and morally exemplary" (Selmini 1987, 98). The court documents analyzed by Selmini support her contention that there existed a rupture between the women's so-called bad reputation and their acquittal by reason of honor. Selmini claims that it was only through judicial procedures that women "took responsibility for their criminal acts," that is, invoked their lost-but-soon-to-be-found honor. Honor was in that sense an invention and an expectation imposed by the courts on the infanticidal mother. The goal of the trials was then to provide an education not just in maternity but also in honor. Women learned to be honorable qua unnatural mothers to the extent that honor was given a social valence, one that could be lost and regained.

Yet the trials were symptomatic of a complicated and contradictory process, a process wherein what was at stake, in fact, was a *de*naturalization of maternal feelings in order to make them more malleable to the intervention by social institutions and extralegal discourses. Such denaturalization allowed for what Jacques Donzelot has called a dematerialization of the offense and for a break between pretrial investigation and judicial decision, whereby the infanticidal mother became the site of continual surveillance and study to the extent that she was removed from the realm of the law (1979, 110). And it also allowed for the transposition of maternity into a different register, that is, from the realm of naturalized right to that of social responsibility, to the idea that maternity, even if illegitimate, was a social duty. At stake here was not simply a return to a previous equilibrium, but the creation of something new. Otherwise, how is one to explain the enormous importance that Ferriani lent to an education through *literature*? It was the *creation* of the infanticidal mother as a literary heroine that welded her to honor, to a passion for society of such a kind to transcend the egotistical love of self. Ferriani's infanticidal mother may be a victim—and indeed society's most glorious victim—but she is not therefore a dupe. She is, rather, modernity's great symbol and therefore its great educator. Ultimately, in his quest for a return to family values, Ferriani gave to such an education a content founded on traditionally conceived prescriptive moral norms. However, there remains in his text an element of fascination or investment in his heroines, a mark of passionate love not containable by his average type of mother to whose creation he avowedly remained committed. In the end, it may be Ferriani's construction of the courts as a scene of and for literature that constituted his novelty, insofar as it removed the infanticidal woman from the legal domain to that of theatrical (self-)presentation. The very "extralegality" of passionate fascination founds Ferriani's project of a conservative modernity as morality play in and because of which the infanticidal woman is required to play a defining role. If in Ferriani's narrative the infanticidal mother is heroic by virtue of her submission to social laws, it will be in the work of Cesare Lombroso that the heroically passionate woman who kills her offspring in order to love society all the better will rise to her full stature.

Cesare Lombroso: The Passion of and for the Social

In her discussion of female crimes of passion in fin-de-siècle France, Ruth Harris has laid out the reasons for the consistent clemency meted out by male juries to women who had killed husbands and lovers in the "heat of passion." Specifically, she analyzes "the hidden dimensions of manipulation and exchange" between male psychiatric assessment and judicial analysis and "the feminine arena of dramatic self-presentation and retrospective rationalization" (Harris 1989, 208). Of particular concern to her analysis is this representation by women of themselves as characters in a melodramatic play of passions, a fact that won them acquittal after acquittal. Not only were the trial documents highly stylized literary constructions, the crimes themselves "were committed in a repetitive, even ritualized fashion," constituting "social dramas which involved passers-by as audience and also as participants" (211). And thus, "the crime of passion was a universally recognised cultural phenomenon in which the outcome was, to a large extent, pre-ordained by the style and form of execution and presentation" (213). Two motives were routinely invoked for such crimes of passion: honor and romantic disappointment. "Love-sickness" was an essential aspect of the self-representation that generated both compassion and an image of feminine irresponsibility. Harris's point is that although the passionate criminal woman was understood as bearing certain masculine traits in her willingness to take up arms and mete out justice on her own terms, she was not understood as either morally deviant or a danger to society. An important factor in this devaluation of feminine crime was that "a woman so closely adhered to melodramatic modes of self-representation. Indeed, the representations of 'romantic distress' in both literary and legal records demonstrate a similar predilection towards an emotionally transparent self-representation and the use of ideal oppositions to explain issues of immense psychological complexity. The extremes provided by both [melodramatic] play and trial offered, at least for audiences, an opportunity for ritualistic catharsis and an affirmation of shared values" (225).

Why, however, should it be that representations of crime and mental disturbance offered the possibility of ritual catharsis, even of identification? This is, in fact, Cesare Lombroso's question in his fascinating essay from 1899, "Il delinquente ed il pazzo nel dramma e nel romanzo moderno." Why, Lombroso asks, "does the world refuse to accept the existence of the criminal type, of the madness of genius . . . that it so willingly accepts in the novel and in the theater?" (1899, 681). For Lombroso, the answer lies in the nature of modernity and in the human economy of passion produced by modern life. Thus, he notes the "enormous difference" between classical and modern literature, the latter of which presents an inordinate number of insane and criminal characters that seem to have been "sculpted by an alienist or by a criminal anthropologist" (665). When these new protagonists, furthermore, "are not insane, they are agitated by such violent and strange passions as never encountered on the streets of real life, and indeed are denied to exist when they appear in a scientific tract" (665). They gain acceptance, however, when encountered in modern literature (665). In classical theater, poets had been concerned with the representative or average type. Characters had not been real but symbolic and had corresponded to the "reduced humanity of the mythical and heroic age" (674). Classical poets had emphasized tradition and declamation at the expense of plot and individual character. The reason for this difference can be found in that "law that demands the movement in all organisms and in all works of art from the simple to the complex. Just as earlier penal law did not study the criminal but only the crime, while now both are studied together, and just as ancient medicine only studied the illness and now above all it studies the patient, so also in the theater, as thought has become more discriminate, one has substituted . . . the observation of the fact with that of the author of the fact" (675–76). Modern literature has reached the maximum of complexity because it both creates characters from the real *and* tries to impart a moral lesson through the representation of a "symbolic idea."

The reality effect in modern literature is produced, according to Lombroso, by the malaise of modern culture, by the fact, that is, that insanity and criminality have increased significantly in contemporary civilization. Stimuli to the nervous system and febrile activity have produced a "mass of neurasthenics, hysterics and . . . morally insane; it had produced people who were profoundly egoistic and devoid of affect, and guided only by powerful passions such as the desire for gold and power, and to which everything, even health, was sacrificed" (677). Civilization has increased the number of insane and quadrupled their importance in society. In premodern societies the insane individual was either "not noticed or was adored or feared as a saint or a witch; he always seemed a phenomenon, a kind of extraplanetary meteor who was an outsider to society" (678). Now, however, the abuses of civilization have created new forms of insanity, forms that reside within society itself: "phobias because of which one was afraid to cross a square or hear pronounced certain words" or "perverse sexual tastes that constitute an entire new world apart and are capable of inspiring new comedic or dramatic possibilities" (678).

Modern life has thus generated insanity and criminality everywhere—"under foot," as Lombroso remarks, not just in books, newspapers, and in the theater, but in politics and in finance, in the streets and in the public squares. But not only has civilization turned crime and insanity into public events. That same release of passion that is at the origin of crime and insanity and that comes to life as a public event *inside* the contours of the social, produces another effect. Passion in modern society allows for a new kind of aesthetic release; it allows for an *experience* of the new as self-creation. "When we are in the presence of real figures, figures that have been made to flash under the strong light of great artists, the awareness of the real that slumbers in all of us but that is compressed and disfigured by the pedantry of education, is roused and it rebels against the conventional prejudices that were forced on it. All the more so in that the seduction of art has magnified the contours of the real; it has rendered the real more evident, and thus has reduced the necessary effort to take possession of it" (681). While aesthetic experience makes possible a libidinal investment in the new, while it destroys conventions and accesses the real, science forecloses such access. "When instead we must draw the consequences from cold statistics or from a skeletal study of the facts, we feel the weight of the past that interferes with and aligns itself to feelings, and even with the aesthetic sense, in order to compel us to deny those same feelings" (681).

The aesthetic experience of passion, for Lombroso, is thus intimately linked to the experience of modernity. It signals both modernity's exaggerated affects and excess, and its driving principle. As also for Ferriani, Lombroso views the excessiveness of modern passion as most effectively mastered through its translation into an aesthetic experience. And yet his own relationship to such a passion for the new is nevertheless complicated; those figures that place themselves beyond the law because of their passion retain for him a status that is always ambiguous, to the extent that they are perceived as bearers of the new. There is something in passionate criminals that Lombroso finds quite irresistible, and he understands their irresistible nature in terms, precisely, of an awakening from the slumber of convention. The aesthetic relation permits an identification between those who transgress the norm and the spectator to that transgression, an identification that Lombroso understands as the unleashing of passion and *therefore* the taking possession of the real.

Taking possession of the real through an aesthetic working-over of passion is not a marginal aspect of Lombroso's work. Lombroso's anthropological method is, as Cristina Mazzoni has pointed out, distinguished by the fact that the somatic is inherently semantic (1997, 243). Lombroso's aesthetic principles provide the basis of his own passion, both regarding his style of writing and his drive to categorize. Thus, in Annamaria Cavalli Pasini's words, Lombroso's style "never falls into the pedantry of a 'technical' kind but rather avails itself of a narrative exposition . . . founded on the most disparate sources . . . in order to establish with the reader a relation of emotive connivance, where scientific 'objectivity' gives way to a winsome parlor chit-chat" (1982, 74).

It is perhaps the very richness of his sources that compels Lombroso to always keep an eye on difference and hence to continuously multiply his categories and groups, to even celebrate their differences. Lombrosan categories are an amorphous flux of divisions and subdivisions that ultimately undermine the very possibility of all categorization. As Giorgio Colombo has remarked, if Lombroso began his scientific project with the desire to place all individuals into classes, he ended up with classes without individuals (2000, 228), because individuals were always already in excess of the class to which they belonged.

Though passion founds and confounds all categories, the passionate criminal is also a specific type, one that Lombroso places between the "born criminal" and the "occasional criminal." While the born criminal demonstrates physiological and psychological defects due to degenerative characteristics that can be read on the surface of the body, and the occasional criminal commits antisocial acts because pressed to do so by the environment, the criminal by passion kills because of an irresistible force within him- or herself that is caused typically by strong feelings of love. The postulation of such an "irresistible force" raises two problems, however. The first pertains to the nature of its attachment to and existence within the body. Is this irresistible force self-generated, or is it the result of an external influence that can have permanent or temporary effects on the body? Where, in other words, does passion come from? The second problem is that passion may take the form of a strong feeling of *legitimate* affect, or even of an irresistible *ethical* force. It is not always easy to draw a line between passionate states that are excusable because they stem from socially accepted values and those passions that can never be excused or that might even compound culpability. For Lombroso, honor is one of those passions that must be considered a strong affective tie to social norms. Because honor binds an individual to society, certain crimes of honor must be viewed as symptoms of an ethical and social hypersensitivity. But how does one know when passion is socially valuable and when it is destructive? Ultimately, the Lombroso school can only assert the difference between good and bad passion by falling back on commonsensical notions of good and evil. Enrico Ferri, for example, in painting a description of the born criminal who is simply indifferent to the fact that he has broken the law, posits the hero's indifference to pain as something diametrically opposite: "And yet, beware, this apathetic attitude of the vulgar deviant is radically different. Its genesis and moral significance are completely contrary to the strong and tranquil heroism with which the blond martyr of freedom smilingly salutes the flash of the guillotine and sacrifices his name to the veneration of an entire people!" (1885, 33–34).[10]

Passion is thus a force that is both irresistible and unreadable. It is simultaneously the bond that makes people adhere to society and the cause of society's undoing. This contradictory characteristic of passion pervades Cesare Lombroso's major work on women, his 1893 *La donna delinquente: La prostituta e la donna normale.* Written as the ostensible companion-piece to his hugely successful *L'uomo delinquente,* the text is a bizarre collection of scientific categorization, statistical systematization, proverbs, literary citation, and commonplaces, all combined in an effort to create the impression of a *commonsensical* representation of woman. Local knowledges and traditions, therefore, join the scientific voice of Lombroso to produce, reorganize, and thus cathartically reaffirm an *experience* of woman as a contradictory being. Commonsensical experience founds knowledge and thereby makes possible direct access to the workings of natural law. It is woman's contradictory nature that proves that nature and law are themselves not logical and that all categories, like women, are themselves subject to deconstruction.

The infanticidal woman occupies a rather limited space in *La donna delinquente.* As Lombroso had already announced in *L'uomo delinquente,* mothers kill their illegitimate offspring "because of an exaggerated sense of honor, a sense of honor caused in turn by the infamy that our society attaches to illegitimate maternity. At the same time, society does not obligate man to make reparations, nor does it stipulate the right to search for the father" (2000b, 589). The infanticidal woman also occupies a somewhat unstable position in the Lombrosan system. While a subspecies of the criminal by passion, she nonetheless is also an occasional criminal, insofar as her criminal act can be traced back to societal factors. The infanticidal woman never exhibits degenerative traits, though Lombroso does hold that she shows masculine characteristics, a fact which Lombroso traces back to her capacity for great passion.

Virile passion is what distinguishes the infanticidal woman from the so-called *donna normale.* The normal woman is to be differentiated from man, in turn, by the fact that she tends to gravitate toward the "average type" of the species; her greater organic monotony is opposed to man's greater evolutionary variability. While man focuses on individual and social life, woman, geared to protecting the species, is nevertheless also more complete, more vital, more self-sufficient (Lombroso and Ferrero 1923, 16). Given this self-sufficiency, she has virtually no sexual appetite and prefers being loved to loving. And while man is, according to Lombroso, predominantly an erotic being, woman is a sexual one: "Man loves woman for her vulva, woman loves in man the husband and the father" (47). Woman is therefore libidinally invested in her *social* relationships with man, relationships that constitute a form of sublimation of man's erotic investment in her organs. While frigidity and monogamy are "normal," they are nonetheless the result of civilization and constitute the basis for woman's insertion into culture. The normal woman is thus the product of the male civilizing process, and hence normality for Lombroso is always already the result of a cultural working-over of nature. And yet civilization has a contradictory effect on woman, for it makes her both more civilized—through the control of her passions—and less so. What in fact distinguishes the normal woman from man more than any other factor is her pity. Pity (*pietà*) lies at the origin of another female contradiction, namely her tendency toward both cruelty and her fulfillment in maternity. Though generally more vindictive, woman tends to pity her victims, and therefore she is essentially more arbitrary in the exercise of power. Woman thus has more pity, but no sense of justice. Two factors arouse woman's cruelty: love and revolution, the first generating crimes of passion and the second a participation in what Lombroso calls "*crudeltà epidemica*" (59). Passionate love for man and for social change define but undermine the normal woman, rendering her crueler and yet passionately pitying in her love.

The infanticidal woman belongs to the category of passionate criminals who, except for their "virility," show no signs of degeneration, be they physiological or moral. On the contrary, she passionately loves society and family. Indeed, her strongest passion tends to be love. Interestingly, the infanticidal woman's passion, her *political passion* as Valeria Babini rightly calls it, is conceived by Lombroso as a true, disinterested, and intense passion, "constructed not on the male model but negatively on that of the female norm where love is, so to speak, a deferred sentiment" (Babini 1986, 458). Lombroso's passionate female criminals have, in fact, a distinguished literary model, one already encountered in Sighele's work: they are woman who love with the passion of Éloise, "violating for [their men] prejudices, customs, and even societal laws. . . . Such intensity in their love passions explains why almost all of these criminals have fallen into love relations that are irregular from the social point of view, though one cannot for that say anything against their purity. Virginity and marriage are social institutions that are suitable, like all customs and institutions, for the average type. That is to say, in this case, they are suitable to the sexual coldness of the normal woman. [Passionate women] love too passionately not to transgress these norms" (Lombroso and Ferrero 1923, 333). And Lombroso goes on to remark melancholically on the "unjust contempt of the world for that which is called their guilt, but which is nothing except an excess of dangerous love in a society whose great strength lies in egotism" (334).

Infanticide is to be placed here, in this conflict between self-abnegating love and social prohibition. Infanticide is always more prevalent in those societies where social norms are most repressive, there where the fear of dishonor is a symptom of a world that leaves no room for passion. The infanticidal woman "loves in man the origin and object of her own passion, and not like the 'honest' woman the 'father' or the 'husband'" (Babini 1986, 458). This is then the meaning of the dishonor projected by society; even if Lombroso famously considers maternity a moral vaccine against crime and evil, he nevertheless detects in the infanticidal woman a possible prying-apart of biological destiny and social desires. The conflictual nature of the relationship between biological destiny and social desires is signaled, in Lombroso's text, by his ambiguous use of a woman's honor. For it stands not only for the unjust imposition of norms, but also for the (revolutionary) passion that attaches individuals to social structures. If marriage works for the average type, this is not so for the passionate woman who feels only the social barriers placed on her by marriage (Lombroso and Ferrero 1923, 356). The infanticidal woman's excessive love, her honor, makes her disinterested, and not, as the normal woman, socially altruistic. And yet she is also not egoistic like man, for what binds her to society through her crime is a *passion for social relations*. As Babini points out, the infanticidal woman represents, for Lombroso, the female figure that combines within herself "both maternity and sexual desire, love and passion." She represents not merely an untamed passion in conflict with a repressive society or "the impossibility, in terms of an introjected norm, to live that feeling of maternity that pushes the woman to infanticide" (Babini 1986, 459). Babini is correct in asserting that crucial in Lombroso's text is the emphasis on the closure of all societies insofar as they forbid transgressions; if for Ferriani, for instance, society has simply forgone its duties and responsibilities, for Lombroso, *no society* can guarantee those values that are different from those on the basis of which it is constituted. But there is more, and this is perhaps an aporetic moment in Lombroso's text. Infanticide, for Lombroso, points not merely to the fact that society cannot accept difference. It *also* points to that which constitutes society as such: its original and originating drive or passion, a love or love-sickness that is more than itself, more than can be contained by its subject, and that reproduces, in its very criminality, the violence of the law that founds all social relations. Lombroso's passionate woman is not merely the heroic victim of social relations; she founds them and provides their energizing and modernizing forces.

Muzio Pazzi and Vincenzo Mellusi: Gynecological Criminology

After 1890, passion came to be medicalized and, therefore, honor increasingly viewed as a function of the body. First and foremost, this meant that "every gesture, every internal sensation, every possible behavior by [infanticidal] women were anticipated and furnished with motivation" (Selmini 1987, 107). Unwed mothers, who before had been protected by the anonymity advocated by the Church, became not only legitimate but indeed necessary objects of scientific-medical inquiry. The medicalization of passion thus represented an important shift from earlier formulations that had linked infanticide to an honorable passion for society. Such a change may in part be explained by the fact that, on its own, the theory of infanticide *causa honoris* was incapable of providing institutional answers to the regulation of passion. Passion had to be made into an object of disciplinary knowledges—in this case, into an object of the medical profession. Nevertheless, some of the theoretical coordinates of the earlier discourses were not entirely abandoned, especially the idea that maternal sentiments were not natural or presocial aspects of a woman's biological makeup; maternity was not to be understood as a self-regulating system, and its imperfections had to be viewed as symptoms of wider psychosocial ills.

While the intervention by the medical profession in the courts became more pronounced, physicians were nevertheless placed in a difficult position. They were compelled to address Lombroso's question, that is, to distinguish between passion and illness, "to determine the difference between exalted sentiments on the one hand, and morbid impulsions, on the other" (Harris 1989, 228–29). An inability to draw clear lines of demarcation ultimately generated legal incoherencies, because, although judges continued to adhere to the honor thesis, this was increasingly linked to a temporary form of insanity produced by the state of maternity itself. As maternity was woman's biological destiny, so was honor a woman's psychological destiny. The latter could produce a temporary madness, one that took the name of puerperal mania in an age that predated the determination of woman's behavior by hormones. While Lombroso held that honor pointed to a woman's choice, in its medicalized version honor referred to an amnesia of the criminal act and thus could only be presumed by the courts as a motive of the crime. In other words, what a woman might state in a court was irrelevant, because she had neither knowledge of nor control over her act. Infanticide as the result of puerperal mania was viewed increasingly as the natural product of woman's organism, a result, fortunately, that was only transitory and that promised her speedy reintegration into the social order. As a consequence, however, the infanticidal mother was from now on deprived of all legal responsibility.

The discovery of puerperal mania, the birth, that is, of a "gynecological criminology," put honor as a motive into second place. Since the battle against secrecy had been largely won, the infanticidal woman now had to be transformed into a socially responsible mother. In a series of pamphlets written at the beginning of the twentieth century, Muzio Pazzi, one of Italy's leading gynecologists, could now explain infanticide on the basis of two premises. First, feminine nature gravitated around a biological function that Pazzi called physiological destiny. Second, in the period that stretched from conception through the time of weaning an infant, women would often, if not invariably, undergo extreme physical and psychological changes that would place their own lives and those of others in danger. "We can say that the normal woman during the period of gestation falls prey to a state that we may term physiological and that is more or less capable of producing psychoanasthesia with vague and oscillating phobias due to the obscure unknowns of pregnancy and birth, a state that like a true nightmare weighs on all pregnant women" (Pazzi 1913a, 7). The state of maternity itself was the true culprit of that inversion of the maternal instinct that led to suicide, abortion, or infanticide. As an example, Pazzi cited the case of an infanticidal woman who had committed suicide while in prison: "This woman, who was unable to restrain the murdering hand against the body of her own child, inexorably struck down herself by an identical pathological psychic process. And human society, which had condemned to infamy the unhappy and apparently denatured [*snaturata*] mother, never gives a thought to the fact that it alone is responsible for the two homicides by virtue of its denatured juridical concept of criminal responsibility of women in the state of maternity" (10). Any other causes habitually given for such a disorder, such as the fear of birth or the desire for honor, were for the gynecologist merely secondary factors. Maternity itself constituted the real cause of infanticide, to the extent that it produced in woman what Pazzi referred to as an *"intossicazione gravida"* (1913d, 5): "If gynecology had already determined that menstruation could produce irascibility, illogical actions, memory disturbances, a fantastic imagination, romanticism, morbid vanity, theatricality, eroticism, mendacity, and suggestibility, one can only imagine the effects wrought by childbirth!" (Pazzi 1913a, 16).

Pazzi detected on the scientific horizon an "unstable weave of biological transformations," transformations that women underwent and that had important consequences in the legal domain (1913c, 4). Once the pathology of women's "genital apparatus" was made a subject of the law, the clear consequence would be woman's legal nonresponsibility, for gestation led to an inhibition of will that in turn led to infanticide, a causal chain that explained the inversion of maternal instinct. The task, therefore, of the criminal gynecologist was to articulate a specifically feminine right founded in woman's natural right. Such a right had to adequately reflect the facts established by science, thus putting an end to "the age-old opportunism" that had viewed maternity as a natural fact devoid of all danger. In Pazzi's view, the feminine personality was enslaved to a psychophysical organization that was more labile than that of man. Infanticide thus had little to do with honor; it was more frequent among single mothers not because the latter desired to save their honor but merely because they tended to be alone during the delivery of their children. Married women, who were always under the supervision of others during the births of their children, could be restrained from those same criminal acts that were bound to be produced by their physical condition. To prove his point, Pazzi reminded the reader that cats and dogs, after all, ate their placentas and thus satisfied their instinctual urges to kill their litters. Women, of course, were denied this option. Maternity, then, was fraught with risks, being the locus of a fundamental feminine instability, precariousness, and insidiousness. Maternity was fragile because, on its own, without intervention by the gynecologist, it was incapable of preserving the destiny dictated by woman's nature. Pazzi's was a vision of maternity founded upon the sacrifice of the individual in favor of the species and as such marked the end of a vision of Italian society based on liberal ideals.[11] While for Ferriani the cause of infanticide lay in society and the seducer, and for Lombroso in the simultaneously created and repressed effects of modernity, for Pazzi's gynecological criminology it was nature itself that was monstrous. Woman became here the embodiment of nature's irrationality and thus was removed from the domain of social laws.

But thank goodness for the clinic! Pazzi proposed as the most important measure against the risks of maternity not just the birth of the clinic, but the clinic of birth. Though not completely abandoning legal reform, where he favored creating specialized courts competent to judge in matters of gynecological delinquency, he had a particular affection for the maternal sanatorium. The *"ginecomio morale"* was to be a specialized female reformatory for those mothers who had committed either abortion or infanticide. These institutions were to be designed to strengthen the psychic personality of women, to reeducate the sexual instinct, and to teach maternal sentiment and domestic virtues, all in order to shape the sons of the fatherland and the civil norms of human society. Pazzi advocated a forced naturalization of woman's behavior, noting both woman's overly natural *and* her unnatural constitution. "The woman who does not know how to dominate the stimuli of the sexual instinct, who has weakened the sentiment on which is founded the complete and marvelous function of maternity . . . and does not feel any pride other than that of vain competition in the domain of economic and civil rights, who prefers personal egotism to the sublime sacrifice of the feminine soul . . . , she is a woman who is socially dangerous and juridically not responsible for impulses that are contrary to her natural temperament, to her special sentiments" (Pazzi 1913b, 5).

Twenty-five years later, though the political and ideological coordinates had changed significantly, Vincenzo Mellusi repeated almost the same words. Mellusi's *Madri doloranti: L'incosciente nella dinamica del delitto* is one of the last major texts in the post-Unification period to be dedicated to mothers who kill their children. Mellusi considered himself a positivist, rejecting the notion of free will, as well as abstract systems of law and right, in favor of a "positive" determination of individual causes and motivations as seen to inhere in the concrete life-histories of criminals themselves. Unlike the earlier positivist criminologists, Mellusi explicitly aligned his own criminology with Christian principles. In her figuration as a *"mater dolorosa,"* the infanticidal woman was once again presented here, right at the center of the fascist regime, as a Christian or pseudo-Christian symbol of redemption, and thereby she furnished proof that new scientific methods of mothering could coexist with the mysteries of Catholic motherhood.

Justice, in this view, was not to be understood as the cynical hatred that lies at the basis of "tragic vendetta," but rather as an informed diagnosis leading to a health-producing therapy. Mellusi advocated a new law and justice that was to be consistent with both Christian morality ("the sweet and holy word of pardon") and a system of social therapeutics ("the coordination of biological and social factors)" (1937, 240). The resultant *"pietà della legge non scritta"* (the mercy of unwritten law) was to become the basis for his critique of abstract law, and hence for a postliberal elaboration of criminological doctrine. "Abstract right," he writes, "is a collection of arid notions and is incapable of addressing pain. Positive right must be a melancholy vision of life; it must be the fount of forgiveness and rehabilitation" (xii). Two figures were central to the functioning of such a new, unwritten law: the infanticidal mother and her melancholy theorist. "When maternity becomes the center of rights and morals, beyond marriage and prejudices, the unwed mother will be able to appear as the heroine in a drama of sacrifice and pain" (293). The theorist of this new justice was to extend a helping hand to the infanticidal mother and, in sharing and giving voice to her shame and pain, write her melancholy history of fall and redemption.

"To my mother with the love that conquers death"—so reads the dedication that prefaces his 1937 volume. Poised between the mother's love and the child's death, Mellusi, who has outlived or conquered his own mother, seeks to distinguish between two loves, female passion, on the one hand, and maternal sentiment, on the other. Both loves lead to the undoing of law, the first because it always produces a crime, and the second because it must lead to the sublation of all codes of law, to the pity of the unwritten law. And both loves are grounded in nature, thus rendering difficult the theorist's task of isolating one from the other, for "what is a code of law when it is confronted with human nature? And when we observe love turning into a crime, we are shocked and ask ourselves: Where is the truth? Where the lie? Thus we come nearer to the mystery with the illusion of deciphering the millenary enigma of sphinxlike nature" (xiii).

As part of such an act of deciphering, Mellusi renames nature the unconscious. Positivist criminology had, in his view, discounted the role of the unconscious not only in the genesis of crime but in affective life more generally. The unconscious, Mellusi holds, is not merely the negation of conscious perception, but one of its inferior levels, and, similar to the tip of an iceberg, conscious life rests on a vast submerged and unknown terrain. The unconscious is an accumulation of atavistic experiences and hereditary leftovers, as well as a reservoir of all those perceptions that are registered in the human brain. Unconscious thoughts are rendered conscious by their progressive assimilation on the part of the mind and by the gradual penetration by collective, that is, cultural and scientific, intelligence into its hidden forces. The process of making conscious the unknown terrain of the unconscious is how Mellusi defines evolution. Evolution comes about through the coordination of biological and social factors predicated on the subordination of the activity of external causes to the activity of internal systematization. Evolution is synonymous to self-regulation (240). While the unconscious is dominated by uncontrolled *emotions* or passions, conscious life is defined as a self-regulating balance of *sentiments*. "The normal state of affective life is given . . . by a condition of relative calm and thus of relative affective indifference. Sentiments are not only regulators of all psychic life; they are also and especially self-regulators. Each sentiment acts by regulating the activity of other sentiments; . . . at the end of this activity a relative and temporary calm is established, thanks to which the action is maintained on a middle ground" (80). Self-regulation appears to be linked, then, to the struggle for existence as a form of adaptation to social existence, and as such generates social altruism (105). Emotions or passions, on the contrary, must be understood as symptoms of a failed adaptation, of an individual's inability to conform to external circumstances (80).

And yet the process of self-regulation is fraught with difficulties. For one, the struggle for existence, or adaptation, is itself a form of egotism (52), and thus passion's conversion to altruistic love is at least problematic. In addition, conscious life "is not a faculty but an extremely variable mode of existence of psychic processes" (96), because conscious life remains founded in and is energized by unconscious passions. Therefore, even in the best of circumstances human sentiments are inevitably besieged and unsettled by unconscious forces. The "bacteria of crime" (97) are always already present in the most self-regulated of individuals, and in everyone there is to be detected at least a trace of egotistic atavism. Crime is the shadow that haunts civilization itself (292); it is the product and symptom of the unconscious. Thus, it is the duty of the anthropologist, the psychologist, the doctor, and the artist to ferret it out of obscurity and explain it.

Crime is thus by definition an act performed unconsciously; it is the result of a malfunction in the self-regulatory or inhibitory function of consciousness. Two factors cause interference in this inhibitory function, though Mellusi will prove that they are in fact one and the same cause: disease (the primary example he furnishes and elaborates on is pregnancy) and passion. The distinction between unconscious and conscious is, in fact, gendered, even if—and this constitutes the motor of Mellusi's argument—it is not immediately obvious what the gender lines are. While disease will be heavily weighted as the province of women, it appears that their passion, at least in certain forms, founds social altruism and thus conscious life. In man, Mellusi claims, love is always transitory and extrinsic to his being and therefore egoistic and closely bound to his deeper involvement with the struggle for existence. For woman, on the other hand, passion has profound and altering organic effects. Her love is intrinsic and altruistic. While for man love is an "excretion" that leaves no trace in the body, in woman it eviscerates itself in her organism. The difference between the sexes is absolute, and equality between men and women an impossibility. It is woman who creates and nurtures the affective ties between family members and therefore between members of society: "not only is the natural bond between mother and child at the origins of collective life, but it is also socially and juridically the only secure one" (47). In other words, male egoistic survival and self-regulation are not sufficient; they must be supplemented and sustained by a bond inscribed within the maternal body. Yet, while Mellusi views the maternal bond as the original and sustaining principle of collective life, he does not for that understand it as a secure and reliable guarantee. To begin with, it is hardly natural, or at least not biologically determined. Maternity implies a suffering and a renunciation at all levels, because it is independent of an organic state (48). It is, in fact, a psychic state and, as such, subject to the transformation from instinct into sentiment. It is only as sentiment, as psychic maternity, that maternity becomes indestructible. Without this transformation, it may reawaken unconscious organic instincts and the imagination (70). When maternity is an effect of a pathological eroticism in conflict with social norms, then maternity turns into a poison, a form of intoxication, no longer a vaccine against social rebellion (53). Maternity is a nightmare that weighs on all women: when a woman is pregnant or nurses her child, she is as if ill, and it is only the most heroic of women who manage to transform this nightmare into social altruism and the propagation of the species (41). If it were not for such heroic transformation, the mother would disappear in favor of the woman who puts her egoistic sexual passion before the requirements of social existence. Thus, "the woman who cannot dominate the stimuli of the sexual instinct, who has weakened the sentiment that lies at the basis of the complete and marvelous maternal function, who exhibits a weakening of her natural prerogatives, who puts personal egotism before sublime sacrifice is morally sick, physically prejudiced, and legally irresponsible" (158).

Such an inversion of maternal sentiment is most commonly present in the act of infanticide. Indeed, infanticide is the prototypical symptom of the relationship between unconscious and conscious life, for infanticide is the result of intense amorous passion and of the instabilities built into social existence itself. Infanticide is a form of transitory madness, a loss of control that must transform itself into an act. The infanticidal woman cannot, under the influence of her condition, remove herself from a dominating unconscious thought, that of a crime. She succumbs to an atavistic, egoistic impulse, to an automatic action, an "illness of the will" (131). Hence, for Mellusi, infanticide is not merely a sociological problem of honor, but one produced by the state of a woman's pregnancy as a result of sexual passion. Honor is here transformed into a fixation; it too is part of the woman's illness of the will. Infanticide is not a crime but a form of insanity that can take many forms. It can produce complete amnesia of the act, or it can be committed in total lucidity. In the latter case, that of "reason in madness," infanticide is produced by a doubling of the woman's personality. The woman knows she is mad, but she has acted under the influence of *autosuggestion.* Indeed, she has come dangerously close, in her madness, to the self-regulating system of socially well-adjusted subjects. Here, maternity points both to a nature that regulates itself, a psychic existence that has transcended nature and makes society possible "beyond the law," and to a nature that is denatured and lawless because it is not self-regulating.

Mellusi's answer to infanticide is the protection of maternity. By this he means not economic and social measures geared to the defense of single mothers, but instead the moral education of women to instill maternal sentiment as *self-regulation.* In an extensive project of mental hygiene, Mellusi proposes a system of social prophylaxis, including earlier marriages, maternal sanatoria, "crime clinics" for the rehabilitation of puerperal mania, and psychotherapy. Hence will arise a new law and justice, a *"pietà della legge non scritta,"* that will cohere with Christian norms of forgiveness: people will hate not Mary Magdalene, but the evil that resides within her. The melancholy son who has outlived his mother will extend his helping hand to the infanticidal mother—that victim of false passion who has tried to gain her pleasures despite her suffering and shame—and take her through his own writing of her passion beyond the law and toward redemption.

Consequences: The Birth of the Welfare Mother

The maternity clinic for birthing and the maternity sanatorium for the construction of maternal sentiment constituted the favored solutions for many contemporary observers to a woman's sociobiological shortcomings. Such institutional solutions to the problems of illegitimacy, abandonment, and infanticide were nothing short of revolutionary. First and foremost, it signified that unwed mothers ceased to be forbidden objects of study. While the Catholic Church had insisted on the anonymity of the unwed mother, by the end of the century policy makers converged to expound the idea that it was unwed mothers who were most deserving and in need of state support. Italian administrators and legislators began to argue that women should be forced to recognize their children and shoulder the care for them. The message was thus from the outset a contradictory one: state institutions were to actively intervene in the private lives of mothers, but were then to turn them over to their (private) fates or to what Mellusi called self-regulation. As Esposito has put it, modern biopolitics dictates that the subject can protect his or her proper identity only by a self-division between "interior and exterior, private and public, invisible and visible." Biopolitics requires that the subject become "at the same time as visible and as hidden as possible" (2003, 116). Mothers were thus "impossibly," as Raffaele Romanelli has called it, commanded to be free (1988, 10).[12] The primary goal was to turn unwed mothers, first, into useful objects of scientific investigation and regulation and, then, into private subjects who would, miraculously, return to the family and out of sight of the public eye.

In an age when few women gave birth in clinics, it was above all gynecologists and obstetricians who were eager not only to obtain statistical information about births and birth's dangers, but also to educate women to raise their children according to the scientific prescriptions of medical discourse. The medical establishment lobbied for closing the wheels and reforming the foundling hospitals on hygienic and medical grounds. One legal battle was fought with particular vigor against the Church: the retraction of the single mother's anonymity. Though the legal battle was not won until Mussolini's accession to power, a series of regulations were passed between 1870 and 1922 that effectively undermined the letter of the law. These regulations were directed at three social categories in particular: prostitutes, midwives, and wet nurses. These three social groups shared, in the doctors' view, two fundamental and interrelated characteristics: their physical and moral contagiousness, and their ability to market a good by virtue of their sex. It was through containing such sexual-economic contagion that the medical profession sought to construct a tight ring around the unwed mother, prying her away from the market economy of sex, and restituting to her her honor. Nowhere is this containment, this tight ring around the sex of woman, better expressed than in the stylized photographs that accompany her official registry in the state (see figs. 5.2 and 5.3).

Figure 5.2 "Biographical Chart" (ca. 1880).

Maternity hospitals had existed in Italy already before Unification. However, women committed themselves only with great reluctance and under extreme duress, because it was a well-known fact that a fifth of all delivering mothers died there of puerperal fever. Given these mortality rates, puerperal fever was, as Gianna Pomata has argued, the

Figure 5.3 "Biographical Chart" (ca. 1880).

factor that most discredited obstetricians in the public eye (1980, 501). Supporters of the theory that puerperal fever was contagious suspected that doctors themselves were its major carriers, and they thus advocated abolishing the clinics, replacing them with home birthing under the supervision of midwives. Indeed, until the 1890s, midwives were decidedly winning the battle against obstetricians. By the last decade of the century, however, public opinion had clearly begun to shift in favor of using hospitals and doctors. The discovery of antiseptic practices brought with it not only a new technical efficacy, but carried also, according to Pomata, social and symbolic weight: antisepsis guaranteed not only the victory over contagion, but also an insuperable difference between midwives and doctors.

Furthermore, puerperal fever could be linked by analogy to another form of contagion, that of syphilis, and especially to the transmission of syphilis through nursing. In the name of the war against syphilis, a campaign was waged for hygienic control over nursing, requiring the creation of reports on unwed mothers and wet nurses of abandoned infants, as well as the direct medical intervention in the nursing practices of poor women.[13] Such intervention was both ideological and political, for the direct intervention in nursing practices had the support of the police through the regulatory measures passed between 1860 and 1888 against prostitution. Availing themselves of the 1860 Cavour Regulation to control prostitution, which gave any police agent the right to denounce any woman as a prostitute and thus subject her to a forced medical examination and, should she be found syphilitic, to send her to a so-called *sifilicomio,* doctors began to apply similar regulations to unwed mothers and wet nurses (Gibson 1999).

Puerperal fever was transformed, one might say, into the more general category of puerperal mania, a term that now carried both biological and moral connotations. Contagion made possible a symbolic analogy between wet nurses and prostitutes, because both were viewed as providing a service to private persons in return for money by virtue of their biological capacities as women. The first brake on "mercenary nursing" came with the 1887 Nicotera Regulation that stipulated that a child be admitted to a foundling institution if and when the mother had proven that she was healthy, in other words, not syphilitic. The regulation, in the form of a decree, was not only the first governmental action that contravened the law against maternity suits, but also one that explicitly linked the promiscuity of mercenary nursing to the sexual behavior of single mothers. Thus, prostitutes, wet nurses, and single mothers came to be linked, as Pomata has argued, via an analogy of sexual promiscuity and contagion, whereby it was doctors alone who could, through the act of regulation and control, guarantee the circulation of "clean merchandise." Contagion, according to Pomata, came to be the analytic lens through which women were viewed in those instances where a norm was transgressed but where that transgression could not be morally sanctioned, because it would enter into conflict with other social requirements. Because the moral infraction was constituted by a woman's promiscuous use of her body in mercenary form within a commodity economy, it was impossible to *directly* prohibit women from lending sexual services, particularly when those services supported other interests. The medical profession was to mediate between two mutually contradictory social requirements: they were *both* to facilitate commodification and to prohibit it by classifying women as the primary agents of contagion. Between 1888, with the deregulation of prostitution, and the 1901 and 1918 regulations concerning the sanitary control of wet nurses, the link between prostitution and wet-nursing had become firmly established and made possible, through the creation of what Donzelot calls a vast tutelary complex, the regulation of women's transgressive behavior. The unwed mother, in particular, was now viewed as a primary vehicle of contagion, and the only solution to such contagiousness was her withdrawal from the sexual and monetary market. By the end of the nineteenth century, it became a requirement for unwed mothers to nurse their own children and, indeed quite paradoxically, they were to be paid for it when necessary. Thus was born the Italian welfare mother, and while her certificate of "syphilitic immunity" permitted investigation into her past, economic subsistence for nursing led to the regulation of her present and future. The new welfare mother was allowed no lapses (other illegitimate children), and she could not live in an unmarried state with the father of her child. No woman could withdraw from her socially imposed maternal duties after World War I, when regulatory measures became stable norms, and after 1923, when they became law.

SIX

In a Dark Continent: Cesare Lombroso's Other Italy

Cesare Lombroso was the explorer of a dark continent, of a space peopled by monsters, madmen, criminals, prostitutes, and spirits, and whose very appearance to Lombroso proved that the past had the capacity to return to the present in the form of what he called atavism. Lombroso's continent was a primitive, nocturnal one, in his imagination as black as Africa or Sicily, as the night of dreams, or the dimly lit scientific laboratories where he devised experiments in order to call forth spiritual beings. Lombroso accessed this continent through a specular, mirroring gaze that—perhaps despite himself—had the capacity to make his objects look back at him. The discovery of his scientific objects was the result of an inward glance at his own body, at Italy, at modernity, where the haunting Other took its place from within the depths of a personal history. And in the process, what Lombroso discovered was an uncanny double of Italy, the "other side" of the project of making Italians.

Lombroso's Style

Lombroso would always experience the objects of this gaze as something dreamlike, hallucinatory, as a kind of mirage. In his diary entry of April 1854, he writes,

> I remember very well the time when I saw myself in a mirror and became conscious of my presence—it awakened in me the most vivid curiosity. I was between 4 and 6 years old. . . . I have observed in myself all the stages of the most diverse manias: hypochondria, manic behavior, lipemania, dementia. Ever since I was four, I feared that I would be drafted. Then I invoked the angels (at age 8). I suffered from all kinds of fears when going to bed and turning off the light; the fear of thieves kept me from sleep at the slightest noise. I believe to have all the ills of which I hear speak. . . . I think I am impotent, that I have a hernia, that I am an idiot. (1932, 4–5)

In his last book—the one that provoked the most opprobrium for Lombroso, because it was dedicated to the scientific investigation and verification of spiritualistic phenomena—Lombroso writes: "In psychical matters we are very far from having attained scientific certainty. But the spiritistic hypothesis seems to me like a continent completely submerged by the ocean, in which are visible in the distance broad islands raised above the general level, and which only in the vision of the scientist are seen to coalesce in one immense and compact body of land, while the shallow mob laughs at the seemingly audacious hypothesis of the geographer" (1988, xvi–xvii). Such mapping activity was not easily distinguished from madness, as Lombroso himself hinted in his 1895 text on graphology. Thus, in one of his cases of graphomania, a man "drew geographical maps by copying the spots on the ceiling of his room and reproducing these spots accurately on a piece of paper; he believed he was making the topographical plan of his dominions, and jealously held on to his drawing, just as a good proprietor would do with the maps of his lands" (1895, 145).

And finally, in 1871 Lombroso saw the skull of the brigand Villella and here he made a monumental discovery, one that would lead to the writing of the work that would make him famous, his *L'uomo delinquente.* The discovery triggered in him an illumination, even a hallucination, that over time became the object of much rewriting on Lombroso's part. Despite all the illumination that Villella supposedly afforded, Lombroso felt compelled to turn him from a rather minor criminal into a monster, whose dangerousness thereby became almost a measure of the importance of Lombroso's discovery itself. At the end of his life, and perhaps in an effort to get as close as possible to an ever-receding object, he even claimed that it was he himself who performed the autopsy on Villella. In any event, this is what Lombroso discovered: in the place where there should have been the occipital median spine, in other words, there where there should have been something, instead there was a concavity, a void, Villella's now famous occipital fossa. According to Lombroso, the presence of such a concavity made Villella's brain resemble that of a fetus in its third or fourth month of development or, alternatively, the brain of a bird, a fish, or an inferior lemur. Villella's fossa, this *nothing* opened up for Lombroso a whole new terrain, whose boundaries were drawn by the possibility of making an analogy between criminals, the insane, and prehistoric races. In 1895 Lombroso recollected this fetishistic replacement of nothing with something, by stating that "at that moment, the whole idea of my future work rose before me like a picture" (2004, 65–66). Similarly, at the Sixth Congress for Criminal Anthropology in 1906, Lombroso would state: "At the sight of that concavity, all of a sudden I saw a vast plain under an infinite horizon, and it illuminated the problem of the criminal, who had to reproduce for our times the characteristics of primitive man down and beyond to the carnivores." Hence was the criminal born, that category of man who was an atavistic throwback into the past of civilization and the missing link between savagery and madness. Significantly, it was this void or negative feature of Villella's brain that, for Lombroso, explained the presence or positive aspect of all the other physical features of the born criminal; his *protruding* cheekbones, his *voluminous* jaws, his *excessive* beard. From nothing comes excess—this discovery lies at the heart of Lombroso's work. Villella's skull—which Lombroso preserved on his desk until his death—functioned, he himself stated, as his totem, his fetish, a filling of the void that he named "criminal anthropology."

Lombroso's work has produced a series of contradictory reactions. Readers of his vast opus—both during Lombroso's lifetime and still today—are quite certain that the impact of his work was profound, both for the history of Italian positivism and for modern theories of deviance and crime. Indeed, it is hard not to see Lombroso towering behind Foucault's sweeping project of tracing the genealogy of a biotechnics of and over the body that constitutes modern relations of power. The idea of the born criminal and the theoretical edifice erected upon him have been regularly understood as an essential component in the development of a disciplinary gaze, intent on marking a body in its criminal essence and thus making it available to a disciplinary network that is largely independent of the individual's actual deeds. Here, the shape of an ear or a chin or the shifty glance of an eye already determine a subject in his or her future actions, thus rendering onto the body a capacity that no "free will" can withstand and that in fact makes this will obsolete. And yet—seemingly—readers of such a theory cannot withstand the power and force of Lombroso's argument, as they oddly succumb to Lombroso's determinism with a determinism of their own. Lombrosan anthropology is seen as capable of determining the course of events; it has ineluctably led to the development of a science of policing and then straight into fascism and—beyond—to the continued powers of a panoptical society.[1]

But this is not the full story. There is something in Lombroso's theory of radical determination that renders unto his theory an excessive quality. Not only is Lombroso himself altogether too garrulous; his objects are equally so. Lombroso's objects, his discoveries, talk back. They produce a kind of choral effect of such power that they are able to make Lombroso's own voice join them to produce a popular language, a language of the people. It is the popular or populist quality of Lombroso's writing that makes him so indigestible as science. When Lombroso's readers react to his *style* as uncontrolled and uncontrollable, it is this quality of "talking back" to which they are reacting. Lombroso is routinely viewed as profoundly antitheoretical, illogical, and unsystematic. Even while he was still alive, Lombroso was the easy target of ridicule, criticized not only by his opponents but also by his own disciples.[2] The latter, while continuously paying homage to their revered *maestro,* set about right away to bring order into his thought, to create a system that on its own was fundamentally unsystematic. They thereby made Lombroso usable for their own needs. Lombroso's style—his bad writing, his lack of system, his obsessive accumulation of "facts"—turned him into an easy target of a debunking that made him into the propagator of a pseudoscience whose basic presuppositions could not hold up to closer inspection.[3]

Lombrosan science, stated Giovanni Papini and Giuseppe Prezzolini in 1906, can be recognized by two signs: bad writing and the fact that it has "discovered something": "When one watches a man like Lombroso developing percentages on the basis of four cases; gathering information about great men from infamous biographical dictionaries; mixing together the latest neighborhood news with European genius; multiplying criminal types in order to avoid exceptions and criticisms; transforming possible explanations of particular cases into universal ones; confusing effects encountered in certain geniuses with the causes of any form of geniality—how can one gain or maintain faith in the Italian school of anthropology?" (cited in Villa 1985, 22). And Enrico Morselli, generally a supporter of Lombroso and an active participant in his "Italian school," remarked in—of all places—the *Denk-*

schrift dedicated to Lombroso at the end of his career: "Perhaps Lombrosan doctrine would have achieved a fuller and less contested victory if somewhere its founder had, for example, defined *genius, talent, mental superiority;* if in other places he had clearly indicated the meaning of his successful, though not very nosographical term *mattoide;* if in other places he had made precise, in respect to clinical and pathological requirements, the value that he assigned to *epilepsy*, to *degeneration*, to *atavism*" (cited in Villa 1985, 23).[4]

Pure indexicality, the fact that the shape of an ear or a protruding jaw points to a criminal personality, was understood by everyone from the very beginning as an obviously inadequate foundation of criminological theory. Lombroso's appeal derived from elsewhere, to wit, from commonsensical or popular-superstitious knowledges that tell us that a shifty, sly look or a certain dress indicate that there is a criminal lurking about. And even popular knowledge itself warns us that appearances deceive. Gramsci, in attempting to capture the Lombrosan appeal, thought that his school was so obsessed by criminality that its members turned it into a *Weltanschauung:* "They fell into a strange form of abstract 'moralism,' to the extent that good and evil were something transcendent and dogmatic, but that concretely coincided with the morality of the 'people,' with 'common sense'" (Gramsci 1975, 1:327). "What is important in order to understand the Lombroso phenomenon," Ferruccio Giacanelli writes, "is the 'style' in which he deals with any problem and that allows him to build a relationship with a new public that has come into being for the first time in Italy since Unification. . . . Polemical, vivacious, and simplifying, he seems to address himself to readers beyond the circles of experts" (2000, 13–14). According to Annamaria Cavalli Pasini, what accounted for Lombroso's success was a style of writing that knew how to appropriate for itself the opinions, the prejudices, and stereotypes of contemporary culture, such that his writing was far more journalistic and sensationalist than scientific and technical (1982, 84). And Luigi Guarnieri views Lombroso's most interesting and enduring feature as located in the scientist's narrative style, one that furthermore expresses a national style: before Freud, "Cesare Lombroso is the greatest narrator of the nightmare, the novelistic apex of horror, the encyclopedist of crime, insanity, and perversion. . . . Lombroso's only real rival is Richard von Krafft-Ebing, author of the extraordinary and astounding *Psychopatia Sexualis*. . . . [However, the two authors' works] could not be more different: as much as Krafft-Ebing is square, aseptic, nitpicking, and impermeable to the picturesque (in one word, Teutonic), Lombroso is approximative, confusing, anecdotal, colorful (in one word, Italian)." It is for this reason that Lombroso made his most enduring mark on late nineteenth-century literature: Zola, Hugo, Poe, and Doyle outside Italy, and within, Praga, Boito, Tarchetti, De Amicis, and Carolina Invernizi, among others (Guarnieri 2000, 117–18).

What if there is a close connection between Lombroso's determinism and his style, a relationship between what he perceives to be the readable, indexical signs of the human body and the writing *surface* on which this body is enveloped in order to gain iconographical meaning? What if there exists an intimate connection between Lombroso's (bad) style and the fact that he discovered something? It is central to state right at the outset that Lombroso was never terribly interested either in law (which, indeed, he sought to marginalize) or in the detection of criminals. He was, however, fascinated by the normativizing, because classificatory, capacities of language, and for this reason Lombroso took the question of style extremely seriously. Style is the language through which the body expresses itself to the extent that the body only exists as a form of writing. The styled body is for him both textual *and* textured, ornamented, or clothed. On the one hand, the Lombrosan body is a blank surface upon which cultures have left their historical messages in the shape of signs and symptoms, a body that can be subjected to a scientific reading. On the other hand, this body is nothing but an envelope, an infinitely pleated or folded texture that is structured or styled around not exactly an emptiness, but an infinite possibility of multiplying types. In his last writings, Lombroso refers to such a body as a *moulage,* or mold; it is nothing but an ornament, a kind of mannerism in the Baroque sense of the term.

The question of style has in no small measure come to be linked to a notion of the Baroque, and I take the idea of the fold or pleat from Gilles Deleuze's discussion of Leibniz, for whom matter "offers an infinitely porous, spongy, or cavernous texture without emptiness, caverns endlessly contained in other caverns: no matter how small, each body contains a world pierced with irregular passages, surrounded and penetrated by an increasingly vaporous fluid. . . . A fold is always within a fold, like a cavern in a cavern. The unit of matter, the smallest element of the labyrinth, is the fold, not the point which is never a part, but a simple extremity of the line" (Deleuze 1993, 5–6). Lombroso's infinite pleating of the subject accounts, then, for his uncontrolled and uncontrollable taxonomy of the subject that will leave, for example and in an exemplary manner, the category of the "normal" subject an empty one. Abnormal types, Giorgio Colombo writes, multiply into infinity, to the point that each one of them becomes a category unto himself: "Where did the normal man go? The passage from the class without individuals to the individual without class is not immediate; one may say that Lombroso works on it all of his life, but in the end . . . the scientist is almost compelled to multiply categories and finally even positively to exalt difference" (2000, 228).

While Lombroso was greatly interested in the normativizing capacities of language, he never provided a definition of the norm. Instead, he reconceived norms as social forces that have the capacity to regulate themselves in a field of relations that he viewed as practices of writerly inscription. The Lombrosan norm is, then, merely an empty placeholder and consequently in itself unable to provide a positive value system. Interestingly, Lombroso would always say that those who uphold the norm are those afflicted by "mysoneism," that is, by a hatred or fear of the new. Only the refusal of normativity, that is, *deviance,* both makes a norm possible and constitutes the motor for historical change. This deviance from the norm, furthermore, can be accessed only through signs, never facts or deeds. Therefore, as Renzo Villa has put it, "The scientific nature of Lombrosan semiology appears . . . to be guaranteed precisely by the fact that it is a convention: by the fact, that is, that those and not others are the elements, the signs that conventionally are attributed to criminal deviance" (1985, 270). The relationship between signs and their objects is conventional, popular, in other words, normative. Nevertheless, common sense is also an *effect* of the relationship between signs and their objects. The tautological circularity of Lombroso's thought constitutes the ground of its ideological effect, its capacity to shore up common sense as scientific knowledge. And yet his thought shifts this ground and thereby creates a new terrain where the objects of Lombroso's discovery have the uncanny power to strike back at the scientific gaze.

During the nineteenth century, the discursive and institutional politics that centered on making subjects placed themselves along the fault line of a divide that I would name a practice of identification, on the one hand, and a discourse of identity, on the other. I use the term *identification* not in its psychological or psychoanalytic sense, but rather in the sense of detection, as denoting a politics whose purpose is to single out individuals in order to first classify them and then either to exact upon them institutional constraints or to incite them to programmed patterns of behavior. Such a politics is at once individualizing and classificatory, specific and taxonomic, and it encompasses that *savoir* referred to by Foucault as the two-pronged disciplines of biopolitics and governmentality.

The second term, the *discourse of identity,* is perhaps more elusive, insofar as it rests less comfortably in institutional practices—even though, because the question of identity cannot be separated from relations of power, such practices are not to be excluded. While the politics of identification hinges in a first instance on forms of visualization, that of the construction of identity depends and elaborates upon the problem of writing, upon a project that posits subjectivity as something grounded in acts of inscription and in practices of writing, because such acts require not an externalized and externalizing visualization but the construction of a self posited as internal and private. If identification is the primary object of the Foucauldian project of tracing the genealogy of modern forms of power in a biopolitics of the observing gaze, then the politics of identity may be fruitfully thought of in terms of Derrida's grammatological project of the critique of metaphysical self-presence. In fact, Derrida's deconstructive project interrogates, as it does for Lombroso, both an anthropology and a style. While in *Of Grammatology,* anthropology provides Derrida with his object of analysis; the deconstructive project itself is explicitly aligned to a question of style. Derrida does this in the context of his argument that there is no linguistic sign prior to writing:

> The concept of sign is here exemplary. We have just marked its metaphysical appurtenance. We know, however, that the thematics of the sign have been for about a century the agonized labor of a tradition that professed to withdraw meaning, truth, presence, being, etc., from the movement of signification. Treating as suspect . . . the difference between signified and signifier, or the idea of the sign in general, I must state explicitly that it is not a question of doing so in terms of the instance of the present truth, anterior, exterior, or superior to the sign, or in terms of the place of the effaced difference. Quite the contrary. We are disturbed by that which, in the concept of the sign—which has never existed or functioned outside the history of (the) philosophy (of presence)—remains systematically and genealogically determined by that history. It is there that the concept and above all the work of deconstruction, its "style," remain by nature exposed to misunderstanding and nonrecognition. (1974, 14)

It is this idea of Derridean deconstruction as style that interests me here, not, however, in order necessarily to counterpose it to the Foucauldian gaze of investigation, but—on the contrary—to think through how, in the writings of Lombroso, these dual projects of interrogation, the "agonized labor" of the last century or so, regarding the analysis of the sign, have constituted a tension but also a site of mutual support. The question, then, is whether Lombroso's stylistics, his narrative about differ*e*nce, is not also linked to the deconstructive stylistics of differ*a*nce.

The term *style* derives from the Latin *stilus* (an instrument of engraving, etching, or writing) and the Greek *stylos* (pillar or column). Style thus refers simultaneously to the instrument and process of making an object, and to the finished form itself. In its dual signification, then, style is the *trace* or the imprint left by an artist on his or her object and the chain that binds the object, in more or less direct fashion, to its creator. In this sense, style is intimately connected to the process of identifying works of art, of attributing them to their makers; style functions as a signature, and thus makes possible the periodization of works through history and the division of objects between authentic and inauthentic, between early and late, between one author and another. Given this close relationship between style and identification, Berel Lang remarks, stylistics would have gone out of business much more quickly if fingerprinting—or for that matter, DNA analysis—had been invented earlier (1979, 177).

Beyond its indexical quality as identification, style is also closely related to the constitution of the modern individual and hence to the idea of free choice. It was, of course, this free choice that Lombroso and his school contested as a factor in the constitution of modern subjects. We recognize style as a trace in an object that can be referred back to an artist's own particularity or individuality, a trace put there by the artist when other choices, conscious or unconscious, may have been possible: "The stylistic trace in the finished artifact should be called one 'alternative' among the set of conceivable alternatives at that place or moment in the work. The artist chooses and his choice registers as an alternative—that is, a stylistic feature" (Chatman 1979, 230).

While style seems, then, something analogous to human character or personality, to a quality that is personal and specific to an individual, in itself style has no meaning; it is merely an *external manifestation* of meaning. Style only testifies to the fact that meaning is present: "The style cannot be said to stand for anything. . . . It may *identify* the artist, but identification is not signification" (Chatman 1979, 230). Style bridges and simultaneously opens up a gap between identity (as that which is particular to the subject) and identification (as that which points to the fact that identity is present). Style is thus a paradoxical phenomenon. It is that element that is most intimate, most personal or individual transferred to an object by an artist, and yet in itself it has no meaning. It is the product of a free choice—a certain writing may have a style, states Leonard Meyer, but someone's breathing pattern does not (1979, 23)[5]—and yet it is also subject to a series of limits and constraints. "Style is a replication of patterning, whether in human behavior or in the artifacts produced by human behavior, that results from a series of choices made within some set of constraints" (Meyer 1979, 21). Because an individual style exists only as a system of stylistic behavior or production, stylistic analysis is thus inherently synthesizing and classificatory, and at the same time, indexical and individualizing. For this reason, there exist essentially two trends in stylistic analysis: while art historians and musicologists, for example, tend to think of style as a *common* element that shapes an aesthetic period (as in: the Baroque style) or a unity of an artist's oeuvre, literary critics tend to conceive of style as a *deviation* from the norm, as a kind of aesthetic and artistic idiosyncrasy or originality. Lang points to these two trends of stylistic analysis by linking style to the process of repetition as constitutive of both identification and identity:

> Repetition is not an act which follows instrumentally from a source already completed or integral, a means employed; the source is by way of being determined in the act, the determination itself communicating its incompleteness. This connection intrinsic to the human source would explain how it is that style is not something apart from the object of which it is the style; it suggests, furthermore, why the discrimination of style provides not merely a label or moment of identification (as would any pattern which is repetitive backwards) but a means of experiencing, of seeing how, from the inside out, a particular identity is asserted in the first place. The repetition that adheres to style, that identifies it, is thus not the *product* of a person or of that person's vision, something made by him, but the articulation of the person or vision itself. (Lang 1978, 728)

Here, in a reading of three of Lombroso's texts, I want to link the relationship between identification and identity to the question of (cultural) style, which I understand here as a form of repetition founded in difference. This means not only that I submit Lombroso's work to a deconstructive reading, but—and perhaps more importantly—that I see the Italian anthropologist's importance and significant impact on Italian nineteenth-century social thought as grounded, first, in an extensive interrogation of the function of writing in the constitution of modern subjectivity and, second, in the fact that the question of style has been intimately linked to what it means to be a modern subject. Lombroso's work has traditionally been read and interpreted as solely an extended and continuously revised attempt at identifying those social subjects that fall beyond the norm. As such, he is understood as one of the founding fathers of a politics of identification that takes the visual characteristics of subjects as the base upon which subjects may come to be categorized and contained. Indeed, already in his own lifetime, Lombroso came to be known as the "anthropologist of the compass and the scales." He has gone down in the annals of history as the inventor of the "born criminal," that type of person who acts in a criminal manner because his or her body, which has become stuck in an earlier, primitive stage of the evolutionary process, dictates that the criminal must do so. Born criminals may be picked out of a police lineup through a series of symptoms or signs that are inscribed on the criminal's body: small(er) skulls, protruding chins, pointed ears, thick eyebrows, a higher or lower sensitivity to pain, to name only a few. But also—and here we begin to move into a very different form of classification—a shifty look, leering grins, so-called moral insanity, a tendency to vagabondism, idleness, overdeveloped or underdeveloped libidinal drives, and, by extension, the tendency to use the argot of the criminal sects, to write on prison walls in hieroglyphics and other contaminations of alphabetic writing, to be prone to religious fanaticism, or to tattoo one's body.

What appears to govern the born criminal, in other words, is his or her biological constitution. In this scenario, criminal behavior is from the very outset predetermined and beyond the capacities of the will to do otherwise. Though such a reading cannot be contested, I would like to propose another reading of Lombroso's work, one that places him into a logic of the grapheme, a logic that does justice to what I see as the overwhelming textual quality of Lombroso's extensive opus. This reading also makes Lombroso into a producer of what Gramsci has called the national-popular, even if Lombroso becomes this—given his self-placement beyond the norm—from the outside, or from an inside that simultaneously marks itself as always already "other." I would, therefore, want to take seriously the quality of his writing, of its prolix nature and even its seeming incoherence, as well as his perception that writing itself has something to do with the constitution of the individual. Lombroso's style, I argue, is a fundamental aspect of his thought and not a "mere" supplement to theories that must be culled from underneath his writings. Lombroso's work must be connected to a broader discourse that, in the late nineteenth century, circles around the aesthetic difficulties of not simply representing the body but also giving it meaning. I have said that Lombroso's objects, the criminal bodies he studied, looked back at him and that they merged their voices with that of their scientist. I would add here that they do this as written or inscribed signs, and that they produce a graphomaniacal effect in which Lombroso is swept up in the very process of describing this effect.

Detail Effects

In his justly famous essay "Clues: Roots of an Evidential Paradigm," Carlo Ginzburg has outlined a genealogy of a model for the "humane sciences" that he calls "conjectural" or "evidentiary." The texture of this paradigm is comprised of a venatic, divinatory, or semiotic method that takes the individual case as its unit of analysis and that must, because it cannot reproduce causes, deduce these causes solely from their effects. Disciplines such as medicine, history, archaeology, and art criticism, and eventually psychoanalysis, rely on such a method, because it is by signs, clues, and symptoms that such sciences seek to draw their conclusions. These signs function within such disciplines as divinatory or predictive mechanisms of the past. While reality is perceived as opaque, it may nevertheless be penetrated with the help of signs. Ginzburg opposes this paradigm to that of the natural, Galilean sciences, where the individualizing perspective is excluded in favor of an empirical and mathematical method that relies on abstraction, quantification, and repetition of phenomena and on the suppression of sensory, bodily data that would necessarily point to the individuality of both the object and the investigator (Ginzburg 1989).

In order to provide a scientific foundation for itself, and in that move, the evidentiary paradigm during the nineteenth century sought to give individual characteristics an additive representation by generating a political arithmetic referred to as statistics. The quantification of individual differences led not to a break with the evidentiary or conjectural model—it did not create a science based on the reproducibility of causes—but instead, as it compiled data regarding a population's birth, procreation, and death rates, it constructed models geared to predicting the behavior of individuals in the future. The calculation of probability, Ginzburg states, "was an attempt to give a mathematically exact formulation of problems which had also confronted divination in a radically different form" (113). And as Ian Hacking has stressed, statistical knowledge gave rise not to a transfer of natural laws to the realms of culture and society, but, on the contrary, to an *erosion* of determinism or causality. The nineteenth century discovered, Hacking argues, that the past does not determine what happens next. Two processes contributed to this erosion. First, "it became possible to see that the world might be regular and yet not subject to universal laws of nature. A space was cleared for chance." Second, statistical laws, the enumeration of people and their habits, came to be expressed in terms of probability. Laws of probability "carried with them the connotations of normalcy and of deviations from the norm. The cardinal concept of the psychology of the Enlightenment had been, simply, human nature. By the end of the nineteenth century, it was being replaced by something different: normal people" (Hacking 1990, 1).[6] It is important to stress the fictional, if not phantasmatic, nature of this normality. The famous "bell curve," or "normal distribution," was used to define the normal human and normal human behavior because its shape matched the shape of large aggregates of social data, not because the normal human could be found in reality. The norm functioned, in other words, as a kind of center of gravity, as a point of convergence not found in actuality. And while Adolphe Quetelet's "deviant" from the norm demonstrated that such deviance was only established mathematically, in other words, as the result of determining social forces, both the deviant and the normal man were inevitably the result of a fiction, or what Silvana Patriarca has called an "allegory of difference" (2003, 18). Allan Sekula comments, "While [Quetelet] admitted that the average man was a statistical fiction, this fiction lived within the abstract configuration of the binomial distribution. In an extraordinary metaphoric conflation of individual difference with mathematical error, Quetelet defined the central portion of the curve, that large number of measurements clustered around the mean, as a force of normality. Divergent measurements tended towards darker regions of monstrosity and biosocial pathology" (1986, 22).

The clustering of "normal man" at the tip of the bell curve and the geographical expanse of deviance on either of its sides, the construction, in other words, of a *standard deviation,* forced statistics back into the evidentiary paradigm, and thereby it left open the question of *who* exactly belonged to those outside the norm. According to Allan Sekula, this led at the end of the nineteenth century to the merger of statistics and optics, of the social sciences with visual representation; according to Ginzburg, it led to new systems of identification founded in a now thoroughly bourgeois notion of propriety and property. It led, in other words, if we take these two observations together, to the creation of the police file.

During the same period, the evidentiary paradigm also made its appearance, Ginzburg tells us, as a new art-historical method of connoisseurship, as the detective novel, and as psychoanalysis. In the mid-1870s a series of articles appeared in Germany that proposed a new method of attributing the old Italian masters. The articles were signed by one Ivan Lermolieff, and they created quite a stir, as in all of Europe's most important museums, the new method proposed sensational new identifications. Lermolieff eventually revealed his true identity: the Italian Giovanni Morelli (1816–1891), Risorgimento patriot, physician, senator of the new Italy, personal friend of Francesco De Sanctis, and art connoisseur. His method of art attribution is still today referred to as the Morellian method.

When looking at paintings, Morelli claimed, a general impression is not sufficient, for, as the Italian proverb stated: "*l'apparenza inganna* [appearances deceive]" (1995, 110).[7] It is, instead, only by gaining a thorough knowledge of the characteristics of each painter that one may distinguish a great master from his imitators or even criminal fakes. Every great artist sees and represents form and color in his own distinctive manner. They are distinctive characteristics of the artist because they are not the result of accident or caprice but derive from internal conditions. According to Morelli, the source of painterly knowledge must be the work itself. "Is there any document more likely to inspire confidence," he asks, "than that bearing the master's own name on a picture, which we call in Italian a *cartellino* [written label, caption]?" However, art and gallery directors are merely duped by these *cartellini,* "just as in the good old days, when passports were an absolute necessity, the police were taken in by the greatest scoundrels" (112). The true site of the *cartellino* is, therefore, not outside the work in the form of a supplement, but part of the body of the work itself.

Morelli's method consists in attributing works by reading the details, identifying art works by the help of marginal signs, in a process that resembles the work of a physician, diagnostician, or anatomist: "Among Sandro Botticelli's characteristic forms I will mention the hand, with bony fingers—not beautiful, but always full of life. . . . It is just this hand . . . which reveals the northern master, for the thumbnail is a form which we never find in Italian pictures, though it frequently occurs in northern paintings. . . . Look at the hand in this portrait, particularly at the ball of the thumb, which is too strongly developed, and at the round form of the ear" (Morelli 1995, 113–14). It is the trivial detail that betrays the artist, his own particular ways of painting a fingernail, a thumb, or an ear. Morelli's treatises on art, writes Edgar Wind, "look different from those of any other writer on art; they are sprinkled with illustrations of fingers and ears, careful records of the characteristic trifles by which an artist gives himself away, as a criminal might be spotted by a fingerprint . . . any art gallery studied by Morelli begins to resemble a rogue's gallery" (cited in Ginzburg 1989, 97).

Morelli's method was soon discredited; it was judged overly materialist, crudely positivist, and mechanical. Critics could not find in Morelli's work an aesthetic engagement with painting. Croce found the approach overly sensual in its response to detail, and these details were furthermore placed out of context (Croce 1946, 15). But it was precisely this attention to detail as the artist's truest, because involuntary, expression that made Morelli's method so modern. Many critics have noted that Morelli's identification of inadvertent gestures as a sign of authenticity links the Italian art critic not only to the crime novel but also to psychoanalysis. Morelli's attention to the detail of ears was fundamental to the physician Arthur Conan Doyle's method for solving crimes on the basis of the involuntary traces left behind at the scene of a crime by the perpetrator. In Doyle's 1893 "The Cardboard Box," for example, it is in fact the shape of an ear that betrays the criminal (Doyle 2001).[8] And in Sigmund Freud's own incursions into the art history field, Morelli is directly cited as a source for Freud's interpretive efforts. In his 1914 essay "The Moses of Michelangelo," Freud says that Morelli "had caused a revolution in the art galleries of Europe by questioning the authorship of many pictures. . . . He achieved this by insisting that attention should be diverted from the general impression and main features of a picture, and he laid stress on the significance of minor details . . . which the copyist neglects to imitate and yet which every artist executes in his own characteristic way. . . . It seems to me that his method of inquiry is closely related to the technique of psycho-analysis. It, too, is accustomed to divine secret and concealed things from unconsidered or unnoticed details, from the rubbish heap, as it were, of our observations" (Freud 1959c, 222). For Freud, as for Morelli, then, individuality is linked to a style, a style that is furthermore considered involuntary or unconscious, that takes place as detail, and that fundamentally *betrays* the specificity or individuality of an author or subject. The analyst, when confronted with this style, must exact upon the object of investigation a process of detection, in the same way one detects a crime. Such an investigation, or divination as Freud states, is then to reveal the secret and concealed things that together make up the particularity of the individual and his or her history.

Ginzburg has rightly asked whether such divination can be called science, not because the results of such an investigation are too impressionistic, but rather because it is a method that posits the specific, the individual, concrete detail as its unit of analysis. In other words, this is a method of investigation that has at its foundation not rules established on the basis of the identity of a certain number of cases, but rather the *differences* that can be called forth when attention is paid to the signifying capacities of the detail. Ginzburg, not coincidentally, evokes here the act of falling in love as the act of overvaluing marginal differences. Freud too spoke of the act of falling in love as transferential desire, the buried desire for the authority of the father, and as the "narcissism of minor differences," that is, as the desire to constitute the self on the basis of an Other that is banished from the contours of a now purified, authentic self. In both cases, however, a knowledge comes into being that is predicated on the existence of the loved *and* refuted object that has the power to return, to speak, and to betray the porous boundaries of the subject in its relation to an outside.

Graphology

Cesare Lombroso belongs to the universe of the evidentiary paradigm. His name must therefore be inserted next to those of Morelli, Doyle, and Freud, for he, too, was obsessed with the ears, fingers, and hair of the modern subject, with all those involuntarily betrayed details that allowed him to read this subject's specificity and history. And for him, as well, all the evidence leads to the discovery of (a) crime. Indeed, he chose the world of crime as his particular field of analysis, a world constituted by the meaning generated by details, by those individual phenomena capable of furnishing him with a model of reading, one that constructs a case, a *"caso,"* understood both as a case history but also a history of chance. The Lombrosan detail as the sign of a crime dislodges or, in Ian Hacking's terminology, *erodes* the structure of causality and determinism from within its own system and thereby constructs what I would call a kind of atavism of everyday life. The greatest sign of atavism is, according to Lombroso, the fact that the sign, and in particular the graphic sign, is both separated from its signified *and* dangerously or criminally identical to it. In this sense, Lombroso's graphology engages an economy of signs structured by the logic of *differance,* that is, by a logic that addresses both difference and deferral. This is the fundamental paradox of Lombroso's thought: the criminal body gives evidence of two contradictory messages. On the one hand, it proves that crime is constituted by a sort of graphism, by the separation between signifier and signified, by signs that are independent of meaning. Here art exists for art's sake; the message transmitted by the criminal body is that there is no message beyond that of the material presence of the sign itself. On the other hand, to the extent that it is the body that speaks, Lombroso also grounds this sign in a radical determinism of the object itself. In this latter sense, he attempts to create an adequate distance between signifier and signified, to generate a form of bodily representation that would both make the body coincident with its capacity to function as a sign of itself and yet allow the sign a stylistic space that is free of its own embodiment. It is said, not coincidentally, that the dying Lombroso spent his days copying out Chinese ideograms, in an effort to return meaning to graphic representation.

Lombroso's *Grafologia* was published in 1895. I begin with this text, for it not only takes up the themes detected in Ginzburg's evidentiary paradigm, but also because it is typical, if not exemplary, of the Lombrosan project and style. Among such characteristics one may count the usual overflow of examples and the virtual absence of analysis or interpretation beyond the commonsensical or intuitive, as well as the power that these examples exert on his own text, a power that turns his examples into a virtual parody of the method itself. The work constitutes—in its form and content—an interrogation of the meaning of a *signature,* a Morellian *cartellino,* placed there by Lombroso himself on his own work, and hence a telling mark of his own identity. To this end, he concludes his introductory chapter on the history of graphol-

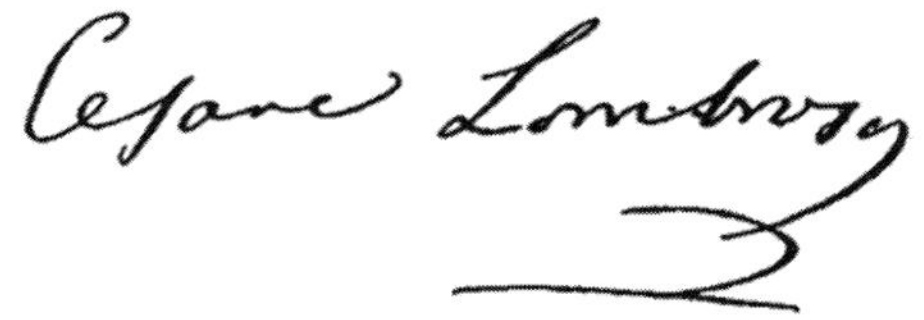

Figure 6.1 Lombroso's signature. (From Cesare Lombroso, *Grafologia*).

ogy by adding his own signature to the text, inviting thereby an analysis upon himself and his theory, as he will then set it forth in the text to come (see fig. 6.1). What is particularly striking in this text is the extent to which Lombroso's own language falls progressively silent and cedes its place to the signatures of "normal people," "geniuses," and "deviants"; the book has no conclusion, but simply the telling writing of the Other. And here Lombroso has no hesitation in adding to his own signature those of a broad array of Italian and European intellectuals and politicians, along with those of an assortment of criminals, hysterics, and insane.

As in all other sciences, so Lombroso begins, Italians were the first to put the original intuitions of graphology down on paper. He cites Camillo Baldo's 1622 treatise on handwriting and character, along with that of the Neapolitan physician Marco Aurelio Severino. However, after that point, apparently, the Italian contribution ceased and was taken over by "foreigners"—Gottfried Leibniz, Johann Kaspar Lavater, J-B Delestre, Jean Hyppolyte Michon, and so forth—as is "typical" of Italian scholarship. What this history of graphology proves, according to Lombroso, is that handwriting transmits the individual character of a man or woman. According to Leibniz, for example, handwriting almost always expresses in some way or other our nature, unless of course—and this exception is crucial—the writing is the product of a calligrapher or professional scribe, that is, of a mere copyist. Whether Italian or foreign, however, after the initial discoveries by scientists of the importance of handwriting, there was a hiatus, a kind of latency period, and the question was not taken up again until the late nineteenth century with Adolphe Desbarolles (a famous soothsayer) and Michon (an abbot), among others (Lombroso 1895, 1–8).

The first characteristic of handwriting is, Lombroso states, its unconscious and involuntary nature, and he cites here the work of Marey and Mosso, who had both been engaged, as I already discussed, in registering the body's invisible and unknown movements. Both had given us an idea "of the various emotional states of the mind and of the conditions of intelligence and of attention; as also some of our neuropathological conditions that may be studied through accurate, graphic observation" (11). Therefore, he concludes, "man, when he writes, *is completely present in his pen,* and therefore also in his hand that acts as writing's intermediary instrument; so that, if a word is the instantaneous manifestation of thought, writing is an equally immediate, if not *more* rapid translation of this same thought" (12; my emphases). And therefore, "unconscious movements are produced by the hand of the subject who writes. . . . Just as language translates psychic impressions in a determinate form, so also does writing, which is another process of translating thought" (12). The site of such writing is located in the left side of the brain, furthermore, because most people—with the exception of idiots and savages—write with their right hands. Differences in handwriting must be attributed to the complexity or overdetermination of the transmitting machinery of the brain: "The apparatus is so complex that it certainly must present a certain number of imperfections, and they each influence writing, thereby differentiating them one from the other. " Furthermore, "the brain is not always in a normal state: it can be in a particularly excited state, according to temperament; and certainly, the brain of an artist is not as calm as that of a mathematician who, in turn, has a brain not as calm as that of a mere copyist, etc." (16). Handwriting can therefore tell us something about character, a relationship that is thus not related to the hand per se—because the same telltale signs could be found in an individual writing with his mouth or foot—but in the psychic and physiological makeup of the writer.

Having established the connection between writing and the individual, Lombroso proceeds to outline the general characteristics of the graphological project. Graphology is made up of an investigation into general signs, particular signs, and the general, interpretive results that may be gleaned about character. General signs refer to the overall picture presented by a handwriting, such as slant, size of letters, regularity, and so on. They are also immediately accessible to the eye: "They are, we should say, the characteristic traits of writing that can be embraced by a glance and be applied with a little good sense and practice without the need of deeper studies" (18). The study of particular signs, on the other hand, requires a more careful and prolonged observation: it requires the study of individual characteristics, such as how *t*'s are crossed and *i*'s dotted; such study requires tact and connoisseurship, in order to apply more general rules of graphology to the particular, individual aspects of writing. Finally, the results refer, according to Lombroso, to observations that tend to be more speculative, because they require individual psychological intuition. And therefore, because "writing, like words, is a manifestation or immediate translation of thought, it is natural that a very slow and uncertain handwriting should belong to an ignorant individual. . . . Punctuation can be executed only by an act of our will; so that when it is absent or misplaced, and when the lines intersect, this is a sign of a confusion of ideas in the person tracing the letters" (19). From this Lombroso concludes that graphology rests on broad scientific bases. It proves, when one inspects the samples provided, that Ferrero (Lombroso's son-in-law), Sighele, and De Amicis are, respectively, a highly intelligent man, a vigorous sociologist and a man of considerable *scioltezza*. Even more, there are times when the habitual and unconscious movements of a person appear "as if photographed" in this person's handwriting. And so, in a move that is typical of his own style, Lombroso moves from the positivity of fact to intuition, from determinate causes and their effects to the vivacious style of a dotted *i:* "All these peculiarities, which seem so empirical, have not only a positive foundation, but almost an instinctive one, so much so that a person newly initiated into graphology . . . can describe the total picture of a person, his or her way of walking, acting, etc., and all that from the vivacity of the dot on his *i*'s" (29).

Lombroso dedicates exactly two pages to the question of interpreting graphological signs and their meaning. They are interesting, however, because they provide an exemplary account of his general theory of how to translate disparate and individual signs into a system of signification. Though undertheorized, these two small pages are remarkably similar to Freud's pages in his *Interpretation of Dreams* on the uses for dream analysis of symbolic images (Freud 1965, 385ff). When interpreting graphic signs, Lombroso warns, it is necessary to pay attention to the fact that our body responds at times in a similar manner to different stimuli, and in turn, also in a different manner to identical stimuli. The examples he gives are those of crying for joy or laughing in response to pain. In a like manner, graphological signs can have one meaning, as also their opposite. Thus, simple handwriting is the sign of "great banality, lack of imagination, as also superiority and simplicity" (30). How then know the true meaning of a sign? The answer lies, for Lombroso, as always, in locating the sign in its wider context. Signs are to be interpreted with the "same method by which we distinguish a happy laugh from a spasmodic laugh: by the mimicry that precedes and follows it. One must, when one studies a handwriting, take note of all the signs and then move by process of elimination" (31). And again later, and here making a direct link to anthropology, he states: "Just as in anthropology pointed ears, long fingers, a threatening look, or protruding cheekbones on their own are insufficient to give us the *type* of the born criminal, and often do not even make us suspect its presence, so also in handwriting one particular sign is not enough . . . to provide us with the accurate psychic examination of an individual" (101). It is, therefore, only in and as a whole that signs function and give meaning. David Horn has pointed out that it was these seemingly infinite possibilities of combining individual features that ultimately frustrated Lombroso's efforts at constructing types or typologies (2003, 15–16). Lombroso's struggle to find the appropriate metaphor for describing the relationship between body and signs made him, for instance, compare the total picture to impressionist painting: "examined from up close, they seem shapeless blotches, while at a distance they prove to be wonderful" (Lombroso et al. 1886, 34). He also compared it to music. The following are the words of his daughter Gina Lombroso-Ferrero, one of the greatest of Cesare's systematizers: "Just as a musical theme is the result of a sum of notes, and not of any single note, the criminal type results from the aggregate of these anomalies, which render him strange and terrible, not only to the scientific observer, but to ordinary observers who are capable of an impartial judgment" (1915, 49).

In *Grafologia,* Lombroso applies a similar method: for example, he states, snaky lines in handwriting could mean, as Michon had already noted, diplomatic ductility. And indeed, it does so in the case of Senator Negri; but the same trait also appears in the handwritings of many peasants. Is the peasant then a diplomat? No, of course not, he is a . . . simulator! Simulators, it appears, present a particularly difficult problem, because they, by virtue of this trait, escape the possibility of an accurate reading: they are both "mere" copyists and criminal fakers. And so, in a characteristic Lombrosan slippage from character as letter to character as individual, Lombroso writes: "Dissimulators, liars, hypocrites, often have an illegible handwriting. Because of this dissimulating character, it is almost impossible to determine their characters" (78). Just as with the liar Pinocchio and his protrusions in the form of a growing nose, Lombroso's signs are essentially unstable indicators of meaning. The cross of a *t* and the dot over an *i* bind together the diplomat and the peasant in a fundamental uncertainty.

Lombroso's analysis is thus condemned to a kind of oscillation between a specific sign as the expression of individuality (or criminality) and the assignation of meaning as the result of a general type (automatic copying). Signs can exist only by virtue of a parentage, and yet such relations can come into being only as the result of signs in their capacity to show difference. The type cannot be determined as a result of the data themselves: it preexists them in the form of common sense and forever eludes the investigator. Ultimately, the graphic sign is nothing but a sign of itself, that is, of the process of writing per se. All graphic signs must then model themselves on that *particular* graphic sign that is excluded as an exception from Lombroso's analysis at the very outset: the sign produced by the "mere copyist" or scribe, who, by virtue of Lombroso's logic, is surely the greatest simulator of all. What truly fascinates Lombroso, states Villa, is the capacity on the part of the signifier to lead an autonomous existence, separated from all signifieds (1985, 275). Therefore, Lombroso can only order writing into commonsensical notions of the kind that state: "The letter *O* is not very important" (48); "The letter *L* is very frequent, and therefore important" (44); "The letter *H,* rare in Italian, gives this letter little importance, and then only when capitalized" (42). This is indeed "intuitive knowledge" in Ginzburg's sense, knowledge that founds itself in folklore and proverbs and that is inevitably anthropocentric and ethnocentric.

It is also unsettling, because it is a knowledge that always verges on madness and because it functions to silence Lombroso's own critical voice. The book ends not simply with a takeover by his examples and the shutdown of an order-giving commentary, but it also becomes increasingly crowded by the writing of the insane. The book explodes into a veritable uncontrolled and uncontrollable graphomania. Graphomaniacs, Lombroso tells us, are perpetual frequenters of courts and they are the despair of lawyers; their handwriting is generally dense and elongated, as also clear and small. The graphomaniac Lombroso, the author of innumerable printed pages and despair of many lawyers, finds ultimately a kind of exhibitionistic pleasure in the display of the printed page. Not coincidentally, the final sentence of his dairy reads: "*piacere a veder i propri scritti stampati* [the pleasure in seeing my own writings in printed form]" (Lombroso 1932, 39). The passage from "proper" individual writing to that of print should give us pause, for it

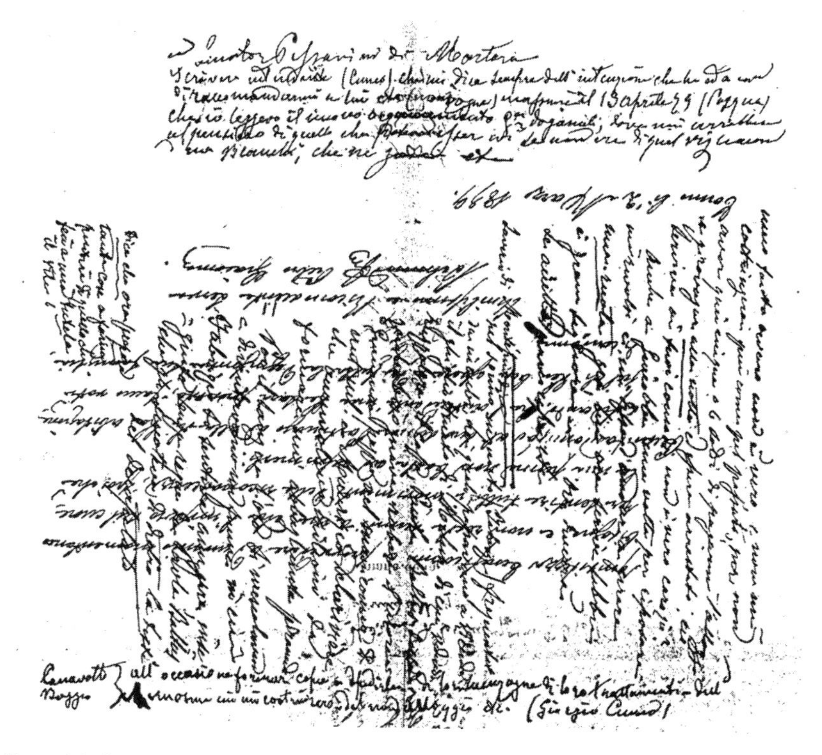

Figure 6.2 The writing of the insane. (From Cesare Lombroso, *Grafologia*).

signifies, as with the writing of the copyist, the emergence of a *type* in its double meaning, and also all the pleasure that such typology may afford.

The graphic spread or sprawl extends into other areas as well. Writing cannot be here contained within the civilizing influences of alphabetic writing and its translation into type. The visual aspects of the text, that is, their *typeface* or setting, take over and convert the alphabet into pictures. Lombroso's graphological apparatus is a writing that returns to its (atavistic) origins in picture making at the hands of the insane (see fig. 6.2), one that Lombroso himself repeats in both the evidential apparatus of the book itself, as well as in his own body of writing (see fig. 6.3). The entire text thereby turns into a pictograph, a giant rebus whose meaning must remain unknown. All writing, both the innumerable illustrations that are scattered throughout and even-

Figure 6.3 A drawing (frontispiece) from Lombroso's diary.

tually take over the book and Lombroso's writing as well, thus become pure style, pure illustration or ornament.

The Tattooed Body

A child is amoral. A Papuan, too, for us. The Papuan slaughters his enemies and devours them. He is not a criminal. But if a modern person slaughters someone and devours him, he is a criminal or degenerate. The Papuan covers his skin with tattoos. . . . He is no criminal. The modern person who tattoos himself is either a criminal or a degenerate. There are prisons in which 80 percent of the inmates have tattoos. People with tattoos not in prison are either latent criminals or degenerate aristocrats.

These words could have been written by Cesare Lombroso, but they in fact come from Adolf Loos's 1929 essay "Ornament and Crime" (1998, 167). They appear on the opening page of Loos's text, which is dedicated to showing that the evolution of culture is synonymous with the removal of ornamentation from the objects of everyday use. Lombroso, too, linked the existence or absence of certain forms of ornament to evolutionary development and to crime. Furthermore, both Lombroso and Loos make tattooing exemplary of atavistic behavior, and both oppose this practice to the simplicity of modern male dress codes: "I have been told that the fashion of tattooing the arm exists among women of prominence in London society. The taste for this style is not a good indication of the refinement and delicacy of the English ladies: first, it indicates an inferior sensitiveness, for one has to be obtuse to pain to submit to this wholly savage operation without any other object than the gratification of vanity; and it is contrary to progress, for all exaggerations of dress are atavistic. Simplicity in ornamentation and clothing and uniformity are an advance gained during these last centuries by the virile sex, by man, and constitute a superiority in him over woman" (Lombroso 1896, 793). Loos states that modern man uses his simple dress as a disguise because his individuality is so strong; Lombroso sees the masculine absence of ornamentation as a clear sign of sexual superiority. Both critics echo here J. C. Flugel's idea that the history of male clothing is marked by the crucial moment of a "great renunciation," that is, by the willingness to give up bodily design in the interest of economy and the political ideals of equality and fraternity (Flugel 1950). The refusal of ornament is, therefore, modern, civilized, democratic, masculine, and individualistic because private; the indulgence in ornament, on the other hand, is atavistic, uncultured, bound to authoritarian power, feminine, and transgressive because it contradicts public decorum. What Lombroso calls a physical insensibility to pain is, therefore, the incapacity of the individual to introject civilizing norms.

Tellingly, for both Loos and Lombroso, the line that separates ornament from simplicity, crime from civilized behavior, and of course man from woman, is the body; to be precise, the inscribed, tattooed body. The body's skin is, as Jane Caplan has pointed out, the site and barrier of an *exchange,* of an interface which, in its function as envelope, gives privacy and keeps the outside out, *and* at the same time is the surface of receptivity upon which marks are left by the outside, that is, by other individuals and by the world (1997, 113).[9] By extension, the tattoo, in the words of Alfred Gell, is a "paradoxical double skin [which], folded over on itself, creates the possibility of an endless elaboration of interacting components of the social person" (cited in Caplan 1997, 113).

Caplan has traced the complex history of the tattoo in Western culture as the history of a practice that may in the Greco-Roman and early Christian periods have had a broad appeal across the social spectrum but that from the Middle Ages through the Enlightenment was linked to the practice of branding criminals, outcasts, slaves, and indentured labor. As an object of knowledge, the tattoo reappeared in European culture at the end of the eighteenth century in a nexus of complex associations. The tattoo became an object of fascination when modern states had rejected the spectacularity of great crimes, such that these states no longer tolerated the marking, branding, and exhibition of criminals in public, but instead withdrew criminals into the "privacy" of prison walls.[10] During the eighteenth century, representations of crime were still closely linked, therefore, to the logic of branding. Once crime ceased to be a public spectacle, however, its representation was textualized and therefore made private. The representation of crime, imitating the move of the criminal from the public scaffold to the private prison cell, migrated to the scientific text, and visual representations of criminals took on the function of illustration to support a textual argument (Villa 1985, 71). The scientific investigation of tattooing also coincided with the period of global expansion and exploration, with contacts (direct, physical, one might even say, epidermal) with the new world, and with the international slave trade. "It is surely not only coincidental," Caplan remarks, "that tattoos became visible in Europe exactly at the point when the commodified body of the non-European slave had become an object of unease and embarrassment" (1997, 116).

The new public interest in and investigation of tattooing led to the discovery that sailors, soldiers, prisoners, and other social outcasts, such as itinerant performers at fairs and circuses, were inscribing their bodies with writings and images. From the point of view of these observers, writes Caplan, tattooing seemed associated with men who existed at the margins of society, who furthermore seemed either too much or too little on the move and who thus tended to be idling vagabonds. Caplan has shown that the various national investigations into tattooing consistently denied the indigenous sources of the practice and instead attributed it to outside influences, for instance, to "savage" or "primitive" societies. The debate, in other words, repeated the anxieties at stake; the possibility, that is, that a national body could adorn itself with and thus be permeated or inscribed by a cultural exchange of skins through an uncontrolled process of imitation (Caplan 2000, 172–73).

The tattoo appeared, then, as multiply threatening: it inscribed the other directly on the skin, it had the capacity to create a kind of group ethos or bond between the members of marginal groups, it seemed the sign of a certain mobility of these groups, and this mobility, in turn, was by analogy related to a mobility of the meaning of the tattoo itself. Finally, the tattoo was self-inflicted, and the displacement of the old branding practices in the form of self-stigmatization performed by men on themselves was particularly disquieting. A physical mark that was neither hereditary nor involuntary but self-imposed entailed of necessity a kind of provocation, to the extent that, in its exhibitionism, it either confused meaning or turned it upside down: the tattoo was painfully inflicted on the body, but in the name of pleasure; it was a stigma worn as a badge of honor; it blurred the lines between writing and pictures; and it confused the exotic with the vulgar. It was in an attempt to respond to this "provocation" that, beginning in the mid-nineteenth century, Europe witnessed a veritable explosion of a sort of comparative tattoo studies dedicated to analyzing the national and transnational characteristics of the practice. While most analyses deemed the practice as stemming from "elsewhere"—that is, as either from another culture, civilization, or social class, Caplan has nevertheless detected differences between the various national schools. British analysts, for instance, found tattooing so common among the members of its own working classes that they were hard put to link the practice to atavism or degeneration. German observers, on the other hand, conducted their researches from within the paradigm of a *Volkskunde* and therefore looked at tattoos not only on the bodies of criminals and soldiers, but also within the milieu of popular traditions. Different were the French and Italians, who spearheaded the movement, for they linked the practice of tattooing specifically to the *modern* world of crime. They thereby made the tattoo into an object that pertained to criminological and medico-legal discourses. The French debate was led by Alexandre Lacassagne, the Italian one by Lombroso, and it was their disagreements that set the parameters of the tattoo question for the remainder of the century.

Virtually all of the research was conducted on the body of convicts, and therefore the idea of the tattoo became firmly linked in the imagination of its investigators to stigmata not only of difference, but also of deviance. In such a function, furthermore—and this was particularly the case in France—it became an identificatory mark, a sign by which the criminal could be detected. The tattoo entered the domain of police science once it was established that it was indelible, that is, that the criminal would carry his self-inflicted identification for life. Italian and French positivists alike were obsessed with tattoos. Pierpaolo Leschiutta has noted that between 1880 and 1918 more than seventy articles on the tattoo appeared in Lombroso's journal *Archivio di psichiatria* alone (1996, 81). All over Italian and French prisons, the skin of dead criminals was cut out and preserved; tattooed inmates were photographed and their tattoos reproduced on paper, collected and catalogued, and, above all, written about in police journals. Most of this work was conducted by prison guards and medical officials in the army. These officials, who all agreed that the prisoner or soldier tattooed himself because he either had too much time or because he was imitating other prisoners, themselves filled their own leisure time copying out tattoos, imitating them, and then going into print with their findings (see fig. 6.4). Caplan has recognized that a bizarre parallel universe was thus established between prisoners and guards, as the guards copied the prisoners' tattoos, and the prisoners, in turn, were virtually incited to tattoo their bodies for the pleasure of the observing scientist (2000, 164).

The main point of contention between the French and the Italian schools hinged on the question whether the tattoo was a sign of identification or, more profoundly, of an identity of the individual. Both Lacassagne and Lombroso attributed to the tattoo a certain legibility, in other words, its capacity to transmit a message. Lacassagne dubbed tattoos "speaking scars," and what these scars communicated was a specific milieu: tattoos were the materialized expression of a lack of education and of the fact that their wearers had spent time in prison. Tattoos thus traced an individual's time and place in history, and as such, they were signs of environmental factors or evidence of culture's impact on the body. Lacassagne's criminal bodies spoke, therefore, but only to the extent that they provided the blank page upon which culture could communicate its messages.

Lombroso in a sense reversed this relationship, for in the Italian's work, the body itself is the one to produce a message. The body does not receive a message, but constitutes the message itself. The Lombrosan criminal body, states David Horn, is like a book open to a scientific reading (Horn 2003, 6). Indeed, for Lombroso the relationship between text and body is not metaphoric but one of homology; just as Lombroso's textual practices, his own writings, are subject to a sort of porosity, so also his criminal body is porous and subject to being read,

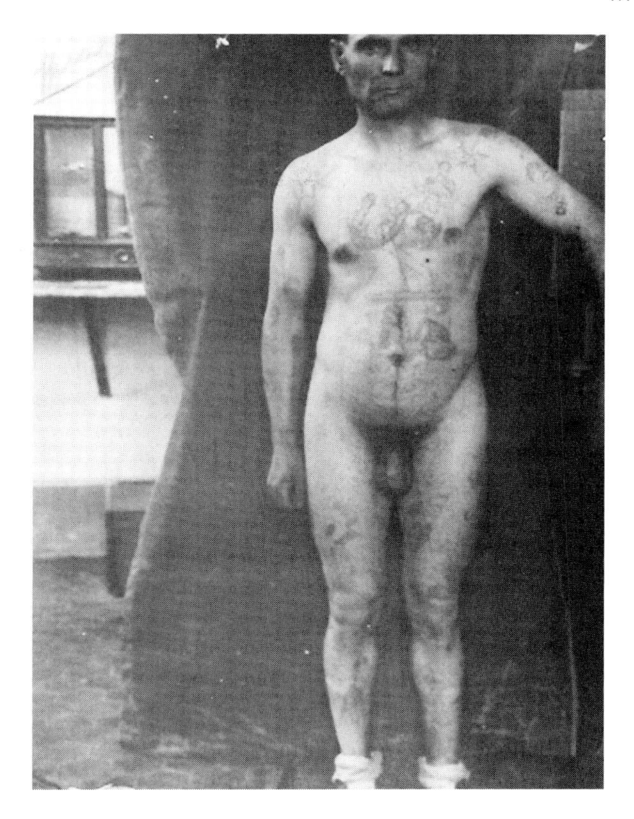

Figure 6.4 A tattooed criminal. (Criminal Anthropological Museum, Turin.)

but—like his texts—resistant and therefore only partly legible. If, for Lacassagne, tattoos speak, for Lombroso they are, first and foremost, a form of writing; and if, for Lacassagne, tattoos place an individual into a specific class and time, for Lombroso the tattoo pertains to the order of an overarching atavism, one sign among many other possible bodily signs, such as cranial deformities or protruding jaws.

Renzo Villa has remarked that the very basis of Lombroso's method is semiological, that what he always examines are the signs per se, the fact of their sheer presence and not their meaning. Lombroso is thus interested in the fact *that* criminals write and not in *what* they write. Even more strongly, one may say that for Lombroso the body is a form of writing itself. Because the writing and written body is linked in his analysis to atavism, so Villa holds, and because therefore Lombroso can only ever replicate this writing, causality, along with determinism, disappear almost entirely from Lombroso's texts (Villa 1985, 195–98). Signs combine in a history of chance encounters, and atavism functions as a kind of last instance: it is structurally necessary as an explanation, while it simultaneously provides Lombroso with a space in which to bring a multiplicity of factors into play. Atavism is both immediate, because it signifies the return of the past in the present, and yet that element that is both buried deeply in our psyche and an ever-receding referent of the body's semiotic system (Villa 1985, 167–68).

Lombroso's interest in tattoos can therefore only be secondarily attributed to the need to identify the criminal. His main concern, when he studies the tattoo, is to provide a semiological and diagnostic reading of the practice. In this sense, for Lombroso the anomalies betrayed by tattooing are exemplary, not identificatory. The presence of the modern tattoo must be explained, according to Lombroso, by two interconnected factors. First, it constitutes a form of hieroglyphic writing and, as such, participates in constructing identity in primitive societies. Second, when the tattoo is encountered in modern societies, it must be explained as an atavistic feature, because it takes primitive societies as its primary *model* of social expressivity: "Nothing is more natural than to see a usage so widespread among savages and prehistoric peoples reappear in classes which, as the deep-sea bottoms retain the same temperature, have preserved the customs and superstitions . . . of the primitive peoples, and who have, like them, violent passions, a blunted sensibility, a puerile vanity, long-standing habits of inaction, and very often nudity. There, indeed, among savages, are the principal models of this curious custom" (Lombroso 1896, 802).[11]

Tattooing is an essential characteristic of primitive humans, and, as Lombroso states, there is not a single "savage people that does not tattoo itself more or less" (801). Here he provides a long list of examples: the various African tribes who used tattoos as distinguishing marks between tribes and between genders and classes; Samoan widows who tattooed their tongues; fashionable ladies of Baghdad who tattooed their temples and lips; men of the Marquesas Islands who wore tattoos as a kind of clothing. Laotian tattooing is "very animated" (801); that of the Marquesas Island women is "drawn with remarkable fineness and perfection . . . and [constitutes] real works of art" (802). Lombroso has a particular liking for the tattoos of the "New Zealanders": here tattoos form a sort of coat of arms and they also serve the purpose of signatures. "The tattooing of the New Zealanders has found an unanticipated use in their relations with Europeans. Thus, the missionaries having bought a tract of land, the facial tattoo patterns of the vendor were drawn at the bottom of the deed, to serve as his signature. . . . Toupes, an intelligent New Zealander, who was brought to London a few years ago, insisted upon a photographer taking pains to bring out his tattoo marks as well. 'Europeans,' he said, 'write their names with a pen; Toupes writes this way'" (802).

Lombroso draws two conclusions from these ethnographic findings. First, tattooing constitutes "the true writing of savages, their first registry of civil conditions." Indeed, and repeating Nietzsche's claim that the passage into social relations is inscribed in and on the body as a branding against forgetfulness, Lombroso adds that "tattoo marks indicate the obligation of the debtor to serve his creditor for a certain time" (802).[12] Second, savage tattooing exhibits a strangely excessive, *stylistic* quality and as such is subject to *variability:* the "figures of the tattooing vary," Lombroso states, "as do the fashion styles with us." This comparison appears about halfway through the essay and is given almost as an aside. Nevertheless, it constitutes the point when Lombroso changes his focus from modern tattooing practices to those of primitive societies; it also evokes the parameters of the entire essay, insofar as it begins, as I have already noted, with the evocation of London society ladies who indulge in the fashion of tattooing, and it ends with the following words: "O Fashion! You are very frivolous, you have caused many complaints against the most beautiful half of the human race! But you have not come to this, and I believe you will not be permitted to come to it" (803).

The problem of fashion and style thus frames Lombroso's argument about tattooing, providing, in a sense, its outer garment, skin, or even stylistic flourish. But what lies at the center of the text, beneath this outer surface? What, in fact, lies beneath the enigmatic "this" and "it" that fashion has not yet come to, because its approach has not been permitted? It is not desirable, Lombroso insists at the beginning of his essay, that "so inordinate an accession to ornamentation as tattooing" should be adopted by modern society (793). This is so because—as he states—he had made an important discovery, to wit, that for more than "5,000 criminals" such a "custom is held in too great honor among them" (793). The "genuine disgust" and horror elicited by the appearance of the tattoo in the "respectable world" (803) derive from the fact that tattooing is in its essence a savage and primitive practice.

While the tattoo in savages is perhaps great art and a form of writing proper to primitive civilizations, when it shows up in criminals, that is, in modern society among "us," then the tattoo must be attributed to atavism, to the return of the past in the present: "The primary, chief cause that has spread this custom among us is in my opinion atavism, or that other kind of historical atavism that is called tradition" (800). The tattoo in the modern era is thus a symptom of atavism as tradition: "The influences of atavism and tradition seemed for me to be confirmed by the fact that we find the custom of tattooing diffused among classes so tenacious of old traditions as shepherds and peasants" (803). Conversely, tradition can only be explained as itself an atavism, as a distorted and hence inauthentic supplement to the properties of modern evolution: the tattoo "performs the services among [criminals] of uniforms among our soldiers" (803). In the very excessive nature of such a clothing, the tattoo also serves "a psychological purpose, in enabling us to discern the obscure sides of the criminal's soul, his remarkable vanity . . . his atavistic character, even his writing" (803).

It is the tattoo as a written transmission of obscurity that most firmly links the tattoo to both the atavistic return of the past and to the "soul" or essence of criminal character: "Never, I believe, had we had a more striking proof that tattooing contains real ideographic hieroglyphs which take the place of writing. They might be compared to the inscriptions of the ancient Mexicans and Indians, which, like . . . tattooings . . . are the more animated history of individuals. Certainly these tattooings declare more than any official brief to reveal to us the fierce and obscene hearts of these unfortunates" (798). The tattoo is, therefore, both a mere surface, an excessive ornamentation that has no meaning and as such must be condemned, and, at the same time, the telltale sign of an individual "soul." It is, in other words, a style, one that functions as both index and icon of the modern individual.

Criminal tattoos have a "strange frequency" but also "a special stamp" (793). They are characterized by the desire for, or rather the promise of, vengeance, by their capacity to act as secret codes and messages for other members of the criminal classes. Criminal tattoos are "a kind of hieroglyphic writing . . . that is not regulated or fixed, but is determined from daily events, and from argot, very much as would take place among primitive men" (794). Tattooing in criminals tends to cover their entire bodies, for Lombroso notes "the strange liking these curious heroes have of spreading on their body, just after the fashion of the American Indians, the adventures of their lives" (795). Criminals wear their histories on their skins, thus betraying their past and their provenance. Tattoos are souvenirs of criminality. The impulse to tattoo oneself is grounded in religious factors, in the spirit of imitation, the love of distinction "styled" as "the embroidery of the skin," vanity, vengeance, indolence and inaction, and even "the stimulus of the noblest human passions," such as love.

Despite what may appear as biological reductionism on Lombroso's part—in comparison to Lacassagne's more "enlightened" emphasis on environmental factors—I would like here to explore the implications of Lombroso's radical stress on the tattoo as writing. Caplan has noted that Lombroso so vigorously adhered to the link between tattooing and criminality because of his anxiety about the persistence of tradition or primitivism in his own, newly unified nation (2000, 165). But it is possible to explain Lombroso's insistence that the tattoo is a sign of criminality from another perspective. Pierpaolo Leschiutta has placed the Lombrosan project in direct opposition to a cultural anthropology in search of the "authentic soul" of the Italian people. Italian folklorists, such as Giuseppe Pitrè, searched for the authentic expressions of Italy's "backward" inhabitants in the popular culture of, for example, Sicilian songs or rituals, that is, in a pacific vision of Italian peasants as embodied in an *oral* tradition of nativist lore. Lombroso, on the contrary, conceived of the "Italian people" as a melting pot of an urban and therefore of a *writing* culture: as the marginalized riffraff that filled the new industrial slums, as the inhabitants of prisons and of mental asylums, as precisely those individuals that deviated from the norms of Italian authenticity. What constituted the novelty and modernity of Lombroso's investigations was, as Leschiutta states, his interest in "the readaptation and refunctionalization of traditional practices," his interrogation of "the changed conditions and new expressive forms" of modern life (1996, 4). Thus, while the religious tattooing at Loreto was for the folklorists a thankfully persistent expression of religious tradition, for Lombroso that same tattooing had to be understood as an atavism, an insistent dysfunctionality in, but also expression of, modern Italian national culture.

Lombroso's world of deviance thus opened up and laid bare in post-Unification Italy a double wound. Lombroso made evident a disquieting *difference,* an urban world of deviance and criminality, a world that he made visible through the recuperation of the detritus and rejected objects of folkloristic anthropology. As his daughter Gina Lombroso would write: "Lombroso was a born collector. . . . He was always looking at something that no one else could see . . . [and] of which no one, not even he himself, could know its value. . . . He conserved everything" (cited in Leschiutta 1996, 27). As an obsessive collector, Lombroso's was a science, as Leschiutta states, that was complex, multicentric, and sensible to stimuli and contributions that came from far away places and that prior to his collecting efforts had not been put into communication (Leschiutta 1996, 44).

Figure 6.5 Italian criminal anthropologists. (Criminal Anthropological Museum, Turin.)

Lombroso obsessively scavenged his "facts" from among the dregs of human society, and he brought them together to produce a picture or mirror of that (his own) society. This was disquieting enough, but perhaps worse was that he also discovered another wound, which he laid bare for all to see, one that belonged to the world of Italian science itself: a sort of complementarity of roles in the process of modernization between the inmate who writes on his body (and in other illegitimate and illegal places) and the anthropologist who collects these writings in his own writings (see fig. 6.5). Many critics have observed that on display in Lombroso's criminological museum are not only the products of crime, but also the discipline of criminal anthropology and indeed the anthropologist himself: part of the exhibit is Lombroso's *own* body, dedicated to the advance of science and preserved in a jar (see fig. 6.6). Lombroso is thereby eerily equalized with Villella's skull, as well as with all those other criminals who have met a fate similar to Lombroso's own (see fig. 6.7). The modern scientific method, so these bodies tell us, demands both wounding and self-wounding, the exhibition of others as an exhibition of the self. Lombroso remains here faithfully but also hauntingly bound to his objects of analysis. As one of the prison inmates would write in a poem dedicated to

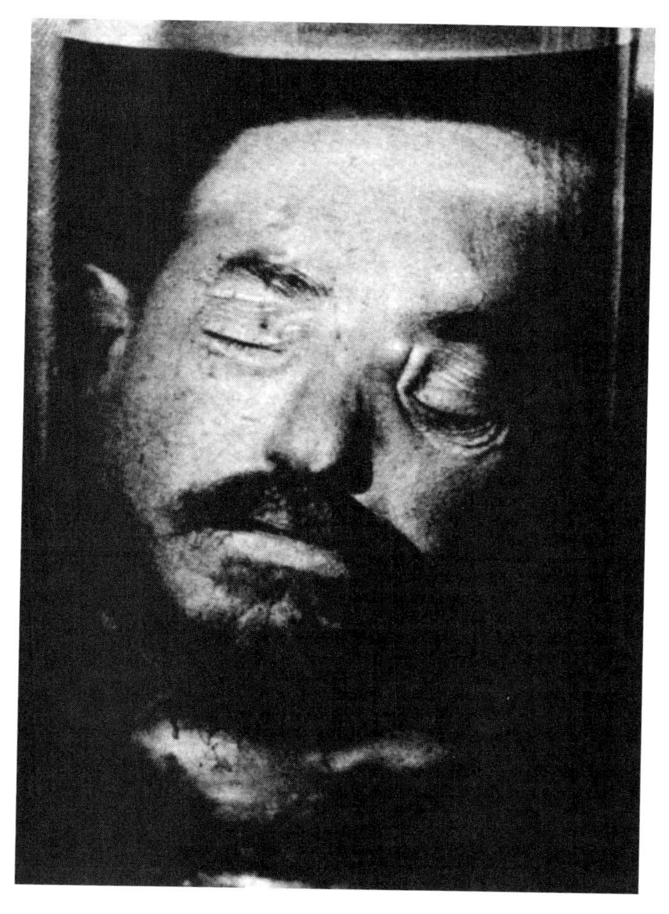

Figure 6.6 Lombroso's head preserved in a jar. (Criminal Anthropological Museum, Turin.)

Figure 6.7 Heads of criminals. (Criminal Anthropological Museum, Turin.)

Lombroso, faithfully copied out in Lombroso's *Palimsesti del carcere:* "He who comes to your laboratory will discover nothing there but traces of death: when thinking of it, he who leaves his dead skull in prison, is horrified" (Lombroso 1996, 145). Villa has stated that for Lombroso the discovery of individuality always immediately leads to the discovery of difference (Villa 1985, 87). But, one may add, the reverse is equally true; the discovery of difference also always guarantees the discovery of individuality.

Writing in an Italian prison was a forbidden act. The Italian prison system during the second half of the nineteenth century resembled, in Leschiutta's words, more Giovanni Battista Piranesi's imaginative representations than the ordered utopia of Jeremy Bentham's panopticon. Its inhabitants were overwhelmingly men and women who had violated the sanctity of private property, those afflicted by vagabondage and idleness, and a large class of literate but marginalized individuals of the tertiary sector whose culture had not guaranteed economic and social stability. Once having entered the penitentiary system, inmates were subjected to strict regulations, all geared to stripping them of their individuality. The new inmate was deprived of all personal articles of clothing, his prison shirt bore his serial number in visible stitching on the sleeve, and he was shaved and forbidden all contact with family and friends. And, as already mentioned, any form of writing was strictly prohibited.

Prisoners nevertheless wrote—their identity, their names. They wrote on the walls, in the margins of books in the prison library, on the terracotta pitchers provided for drinking water, and on their own bodies, as tattoos, where the body functioned as a sort of indelible blackboard upon which were inscribed personal histories, memories, and desires in a desperate attempt to confirm and reaffirm the presence of a self (see fig. 6.8). The masses, as also the scientific community, writes Lombroso,

> believe in good faith that prison, and in particular the prison cell, is an organism that is mute and paralyzed, or deprived of language and hands, because the law has imposed a rule of silence and immobility. But because no decree, even if backed up by force, can go against nature, so this organism too speaks, moves, and at times wounds and murders despite all decrees. Only that, as always happens when a human need is in conflict with a law, it expresses itself through means that are less familiar, always subterranean and hidden: on the prison walls, on the drinking pitchers, on the slats of a bed, in the margins of books that inmates are allowed to read so that they may be moralized, on the paper in which are wrapped their medications, even in the mobile sands in the open walkways, even in the clothes where they inscribe their thoughts in embroidery. (Lombroso 1996, 37)

That today we know anything of this submerged history of a writing in order to be somebody is due to a large extent to Lombroso's obsessive collection of these prison writings, assembled in his 1888 *Prison Palimpsests,* Lombroso's own, idiosyncratic version of a later Italian *Prison Notebooks.* What Lombroso collected and published in this book were forbidden objects, criminal objects in a double sense: they were produced by criminals and they were transgressive because they violated prison regulations. From thence derived, as Lombroso states, "a collection of autobiographies that lack pretense" by a race that lives next to us, without us being aware either of their presence or their characteristics that make them different from ourselves (1996, 37). Lombroso is eager to demonstrate how prison writings exhibited "not only the criminals' hearts that have thus laid themselves bare in documents," but also the totalitarianism of the "carcerary organism, created, just like penal laws, by a priori systems without serious and experimental study, and that therefore had to produce its own bad fruits" (38).

Figure 6.8 Water pitchers from prison: "God! Religion! Justice! Big words." (Criminal Anthropological Museum, Turin.)

These words come from Lombroso's preface to his *Palimsesti del carcere*—a book, as he states, written only for scientists—and they betray a certain anxiety about replacing, with his own words, the words of the prisoners themselves; he would prefer a *spontaneous* and unmediated emergence of their writings, an impartial and dispassionate presentation where Lombroso's own voice must necessarily fall silent. Nevertheless, his own voice must at times be present, for criminals "do not know how to speak the language of honest men, even less do

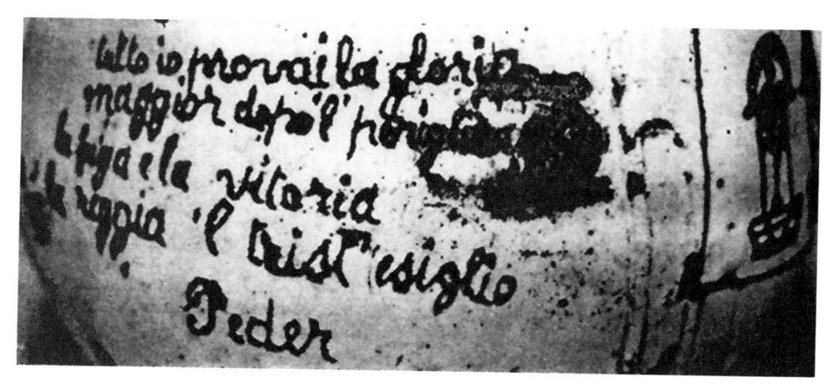

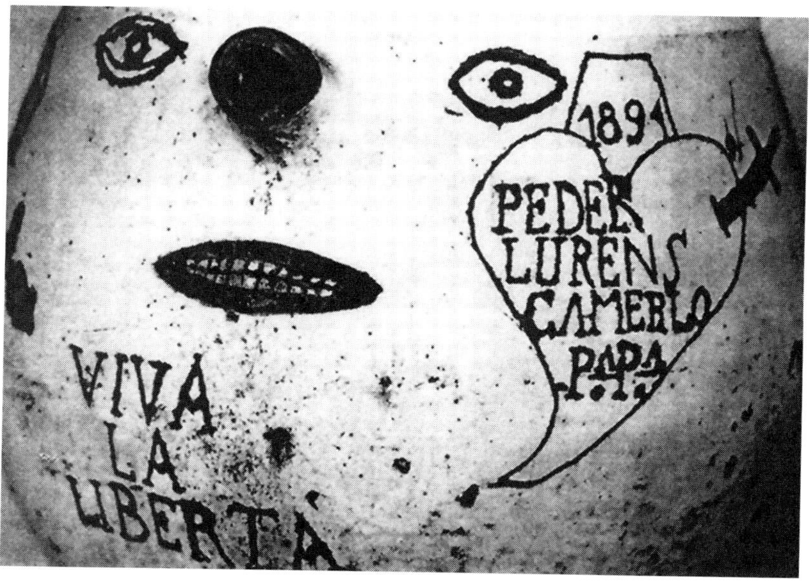

(Figure 6.8 continued.)

they know how to show that reserve that is conventional in the writings of all proper people" (38). To understand prison writings, readers require guidance. The scholar presenting these writings must arrange them and sometimes even take poetic license in order to show their strange contradictory nature, their "inspiration in reverse."[13] And here Lombroso makes one of his many references to Dante: just as the Poet had to imitate the filthy language of the demons of hell, so Lombroso too had to remain loyal to the expressive forms of his infernal space.

Giuseppe Zaccaria points out in his introduction to the text that the novelty of the *Palimsesti* consists in "its perspective 'from the bottom up' (and not 'from the top to the bottom'), in its alternative vision that does not sit well with the values and conventions of official society. From whence derives the confusion of voices in what we can imagine as Dante's hell" (Zaccaria 1996, 21).

Moulage: The Body's Mold

Now if in front of me no shadow falls, do not marvel more than at the heavens, which give no obstacle to each other's rays.
DANTE, *PURGATORY*, 3:28–30

With these words, Lombroso seeks to explain the complex nature of an ethereal substance that is invisible and hence not perceived by us as a corporeal entity, but that is nevertheless a substantial matter and therefore the stuff of bodies. Lombroso, like Virgil in purgatory, conceives of the body as an ethereal matter that at times may become visible, while yet remaining transparent. Indeed, Lombroso's most extensive, posthumously published text on hypnotic and spiritualistic phenomena is strewn with references to Dante's own trip to the other world, most famously in his reference to the Farinata episode of Inferno's canto 10, where the resurgent body can appear only from the waist up to speak in the prophetic power of shades (Lombroso 1988, 28). In this sense, Dante functions as a guide to Lombroso's own investigations into the realm of spirits. Anticipating critical reactions by the scientific community to his claim that there are living bodies beyond death, Lombroso thus takes as his motto Dante's words on the complex relations that exist between truth and words: "Always to that truth which has the face of falsehood one should close one's lips as long as one can, for without any guilt it brings shame" [Inferno 16:124–26]."[14]

Lombroso's researches into hypnotic and spiritualistic phenomena at the end of his life are dedicated to a positivist analysis of phantasms, luminous materializations, and ectoplasms. Such researches were not Lombroso's first encounter with scientifically unexplainable phenomena, however. Already in 1886, he had taken a keen interest in Donato's experiments with "fascination" and conducted his own research into hypnotic and other paranormal phenomena. The resultant *Studies in*

Hypnotism in 1886 bore down hard on theatrical presentations of such bodies. Lombroso's forensic evidence was crucial in making Donato's performances illegal; and he stated that any belief in spirits constituted an atavism, a return to fetishism and totemism, and therefore had to be stopped by all available means, including legal prosecution. During the 1880s Lombroso thus arrived at two mutually contradictory conclusions: on the one hand, spiritualistic phenomena had to be wrenched from the control of popular magnetizers and soothsayers and handed over to the realms of science and medicine; and on the other hand, these same phenomena were nonetheless beyond the realm of science, because belief in them pertained to atavism. In this context, then, Lombroso took a far harder line on spiritualism and hypnotism than did Enrico Morselli, who, as I already discussed, was more open to the lessons imparted by Donato's performances.

In March of 1891—and somewhat on a dare—Lombroso had his first of many encounters with the famous medium Eusapia Palladino. The standard narrative of these events presents Lombroso passing from the practice of a shaky but nevertheless real science to its total abrogation. Yet the relationship between Lombrosan positivism and spiritualism is not necessarily one of opposition. All over Europe and the United States, scientists and especially doctors were providing the grounds for a fertile cohabitation of positive and magical facts. The Society for Psychical Research was founded in Britain in 1882, and its members, including Lombroso, were busy in steadily assembling the "facts" that pertained to spiritualistic life. The first great archive of phantasms—the *Phantoms of the Living*—was published by the Society in 1886. And it was a physician, the Frenchman Charles Richet, who invented the term *ectoplasm*. Richard Noakes has pointed out, furthermore, that many investigators and supporters of spiritualism were also firm supporters of modern, technological culture and that technology was repeatedly enrolled in the service of spiritualistic science (2002, 126). Alessandra Violi, in her superb study of Lombroso's spiritualistic experiments, describes his final text as less a passage from science to the realm of spirits than an "internal torsion" of positivist knowledge itself. What we are dealing with, she states, is the "emergence of an imaginary that is already inscribed in the project of the positivist sciences, an imaginary that Lombroso pushes to its extreme consequences, rendering unto it the contours and character of a phantasmatic revelation" (2005, 44). And: "This positivist phantasm of total possession is obviously also the sign of its maximum reversal into the imaginary, the highpoint of that torsion that in fact constitutes its most conspicuous legacy to artistic experimentation at the beginning of the twentieth century" (62).

The series of encounters and experiments with Eusapia Palladino were materialized, or given texture, in Lombroso's 1909 *After Death—What?* a text itself dedicated to analyzing the texture and materialization of spirit. For Lombroso, the scientific nature of such an enterprise depended, crucially, on this idea of textualization, which he understood in a double sense. First, the scientific proof of the existence of spirits had for him to be constructed as a web or weaving. This is a point he insists upon repeatedly. "But note this well," he states in his introduction, "that, however doubtful each separate case may appear, in the ensemble they form such a compact web of proof as wholly to battle the scalpel of doubt" (1988, xvi). Again later, Lombroso asserts: "Doubtless many of my readers will be astonished to see here cited and gathered together cases that seem almost to lack verisimilitude. But what renders them less doubtful is their mutual adaptation and interrelation, which are such as to make of them a complete and coherent whole" (234). And a few pages later: "Many of these occurrences, when considered alone, may give rise to doubt, but viewed in the ensemble they become a solid reality and certainty,—a certainty which arises from seeing life incidents revealed, small in themselves and unknown to everybody, but of supreme interest nevertheless" (243–44). I have already described such a move before: Lombroso's insistence that a sign gains meaning only by virtue of its placement in a system of signs. Here, however, this system is explicitly aligned not only to the Lombrosan method itself but the very texture of the body.

Second, Lombroso's idea of textualization relies quite literally on the idea of clothing. Eusapia Palladino's success in evoking spirits seemed to depend, Lombroso tells us, on the contact of her garments with the floor (47). Indeed, it is the tactility of the spirits' texture as garment that not only proves their existence but also constitutes their very essence. Phantasms, according to Lombroso, are covered with a white woven fabric, one that is very fine and that sometimes is doubled, tripled, or even quadrupled. This texture they seem to draw out of the body of the medium. It is an envelope of their fluidic organism that keeps the phantasm from dissolving. Frequently they also borrow their texture from the curtains of the spirit cabinet, weaving a cloth that also appears in the imprints they leave in their sculptures and photographs (see fig. 6.9). Phantasms are like radioactive bodies that dissolve under

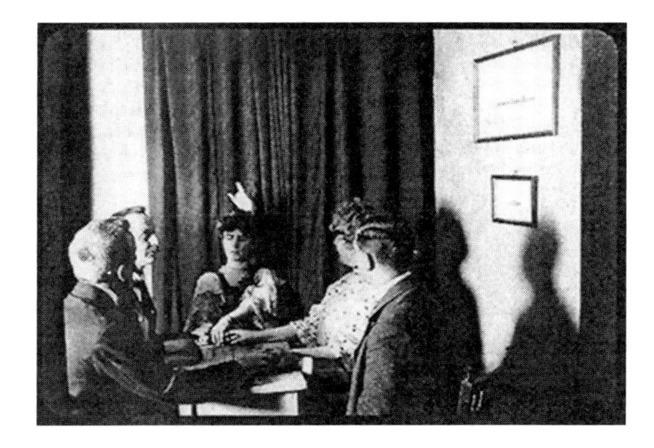

Figure 6.9 Spirit photograph. (From the Imoda series of spirit photographs, Criminal Anthropological Museum, Turin.)

a strong light, but that in the semidarkness of the séance always appear as a fabric, a fabrication, a textual weave.

The question of the body dominated the scientific investigation of spiritualism in the last decades of the nineteenth century. Both supporters and detractors of phantasms were intent on making claims about the reliability, or not, of the body's capacity to act as an instrument of another world. "The séance," states Noakes, "was undoubtedly the most revered institution in spiritualism, and spiritualists worked hard to negotiate and enforce 'rules and conditions' of séances that would improve the chances of contacting, exhibiting, and investigating spirits who appeared to be as capricious and 'self-willed' as living humans or who might . . . 'choose not to manifest themselves'" (2002, 128). Scientific observers of spirits claimed that they used electrical and magnetic powers to both constitute and manifest themselves, and therefore the metaphors by which spirits were described derived largely from the world of modern technology. "Just as the electric telegraph annihilated spatial and temporal gulfs between continents, so the 'celestial telegraph' was upheld as a bridge between this world and the next; and just as photographs, telephones, and phonographs embodied the voices of the distant living, so mediums were seen as instruments that embodied the appearances and utterances of the distant dead" (125). For this reason, and as I will show, technological instruments for measuring and registering spirits came to be the primary means by which these troublesome bodies could be registered and thereby controlled.

Three bodies meet in the séance: that of the scientific séance-goer or observer, that of the phantasm, and that of the medium. While Lombroso exerts great care in giving these bodies the contours and distinctions that are proper to them, nevertheless they exist only in reference to each other in a "borrowing," leaning, or anaclitic relationship. During the first five to six years of her activities, the medium Eusapia Palladino was, according to Lombroso, limited to producing only self-moving objects, a phenomenon that he summarizes under the category of the externalization of motivity. These procedures included, among many others, oscillations and levitations of the table of the séance cabinet; typtology (the pounding out of messages through "raps" by objects); movements, undulations, or inflations of the curtains in the cabinet; movements and inflations of the medium's garments; and functional movements of mechanical instruments at a distance from the medium's body (such as guitars and pianos, but also a panoply of Marey's and Mosso's instruments to register invisible movement). During this period, the medium was also able to produce a range of noises and human sounds, intense cold, wind, "direct writing" made without the intervention of Eusapia's hand, imprints on plastic or photosensitive materials, and other mysterious marks made from a distance.

It was only in later years that Eusapia produced so-called materializations, what Lombroso calls "*ex novo* creations" (Lombroso 1988, 96). These materializations are beings capable of resisting touch and muscular sense, hence, tangible beings that are endowed with self-light, luminous existences that have the capacity of "arresting the exterior rays of light (rendering themselves visible)" (96). These apparitions are genuine human organizations that have a solid form and look like parts of the human body. They touch, stroke, tickle, kiss, and bite and are hindered in their actions only by the fabric of the curtain. "Sometimes they appeared solely for the purpose of showing themselves—frequently being pale, diaphanous, of a pearly tint" (65). If touched by one of the séance-goers, they dissolved as if composed of a semifluid substance. Luminous phenomena—resembling "little flames" or "tongues of fire" or white mist (99)—seem prolongations of the medium's body: they are incomplete materializations and constitute neoplastic appendages of Eusapia's body. They result from a stratum of sensitivity around her body and produce a phantasmal enlargement of her appearance, one that Lombroso likens to "the garment on a manikin" (247) and that resembles a diaphaneity on the contours and periphery of the fingers, thereby forming a second, vague skin. The final and most "complete materializations" (101) occur rarely; they are apparitions that have a human appearance or character. These forms are "faces accurately delineated, heads and figures and half-busts of personages who are identified and named" (101). Indeed, these full materializations are remarkably similar to the appearances of Dante's Farinata and Cavalcante.

According to Lombroso, there are all sorts of mediums: typtological or motor mediums, healers, automatic writers, painters, musicians, photofors, photographers, glottologues, prophets, and incarnators (123–26). Nevertheless, a common ground can be found for all these variations through a clinical and physiological analysis of the medium's body. Eusapia, like most mediums, comes from a village culture and thus from the lower social order. Mediums frequently lack good common sense but abound in subtlety and—like Lombroso—in intuition. Despite their bad education, they are good judges of people and they have a keen visual memory. They generally also exhibit morbid characteristics that border on hysterical insanity, such as hallucinations and the capacity to exteriorize bodily sensitivity. Mediums demonstrate true hysteria, "but under a new form" (119), a creative frenzy exhibited also by geniuses who operate with similar neurotic concomitants. The medium is creative, in that the spectral bodies she makes visible are formed at the expense of her own body. It is for this latter reason that the medium and the phantasm so often resemble each other.

In this sense, the medium's body constitutes a switching point between pure matter and the technology to register that matter. She is an apparatus of registration without thought or consciousness and as such constitutes an atavistic regression to matter. Yet it is this primitive regression, argues Violi, which guarantees that the medium's body produces an extraordinary technology of the spectral. The medium is a photographic machine where the past of matter, that is, all that is dead but survives in invisible form in the ether, returns in order to make an image of itself. Quite fundamentally, the medium's corporeality is one where primitivism and technology come to meet (Violi 2005, 54). In the psychological atmosphere of the medium in trance, Lombroso states, the conditions of matter are modified relative to both time and space (Lombroso 1988, 126), and, indeed, it is such an atmosphere that makes possible the transformation of time *into* space.

If the medium's body alone gave shape to invisible matter, however, there would be no room left for either the scientist or the autonomous effectivity of the phantasm itself. The body of the medium, Violi states, gives access to death, but from the point of view of life (Violi 2005, 50). Death is rendered visible through life, through its vital signs, which means that the body always re-presents the spectral: "death that returns as life, as an ensemble of traces that can be registered, measured, catalogued and therefore possessed. Prior even to ectoplasms and apparitions, the scientist thus finds the logic of phantasmatic revelation in the medium's body itself and in the mechanical traces that already shape specters, thereby drawing a physiognomy of the invisible" (50). Spiritualist investigation does not replace positivist science, but realizes its greatest ambition: to make death visible as a vital process traversing all matter. The medium must therefore be made obedient to positivist principles and create—*ex novo*—autonomous and physical beings that cannot be simply reduced back to the medium's or the scientist's fantasy or unconscious. The medium is, Lombroso states, an aid to, but not the exclusive creator of phantasms (1988, 170). Indeed, most of the medium's actions are *automatic,* machinelike, as is proper to her status as recording machine. And who, Lombroso asks, animates this automaton? "How reconcile with the automatism of the medium her multiplex activity and her artistic productivity? Outside intervention is required; and is not that of the spirit precisely what would be demanded—a spirit for the most part powerless by itself, but which becomes powerful by associating itself with a living body of the medium under the conditions of the trance? It is in vain to assert that the unconscious action of the medium explains all; for when it is a question of a language, an art, totally unknown to the psychic, or medium, pray, what has this got to do with it?" (182; translation modified). A "complete explanation" can only be provided if one integrates the mediumistic force with "another force," one that is more fragmentary and transitory, but that through identification with the medium, acquires—vampirelike—greater potency and consistency. This force is authenticated both by tradition and by experimental observation and is found in the residual action of the dead. The scientist approaches the medium's body with a battery of scientific tests and instruments, in order to ensure that she will be kept separate from other bodies and thus not contaminate their existence and integrity. The medium must be quite literally shackled and hemmed in by the scientist's instruments and tissues to allow for the phantom's autonomy (see fig. 6.10).

Quite spectacularly, the separation anxiety so rife in these darkened spirit cabinets seems obsessively to revolve around dead mothers. Indeed, the very material proof that spirits exist appears to hinge, in Lombroso's text, on the possibility for the mother to make an appearance. "I have myself been a witness of the complete materialization of my own mother," Lombroso states confidently and thereby becomes

Figure 6.10 Medium in a net. (From Cesare Lombroso, *After Death—What?*)

an ardent supporter of spiritualism (196). In the presence of some of Italy's finest minds, including crucially also Enrico Morselli, Eusapia promises, if not threatens, to have Lombroso's mother to make an appearance. And so Lombroso writes:

I was seized with a very lively desire to see her promise kept. . . . And soon after . . . I saw detach itself from the curtain a rather short figure like that of my mother, veiled, which made the complete circuit of the table until it came to me, and whispered

> to me words heard by many, but not by me, who am somewhat hard of hearing. I was almost beside myself with emotion and begged her to repeat her words. She did so, saying, *"Cesar, fio mio!"* (I admit at once that this was not her habitual expression, which was, when she met me, *"mio fiol"*; but the mistakes in expression made by the apparitions of the deceased are well known, and how they borrow from the language of the psychic and of the experimenters), and, removing the veil from her face for a moment, she gave me a kiss. (68)

Morselli's mother, too, made an appearance: she kissed him, dried his eyes, and spoke a few words to him. Despite the dialectal anomalies exhibited by Lombroso's mother, he is convinced by the event. Morselli, by contrast, hesitates before these mistakes. What Morselli does not comprehend, according to Lombroso, is that "spirits . . . speak vilely [*negro*]" (198), that "they always make these mistakes. [Morselli] lays stress also upon the fact that the phantasm had a fuller bust than his mother, not remembering that the phantasms assume the words, gestures, and the body of the medium. This should have also explained for him the vulgar habit of playfully biting the beloved one which is common to all other phantasms evoked by Eusapia and from whom they borrow it" (199). Morselli, then, in the throes of Oedipal angst, wavers in his full assent to such a materialization, while Lombroso appears to have no such inhibitions. Lombroso has seemingly no difficulty in owning his transferential desire. "There can be no doubt," he states, "but that the thought of the participants in a séance exercises a certain influence upon phenomena. It seems as if our discussions were listened to in order to get from them a suggestion for the execution of the various performances" (62).

Two factors seem to divide Morselli and Lombroso: whether or not spirits have an identity and, as a consequence, whether or not they have an autonomous provenance, whether, in other words, they have the power to generate sons. According to Lombroso, Morselli is wrong in believing that spirits do not have their own separate identity and that they are therefore simply the creations of a medium, or—and more disconcertingly—of the scientist himself. While it is true that many spirits—like Morselli's mother—do not like revealing their proper identity, and while it is true that they tend to disguise themselves, still, "in *intimate conversation* . . . they end by revealing themselves in their proper identity" (221; my emphasis). Despite the role of the unconscious at work in medium and experimenters alike and despite the errors of speech, the confusions, and even tricks played by some of the mediums, for Lombroso, all these factors constitute, quite paradoxically, a

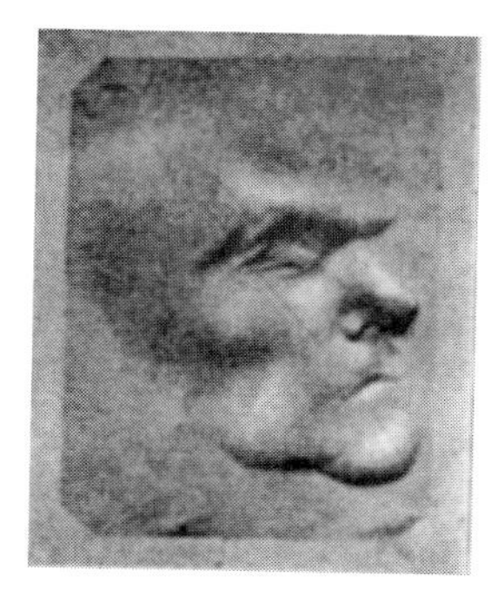
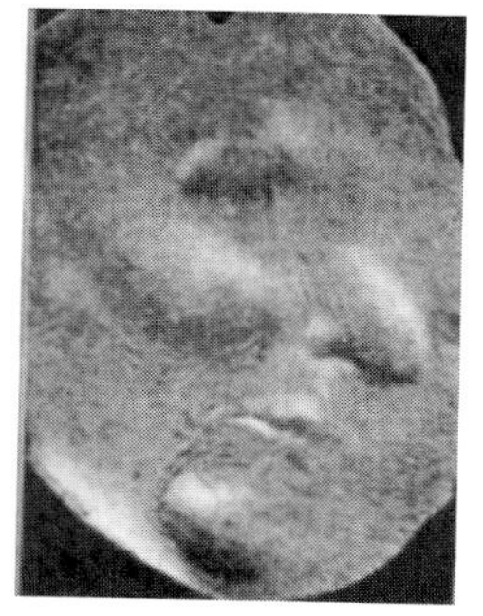

Figure 6.11 Spirit bas-reliefs. (From Cesare Lombroso, *After Death—What?*)

proof that spirits have a separate identity. They are fragmentary and incoherent beings "which at best think and feel as we think and feel in dreams, and which, if they are of weak mind when living, we should expect to be so much more so after death" (227). And in any case, the proof that appeals to Lombroso "with most insistent force" (198) is the universality—*pace* Morselli—of belief in the spirits of the dead, a piece of information Lombroso gets from a study of ancient and primitive cultures. In fact, as Violi remarks, Lombroso's ghosts look remarkably like primitive humanity (see fig. 6.11). They also look much like modernist art (see fig. 6.12).

In one of the first complete materializations witnessed by the intrepid explorers, Morselli is the one to "give notice" that he has discovered someone behind the cabinet curtain. He feels its body resting against him, and the observers see the spirit's arms enveloped in the curtain. Without warning, another observer pokes his head into the opening of the curtain in order to see what is going on in the cabinet. It is empty. And here Lombroso, in his first encounter with death, formulates his idea of the *moulage:* "The curtain is swelled out and its voluminous folds are empty. That which on one side seems to be the form of a human body in relief, on the other appears as an absence [*carità*] in the fabric—a *moulage,* or mould" (Lombroso 1988, 163; translation modified). Here, the emptiness behind the curtain repeats the void discovered in Villella's skull. And hence the phantasm constitutes for Lombroso not an undoing of positivist theory, but, in fact, its ultimate proof, because it most adequately reflects, as *moulage,* the torsions or pleats of scientific theory. Spirits have subtle and refined bodies, he tells us, which are imponderable and invisible except in special circumstances. They are, he says, like mollusks that extract from water

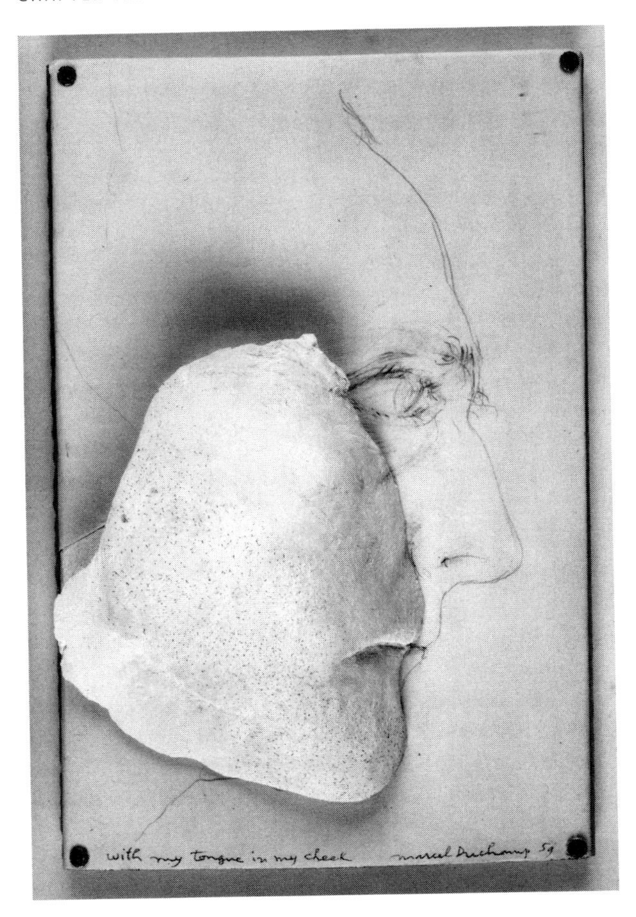

Figure 6.12 Marcel Duchamp, *With My Tongue in My Cheek* (1959). Plaster, pencil on paper mounted on wood. AM1993-123. (Photo: Jacques Faujour. Musée d'Art Moderne, Centre Georges Pompidou, Paris, France. Photo credit: CNAC/MNAM/Dist. © 2006 Artists Rights Society (ARS), New York/ADAGP, Paris/Succession Marcel Duchamp. Réunion des Musées Nationaux/Art Resource, New York.)

the materials to make their shells. Spirits, in a like manner, are ethereal bodies that are capable of temporarily utilizing terrestrial molecules in order to gain matter and thus visibility. Such bodies are rarely complete; usually they are composed only of certain limbs—hands or arms, mostly—which detach themselves from the medium or from the curtain of the spirit cabinet, "exhibiting always an instinctive tendency to wrap themselves in the curtain as well as in their astral veil" (191). And most of the times, "we see emerging from the curtain or from the skirt of a medium a true fluidic body which is deflated and weakly dissolved when we apply pressure to it" (191). In order to exist, spirits take on temporary loan a part of the substance of the medium (see fig. 6.13). Nevertheless, and Lombroso insists on this repeatedly, borrowing does not signify identity: "That which we think we comprehend when we speak of anything as incorporeal is only the product of a fictitious misconception. We mean at the utmost a kind of *attenuated fabric, or consistency,* incapable of longer affecting our senses" (192; my emphasis).

The spirit constitutes a kind of bas-relief, a living mold that makes visible the invisible. The invisible ether is viewed by Lombroso, Violi says, as a huge archive of invisible traces, as a crypt in which are preserved the sensible footsteps of the past. The séance provides a panoptical vision of dead things and confers on them a vitality and immediacy that is paradoxical because they are rendered as both past (far away)

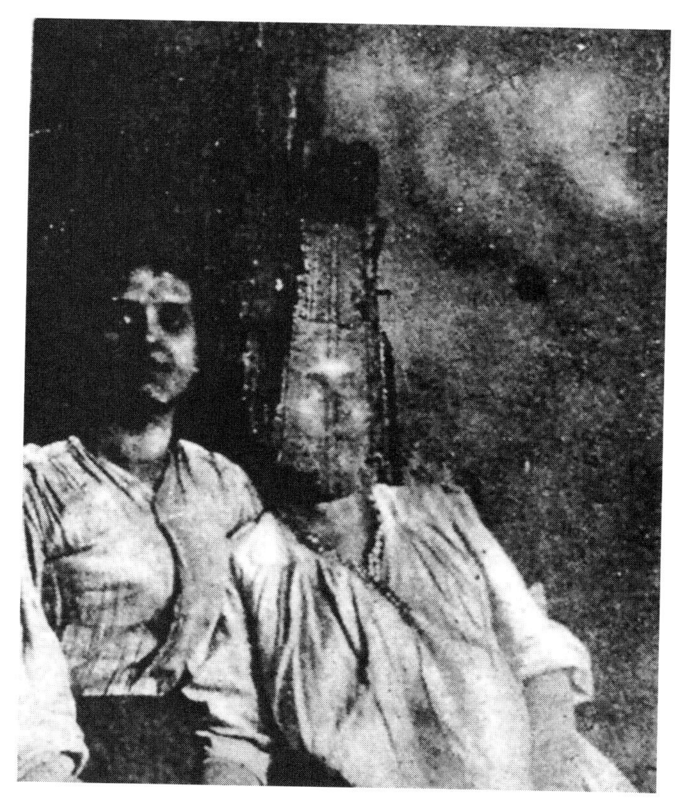

Figure 6.13 Spirit borrowing. (From Cesare Lombroso, *After Death—What?*)

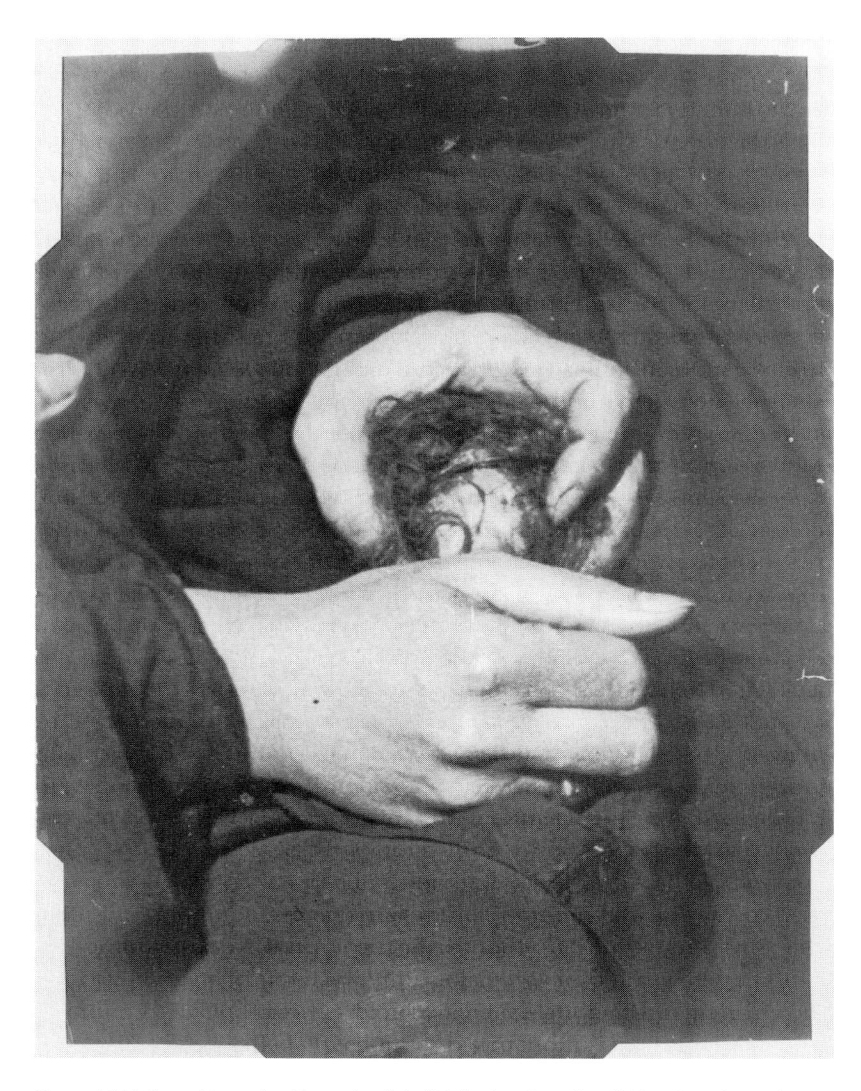

Figure 6.14 Juliette Alexandre-Bisson (attrib.), "Birth of an Ectoplasm" (detail). Gelatin silver print. (Metropolitan Museum of Art, Gilman Paper Company Collection, Purchase, The Howard Gilman Foundation Gift, 2001 [2003, 10]. Image © The Metropolitan Museum of Art.)

and present (intimate). Lombroso's spirits are also an exteriorization of the medium; they are made up of a fabric of nerves with all the imprints of the past, imprints that show themselves as an aura, as a double externality. By invading space, interiority gains an exteriority, that is, a skin. The ethereal body is, for Lombroso, a cloth that envelops itself in and as a multiple fold. The fold makes up the structure of the body; it unites inside and outside, here and elsewhere, past and present, and life and death. "In the pleats of the ectoplasm," states Violi, "the positivist utopia of a total imprint seems thus to become a reality, a living *moulage* of the body of the universe that, above all, and thanks to the technology of the medium, does not limit itself to returning as an image . . . but re-creates itself as a sensitive double, thus offering itself as an experience that is not only visual but sensorial" (2005, 62). The observer himself is enveloped in these folds because the séance space constitutes a sort of virtual reality, an anatomical space-body where the observer can explore, from the inside, an exteriority that touches him and where in turn he can touch. And given the centrality of the spectral mother in these visitations in the dark, womblike cabinets, one may well wonder the extent to which such explorations in and of the space-body do not constitute a fetishistic disavowal of loss. "The cloth," according to Joan Copjec in a different but related context, "is not a presentified image of loss, but rather a solid *presence,* a barrier against any recognition of loss" (1994, 113). And the motherly quality of the spectral may also explain the ectoplasmic effusions witnessed by so many of those present at spiritualistic séances (see fig. 6.14).

The Rent in the Veil

I dreamed the evil dream that rent the veil of the future for me.

DANTE, INFERNO, 33:26–27

"The imprint of the hand was a permanent proof that we had not been under an hallucination" (Lombroso 1988, 56). So Lombroso articulates the very essence of the spirit's matter and materiality in a text dedicated, first and foremost, to the question of permanence and to proof as an antidote to hallucination. The imprint left by the spirit's hand, and not the hand itself, constitutes the proof that tears the veil from illusion at the very moment when the invisible is made visible as veil. For this reason, Lombroso not only insists on the sculptural activities left behind by phantasms, but above all on their photographs. The matter of photography is a complex one in this last text of Lombroso, as it is in his work more generally. David Horn has remarked that Lombroso uses photography "differently" (2003, 20). Two chapters in *After Death—What?* are dedicated to such uses. The first folds into the use more generally of scientific instruments to prove the existence of phantasms, among which also count Marey's cardiograph and other devices to register and measure the presence of invisible matter. The other chapter more directly addresses itself to spirit photography and the latter's capacity to make visible on photographic plates the presence of otherwise invisible forces in space and time. Nevertheless, such photographs are not simply limited to their demonstrative or indexical capacities in this chapter. Spirit photographs pervade the text from beginning to end and take on a phantasmatic character of their own vis-à-vis Lombroso's text. Therefore, photography functions here not simply as one technical example among many, but is in fact exemplary of the phantasm itself. Thus, phantasms not only appear on photographic plates (with or without the help of a camera), but themselves exist in photographic form: phantasms are, quite simply, photographs. Furthermore, their veiled, pleated aspect seems to bear some kind of close connection to their photographic nature. One 1911 text even reported that spirits often "consulted" photographs as often as mediums, in order to find for themselves a model of embodiment or an identity (Coates 1973, 160).

Nineteenth-century photography constructed, according to Tom Gunning, a new realm of visuality that undermined the standard idea that what is conceivable is visible and therefore an object in reality (1995, 42). At a first glance, this would appear a strange idea, for photography played a key role as a material support for positivist claims that this medium could provide images by a purely physical or mechanical process over which human will had no decisive role; it was an automatic procedure that was therefore capable of producing objective results. It comes as no surprise, then, that Lombroso would, in his project of derailing a decisive function for free will, compare the mind itself to the operations of a photographic medium: "We resemble an electric wire that transmits the sign, but that does not recognize what this sign means, nor what it will say when combined with other signs. We transmit a sensation to the brain, which is then elaborated upon and transformed into thought. In other words, man is a sort of *medium* for the brain" (Lombroso 1902, 89).

The photograph is first and foremost defined by its indexical function, as a trace left behind by a past event; it is a mark that "bears a connection to the thing it represents by having been caused, physically, by its referent" (Krauss 1978, 34). Rosalind Krauss speaks of a kind of physical intimacy between the body and its photographic trace, of the sense that photography, more so during the nineteenth century, could operate only with the directness of a physical graft. Like footsteps left in the sand, photography was the activity of a direct impression. The question that beset photography from its inception, however, pertained to the nature of the photographic object produced as a *reproduction* of the original object: From where did it derive its materiality? In other words, did the photograph take something away from the original object? Or, alternatively, did the photograph generate its own materiality—*ex novo,* as Lombroso would put it? In fact, the problem of the photograph's materiality is identical to the Lombrosan problem of the spirit's materiality. Both the spirit and the photograph depended on their medium for their existence, and yet they were also independent, capable, that is, of producing something new.

Such is the import of Rosalind Krauss's reading of Fox Talbot's 1844 *The Pencil of Nature,* where photography functioned as the first demonstration that light could "exert an *action* . . . sufficient to cause changes in material bodies" (Krauss 1978, 39). Thus, if a book was a container of written language, the space for not natural but cultural signs, then language had the power to conceptualize and outdistance the objects available to vision. Writing had to be understood—and Lombroso would echo this sentiment—as a transcription of thought and not as the mere trace of a material object. For Talbot, the photographic trace worked like language: it too constituted a transcription of thought, of a psychological transaction that was normally hidden from view. Photographs were taken with "invisible rays" and could reveal activities that took place from within a darkened chamber: in other words, for Talbot, and this is crucial, invisible photographic rays not only made manifest behavior but also gave expression to meaning. "In this scenario of a trace produced by invisible rays, the darkened chamber seems to serve as a reference both to the camera obscura, as an historical parent of photography, and to a wholly different region of obscurity: the mind" (Krauss 1978, 42). Talbot thus believed that light had the power to transmit the invisible and imprint it on phenomena: it could *make* a body out of nothing.

Felix Nadar was one of the earliest photographers to experiment with this idea, to wit, that photography was capable not just of transcribing a visible trace but also of generating meaning. In Krauss's interpretation of Nadar's *Pierrot* series of photographs of the mime Charles Debureau, what Nadar made visible was not only a record of

Figure 6.15 Felix Nadar [Gaspard Felix Tournachon], "The Mime Debureau: Pierrot Pleading." (Photo: Herve Lewandowski. Musée d'Orsay, Paris, France. © Reunion des Musées Nationaux/ Art Resource, New York.)

the physiological trace, but the process of that recording itself. Nadar, therefore, staged a performance that fused the physiological specificity of the character-revealing trace with the highly conventionalized gesture of the traditional mime (see fig. 6.15). He passed the phenomenon of the indexical trace through an aesthetic filter, thereby transforming the trace's automatism, its mechanical quality, into a willed and controlled gesture, indeed, into a form of writing (Krauss 1978, 43–45). Nadar thus thematized the process of doubling that seemed to inhere to the photographic medium: its function as an index or a trace left by a past event *and* its ability to function as an icon, that is, as a bearer of meaning. The photograph both provided the material, identificatory support for positivist proof and had to be experienced as an uncanny phenomenon that simultaneously constituted and undermined the unique identity of objects and people.

It is in this double manner that—I believe—one must also view Lombroso's vast archive of photographs collected in his Criminal Anthropological Museum: as a support or positive proof of identity, for sure, but also as a bearer of meaning—indeed, as a producer of meaning. Thus, the image of the pederast Soldier Ghiglione (see fig. 6.16)—one of many such images in the Lombroso collection—is to do both: it must function as an indexical trace left behind by the past and in that

Figure 6.16 "Soldier Ghiglione: Pederast." (Criminal Anthropological Museum, Turin.)

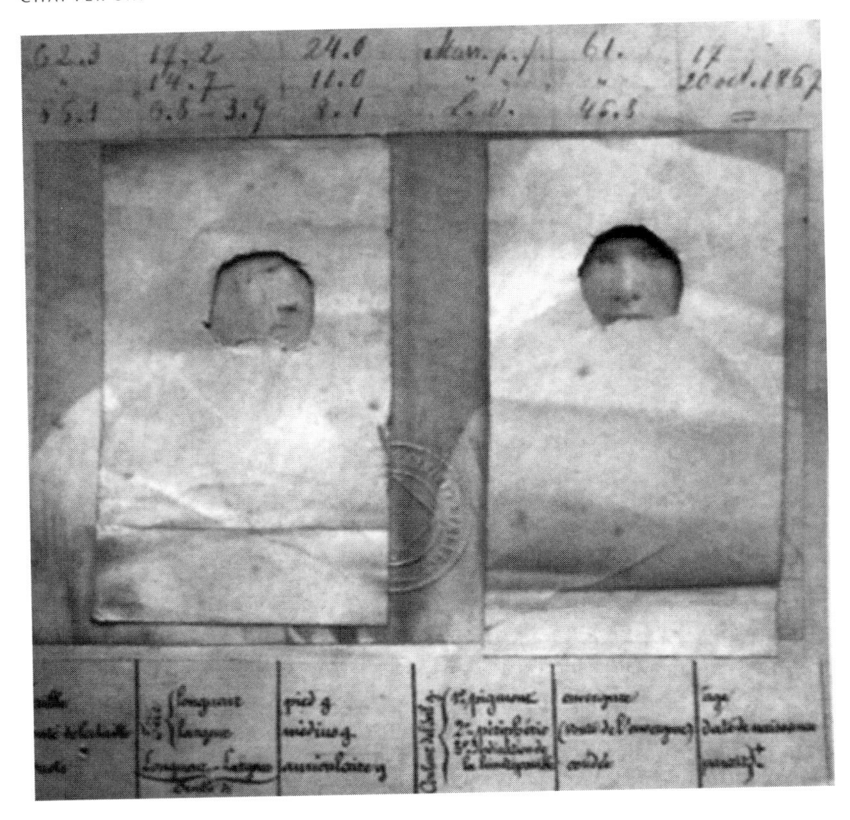

Figure 6.17 From a police file. (Criminal Anthropological Museum, Turin.)

move, in the very reproducibility of the object introduced by the modern, photographic medium, stage, and hence prove, the fact of atavism. And the image must also produce meaning—*ex novo,* so to speak—insofar as, like Nadar's *Pierrot, Soldier Ghiglione* combines a physiological trace with a conventionalized, even theatrical, gesture in order to produce the subject's identity as phantasmatic effect.

The idea of making something out of nothing was central to both photography and spiritualism. Spirit photography certainly depended on its indexical claims, to wit, its ability to provide proof that there were materializations from the other world that were invisible to the naked eye. Nevertheless, spirit photography claimed more. It functioned as a model, one usable by spirits for their materializations. And photography, through its engagement with spiritualism, grew increasingly independent of its indexical function, because it was also capable, as Lombroso insists, of producing *ex novo* creations, of making something out of nothing. In this sense, photography had to work, as Gunning notes, at cross-purposes with its indexical or identificatory function: photography "as mechanical reproduction may undermine identity through its iconic power to create doubles of an unfaltering similarity" (1995, 66).

Lombroso's spiritualist photography resides in such a cross-purpose. But what is more, his entire *oeuvre* does so and thereby constitutes a strange project of "making Italians." It is indeed an *ex novo* creation, one that posits a void at the center of the modern subject—hence the extraordinary importance Lombroso always lent to the brigand Villella's

Figure 6.18 "Gatti, 91." (Criminal Anthropological Museum, Turin.)

occipital fossa. His drive was that of restituting to modern life a new form of aura, and he found this aura in the detritus of Italian society, that is, in the writing and written bodies of the criminal, the insane, and the marginalized. It was these subjects that spoke in the language of "the people," though this language—one that he thought of as the "black" [*negro*] dialectal language of such venatic subjects as Eusapia Palladino—had little to do with an attempt to reclaim an authentic language of the past. Lombrosan semiology takes place within a network of atavistic signs which themselves exist only by virtue of the fact that they borrow their models from the past and clothe themselves in them as if in a garment. The modern body as a style makes the body into nothing but an infinitely pleated surface, while also returning it to an imaginary or specular relation with its Other. The return of the past in the present as a form of a haunting motherly spirit that is accessed only through a modern medium has the power both to make a body as *moulage* and simultaneously make visible that object rendered invisible by the symbolic order. Lombroso in some sense tries to give a face, in his obsessive collection of the outcast objects from society, to what Lacan has called the *petit objet a:* that which cannot be symbolized but which nevertheless makes all symbolization possible. Two photographs from Lombroso's collection in his Criminal Anthropological Museum may well articulate this Lombrosan desire. The drive and simultaneous refusal of identificatory photography coalesces in the veiling/unveiling gesture of an example of a police file covered with paper in order to highlight certain features but only with the effect of rendering the subject unrecognizable in its ghostly but expressive or expressionist quality (see fig. 6.17). The second photograph, entitled "Gatti, 91" (see fig. 6.18), produces no other meaning beyond a name, a signature.

SEVEN

Social Maria: The Scientific Feminism of Maria Montessori

From innumerable towns and cities, teachers, ambitious to be in the front of their profession, are taking their horded savings from the bank and starting to Rome with the naïve conviction that their own thirst for information is sufficient guarantee that someone will instantly be forthcoming to provide it for them. DOROTHY CANFIELD FISHER, *A MONTESSORI MOTHER*

When Maria Montessori opened her first *Casa dei bambini* in Rome in 1907, the events taking place inside the nursery school caused a sensation, for here a group of slum children between the ages of three and six turned—seemingly overnight—into clean, disciplined, and literate little Italians. What is truly astonishing in this story is not simply the rapidity by which three-year-olds learned to read—though this, too, requires investigation—but the speed by and extent to which the event took on the tones of a religious miracle. As the epigraph to this chapter makes clear, Montessori's *Case* and their promise of instant gratification generated pilgrimages to the Holy City, not only to dispel doubts but also to allow converts a part in the miracle. That Maria Montessori herself was deeply implicated in such a religious construction of the event is proved by her subsequent writings about her pedagogical discovery, as well as by the nature of the international movement that resulted from the 1907 events. The international Montessori movement still today stresses strict methodological orthodoxy and obedience to and veneration of its first "directress." Furthermore, the mythic structure of Montessori's life work was always understood by its founder and followers alike as almost religious in nature, based not only on the supersession of the Old Testament (Eve) with the New (Maria), but also on a rewriting of the embodiment of femininity as a sexualized wife into that of a Virginal mother of humanity. Finally, however, a dissonant note can also be heard in the epigraph: as pilgrims emptied their bank accounts and made for Rome, expecting to find there an immediate return on their investments, what if there was no such instant gratification? What if the miracle was nothing but a projection, a transference of personal and even broader social and cultural desires—for instance, the desire for a renewed, resacrilized life?

Maria Montessori created and was created by a cult. In this sense, her educational method takes us deep into the territory of the myth-making structures of Italian post-Unification society and culture. Indeed, the very power of her own myth-making allowed her to productively engage, though not necessarily overcome, several key myths that have sustained Italian national culture ever since Unification. These myths regard in particular Italy's trajectory through the secularization process, specifically the modern state's confrontation with the "Roman question" and the pervasiveness of Catholicism in Italian civil society. Montessori sought to provide an engagement with Catholic culture in the form of a displacement rather than a replacement, and she did this not at the level of institutions but at the level of culture and civil society. I engage here, broadly speaking, four interconected myths that she confronted and rearticulated to that purpose.

First, I would cite the myth of Italian backwardness. In this scenario, as it is generally described still today, Italy simply failed to modernize along lines similar to other Western societies, economically, socially, and culturally. Italy failed to produce, as Silvio Lanaro has summarized this theory, a "real" bourgeois culture, or to the extent that it underwent economic modernization, it created a Lumpen capitalism and a transformist ethos that depended entirely on compromises with traditionalist structures. The resultant culture was imbued with the neo-idealism of Benedetto Croce and Giovanni Gentile and hence left little room for a professional technical culture. In other words, so the narrative goes, a modern scientific culture that in Italy found its widest diffusion in positivism simply collapsed and, by the beginning of the twentieth century, ceded hegemony to the political and cultural nostalgia of neo-idealist thought (Lanaro 1980, 12).[1] One does not have to adhere to Lanaro's thesis that Italian state and society were from their inception nationalist, protectionist, imperialist, and tendentially authoritarian, or that the real parenthesis in Italian history was not fascism but the Giolitti era.[2] Nevertheless, it does require us to acknowledge that Italian society underwent significant industrialization and modernization during the period under discussion, doubling its industrial output between 1896 and 1914 and doubling the working-class population actively engaged in industrial production between 1903 and 1911, when it reached 21 percent. Lanaro claims that the ideology of modernization in Italy often took on the tone of an exaltation of the "Latin" compatibility between precapitalist social relations and technical progress and that, therefore, this ideology does not inevitably point to the legitimation of the new through the old, nor to the slowing down of economic development in favor of political and social stability. Indeed, at times the traditionalists in Italy saw farther than the modernists (Lanaro 1980, 111–12). Lanaro speaks of an intertwining of traditionalism and modernism (89), consolidated by a productivist ideology that was founded in a conception of work understood as "*lavoro-fatica*"—an ideology viewed by many critics as the fundamental coordinate to move Pinocchio—that is, as a motor activity occurring under the sign of fatality typical of rural labor. This ideology was furthermore sustained by an industrial pedagogy of self-help founded in submission, conformism, deference, paternalism, and diffidence toward politics (114–17). Beginning in the 1880s and coinciding with Italy's greatest economic growth, Italian capital left the cities and moved to the countryside, where labor was cheap and obedient and where industrial capital could rely on the patriarchal structures of the domestic economy (the cheap labor of women and children) and a traditional culture that insisted that "one does not become, one simply is."

As I will show, Montessori made use of the rearticulation of precapitalist structures into a technical, modern language, as well as of this productivist, self-help ideology in order to make it operable for an urban environment. She created a modern culture in the name of a kind of ruralism or nativism, a rootedness in the soil, though now in the form of potted plants. Her peculiar mixture of technological know-how and watering plants in the context of a kindergarten goes far to explain the appeal her method had during the initial years of the movement, not only in Italy, but also in countries, such as Spain, Russia, or India, that confronted similar problems of modernization. It explains, as well, its initial failure in the urban centers of the United States.

Second, through the myth of the traditionalist nature of the Catholic Church, it is routinely claimed that Italy failed to become a modern nation because of the presence of the Vatican and the deep-rooted Catholicism in the Italian nation. The Vatican refusal to recognize the new state, Pius IX's *Non expedit* in 1874 prohibiting the participation of Catholics in the political life of the state, as well as the secular state's concessions to and compromises with the Church in order to prevent the alienation of an essentially Catholic electorate—and here the emotionally charged problems of the control over education and sexual relations are particularly relevant—all these factors speak to the retarding effects of the Church on the process of modernization. And yet, it was the Church, I contend, that made the most significant inroads in constructing a modern mass politics. References to Catholic culture and beliefs cannot, at least in the Italian context, be understood as necessarily antimodern, even if they can be read as politically reactionary; before fascism, that is to say, reactionary modernism was occupied principally by the hegemonic social and cultural politics of the Catholic Church. We are faced here with an extremely complicated form of secularization that, quite paradoxically, was in the hands of Catholic intellectuals, be they ordained or lay. While in the initial phases of Unification and state formation the Church concentrated all its energies on the struggle against those changes it deemed dangerous—the promulgation of Pius IX's encyclical *Syllabus of Errors* in 1864 and Leo XIII's encyclical *De rerum novarum* in 1891 are clear indications of this—and while the Church found itself clearly displaced by the new power elite and no longer a principal ally of the ruling class after 1870, the Church soon formed an alliance, as Lucetta Scaraffia has argued, with the two "losers" of the newly established society: peasants and women (Scaraffia 1999, 249). It thereby created the grounds for a modern, populist mass movement. At a time when the state was preoccupied with the secularization of its institutions, the Church's "social Catholicism" made possible the Christianization of civil society along new lines. As Antonio Labriola put it in 1903, "While the liberals were worried about the legitimacy of the new lay state, the priests, having changed course and adopted a new tactic, set themselves to clericalizing society." Furthermore, "Rather than crystallizing in a true and proper political party, clericalism has come to take on the characteristics of a widespread infection" (Labriola 1970, 506, 505). It did so by relying above all on women, in particular mothers. It was because of their roles as mothers that the Church came to realize the strategic importance of women's role in defending the Church and its rights against male secularization. Montessori's work may be understood as a deconstruction of the opposition between state and Church whereby she proposed a resacrilization of life but in the form of a displacement of older Catholic meanings. While never herself becoming an operative of the Church nor espousing Catholic doctrine, she delved deeply into a kind of cultural unconscious and made it serviceable for modernity and for the secular state. In effect, Montessori took what Annarita Buttafuoco has called the essentially Catholic feminist "philanthropy as politics" and offered it to the secular state (Buttafuoco 1988).

The third myth is founded in the idea that patriarchalism is contrary to modernity. The replacement of religious culture with secular culture is commonly viewed as consonant with the replacement of patriarchal structures by a governmental logic geared to the management of families and with the replacement of personalized metaphors of power with the inscription/creation of subjects via the disciplinary mechanisms of capillarily structured knowledges. Yet, and as Pavla Miller has persuasively argued, the logic of governmentality must not necessarily dispense with patriarchal structures (Miller 1998). More commonly, the latter are displaced and made usable in new ways. In particular, the invention of the male breadwinner and of the family income at the beginning of the twentieth century upheld patriarchal power structures within the family because the mother was now taken out of the labor market and confined to the home.[3] On the other hand, however, structures of governance and management were put into effect, in particular through the idea of "saving the child" from mismanagement by bad parents through limitations on the child's ability to work, compulsory education, and direct state intervention in the control of domestic violence (Miller 1998, 280ff).[4] Montessori's particular blend of positivist science and Catholic ethics shaping her own version of maternal feminism made good on Miller's claim. Above all, her "discovery of the child" as the most important modern subject carried with it a reconfiguration, and at the same time a reconfirmation, of the key position of the family. And here Montessori was able to draw on not only the Pinocchian metaphor of Italy as child, but also on the work of those positivists, like Sighele, who viewed the "protection" of children as central to the project of making Italians.

The fourth myth, that of the Italian cult of the Mother, is especially important for understanding the work of Maria Montessori. One of the most enduring and resilient myths in Italian culture is that of the great Mother and her offspring—the image of Italian men as perennial Mamma's boys. That the Italian mother had deep roots in Catholic culture and was modeled on the Virgin and a rather militant army of female saints is clear even from such a secular commentator as Paolo Mantegazza. According to this observer, "woman is always a mother: mother also when she is a virgin. All things and all creatures that woman loves are for her also sons. The doll in childhood, the brother in adolescence, the lover in the spring of life are always woman's children. . . . Woman is soaked in maternity and she bears its sacred imprint in her entire organism" (cited in Bravo 2001, 79). Nevertheless, neither her "Latin" identity nor her thorough soaking in maternity guaranteed that the Italian woman would not veer off the course of her biological destiny. This was because woman, as religious and secular commentators repeatedly emphasized, was incapable of reflection and judgment and was therefore an easy prey to emotions and first impressions. For Catholic critics, this meant that she could and would yield all too easily to novelty or modern ideas—whether these came from abroad or whether they were homegrown—which had the effect of de-Christianizing the family and assaulting the power of husbands. Beginning in 1854, when Pius IX pronounced the dogma of the Immaculate Conception, the Church made intensive uses of the Marian cult and the beatification and canonization of women in order to generate powerful models of emulation for women and to teach them their duties in staving off the ill effects of modernization (Fattorini 1999a and Fattorini 1999b).

Secular theorists of Italian mothers did not disagree with this analysis, except that they feared that women's volatility would make them prone to religious and superstitious influences. They responded to this problem in an essentially contradictory manner. On the one hand, Italian women were to be educated in order to become modern mothers who fulfilled their duties according to the precepts of modern science. The standardization of child-rearing practices led to the mother's increasing privatization and withdrawal into the nuclear family: while in 1888 women made up 40 percent of the workforce, by 1911 the percentage had dropped to 28. But, conversely, these private duties had to rely on state legislation (for instance, limiting the woman's work day or guaranteeing adequate maternity leave) and women's education to put the scientific management of the family into practice. In other words, the state had to intervene in the privacy of the family, while the mother had to invade the public sphere. In the event, as many feminist historians have pointed out, the state ultimately failed to build viable structures for creating scientific motherhood, thereby relegating women—unless, of course, they committed infanticide—to the virtues of Catholicism and limiting the "making of Italians" to the construction of masculinity. According to Anna Bravo, the "diffuse religiosity, the capillary presence of the priests, the still largely rural character of society, the importance of the family—and the *Mater dolorosa* . . . that dominates a national cult . . . which even nonbelievers have difficulty resisting"—all these factors became the foundation for a compromise that had the holding power of a great stereotype. This compromise took the form of an alliance, a marriage between the "*mangiapreti* [priest-eating]" husband and the devout wife. They could coexist because she did not contradict him in public and he did not interfere with her choices in the private realm (Bravo 2001, 92, 111).

The historian Ilaria Porciani has been occupied with analyzing the "invention of tradition" in the post-Unification context, in particular with the construction of political symbols capable of representing the nation as a unified body (Porciani 1997). She notes in this context that an Italian equivalent of the French Marianne, the German Germania, or the American Liberty was virtually absent in Italy. The figure of Italia tended to remain in a subaltern position and be entirely overshadowed by the representation of the nation in the body of the monarch Victor Emanuel II (Porciani 1993, 386). She notes the inability of Italia to take on stable meanings, because she is variously recalled as symbol of the Roman tradition of state and empire, as well as symbol of the Medieval traditions that evoked Italy's civic past in the "*cento città*." And Italia also had competitors: the goddess Roma and the Virgin Mary, together with a long line of Catholic saints (Porciani 1993, 400, 422–25). However, the reconstruction of Italian national history as embodied in the figures of the King and eventually Cavour, Garibaldi, Dante, or Mazzini did not, according to Porciani, work effectively. Such representations remained cold and distant, making the nation visible, as Carducci put it, as a "people of statues." The builders of national monuments and sites of historical commemoration—and this was especially the case in the capital, as I have already shown—understood all too well that it was the Catholic Church that most effectively managed the rituals of collective life and controlled its symbolic spaces, because it was Catholic representations that most directly addressed the senses and the heart.

Porciani has also pointed out in a related context that the creation of a nationalist memory was obsessively concerned with reconstructing and propagating the lives of Italy's founding heroes of the Risorgimento. She traces the history of an equivalent literature dedicated to constructing Italian women, a literature geared to the consolidation of the figure of the self-sacrificing mother in a patriotic and national context (Porciani 1991). Her main point is that such texts dedicated to the memory of Risorgimento heroines are closely modeled on the lives of saints, whereby Risorgimento women became models for both civic virtue and civic martyrdom. "The counterposition vis-à-vis the Church," she states, "that is evident in the desire to stress the civil and national aspects of [the pantheon of great women], nevertheless did not take on the character of a frontal attack [on the Church], but rather adopted multiple forms of mediation. These forms were seemingly necessary insofar as it was impossible to ignore the old ecclesiastical and religious hegemony in the delicate terrain of female education" (308).

Because female education was at stake, Italian women were to model themselves not solely on the image of the Virgin and the lives of the saints, however. They had also to become teachers, in particular, elementary schoolteachers. A mechanism of mutual emulation developed between mother and teacher, whereby the good teacher was held to be "like a mother," but where in turn, as Carolyn Steedman has argued, the figure of the good mother was modeled on the presumed characteristics of the elementary schoolteacher (1985). As Friedrich Froebel, the founder of the kindergarten put it, a good teacher is "the mother made conscious." Johann Pestalozzi, the Swiss reformer of elementary education and, with Froebel, an important influence on Maria Montessori, believed that teachers had to learn from mothers, even if few mothers could live up to what they naturally should be for their children, without taking their lessons from teachers (Miller 1998, 163–64).

The motherly gaze that is constant and loving became, during the second half of the nineteenth century, the model for the education of young children. In Italy, such a model was supported by, and in turn also created, a renewed and invigorated image of the Madonna.[5] Tellingly, every "real" Montessori classroom still today, under the explicit instructions of its inventor, has a reproduction of Raphael's *Madonna della Seggiola* hanging on its walls.

> A large painting in color that is a reproduction of Raphael's *Madonna della Seggiola* is enthroned on the walls [of the Case dei bambini in Rome], and we have chosen it to function as the emblem, the symbol of the "Case dei Bambini." Indeed, the "Case dei Bambini" represent not only social progress, but the progress of humanity; they are closely linked to the elevation of maternity, to the progress of women, and to the protection of posterity. The Madonna as conceived by Raphael is not only beautiful and sweet like the sublime mother with her child that is adorable and better than her, but next to this perfect symbol of living and real maternity stands the figure of John, who represents humanity. . . . Thus, in Raphael's painting one may see humanity that renders homage to maternity, a maternity made sublime through

its definitive triumph; and at the same time he shows how such sublime humanity no longer simply ties the son to the mother, but conjoins the mother with all of humanity. Furthermore, this is a work of art by a major Italian artist—and if one day the "Case dei bambini" should spread throughout the world, Raphael's painting would eloquently speak of the country from which they originated.

The children will be unable to comprehend the symbolic meaning of the Madonna della Seggiola; but they will see there something larger than in other paintings that represent mothers, fathers, grandparents, and children; and they will embrace it within their heart in the form of a religious impression.

This is the environment. (Montessori 2000, 186–88)[6]

Mediator and ambassador, the Virgin-mother functions as both national representative and universal symbol of human progress; as both maternity triumphant and sublime object of a son whose desires already overshadow the mother's and who will sublate her on the path of progress. Nevertheless, Montessori's peculiar translation or use of the Virgin mother testifies also to a certain break in this tradition. As Paola Trabalzini has noted, the Montessori teacher is no longer simply a teacher-mother for whom it had been sufficient to apprehend a few notions of general culture and, above all, the human characteristics of understanding, gentleness, and courtesy. The Montessorian teacher—and this constitutes her foremost novelty—is a teacher-scientist who combines education with the discovery of the laws of human development (Trabalzini 2003, 10).[7]

Social Maria

The Eve of old who lived for man within domestic walls has been replaced by a social Mary, purest and most powerful, who lives for her son and for humanity.

MARIA MONTESSORI, "LA VIA E L'ORIZZONTE DEL FEMMINISMO"

Modern myth-making depends on an intricate relationship that is established between public and private because it must account for acts of heroism as grounded in the affective mysteries that take place in the depths of the self. In this sense, it requires a biography. It has become commonplace on the part of those not within the inner circles of Montessorianism to begin all discussions of Montessori's life and work by remarking on their hagiographic construction. It is equally commonplace for every committed Montessorian to begin any encounter with the pedagogue's life and work with Edwin M. Standing's *Maria Montessori: Her Life and Work,* the authorized version (by Montessori herself) of her life. Actually, the British Standing, a convert to Catholicism as a result of his encounter with Montessori, had been rebaptized "Benedetto" by her, while he, like other disciples, referred to her as "Mammolina." I am not sure how we get from Edwin to Benedetto, but "Mammolina" definitely suggests that "mamma-ism" had export potential to foreign soils.

We too shall begin here, with Benedetto and Mammolina and the disciple's construction of her life, the preface of which was written on the Feast of the Epiphany in 1957—"exactly fifty years, to the day, from the opening of the first Casa dei bambini in Rome." Standing begins his *Life* with a chapter meaningfully entitled "Preparation"—a presage of things to come—and a quote from Montessori, pointedly describing Montessori's own encounter with the lives of great women, the imitation of which she must refuse in her own biography. "When I was at school we had a teacher whose fixed idea was to make us learn by heart the lives of famous women, in order to incite us to imitate them. The exhortation which accompanied these narratives was always the same: 'You too should try to become famous. Would you not like to become famous?' 'Oh no,' I replied dryly one day, 'I shall never be that. I care too much for the children of the future to add yet another biography to the list' " (Standing 1957, 21).[8]

Maria Montessori was born in Chiaravalle (Ancona) in the same year that Italian troops breached the Porta Pia and thus conquered Rome as the future capital of the new state. In 1875, when Maria was five years old, her father, a successful government bureaucrat, was transferred to Rome. Maria opted early in life for a technical-scientific education, and in 1890, it appears, she made the decision to study medicine. In her later constructions of her intellectual trajectory, Montessori recalls this decision as a "calling," something close to a mystical experience. As told to her friend and disciple Anna Maria Maccheroni, she was "walking in a street when she passed a woman with a baby holding a long, narrow, red strip of paper. I have heard Dr. Montessori describe this little street scene and the decision that then came to her. At such times there was in her eyes a long deep look, as if she were searching out things which were far beyond words" (cited in Kramer 1988, 34).[9] As I will show, the mystery of obeying a calling will become a fundamental aspect of Montessori's later conception of the role of science, as well as of her understanding of discipline: her scientific pedagogy will be founded in a voice that comes from beyond.

Montessori began medical studies in Rome in 1893. Her enrollment in the medical faculty of the University of Rome has been a cardinal point of Montessori mythology. Legend has it that she was the first Italian woman to obtain a medical degree,[10] that she did this all alone and against all rules and regulations. But part of this lore is also that the high and the mighty intervened on her behalf to help her on her path-breaking activities. Thus, Montessori later claimed that she gained entry to the medical college because of papal intervention. Whether this is true or not cannot be determined. But it is clear that Montessori had close ties to those in positions of power and that this would prove not insignificant to her whole career.

At the turn of the century, the Rome medical college was staffed by some of Italy's most important thinkers. Close to the government circles of the Sinistra Storica, they conceived of medicine as a tool of social intervention and as a method for denouncing social injustices. Jacob Moleschott's alimentary physiology and his studies of pellagra, Angelo Celli's investigations into the control of malaria and the living conditions of the peasants in the *Agro romano,* Clodomiro Bonfigli's studies of degenerate children, as well as his interests in education and childhood, and Luigi Pagliani's creation of a scientific social hygiene—these constituted the intellectual coordinates within which Montessori moved in those years.[11] Montessori's interests, therefore, did not move toward gynecology or pediatrics, as was expected of her, but toward psychiatry. This was a psychiatry influenced by Bonfigli and Sante De Sanctis, who were both arguing, on the basis of Wundt's experimental psychology and British associationism, for an investigation into the socially caused aspects of insanity and degeneracy, as well as for the need of educational policies that would counter mental illness and develop moral sense and character.

Montessori obtained her medical degree in 1896 with a thesis written under Sante De Sanctis and entitled "A Clinical Contribution to the Study of Delusions of Persecution."[12] She explained persecutory delusions in the psychological terms of British associationism, rather than as a functional independence of the two brain hemispheres. It appeared that the doubling of personality was an effect rather than a cause of hallucinations and that such a pathological phenomenon could be encountered also in normal psychic life. Montessori thus detected here a hallucinatory, uncanny power akin to the Freudian superego, one that split the human subject between inner needs and externally imposed orders that derived from culture and society. Many years later, Montessori would speak of a kind of secret violence, an oppression that is dressed up as love within the family. She conceived this "love" as the diabolical, invisible power of adults and named it OMBIUS (Organizzazione del Male prendendo la forma di un Bene Imposta dall'ambiente su tutta l'Umanità tramite la Suggestione).[13]

Also in 1896 Montessori joined a Roman association for women, one geared to instilling in women feelings of solidarity and "fraternity" and to encouraging women to protect their interests (Babini and Lama 2000, 49). It would be this association that would send Montessori as Italian delegate to the International Women's Congress in Berlin. Both within the association and at the Berlin Congress, Montessori espoused a "scientific feminism" that brought into alignment her medical training and her deep involvement in the "practical feminism" of turn-of-the-century Italy. Annarita Buttafuoco has argued that the ultimate failures of the intransigent paritarianism à la Anna Maria Mozzoni was superseded at the end of the nineteenth century by a "philanthropy as politics" that described the reformist feminism hegemonic in Italy until the rise of fascism. Thus, given the failure of emancipationism to make concrete gains in the field of voting rights, active political participation, and family law, practical feminism refused abstract subjectivity and rights in favor of a concrete, "positive" intervention in the everyday lives of women, as well as the positive valorization of what were deemed "feminine characteristics." Women's organizations, therefore, became actively involved in education, hygiene, and the moralization of the family. In fact, given the movement's largely antistate position, such activities tended to be limited to a war for "public morality."[14]

This shift in focus within the women's movement coincided with the Church's creation of new organizations for women, as well as with its growing concentration on the Marian cult that both led and reacted to the growing feminization of Catholicism. The first Marian Congress was held in Livorno in 1895. As Emma Fattorini has argued (1999a), up to this point the Church had been relatively uncertain as to what Marian devotion was to actually do for women. At the Congress, and consistently since, the Church claimed that the Madonna wanted women to develop into modern but Catholic subjects. Women were to model their lives according to the Virgin and all those newly created female saints by becoming engaged in social activism: by educating the young according to Christian principles and by doing charitable work among the poor and the sick in order to counter rising class conflict. The immediate result was a rapid increase in the beatification and canonization of young women and housewives, whose miracles consisted not in acts beyond human understanding, but rather in their exemplary biographies (Fattorini 1999a; see fig. 7.1).[15] Fattorini, like other feminist historians, stresses that though the creation of Catholic women's asso-

Figure 7.1 *Saintly Housewives: Beata Anna Maria Taigi, Mother of a Family.*

ciations was geared to slowing down change and to reaffirming the traditional family, that although the most significant Mariophanies were in response to the crisis produced by modernization, nevertheless, the resultant mass movements relied on and also produced new technologies of mass politics and communication (1999b, 283).[16]

Both practical feminism and Catholic, Marianic feminism were deeply sympathetic and responsive to "female subjectivity," that is, to a form of subjectivity that refused the abstract rights of modern male citizens. Instead of abstract equality, both movements stressed the equivalence of functions. The virginal motherhood of Mary, for instance, provided opportunities for women to disjoin sexuality and procreation, to have the son without having to pass through the father. Such activism provided legitimate means by which women could participate in the public sphere. It proposed a form of politics that took the "private" subjectivity of women into account; it also offered a new model of spirituality for women that was articulated as specific and different, even if it remained subsumed in a male institutional hierarchy.[17] As Anna Bravo has put it, both the Church and practical feminism constructed a model of femininity that was simultaneously submissive and militant, where suffering became a merit and sacrifice a weapon. This was a femininity that was of necessity anti-institutional—a kind of *non expedit* as virtue—but also capable of resistance and survival under the worst conditions (Bravo 2001, 93). Paradoxically, however, and despite their anti-institutional ideology, these movements ultimately had the effect of integrating women into the administrative machinery of the state, precisely because they were ineffective in bringing about legal and institutional reform.

Montessori's scientific feminism was dedicated to teaching women a scientific approach to life and to encouraging women to themselves become scientists. She wanted women "to fall in love with science" and to use science as a guide for even their most intimate decisions. According to Schwegman, Montessori's love of science founded a new relationship between knowing subject and the object of study (1999, 35). This was a transferential, Oedipal relationship, structured like that between mother and son. For this reason, Montessori's woman was always already a mother. The privileged relation that existed between scientific knowledge and the mother redeemed the mother for a pivotal role in social regeneration and in the fight for justice. It was the new woman qua mother who would reform the family through her scientific knowledge of nutrition, hygiene, and even eugenics. Montessori's motherhood was, according to Babini and Lama, both the signifier and the principle of social solidarity, as well as the very essence and origin of the medical "arts" (Babini and Lama 2000, 88–90).

Yet Montessori shifted the parameters of maternity in important ways, and in that shift she brought it closer to the reformulations of maternity that were taking place at the same time among Catholic thinkers. Both moved away from notions of biological maternity to one that was viewed as socially grounded. "Social maternity" stood behind women's calling in philanthropic activism, as it also constituted the basis for Montessori's critique of the biological determinism prevalent among her fellow positivist scientists' writings on women. Indeed, all social activism became coded by Montessori as "feminine," to the extent that such activism worked against degeneration and the failures of modernization, that is against the negative effects of the biological order. Montessori's new mother, her "social Mary," was to socialize and make social all private domestic virtues and infuse the world at large with the values of progress. The socialization of maternity would destroy the old patriarchal family, along with the traditional couple. Within the new society of equals, humanity would become one big family, and woman would be transformed into man's "social sister." Montessori thus fundamentally de-eroticized woman in favor of the sublimating capacities of modern, social motherhood and thus posited, paradoxically, a quasi-virile women at its foundation.[18]

After obtaining her medical degree in 1896, Montessori began work at the neurologist Ezio Sciamanna's psychiatric clinic, where she worked with De Sanctis and the young physician Giuseppe Montesano. Montesano, whom she had met a year earlier, was involved in the study and reeducation of mentally retarded children, and it is assumed that Montessori became interested in these children through him.[19] The two years between 1896 and 1898 were to prove critical for Montessori. Little concrete is known of her relationship with Montesano, except that it was an intimate one, that it produced a child but did not lead to marriage. Mario Montessori Montesano was born in 1898 and sent immediately to the countryside, where he was raised by foster-parents. He would be reunited with his mother only fifteen years later (as her "nephew"), when he became inseparable from her and eventually, after his mother's death, took over the international movement. Montessori and Montesano broke in 1901. The impact of her secret love affair, pregnancy, and motherhood has been the source of much speculation, especially regarding Montessori's sublimation of biological maternity in favor of its socialization. Of course, her hagiographic biographers do not mention these events at all.[20] Anna Bravo has suggested that, like her contemporary and friend Sibilla Aleramo, Montessori's myth-making was centered on the presence/absence of a child and that her own nontraditional motherhood founded an almost impersonal but universal love, one that was spiritual rather than carnal, and that detached maternity from relations within the family (Bravo 2001, 115, 122). Similarly, Marja Schwegman has insisted that Montessori's discovery of the child was not simply a sentimentality or a substitute for Mario. Her work consisted, rather, in an impersonal reflection on the universal drama of abandoning and of being abandoned (Schwegman 1999, 67).

The scientific discovery of the child occurred relatively late in Italy, that is, during the last two decades of the nineteenth century in the fields of anthropology and social hygiene (Babini and Lama 2000, 53). Giuseppe Sergi at the Anthropological Institute in Rome was a crucial player in the new initiatives taken to involve doctors and educators in large-scale projects of scientifically educating the characters of young Italians and thus improving the Latin race. The operative word here is precisely *education,* for the stress in social medicine and hygiene was on educating those subjects that had fallen through the cracks of the social system, and thus of recuperating them for the future. Valeria Babini has argued that in Italy it was through the problem of the so-called phrenasthenic children that medicine entered the school system (Babini 1996). Sergi shifted the focus, not only from adult to child, but specifically to the mentally retarded child, and argued that such a child, when integrated into "normal" society, that is, removed from the insane asylums to which these children were confined, could and indeed did learn. Sergi therefore argued that "moral education" was a part of, indeed, fundamental to, any cure.[21]

What Montessori had done in her critique of positivist biological reductionism in regard to women, she repeated with mentally retarded children. In that move, she made them available for socialization. The repetition of this gesture was accompanied again, as with her "vision" of the child playing with the red piece of paper, by another "vision" of playing children. As I will discuss shortly, Montessori would later rewrite such playing into work. For now, however, this is how Standing describes the scene:

> In one of the lunatic asylums she came across a number of these unhappy children herded together like prisoners in a prisonlike room. The woman who looked after them did not attempt to conceal the disgust with which she regarded them. Montessori asked her why she held them in such contempt. "Because," the woman replied, "as soon as their meals are finished they throw themselves on the floor to search for crumbs." Montessori looked around the room and saw that the children had no toys or materials of any kind—that the room was in fact absolutely bare. There were literally no objects in the environment which the children could hold and manipulate with their fingers. Montessori saw in the children's behaviour a craving of a very different and higher kind than for mere food. There existed for these poor creatures, she realized, one path and one only towards intelligence,

and that was through their hands. Instinctively the poor deficient mites had sought after that path by the only means in their reach. (Standing 1957, 28)

The "craving of a very different and higher kind than for mere food," the transubstantiation of bread into spirit—this is the mechanism that lies, states Schwegman, at the center of Montessori's thought (1999, 8, 68).[22] In her 1910 *Antropologia pedagogica,* Montessori states: "The necessity of eating is proof that the matter of which our bodies are composed does not last, but passes like a fleeting moment. And if matter thus flees, what greater symbol of immateriality and spirituality than the banquet?" (1910, 106). Schwegman has stressed the importance of the kitchen in Montessori's life, the cure of a good steaming bowl of pasta for many ills. Montessori was apparently a good cook and an even better eater, and she imbued those activities with a sacredness that would later find their place in the *Case* and in the Montessorian classroom (see fig. 7.2).[23] Transubstantiation was at work equally in Montessori's need to transform ugly facts (including those of her own personal life) into something "nice" (Schwegman 1999, 68). It is for this reason that her writings tend to lack pain, anger, or conflict. Similarly, the children of the *Case* were to be free in their movements and their self-expression, with the exception—and here Montessori's language takes on its own kind of violence—"of useless or damaging

Figure 7.2 Transubstantiation of bread into spirit. (From Maria Montessori, *Metodo della pedagogia scientifica.*)

actions, precisely *because* these must be *suffocated, destroyed*" (Montessori 2000, 193). And regarding their language, as well, the children are asked to speak of pleasant things only, to learn the *art of conversation:*

> [The teacher] invites the children to speak—she asks them about what they did the day before—disciplining herself in such a way so that they do not have to speak of the intimate events within the family, but only of their own attitude toward their parents etc. . . . Particularly detailed should be those conversations on *Mondays,* that is, after the break: in that case one should have them tell what they did with the family "outside the home": whether they drank *wine,* as it so often happens, and to exhort them not to do so, to teach the children that wine is bad for them. These conversations are an exercise for the *ease* [*disinvoltura*] of language—and they also prove to be educational, because the teacher, by *preventing* them from talking about the details of the home or of the neighborhood and by choosing instead topics appropriate for conversation, teaches children what is proper to say—that which life should engage. Public facts that have perhaps taken place within the tenement, especially if they concern children, a baptism, a fall, etc.; these will serve as casual conversation, and the facts should be told by the children themselves. (Montessori 2000, 244–45)

Montessori's work with mentally handicapped children led to her extensive reading between 1896 and 1898 of all the most fundamental texts of pedagogy published to that date: Jean-Jacques Rousseau, Johann Pestalozzi, and Friedrich Froebel, as well as the Italian anthropologists Sergi, Lombroso, and Achille De Giovanni. Of most lasting importance, however, would be her encounter with the works of Jean-Marc-Gaspard Itard and Edouard Séguin. Itard, a physician at the institution for deaf-mutes in Paris, received in 1800 a patient who has come to be known as the "Wild Boy of Aveyron," a child who had been exposed to the wilderness since infancy and who thus lacked the most rudimentary education, including the ability to speak. Itard's teacher, Philippe Pinel, considered the boy beyond education, but Itard worked with the child in order to stimulate the boy's senses with the goal of teaching him speech and of ultimately civilizing him. It was this training of the senses that interested Montessori. Itard constructed sets of colored cardboard shapes and eventually letters, all with the goal of developing the boy's sensory reactions through a method that he called "medical education." Séguin studied with Itard and in time founded a school for mentally retarded children. His *Moral Treatment, Hygiene, and Education of Idiots and Other Backward Children* was published in 1846.

Here Séguin laid out the foundations for a method of teaching that could be applied to mentally deficient children. In this, he aimed for an education that would respect individual differences and that would, therefore, be more effective than the "violent sameness" of ordinary education. In this first work, together with his 1866 *Idiocy and Its Treatment by the Physiological Method,* Séguin, as Kramer has described it,

> divided the education of the child into a sequence of stages of development from physical movement to intellect, beginning with "the education of activity." He developed a series of graduated exercises in motor education and used simple gymnastic apparatus . . . as well as tools used in daily life . . . to stimulate the sense perceptions and motor powers of the child. He used different sized nails placed into corresponding-sized holes in a board, geometric figures to be inserted into corresponding spaces of the same shape, beads to be threaded, pieces of cloth to be buttoned and laced, to train the children's senses and teach them the skills of everyday life. He developed the child's sense of touch by providing objects of different texture, his sense of sight by the use of colored balls to be placed in holders of the same color and sticks of graduated length to be arranged in a series from longest to shortest. His children progressed from drawing lines to copying letters, a method which—contrary to what was done in schools—led to writing before reading. (Kramer 1988, 61)

Montessori took from Itard the idea of a "medical education," from Séguin his method of graduated exercises that were grounded in physiological training. It was with this new theoretical apparatus that she was sent by Bonfigli to the First Congress of Pedagogy held in Turin in 1898 to represent the interests of mentally retarded children and argue for the creation of special schools that would free them from the insane asylums. The congress, which gathered approximately three thousand educators from all over Italy, signaled the rise of a scientific pedagogy in the country, one deemed more capable of addressing both theoretical and practical problems within the national educational system. For some participants, a scientific approach to education meant introducing medicine into schools. The supports of this initiative were to be the mentally retarded children, to the extent that they were to be moved out of the hospitals and into the educational system. From now on, education was to function as a cure. As I will show, Montessori would later take a further step: she would make all children the bearers of this change, and in that move she would bring the school into the home. At the 1898 congress, however, this was an absolute novelty. As Montessori would later describe the event: "It was 1898: the First Italian Congress of Pedagogy had been called in Turin. . . . And I, impelled by a new passion, like the one that made me intuit the mission and transformation of an elect social class on the path of a great redemption: the class of educators—I participated in the Congress. At the time I was an intruder there, because the happy marriage between medicine and pedagogy was still unsuspected in the thoughts of the times" (1910, 11–12). At the congress, Montessori argued for a medical pedagogy that was capable of modulating teaching methods according to the individual needs and abilities of the biological and social conditions of each child. Hers was essentially a campaign speech for the establishment of special schools for "phrenasthenic" children, together with training courses that would prepare teachers for their new pedagogical tasks (Montessori 1995f and 1995g). As Babini and Lama have argued, in this campaign Montessori brought with her, through her connections to the feminist movement in Rome, an army of "practical feminists," philanthropists, and benefactresses who were eager to become actively involved in the sanitary and social field of marginalized subjects (2000, 58). That Montessori got a hearing at the congress may be attributed more generally to the recognized crisis of the Italian education system, but also more specifically to the fact that the congress was held under the shadow of the assassination of the Empress Elizabeth of Austria at the hands of an Italian anarchist. Scipio Sighele, for instance, who was present at the meeting, urged more active intervention in the cure of degenerates in order to stem the rising tide of anarchism. Growing pressures for a specialized medical intervention in the educational field did indeed lead to the establishment of the *Lega nazionale per la protezione dei fanciulli deficienti*, to the founding of the first nursery school for mentally retarded children under the directorship of Sante De Sanctis in 1899, and to the creation of the Orthophrenic School in Rome in 1900. Montessori was an active member of both the *Lega* and the Orthophrenic School, where she taught anthropology.

Montessori gained considerable notoriety for her activities both on behalf of the mentally retarded children and of women. It is in these last years of the century that the public image of her was constructed of a woman selflessly dedicated to the needs of others, of a "modern nun" who had sacrificed personal happiness for the medico-social reform of the nation. What is striking about this public image is the amount of media coverage Montessori received for her activities, as well as the extent to which she had the endorsement of the state.

Montessori was and always would be close to power, and in this she shared characteristics with Florence Nightingale (Poovey 1988). Hers was indeed a militant subordination. It was not merely that Montessori worked in the circles of Italy's most prominent intellectuals, such as Sergi, Morselli, De Sanctis, Gentile, Labriola, Bonfigli, and so forth. During the years of the turn of the century, she also had the ear of the government, in particular that of the then minister of education, Guido Baccelli, who supported her in her work in the Lega and the Orthophrenic School, as well as in the Italian feminist movement. Baccelli, in fact, saw a clear link between these two activities, and it was he who sent Montessori to the 1899 International Women's Congress in London. As a *national* representative, Montessori dutifully upheld the idea of feminism as above party politics, thus severing her own brand of feminism from, for instance, the socialist movement.[24]

And yet the picture is a more complex one. Paradoxically, and despite the fact that Montessori not only maintained close relations to state authorities and indeed believed in the legitimacy of the state qua state, she nevertheless also consistently refused the idea of an external authority with the right to punish and reward. In this sense, the very goal of education was for her the moralization of power via its interiorization. This contradiction acts as a continuous thread throughout her work. If on the one hand, Montessori wanted children to stop having to imitate their parents and teachers in order to develop their own talents, it was equally true that Montessori turned herself into a mythic hero who brooked no contradictions. Similarly, in a 1906 debate in the feminist journal *La Vita,* while other voices were dubious of the positive effects of institutional reform, Montessori believed in the redemptive role of the state and in its capacity to bring about change (Babini and Lama 2000, 186). Yet her positivist background had taught her that it was only the engagement with and management of material, empirical, or biopolitical reality that would bring about social change and justice. Thus, in a telling passage from 1904 she stated:

> In order not to be influenced [*suggestionata*] by the measurements, I wanted to ignore who [among the schoolchildren] had been judged the first and who the last of the class. I thus examined groups of children of whose scholastic history I was completely ignorant. And as I measured their heads, I was induced to meditate on that mixture of privileged and rejected children. Among them there surely were those who were strong and proud, the gatherers of praises and prizes—the first in the class!—and others who were the last; that is, one in each class, *the last,* no

one below him: most certainly the victims of intellectual differentiation that accumulated upon their heads reproach and derision. It was thus that—*almost as if I wanted to render an act of justice*—I decided to inquire into the criteria by which our schools judge the intellectual level of their students. (Montessori 1904, 234; second emphasis mine)

Montessori's famous "education to freedom" was firmly rooted in the scientific, medical, and feminist communities of fin-de-siècle Italian culture. Her passage, argue Babini and Lama, from medicine to pedagogy was made possible by her militancy, that is, by her ability to bridge the concerns of medicine, social policy and practical feminism (2000, 13). In this sense, Babini and Lama's reading of Montessori regrounds the pedagogue within her environment, thus resisting her "spiritualization" and sentimentalization, indeed denationalization, such as took place in the context of the Montessori movement.

Montessori spent two years at the Orthophrenic School, a sort of medical-pedagogical teaching laboratory for the education of both mentally retarded children and their teachers. Montessori trained future teachers, observed and taught the children, and refined the pedagogical apparatus that she had inherited from Séguin. Her work with the children was so successful that these "unteachable" children were soon able to pass the state examinations of normal schoolchildren. Montessori's success at the school was hailed as a miracle and gave rise to the first wave of pseudoreligious effusions. Montessori aided these representations of herself in remarks about these early educational successes in the *Metodo*, showing already at that time what Kramer has described as Montessori's "peculiar tension . . . between scientist and mystic, between reason and intuition" (1988, 91):

[Séguin's] didactic material . . . was a marvelous instrument, excellent in the hands of those who knew how to use it. . . . But [in order to use it properly] one must know how to call to the soul of the child, to the man who lies dormant there. And I had this intuition: I think that not the didactic material, but my own voice that called to them awakened the children and pushed them to use the material and to educate themselves. . . . [Séguin] has something very original to say about the training of teachers of deficients: it seems advice given to a person all set to become a seducer. He would like teachers to be beautiful, to have a charming voice, and for them to take every care to make themselves full of attractions. Every gesture and the modulations of their voices should be prepared with the same care used by great stage actors when they prepare their performances, because they have to conquer tired and frail souls for the great sentiments of life. (Montessori 2000, 119–20)

We will have to return to the central role played within this system by this (megalomaniac) voice. Schwegman has argued that the Montessorian voice constituted the most fundamental break with positivism (1999, 91), to the extent that it renegotiated the relationship between subject and object. This new relationship was, on the one hand, a recognition of the transferential nature of all relations of knowledge—Montessori was in the habit of beginning her lessons at the *Case* by writing on the blackboard: "*Mi volete bene?* [Do you love me?]" And there was also a dim recognition at play of an unconscious communication between subjects, akin to the talents of what Alice Miller has called "gifted children," the ability, that is, to (unconsciously) recognize and respond to the desires and feelings (unconsciously) projected by the parents onto the child (1981).[25] On the other hand, Montessori predicated this new relationship between subject and object on its re-Christianization, or, perhaps more accurately, on a displacement of the secular terms she worked with into a modernized Christian terminology. A relevant example of this was her rereading of Lombroso—a thinker to whom she was beholden as she entered the anthropological field. Montessori claimed that Lombroso's theory was "all love," and she thus "saved" him from his determinism in order to recuperate him for a scientific Christianity (Babini and Lama 2000, 142ff).

1901 was a year of breaks, with the Lega and the Orthophrenic School, as well as with Montesano. Above all, it was a decisive year for Montessori's passage from medicine to pedagogy. She shifted her institutional affiliation to Rome's Magistero femminile, where she taught hygiene and pedagogical anthropology; she also enrolled in courses of anthropology, philosophy, and experimental psychology, with the ultimate goal of obtaining a chair in anthropology. During that same year, at the Second Pedagogical Congress, held in Naples, Montessori presented her first reflections on Séguin's work. She criticized him, above all, for overstressing the intellect in education. While Séguin had proposed a progression from the education of the senses to that of the intellect to moral education, Montessori insisted that morality was achieved neither through the intellect nor the will. Instead, she emphasized the roles of sentiment and affect, to which she assigned a primary role in education. All education was hence fundamentally a sentimental, even DeSanctian, education. Séguin's method lacked such an education, which "may, when founded in religious education, act as a stimulus, a brake, and a guide in matters of will; [Séguin] forgets the role of example, which is not merely dry imitation of the teacher . . . but is that which may strike sentiment through symbolization and art—for example, in the dramatic arts that take place in a little theater among music and lights of gentle colors; or in the sacred arts, which represent the apotheosis of moral victory" (cited in Babini and Lama 2000, 130).

These are, to say the least, loaded terms, for the reference to the centrality of religious education had to send shivers of horror down secularizing spines and of pleasure down Catholic ones. And these comments opened up a hornets' nest, one that had not been addressed successfully either at the political or the legal level. As Dina Bertoni Jovine has argued in her important study of the history of Italian public education, in the separation between state and Church—and especially in the field of education—it had always been difficult to establish "where, in the spiritual formation of man, the needs of the believer ended and where those of the citizen began. For this reason, among all the struggles between the two authorities, the struggle over schools did not end with the constitution of the unitary state, but prolonged itself into the present. For this reason also, the formula of 'freedom of instruction' did not resolve the problem at any point in [Italian] history, because it lent itself to interpretations that each contestant sought to bend to its own advantage" (Bertoni Jovine 1965, 115). Ever since the passage of the first legislation to be applied to the entirety of the kingdom (the Casati Law of 1859), national educational policy had run headlong into a fundamental contradiction. On the one hand, it made education compulsory with the explicit goals not only of fighting one of the highest illiteracy rates in Europe, but also of limiting clerical control over education and of shaping citizens by giving education a moral content capable of creating a new collective conscience. The compulsory nature of education had to be buttressed by the state's willingness to impose sanctions on the Communes (who were in fiscal and administrative control of the schools) and on parents who were not complying with the laws. This policy was reconfirmed by the 1877 Coppino Law. On the other hand, such legislation also remained committed to the so-called "freedom of instruction," by which was meant both the rights of existence of private schools (almost all of which were in the hands of the clergy) and the teacher's freedom to express his or her own opinions. It was the conflict between the compulsory nature of school attendance and the liberal content of schooling that allowed the Church considerable space for maneuver. The Church was able to persistently challenge the state's right to interfere in the running of the private schools and—particularly in view of the state's failure to produce a secular "moral" education for its student body—to contest the quality of religious education. While the Casati legislation had stipulated a compulsory religious education taught by lay and secular teachers, as well as the possibility for non-Catholics to not attend religion classes, the Coppino bill upheld the compulsory instruction of the Catechism, but conceded to the students the right not to attend if they so wished. The result was that entire Communes stopped offering religious instruction, against the protests of the Church. The consequent legal confusion was only partially addressed by a Regulation of 1908 that simply put a fact into law. Communes were now given the choice to offer religious instruction, and they had to provide it only if explicitly requested to do so by parents. That same year, the Socialist Party proposed a bill in Parliament that would abolish all religious instruction throughout the nation. The proposal was defeated in Parliament and in public opinion. The question of religious instruction also split the First National Congress of Italian Women held in 1908. Maria Montessori abstained from the debate.

The years between 1904 and 1908 were the most active and impressive years of the Italian feminist movement. It was in these years that pressure mounted in the campaign for female suffrage. They coincided with a period of significant economic growth and modernization, trends that were affecting the entire population through Giolitti's politics of higher salaries. In 1906 a mathematics teacher from Mantua asked to be put on the electoral ballot. She was successful, and her example was immediately followed in Rome by two more women: Teresa Labriola and Maria Montessori. Later that year a Petition of Italian Women was submitted to Parliament; at the head of the thousands of signatories was the name of Anna Maria Mozzoni, the aged leader of the suffragist movement. The petition demanded the vote for women, arguing that it was women's maternity that would moralize politics and thus regenerate it. The petition thus represented the most perfect blending of the two strands of Italian feminism, its political wing and its practical wing. And yet, at the 1908 Women's Congress, Maria Montessori not only abstained from the vote on religious education, she also remained silent on the question of female suffrage. Instead, her talk centered on the question of sexual morality. She stressed the need for women to control their desires with the aid of science, which would allow them to be guided by love rather than sexual desire. Self-control was to be at the center of woman's sexual education. The two most important pedagogical subjects, she argued, were the mother and the school, and they were to be guided by eugenics rather then sentiment. It was this guiding principle that would create the man of tomorrow, a man that, like the son of Zarathustra, would resemble Christ (Montessori 1995c). As she would say in *Antropologia pedagogica* a few years later, the men of the future would be moralized men of sentiment because they would shape themselves on the model of mothers.

Montessori's presence at the Women's Congress would constitute her last public connection to the Italian feminist movement. Two years later she had also resigned from the University of Rome and quit her medical career. The reason for these breaks was, of course, that in 1907 she had opened the first *Casa dei bambini* in Rome. The rest of her life would be dedicated to spreading and consolidating the movement that came into being as a result of the growing fame of the schools. In 1909 Montessori wrote the founding text of the Montessori system, the *Metodo,* a text that was to act as guide for all the schools that began to open throughout Italy and the rest of the world. After the publication of the *Metodo,* though Montessori was extremely prolific, she wrote only three more important books: the *Antropologia pedagogica* in 1910, which constituted, in a sense, a summary statement of her years of involvement with Italian positivism; the *Advanced Montessori Method* in 1917, a guide for teachers of children beyond the age of six; and *The Absorbent Mind* in 1948, which treated the development of infants. After the initial successes of the Rome schools, Montessori spent the rest of her life protecting her creation from unorthodox applications. She also became increasingly embroiled in the copyright protection of her didactic apparatus, most immediately because her material livelihood now depended on it. The Association Montessori Internationale (AMI) was founded in 1929, in large part to protect these interests. It still does so today.

Montessori was always eager for her pedagogic method to be applied on a large scale, in other words, for it to become the foundation of a national educational system. And yet she was unwilling to lose control over her product. In this sense, it was inevitably doomed to a kind of privatization. While she made two trips to the United States, one in 1913 for a lecture tour and the other in 1915 for the San Francisco World Exhibition,[26] Montessori eventually turned down offers to "Americanize" the movement. During these same years, a commission in Italy mandated to bring some order into the pedagogical and institutional structures of preschool education at a national level published its findings in the form of a Royal Decree in January 1914. The commission, in its *Instructions, Programs and Schedules for Nurseries and*

Kindergartens, was unanimous in holding that preschool institutions in the nation should not move beyond the framework and methods established by Froebel, a methodological approach to the care of small children that in Italy had had its most effective propagation through the Agazzi sisters.[27] The commission argued for the Agazzi method on two grounds. First, it upheld the basically ludic quality of Italian nurseries and kindergartens because, in its view, the preschool child experienced the world primarily through its senses and its imagination. Such a child thus did not require the skills of reading, writing, and the calculation of numbers. Indeed, the teaching of such skills was harmful, because it led to precocity and to the mechanization of infantile activity. Montessori understood all too well that this position constituted a veiled but direct attack on her own method, for the negative comparison to the Montessorian child—who, in Trabalzini's words, "is cognitive, industrious; who conquers the instruments of knowledge and is competent in his or her relations with the environment and with adults"—is obvious (2003, 83–84). Second, the commission found that the young child who played but did not learn was more in tune with the inner nature of the Italian child, a child born into a predominantly agricultural society and whose family still functioned as the primary model for the education of small children. Montessori's educational approach, by contrast, one that in this context assumed the valences of mechanization, scholasticism, inappropriate precocity, and false assumptions about freedom, contradicted the nature of the Italian child. It would be this conflict between a kind of national "scioltezza" and Montessorian internationalist modernity that, according to Trabalzini, would weigh on the future of the Montessori method in Italy (84). Similarly, Gaetano Bonetta stresses not only an inherently internationalist quality in Montessori's work, but also the fact that her modernity placed the Italian educator at the vanguard of her own country: "The Montessori method, when compared to the Agazzi one, points to an educational perspective that is more pertinent to the modernity of the times, to the extent that it is more in tune with the social needs of an urban and working-class infancy. . . . The Montessorian child . . . seems to represent the child of a more progressive Italy, dedicated to overcoming a traditional agricultural society that was heading toward its natural 'antithesis,' toward . . . an industrial one, conceived on the basis of a different utilization of human resources. Such resources were to be prepared not by an ideological and aesthetic, a spiritual and religious education, but essentially by an operative and cognitivist education, one realized in a climate of engagement and freedom, activated through the interiorization of the values of the individual and the social discipline of a society that was becoming increasingly more complex" (Bonetta 1990a, 29).[28]

While Bonetta and Trabalzini are both right in stressing Montessori's modernity, as well as her profound embeddedness in modernist culture both in Italy and abroad, I am less convinced that this fact *therefore* separates Montessori from ideological, aesthetic, spiritual, or religious education, an education that both critics view as almost *too* Italian. Indeed, both rely here on the myth of Italian backwardness and an overly simplified binary opposition between traditionalism and modernity. Instead, I would propose, it was Montessori's ability to bridge these oppositions, to articulate into one coherent discourse both a modernist, technical language and a spiritual, religious, aesthetic, and "Italian" language that would make the Montessorian method eventually so successful and enduring.

Montessori's second chance at creating a national system of education came in Italy in the 1920s. Her involvement with the fascist regime has, of course, been completely elided in the hagiographic literature on Montessori. Her connections to the regime began early, in 1923, and they were initiated by her son Mario in a letter to Mussolini that asked for governmental sponsorship of the movement in Italy.[29] After making inquiries to embassies and consulates abroad to learn of the international stature of the Montessori movement, Mussolini, largely through the mediation of the new Minister of Education Giovanni Gentile, met personally with Montessori in 1924. It appears that Mussolini was willing to hand over the education of young children to Montessori.[30] What interested Mussolini was certainly not Montessori's "education to freedom." He was, however, very interested in the fact that the Montessori classroom created disciplined and clean children who "exploded" into reading and writing at the ages of three or four. He was also drawn to Montessori's international fame, which would give cachet to his own new government. Montessori's "return to Rome" as a national heroine became a consistent theme in the press reports of the time. In addition, Montessori had been successful in making her method palatable to the Vatican. In 1918 Montessori was received in a private audience with Pope Benedict XV, with the result of a papal benediction of her method and the inclusion of her books in the Vatican Library. Her *I bambini viventi nella Chiesa* dates from 1922, as also a laudatory essay in *Civiltà cattolica* that claimed that her pedagogical principles adhered to Catholic dogma. It is entirely possible, then, that the regime's efforts at coming to an agreement with the Church aided Montessori's own relationship with Mussolini. Finally—and this would become more pressing after the Matteotti assassination in late 1924, followed by Croce's Anti-fascist Manifesto and Gentile's Fascist Manifesto in 1925—Mussolini was intent on building a cohesive fascist intelligentsia, largely by targeting those who were as yet "undecided" (Lama 2002, 320).

Montessori's own claim that she was above politics—she in fact signed neither Croce's nor Gentile's manifestos—a position she had already taken earlier in the feminist movement, was now justified by the belief that the "cause of the child" transcended parties and national borders. Fascism's emphasis on youth and education may have also led Montessori to believe that the "century of the child" had arrived in Italy. She furthermore hoped, successfully, for significant financial support for her work. The Italian society *Amici del Metodo* was renamed *Opera Montessori* in 1924 and it was authorized to "raise funds and carry on the reform of education by this method and to demonstrate the method in its purity and entirety." In 1926 Montessori became an honorary member of the Fascist Party, and in a 1927 letter to Mussolini, she stressed the Italian nature of her educational method. In 1927, as well, plans were made to establish a Montessori training school in Rome, and government sources publicly announced the inherent relationship between fascism and Montessorianism. Both restored Italians to the "sacred sense of life" and both stressed spiritualism rather than materialism. In 1929 the doors to a teacher training school were opened in Rome, and part of its curriculum was a course on "fascist culture."

Nevertheless, this may well have been the apogee of Montessori's influence in her own country, for by 1934 this marriage had soured. The conflict came, as usual, over the internationalist tendencies of the movement and over issues of control. The Association Montessori Internationale (AMI) was founded in 1929, with its headquarters located significantly not in Italy, but until 1935 in Berlin, then in Amsterdam. The AMI had the international support of Sigmund Freud, Giovanni Gentile, Guglielmo Marconi, Rabindranath Tagore, and Jean Piaget among its many signatories. Montessori was unwilling to bear interference in her classrooms and, though she had conceded to the teaching of "fascist culture," she balked at the wearing of fascist uniforms and, more importantly, at the persecution of her largely antifascist teaching body. Beginning in 1932, Montessori herself and a large number of her teachers were put under police surveillance. As her books were burned in Berlin and as in Rome government documents began to hint at the possibility of a Montessorianism without Montessori, she and her son asked to have their names removed from the *Opera*'s Committee. Most Montessori schools, as also the teacher training school, were closed in Italy by the mid-thirties. Montessori left Italy in 1934—standard biographies describe this as a flight into exile, though she had never indicated any ideological, political, or ethical conflicts with the regime prior to that date. Montessori spent most of the rest of her life living abroad. Until her death in 1952, she lived in Spain, Holland (the location today of the AMI), India, and Pakistan. Until the recent replacement of the lira by the euro, her image circulated on the 1,000-lire bill.

Functional Maternity

As the first Case dei bambini were opening in Rome in 1907, Ernesto Nathan was actively campaigning to become the first liberal-democratic, non-Roman and non-Catholic mayor of the capital. His Popular Bloc came to power later that year and ruled the city until 1913. Nathan, a naturalized Italian (he was British by birth), Mazzinian republican, Jew, and Freemason, formulated his program on the basis of four main points: increasing the number of elementary schools and removing them from religious control; expanding public hygiene; instituting a housing policy to limit speculation and curtail monopoly control of land and buildings and to support public housing projects; and, finally, creating a broad, popular electoral base at the foundation of the city's administration (Caracciolo 1956, 266–67). Ideologically speaking, what unified Nathan's Popular Bloc was anticlericalism and education, two threads of a discourse that founded his vision of a "Third Rome" (Nathan 1998) and soldered him to the Roman intelligentsia.

The Popular Bloc came to power as the result of a series of conjunctural factors: growing dissatisfaction within the Roman bourgeoisie, whose economic activities had been consistently hampered by a national policy of keeping Rome a backwater of economic development;[31] a temporary split within the conservative and Catholic forces that was provoked by the crisis in the Church in its fight against Catholic modernism;[32] and, finally, the cautious and conditional support of the Giolitti government. The relationships among all these players—liberal democrats, conservative Roman nobility, the Church, modernizing Catholics, city officials, and the Giolitti government—were extremely complex and became the basis of often mutually contradictory alliances. For instance, while Giolitti supported Nathan and his anticlerical program, he was also intent on making peace with the Vatican. Liberal democrats, on the other hand, ever since the beginning of the century had been in dialogue with progressive forces within the Catholic camp and hoping for a broad base of support for their own reformist politics. The Church itself had been deeply involved in city politics since the 1870s, and this despite the rigorous enforcement of the *non expedit* in the capital and despite the widespread expropriation of Church lands that directly affected the papacy. While refusing direct representation on the Campidoglio, the Church had become a major actor in the "government of things" (Belardinelli 1986, 6), that is, in housing and land speculation and in the private ownership of public service companies. The Catholic camp was itself split between conservative forces intent on protecting these economic interests and Christian democrats who sought to open up the city government to urban reforms and renewal.

Nathan brought limited reform to the city, though whether his Bloc was a defensive gesture against Catholic hegemony or an offensive move that truly democratized the city administration remains an open question.[33] The Popular Bloc municipalized public transportation and services, and it succeeded in making inroads in constructing public housing and in reorganizing and often creating the facilities for public hygiene (Ciampi 1986; Pacifici 1986). Nathan's most important legacy, however, was in the field of education. Not only did his administration build a significant number of schools both in the city and in the *Agro romano* and—availing itself of the 1908 Regulation—eliminate religious instruction in elementary schools. Nathan also brought into city politics some of the most important Roman democratic intellectuals, who were thereby allowed to apply some of the reforms of which they had so long dreamed (see fig. 7.3).[34]

Maria Montessori's connections to Nathan were personal and longstanding, for she had already earlier worked with Virginia Nathan, Ernesto's wife, in the Roman feminist associations and in the *Lega* for handicapped children. Probably she also knew Nathan through her father's Masonic connections. In 1906, before the elections, Montessori was approached by Edoardo Talamo and asked to participate in a project of urban renewal in the slums of San Lorenzo. Talamo was the president of the Roman Association of Good Building, a holding company for the Banca d'Italia's real estate interests, and he had been delegated to turn Roman slum buildings into a more profitable investment for the bank. Talamo, an engineer who had been nurtured on the social sciences of Italian positivism and the utopian socialism of Robert Owen, Charles Fourier and Henri de Saint-Simon, envisioned in San Lorenzo the construction of an ideal city for the poor, where so-

Figure 7.3 Giovanni Cena's school in the *Agro romano* (1907–1908).

cial services would be collectivized and where the management of the apartment complexes would devolve to its inhabitants. The ultimately conservative utopianism of the San Lorenzo project combined self-government with paternalistic and intrusive social control, a peculiar mixture that would have great appeal for Montessori.[35] As she herself would put it in her "Inaugural Address" for the opening of the second Casa, the Roman Association was to "acquire city tenements, remodel them, put them into a productive use, and administer them as a good father of a family would" (Montessori 2000, 145). The San Lorenzo project was certainly one of the most successful marriages in Rome between social scientific principles and social intervention, between autonomy and state control.

Talamo hired Montessori out of a practical necessity. If San Lorenzo parents were to be productively employed, the youngest, preschool children required supervision, particularly to prevent them from running wild and defacing and vandalizing the Banca d'Italia's recent investments. Montessori was essentially engaged to babysit these children, and it would turn into a fine irony that her future claim to fame would rest on the transformation of scribbling on walls into an act of writing that would take the form of another, more ordered explosion. Montessori was enticed to accept the offer because it allowed her to experiment with her theory that the teaching method she had used with mentally retarded children could also be applied to normal children. With a minimal operating budget and one room on the ground floor of one of the apartment buildings, Montessori opened her first *Casa dei bambini* on January 7, 1907, for approximately fifty children who lived in the tenement. Montessori lore has it that the lack of funds for either school supplies or trained teachers was part of the miracle that she brought into being in the school, for she was forced to make the furniture and teaching materials herself, as well as hire young women who had not been spoiled by the teaching methods in effect in the public school system.

Montessori's "Inaugural Address" is a meditation on the modern home and on the peculiar, new economy that sustains it. The Italian word *casa* bears the meanings of both "house" and "home," and it is as "home" that Montessori's references to *casa* must be understood, including the *casa dei bambini*. Indeed, it is the transformation of house into home that describes the work of redemption in process in San Lorenzo: "The poor [of San Lorenzo] are to have an ideal home which shall be their own. In quarters where poverty and vice ruled, a work of moral redemption is going on. The soul of the people is being set free from the torpor of vice, from the shadows of ignorance. The little children too have a 'Home' of their own" (Montessori 2000, 137). The Association of Good Building, by demolishing "in every building all portions of the structure not originally constructed with the idea of making homes" (146), by providing more air and light, and by increasing the stairways and dividing the room space in a more practical manner, had been able to instill in the tenants a "gentle sentiment of feeling themselves free within their own homes, in the intimacy of the family" (147). Prior to these interventions, however, the San Lorenzo buildings had certainly not lacked an inside, though this inside was closer to what Matilde Serao had described as the "*ventre*" (stomach, womb) of a place that bore all the claustrophobic characteristics of overcrowding, filth, promiscuousness, and immorality. Montessori refers to this dirty, indeterminate place as an "*intérieur,*" known only when an outside gaze notifies us of its existence: "Every little while the newspapers uncover for us one of these *intérieurs:* a large family, growing boys and girls, sleep in one room; while one corner of the room is occupied by an outsider, a woman who receives the nightly visits of men. This is seen by the girls and boys; evil jealousies are kindled from bed to bed that lead to crime and bloodshed and unveil for a brief instant before our eyes, in some lurid paragraph, this little detail of the mass of misery" (139–40). This interior space is one of "poisonous shadows that envelop overcrowded humanity" (140), where there is no privacy, modesty, or gentleness; and this because there is no light, air, or water. According to Montessori, the interior space of shadows is caused because poverty has become isolated, closed off: "in the Middle Ages, leprosy was isolated; the Catholics isolated the Jews in the Ghetto" (142). And so also, in the modern age, "spectacles of extreme brutality are possible . . . at the very gate of a cosmopolitan city, the mother of civilization and queen of fine arts, because of a new fact which was unknown to past centuries, namely, *the isolation of the masses of the poor*" (142).

What the Association of Good Building had brought to San Lorenzo was a kind of birth: the creation of an interior space that no longer had its walls in the unreadable because indefinable, ungendered space of the womb. A family is thus born through an act of elevation that takes the form of a national project of civilization understood as "*incivilmento*."

> When we recall the poetic and dogmatic idea that we have constructed for ourselves of our word *casa* as one elevated to the almost sacred significance of the English word *home,* the enclosed temple of intimacy . . . accessible only to dear ones; and if we reflect on the great contrast, and on the cruelty of instilling this idea of the home . . . in everyone—when there are too many who don't have a *home* but only lurid walls within which the physiological acts of life . . . are exposed to ridicule, within which there is never intimacy, gentleness and often no light, air, or water—then we must conclude that we cannot speak of the home as an abstraction, . . . nor use it as a foundation that may, along with the family, provide a solid basis of social existence. For we would be not positivists but fanciful poets. (141)

The "life of a community interrupted, broken" (143) is transformed through "a broad and comprehensive work directed toward the redemption of the entire community" (144). Redemption is based, first of all, on the Association's provision of air, light, and cleanliness, a space that is "perfumed with purity and virginity" (147). All this nicety, all these "good things" become the basis of a new kind of interiority, one founded in the responsibility of the tenants that is exacted in the form of a "tax of *care* and *goodwill*" (147). The poor tenants, when given air, light, and cleanliness, *necessarily* respond by conserving their environment: "Here indeed is something new. . . . The people keep the house in perfect condition, without a single spot. . . . The people acquire together with the love of homemaking, that of cleanliness. . . . They not only live in a house, but they *know how to live,* they *know how to respect* the home in which they live" (147–48). The people, in other words, come to respect private property and to name that property home.

Into this picture of perfect redemption enter the vandalizing children, for as yet they have no home. In fact, they destroy and undermine all this wonderful cleanliness by painting on the whitewashed walls. The Children's Home provides the answer; it constitutes, in fact, "the most brilliant transformation of a tax which progress and civilization have as yet devised" (149). Indeed, the economics work out beautifully: "The 'Children's Home' is earned by the parents through the care of the building. Its expenses are met by the sum that the Association would have otherwise been forced to spend upon repairs" (149).

While no coins or bills change hands (attendance in the Casa is "free of charge"), the price for the daycare is "goodwill"—"a willingness to meet the demands of the Association," and in case the tenants do not quite understand the content of this goodwill, it will be the "Directress" of the Children's Homes who teaches it (150). And here lies the center of Montessori's entire pedagogical project, to the extent that all living by the poor is to come under the purview of a "teaching." The Montessorian teacher is renamed "directress," and it is through her that the modern family is to be redefined. It is the directress who socializes the family in both senses of the word: she civilizes its members and opens its walls to make its scientific management possible. The directress is

> a constant example to the inhabitants of the home, for she is obliged to live in the tenement and to be therefore a cohabitant with the families of all her little pupils. This is a fact of immense importance. Among these almost savage people, into these houses where at night no one dared go about unarmed, there has come not only to teach, *but to live the very life they live,* a gentlewoman of culture, an educator by profession, who dedicates her time and her life to helping those about her! A true missionary, a moral queen among the people, she may, if she be possessed of sufficient tact and heart, reap an unheard-of harvest of good from her social work. (150–51)

From this fact derive the two revolutionary characteristics of the Montessorian method: the self-improvement on the part of the tenants, who tend to their homes because they recognize a common advantage or interest; and the pedagogical principles in the *Case,* which are grounded in "rational principles of scientific pedagogy" (151). Self-improvement and scientific management, all occurring under the watchful eyes of the directress, constitute the two necessary poles of Montessori's educational revolution, for together they make possible the union of the family and the school. Montessori's method makes the family available to socialization, though the process is a peculiar one, because it does not signify the move of the family into the public, but—and quite paradoxically—the move of the public sphere into the realm of the family. And it is this move, furthermore, that allows for a structure of mutual surveillance.

> [The family] is a species of phantom upon which the school can never lay its hands. The home is closed not only to pedagogical progress, but often to social progress. We see here for the first time the possibility of realizing the long-talked-of pedagogical ideal. We have put *the school within the home;* and this is not all. We have placed it within the house as the *property of the collectivity,* leaving under the eyes of the parents the whole life of the teacher in the accomplishment of her high mission.
>
> This idea of the collective ownership of the school is new and very beautiful and profoundly educational. (152)

Montessori has been often criticized for creating a radical separation between her pedagogical method within the *Case* and her earlier social activism. Indeed, she has been accused of constructing a pedagogy that isolates the child in his or her private pursuit of knowledge from a more global, social awareness of the world.[36] This is, to my mind, a misreading of her project, or at least it constitutes a simplification of an extremely complex relationship between private and public in her work. I would argue instead that one must understand interiority or privacy in Montessori's writings and practice as always already turned toward the outside, that it is in fact its result. Privacy, for Montessori, is always—or at least in its ideal form—a collective, communal, or socialized privacy: one of the *Case*'s greatest triumphs is that they mark "the first step toward *the socialization of the home*" (153). And in this, the *Case* are merely following other modern trends: "We are all familiar with the ordinary advantages of the communistic transformation of the general environment. For example, the collective use of railway carriages, of street lights, of the telephone, all these are great advantages. The enormous production of useful articles, brought about by industrial progress, makes possible all, clean clothes, carpets, curtains, table-delicacies, better tableware, etc. The making of such benefits generally tends to level social caste. All this we have seen in its reality. But the communizing of *persons* is new. That the collectivity shall benefit from the services of the servant, the nurse, the teacher—this is a modern ideal" (154–55).

The new socialization of persons is in fact quite specific, for what the *Case* make communal is the "maternal function." Because women now leave the home to go to work, society must assume their tasks by educating the children, by setting up infirmaries, eventually even by setting up communal kitchens. The socialization of the erstwhile private maternal duties does not, however, lead to the collapse of the family. While it certainly functions as a compensation for a loss of the mother inside the domestic walls, Montessori's peculiar dialectic between private and social spheres leads not only to the socialization of the private, but also to the privatization of the social. The school goes to the home, after all: "the home will become a center, drawing into itself all those good things which have hitherto been lacking; schools, public baths, hospitals, etc." (156).

The transposition of the mother into a social function stems from Montessori's practical feminism, a feminism grounded in the centrality of that function for the modern era. This transposition is furthermore grounded in the modern idea of *renting a home:* "We are, then, very far from the dreaded dissolution of the home and of the family, through the fact that woman has been forced by changed social and economic conditions to give her time and strength to remunerative work. The home itself assumes the gentle attributes of the domestic housewife. The day may come when the tenant, having given to the proprietor of the house a certain sum, shall receive in exchange whatever is necessary to the *comfort* of life; in other words, the administration shall become the *steward* of the family" (157). And here the Italian *casa* surpasses all other efforts of modernization, tending "to assume in its evolution a significance more exalted than even the English word *home* expresses" (157). The *casa* is a living but rented home, for it is capable of embracing its inmates with the "tender, consoling arms of woman" (157), arms now considered as rental property. The reformed and socialized home frees woman from those attributes that had once "made her desirable to man only as a source of the material blessings of existence" (158) and makes her available for the workforce without threatening the existence of the family.

EIGHT

Maria Montessori: The Writing Subject

Montessori's *Il metodo della Pedagogia Scientifica applicato all'educazione infantile nelle Case dei Bambini* underwent five editions in Italian. The publication history of the work is in itself a fascinating topic and could tell us much about Italian history during the first half of the twentieth century.[1] Questions of interpretation become especially complex when the Italian version of the *Method* is compared to its fate in other languages. The first Italian edition appeared in 1909, on the heels of the experiments in San Lorenzo, and it not only described these experiments, but announced itself as the foundation for a theory of education of the future. A second edition appeared in 1913, which kept the earlier text fairly intact but added two new chapters on the presentation of the didactic apparatus and on the question of discipline in the Children's Homes. One may also notice, according to Trabalzini, the inclusion of more foreign names and photographs from *Case* established abroad, as well as an expansion of Montessori's interests beyond the walls of the school proper to more general issues of child development (Trabalzini 2003, 166). The more international character of the *Case* would, as I discussed in the previous chapter, cost Montessori dearly in the 1914 assessment of the method as inadequate for the education of Italian preschool children. The third edition, dating from 1926, is clearly the most vexed, while also the most interesting, record of Montessori's relationship to fascism and to the Catholic Church. This edition underwent significant changes, both adding and subtracting entire chapters, as well as paragraphs and wording, all in an attempt to bring the work into closer alignment with fascist and Catholic principles. Here, for instance, Montessori added a new chapter on religious education but eliminated the "Inaugural Address" with its many references to economic reform, social activism, and feminist politics. This edition also includes an introduction, in which Montessori stresses the specifically Italian nature of her method. She also considerably expanded here the photographic apparatus of the work, though, as Trabalzini has perceptively noted, the new photographs tend to exhibit a remarkable absence of the teacher or at least her confinement to the margins. I will return to this disappearance of the teacher at the end of this chapter. The fourth edition of 1935 is essentially a reprint of the third edition. The final edition of 1950 was retitled *La scoperta del bambino*, echoing here the title of the third English-language edition, *The Discovery of the Child* (1948), a title designed to avoid the impression of a closed, rigid, and personally owned system, as possibly conveyed by the title *The Montessori Method*. This fifth edition has remained the standard, paperback version of the text read by Montessori teachers and parents. It reinstates the "Inaugural Address" as an appendix, presents religious education along more open, ecumenical lines, but leaves intact most of the chapters added to the 1926 edition. Interestingly, and already reflected in the new title, Montessori's general wording tends to tone down her past in Italian positivism. Her older positivist desire for a scientifically grounded social interventionism is here replaced by a more "psychological" or personal approach to child development. Most recently (2000), the Opera Nazionale Montessori has reissued the *Metodo* in a critical edition that restores the original title and reproduces the first edition of the work, while indicating the later changes in footnotes. While the critical and interpretive interventions of this new edition are relatively sparse, it has the merit of bringing to the reader's attention the extent to which the text is deeply embedded and implicated in the cultural and political context of modern Italy.

To accuse Montessori of political and intellectual opportunism would be very easy indeed, especially if one confronts her first edition of the *Metodo* with its "fascist" version of 1926. Even such subtle changes as her rewriting "education *to* freedom" into the more bland "education *and* freedom" lend themselves to immediate and obvious criticisms. In other words, Montessori's method seems eminently pliable to any given political environment. Equally, however, stand those frequent accusations against her method that raise issues of rigidity, of an unwillingness

Figure 8.1 "Solid inset pieces." (From Maria Montessori, *Metodo della pedagogia scientifica*.)

to bend to the environment. An anecdote, as related by the Montessorian Rosa Covington Packard, illustrates this latter point:

> An excellent nursery school I visited had one piece of the traditional Montessori equipment: one of the cylinder inset blocks. It was placed with the building blocks for the use of the four year old. They, too, called their environment "prepared." The director commented that some of the children had used the cylinders and the inset block for some wonderful play as men in a train. She was implying that it was a restriction of the child and a missed opportunity to limit his use of them to taking the cylinders out and mixing them up and putting them back in the appropriate holes, as the traditional Montessori exercise indicates. Her comment was central to her disagreement with Montessori, and was a disagreement that others share. Montessori designed the cylinder inset blocks as a precise tool, not as a dramatic prop. (Covington Packard 1972, 41–42)

Covington Packard goes on to explain the "proper" use of the insert blocks (see fig. 8.1). They are to teach the dimensional distinctions of adjectives, as well as the comparative and antonymic forms of language, and they are to give a graphic representation of numerical, algebraic, and geometrical progression. "Like the other sensorial materials, they prepare the concept of more and less in relation to the concept of same and different . . . [and] they are to develop the child's conceptual ability" (43). The cylinders must be used precisely, not ritualistically and not dramatically, or they cannot fulfill their role as an opportunity to discover truth. One might even say that they may not be used interpretively. Children should play, of course, but with the proper materials: "There is a difference between structured and unstructured materials, between observant and precise analytical work and dramatic or humorous expressions of one's observations or feelings" (48).

Montessori has been routinely accused of a certain *violence*; or, more accurately, her method has been accused of a complicity in violence, wherein the method is, variously, either the producer of this violence or its product. In its complicity with power—and this especially in regard to Montessori's willingness to adapt to the fascist environment—the *Metodo* is the puppet of a violent regime. And by the violence it itself exacts on children—forbidding them to use the inset cylinders as a train—its system functions as a master puppeteer and ensures that children move only according to its own dictates. And so, in fact, the first encounters between the child and the Montessori teacher read like pages describing the relationship between Pinocchio and the Blue-Haired Fairy: "Take, for instance, the lack of discipline of the small child: this is fundamentally *a lack of muscular discipline*. The child moves *constantly* and in *disorderly fashion*: he throws himself to the ground, makes strange moves, screams, etc. Behind all this lies a latent tendency to *look for the coordination of movements* that will only later become stabilized: the child is a man who is not yet sure of movement and language. . . . Instead he is abandoned to his own experience that is *full of errors and laborious efforts toward the just end* that lies dormant in the instincts but is not clear to his consciousness" (Montessori 2000, 662). Both Pinocchio and the Montessorian child have as their essence their bodily movement; unlike Pinocchio, however, the Montessorian child becomes a real boy not through an act of obedience to the outside but because he obeys an inner principle, an instinct toward order and discipline.

Because the essence of the child is composed of an inner principle of movement, Montessori's two main criticisms of the educational system are its reliance on Pagliani's school desk and its method of exacting obedience through externally imposed punishments and rewards. The school desk that pins children into immobility, like butterflies pinned into a glass case (88), is proof of falsely understood scientific materialist pedagogy; it is "built in such a way as to make the child as visible as possible in all his immobility: all this separation has the hidden purpose of preventing acts of sexual perversion in the full classroom" (90–91). The system of punishments and rewards, on the other hand, is nothing but the "school desk of the soul" (97). Punishments and rewards, insofar as they come from the outside, are instruments of enslavement because they force the child to make efforts in directions for which he or she is not yet prepared. For this reason they also falsify the experimental nature of scientific pedagogy, because the child acts in response to these external stimuli, not because of an inner need.

A scientific approach to pedagogy cannot be confused with a scientific anthropology, though the latter certainly may learn from the former. Knowing a child is not teaching a child, and the act of teaching can take place only when the teacher has been educated for this new task. First of all, this requires that the teacher observe the child in his or her natural habitat—this is the meaning, as I will discuss, of Montessori's "prepared environment." Observation of the child requires two other aspects, however: a bond between teacher and child, and the child's freedom. Thus, unlike the botanist's or the zoologist's relationship to his or her objects of study, the pedagogical relationship "must be of a character that in a most intimate manner connects the observer with the object observed. . . . Man cannot love an insect or a chemical reaction" (85). The teacher must love the child; he or she must combine "in one soul the spirit of harsh sacrifice of a scientist and that of the ineffable ecstasy of the mystic" (86–87). The "essential reform" (88) of scientific pedagogy must, however, be the child's freedom; it is this freedom that provides the experimental science of pedagogy with its proper *method*: the full and spontaneous activity of the object of study. And therefore, "we cannot know the consequences of a suffocated *spontaneous act* when the child is just beginning to act: perhaps we are suffocating *life itself.* The *humanity* that manifests itself in all its intellectual splendor when the child is of a tender and gentle age . . . must be *respected* with religious veneration; and if the educational act is to be effective, it can do so only if it tends to *help* the full revelation of life" (193). The interiority that Montessori claims for the child is absolute, in fact, biological. She calls it the "biological concept of freedom in pedagogy" (215); it is a freedom that resides entirely in the body. "The child is a body that is growing and a soul that is coming into being—this double physiological and psychic form has an eternal source: life. We may not eviscerate or suffocate its mysterious potentials, but only *await* their successive manifestations. . . . The origins of *development* . . . are *interior.* The child does not grow *because* he eats, *because* he breathes . . . ; he grows because the potential of life acts within him and makes itself actual" (215–16).

A scientific pedagogy must under all circumstances avoid arresting this life, this spontaneous movement, and avoid imposing acts that derive from beyond the child's inner needs. It must also analyze this inner principle, break it down, that is, into its constituent parts so that these parts may be trained, worked, and then purposively brought together later as an act of coordination: "[The child] responds to nature insofar as he *moves*; but these movements, because they have a purpose, no longer appear as disorder, but as work. . . . The child thus disciplined is not the child of old who knows how *to be good*, but an individual who has perfected himself. . . . The *goodness* he has conquered for himself no longer allows him to stand still in inertia; his goodness is now made up entirely of *movement*" (663). Disciplined movement achieved by the child's muscular coordination through work produces both an ethical subject and a subject that cannot be depleted: "The *repose of the muscles* destined by nature to move derives from *ordered movement*, just like the lungs rest through the ordered rhythm of respiration taken in pure air. To deprive completely the muscles from movement means to *force them away* from their motor impulse and thus, more than exhaust them, to condemn them to the nothingness of degeneration. . . . *Repose of that which moves* is a determinate form of movement and thus corresponds to the finality of nature. To move in an orderly fashion, in obedience to the occult dictates of life—this is repose" (664). It is such orderly movement qua repose that, paradoxically, multiplies energy; it constitutes a rational division of the body's labor, and it does so because guided by the spirit of self-discipline: "The spirit aids the body in its growth; the heart, the nerves, the muscles find their best evolution in its path. For there is one path only" (664).

Not all roads lead to Rome, it appears. There is one path only to the disciplined body, and this path is additionally a secret one. Montessori calls it a "secret key" (121); Covington Packard not coincidentally entitles her textbook for American Montessorians *The Hidden Hinge*. At stake, then, is a secret, hidden bond that binds children through the work of movement to the world and thus turns them into women and men. The nature of this bond founds the "miraculous" nature of the Montessorian method. It makes the method work and thereby turns children into workers. But what exactly is the nature of this bond, a bond that is also one of love? And does its secret nature not hide a violence of some new kind?

We know that the secret, hidden hinge is not that of a string that attaches the child like a puppet to its puppeteer:

> We like to believe that children are similar to inanimate puppets; we wash them, we feed them, just as the children do with their dolls. . . . The mother who feeds her child without exerting the minimum effort of teaching him how to use a spoon

> and search for his mouth, or at least of eating herself and thereby inviting him to watch how she does it—is not a good mother. She offends the human dignity of her son—she treats him like a puppet. . . . Who does not understand that *to teach* a child to eat, wash himself, dress himself is a job that is more prolonged, difficult, and patient than feeding him, washing him, and dressing him? The first is the job of an educator, the second that of a servant. (207)

The Montessorian child has been cut loose from such strings and he or she thereby exhibits freely the old Italian characteristic of "*scioltezza*": "Our children are never timid; one of their most fascinating characteristics is the ease [*scioltezza*] with which they treat people, with which they work in the presence of others and exhibit, with frankness and the desire for participation, the products of their labor" (671).

I have said that there is no violence in Montessori's writings, no anger and no conflict. Everything for her is explicitly nice, courteous, and clean. And indeed this is the experience of anyone who has observed a Montessori classroom. The *effectiveness* of her method, the translation of her pedagogical text into the reality of the classroom, and conversely the translation of her experiences in the *Case* into the text of the *Metodo*, is indeed striking and, quite understandably, has been interpreted as a kind of miracle. It is the absence of violence, coupled with the effectiveness of this translation between theory and practice, that I wish to engage in the pages that follow, for I see these two aspects as fundamentally bound one to the other. On the one hand, then, I contend that violence is not absent from the Montessorian method, but that instead such violence is structured *as absence*. On the other hand, Montessori's absent violence (as also violent absence) depends on, and in turn also produces, a body and a bodily memory that exist by virtue of the body's capacity to write. Hence the extraordinary emphasis given to the "explosion into writing." This explosion gives birth to a quintessentially modernist body, one that can be broken down, even fragmented, into its constituent elements; it also gives birth to a text, the analysis of these bodily elements, both of which—body and text—are structured around an absence that Montessori variously names silence, zero, nothingness, nonaction. Montessori's body is a writing body; it exists by virtue of an inscription and as a writing practice. Furthermore, it is such an inscription that makes it available for speech, socialization, and ethics. In this quality, and this despite all her talk about spirit, Montessori's method is founded in a modernist discourse, one akin to Nietzsche's writerly practices or even to the Italian futurists' exploding bodies of speed.

"Le lezioni sullo zero"

The chapter "Manual Labor," subtitled "The Potter's Art and Building," appears in the first two editions of the *Metodo* but disappears with the 1926 version, never again to be included thereafter, though it is reproduced in the American translation current today. This relatively short chapter is thus uncannily implicated in a kind of presence/absence or *Fort/Da* structure. The difference, so Montessori begins these pages, between manual labor and manual gymnastics is that the first has as its goal the construction of a specific object that is socially necessary, while the second has as its aim the exercise and training of the hand. The latter perfects the individual, and the former enriches the environment. Nevertheless, "the two are connected because, generally speaking, only he who has perfected his own hand can produce a useful object" (327). I will return to the centrality of the hand in Montessori's *Metodo* later. Of interest here is the nature of the hand's first product: the vase. Montessori is in search of a work [*un lavoro*]—understood as both activity and object—that is "most rational" for the engagement of young children. She rejects the "*lavorini*" devised by Froebel, because they are exercises (i.e., gymnastics) and not work, but she does take up his suggestion of having children work with clay out of which they are to fashion objects. She makes one modification, however, and this is an important one: "I, however, on the basis of the system of freedom that I have proposed, did not want children to copy anything [non amavo di *far copiar* nulla ai fanciulli]" (327). At the same time, however, to allow children to shape objects "*a capriccio*" (318) would also undermine the usefulness of the experience, because such an activity, somewhat like inkblot tests, would perhaps lead to interesting revelations about the children's psyches but hardly to useful work and would thus not contribute to their education.

It is through her encounter with the "*geniale artista*," Professor Francesco Randone, founder of the "Scuola di arte educatrice" and the Society "Giovinezza gentile," that Montessori resolves her problem.[2] Randone's Society had "the goal of educating children in gentleness in their treatment of the environment—that is, in respect for objects, buildings, and monuments: an important aspect of civil education. This was an education of particular interest to me in the *Case dei bambini* because this institution had the fundamental goal of teaching, precisely, the respect for walls, for the home, for the environment" (328). It was to Randone's credit that, as part of this civico-ecological education, he had revived a form of art that "had been the glory of Italy and Florence: the potter's art—that is, the art of building a vase" (329). The vase is the ideal object for children, because it is the first object of humanity, born together with the taming of fire, with humanity's first cooked meals, one of the earliest sacred objects, and the first sign of an aesthetic taste among the nascent civilizations. Thus, "the history of the vase proceeds with human history itself. Beyond the civil and moral importance of the vase, it also has a practical function: that of *lending itself* to any modification of form, of bearing any kind of ornament—that is, of freeing up the individual work of the artist" (330). The child thus reproduces or repeats, in her or his work, the work of the childhood of humanity—"when from its nomadism it made itself stable, begged the earth for its fruits, built itself shelter, and made vases to cook the foods offered up by the fecund soil" (331).

Ontogeny recapitulates phylogeny, through work and through the creation of objects. This is a familiar story and has the power of an original myth or fable. Considerably odder is the phrase "*far copiar nulla*," the imperative to copy nothing. It recalls Lacan's discussion of the vase in *The Ethics of Psychoanalysis*, in his chapter on creation *ex nihilo*. "I posit the following," he states: "an object, insofar as it is a created object, may fill the function that enables it not to avoid the Thing as signifier, but to represent it. According to the fable handed down through the generations, and that nothing prevents us from using, we are going to refer to what is the most primitive of artistic activities, that of the potter" (Lacan 1992, 119). This vase is certainly a tool, a utensil, and one of its uses is "to make us conceive the mysteries of creation by means of parables, analogies and metaphors" (120). For this reason, it is both utensil and signifier, indeed, the first signifier "fashioned by human hand": "It is in its signifying essence a signifier of nothing other than of signifying as such or, in other words, of no particular signified" (120). The vase makes, gives rise to, copies this "nulla" and thereby introduces the possibility of eventually filling it—that is, representing it and decorating it. The point for Lacan is that such a filling is inseparable from absence, from the nothingness or emptiness that makes up the structure of the signifier. The vase is "an object made to represent the existence of the emptiness of the center of the real that is called the Thing," and "this emptiness as represented in the representation presents itself as a *nihil*, as nothing. And that is why the potter . . . creates the vase with his hand around this emptiness, creates it, just like the mythical creator, *ex nihilo*, starting with a hole . . . the fashioning of the signifier and the introduction of a gap or a hole in the real is identical" (121).

One cannot stress enough the centrality of this "nulla" that lies at the heart of Montessori's system, of a fundamental void structuring all signifying practice. Her entire didactic apparatus is animated, set into motion, by its effects. In this sense also her educational imperative, her *"far copiar nulla,"* is profoundly *anti*mimetic, a fact already presaged in her insistence that children are not to imitate—parents, teachers, or objects. This antimimetic imperative is also in play in the anecdote of Montessori's own refusal to imitate the heroines of Italian national history. Mimesis reduces children to puppets who, on cue, copy a reality that preexists them. Yet, and quite paradoxically, the rejection of slavish imitation in favor of creation *ex nihilo* does not lead to a free-for-all or fantastic creativity; it does emphatically not preclude structure. As I have already noted, such activity would be *"a capriccio"* and thus not educational. The "nulla" that resides at the center of all signifying practice produces a structure, one that cannot be modified or changed: it *must be* a *"copiar di nulla."*

This "nulla" has the mathematical certainty of the zero, that point in our numerical system that makes all numeration possible. In its graphic representation, it also reproduces that hole shaped by the writerly hand of the potter's art. From this derives the importance of mathematical training in the Montessorian method and, beyond this importance, also its ability to produce pleasure. In the chapter on the teaching of numbers and the decimal system, we find the "lessons of the zero." At this point in the text, the children have already manipulated the materials that have introduced sameness and difference, they can already count, change money, and recognize the graphical representations of numbers. I will return to this prehistory of the zero, to its life in nonmathematical form, later and for now attend to the child's discovery of "nulla": "We wait until the child, pointing to the compartment containing the card marked zero, asks: 'And what must I put in here?' in order for us to answer: 'Nothing; zero is nothing [*nulla; zero è nulla*].' But often this is not enough—it is necessary for us to make the child *feel* what is nothing. To this end we make use of exercises that greatly entertain the children" (623). Something: nothing must be put in the compartment and it is this impossibility that children must come to *feel*. In order to teach the value of zero, these exercises must be structured along lines of a *positive* command of nothingness, using, as Italian requires, not the infinitive of the verb but its conjugated form. Montessori seats herself among the children and calls to them:

"Come, dear, come to me *zero* times." Almost always the child comes to me and then returns to his place: "But, dear child, you came to me one time and I had told you to come *zero* times." The children begin to marvel: "But then what must I do?" "Nothing; zero is nothing." "But how does one do nothing?" "One does not do it. You should have stood still, you should not have moved; you should have come no time: zero times, nothing times." (624)

And:

We repeat the exercise: "You, dear, with your little fingers, send me zero kisses": the child trembles, laughs, and does not move. "Have you understood?" I repeat in an inviting, almost passionate voice, "Send me zero kisses, zero kisses!" No movement. General laughter. I raise my voice as if getting angry at their laughter and in a severe, threatening tone I call to one of them: "You, come here zero times! I say . . . come here immediately zero times; do you understand? I tell you: come here zero times!" He does not move. The laughter becomes louder, excited also by the change in my countenance, first of prayer, then of threat. "Well," I moan in a sobbing, pained voice, "why don't you kiss me, why don't you come?" and they all yell in a loud voice and with sparkling eyes, almost in tears with joy and laughter: "Zero is nothing! Zero is nothing!" "Is that so?" I say and smile serenely: "Well, then, all of you come here one time!" and they throw themselves at me. (624–25)

It is difficult to miss the violence and cruelty of this scene that makes children laugh so as to avoid its potential terror. Montessori's doctrinal differences and her later distantiation from the Catholic Church centered on the dogma of original sin. She refuses the idea of original sin because, for her, the child is essentially *empty* and therefore has no need to be freed from guilt (Schwegman 1999, 102). Consonant with this belief is also her rejection of Freudian psychoanalysis, because she refuses the idea of infantile sexuality, which, when demonstrated by children, is merely a sign of perversion that comes from a corrupt environment. Nevertheless, I would contend that these "lessons of the zero" are nothing but an enactment or staging of a constitutive trauma or fall, a scene whereby the child, through its act of non-coming, enters the world of signifiers, the symbolic order, to the extent that this order is structured by an absence, a not-being. The lessons of the zero bear witness to this gap or hole in the symbolic order, and they thereby make the child a subject to and of the rule of Law. The zero lessons teach the Law in the form of an impossible command: "Come to me zero times. Kiss me zero times," which, by virtue of that same command, makes all other commands possible as a voluntary, pleasurable submission because experienced as a *relief:* "Come to me one time, then, and kiss me one time." Where before there had been no Law, no commandment, because there was no conscious or conscientious subject, now there exists the command: "Of this thou shalt not eat." The subject is born of this noncommand, never dreamed of before, and with it come knowledge, desire, and the positivity of both "kissing" and "coming" one time or more *and* the prohibition against "kissing" and "coming" at all.[3]

That this primal scene has the structure of a calling, the calling of desire, is not fortuitous. It is a scene akin to Althusser's calling that interpellates individuals as subjects and thereby drives them into the symbolic world of ideology. Similarly, Žižek claims that the escape into ideology protects the subject from the horror of the Real, the Thing, the Zero. But Montessori's scene is one that *precedes* Althusser's moment of interpellation: the policeman who calls to the subject with a "Hey, you, come here," to which the subject, in fact, turns round, this subject reacts already at the level of a certain positivity. Thus, despite Montessori's own rather overbearing presence in this lesson, she herself, and quite explicitly so, views her presence as structured by absence. I am persuaded to believe her. The fundamental *passivity* of the Montessori teacher is that of the Freudian/Lacanian psychoanalyst who does nothing but elicit the transferential desires of a subject who can exist only by virtue of those same desires. The Montessorian teacher is passive certainly because of her function as scientific observer, but she is also "apparently passive" (194), to the extent that she *directs* the child's relationship with the zero, with nothingness.

The teacher's or directress's own affinity to nothingness is what makes the Montessorian method a religious miracle or even an act of magic. It also provides the method's grounding in science. Scientific pedagogy, the art of disciplining and educating children, is born through the understanding of nothingness, which in a Montessori classroom takes on the mantle of silence, as also the mantle of a Pinocchian fairy:

> This *art* must accompany the *scientific method*—which makes the simplicity of our lessons resemble experimental psychology. When the teacher has touched each soul of all of her pupils—reawakening and reviving in them life just like an invisible fairy—she will own those souls, and one sign, one word will suffice—so that every one of them will feel her clearly, recognize her, and heed her. . . . They will look to her who allows them to live—and they, famished, hope to receive new life from her. . . . Collective discipline is achieved as if by the force of magic. Fifty to sixty children between the ages of two-and-half and six—all together, at a mere sign, know how to be silent so perfectly that this absolute silence seems as grave as the desert; and when a sweet order, expressed in a low voice, says to the children: "Get

up, walk for a little on your toes, and then return to your seats in silence"—all together, like one single person, they get up and execute the order with the least possible noise. The teacher, by that voice alone, has spoken to each child; and each child desires from her intervention some internal light and joy—and goes, intent and obedient, like an anxious explorer who follows his path. (232–33)

The "lessons of silence" have long become a kind of trademark of the Montessorian method. In this, they are intimately connected to the zero lessons, as well as to Montessori's fixation with food. Together they make up, according to Schwegman, the essence of the Catholic mass: silent prayer and the Eucharist. I have already mentioned the centrality of food as an act of transubstantiation of matter into spirit and will return to it when speaking of Montessori's idea of bodily training. Silence makes its appearance repeatedly in the *Metodo*, for it constitutes the cardinal principle of her vision of power, as well as her theory of the relationship between nature and culture. In a footnote that appears for the first time, significantly, in the 1926 edition of the *Metodo*, for instance, Montessori notes that "silence has become one of the most recognized characteristics of the Montessori method. . . . The Montessori spirit has thus widely penetrated the common schools in one form or another. It has also been this influence that has allowed its penetration into the public demonstrations of the social and political order in the form of the 'immobility of silence' " (428n326).

The most extended discussion of the "silence lesson" appears in the context of the "*saggio*" of auditory acuteness, a "*saggio*" that must be understood here as both essay and taste, linking it thereby to both the ear and the stomach, in other words, to a kind of swallowing of the message. One of the greatest successes of the *Case*, Montessori states, has been the experiment centered on the "clock and the aphonic voice" (419). The lessons of silence teach that there are many degrees of silence, but the goal of such lessons is to teach absolute silence. As usual, Montessori is the center of such activity, as she seats herself among the children in total silence and immobility.

There is *absolute* silence where nothing, absolutely nothing [*nulla*] moves. The children watch me in astonishment as I put myself in the middle of the room, erect and truly as if "I did not exist." And then they all compete to imitate me and do the same thing. I, here and there, teach when a foot, almost inadvertently, moves. The children's attention is focused on every part of their bodies, anxiously willing themselves to achieve immobility. As they exercise themselves in this activity, a silence comes

Figure 8.2 "Silence lessons." (From Montessori, *Metodo della pedagogia scientifica*.)

into being that is truly different from that which we superficially call *silence:* it is as if life were disappearing, as if the room were becoming empty, as if there were nobody left. At that point the tick-tock of the clock on the wall makes itself heard. (421)

And in this silence, when nobody is left, Montessori calls each child separately by name in an aphonic voice (see fig. 8.2). As in the zero lessons, this constitutes another calling to the child. Each one

raises his head, opens his eyes as if in a dream but also happy; he rises silently . . . and tiptoes almost imperceptibly . . .; nevertheless, his steps resonate in the absolute silence that continues and in the immobility that persists. . . . He suffocates his tiny explosions of laughter, or attaches himself to my dress by resting his face against my body. . . . The called one feels almost a privilege, a gift, a prize. And yet he knows that all will be called. (423)

And hence the result:

After such exercises, it seemed that they loved me even more; they certainly had become more obedient, more sweetly tamed. Indeed, we had isolated ourselves from the world and had spent a few minutes together, united amongst ourselves. I desiring them and calling to them—and they receiving, in the profoundest silence, that voice directed to them each personally. (425)

The relationship between silence and voice is a complicated one in the Montessori classroom. It can under no circumstances be reduced to the child's silence and the teacher's voice, even if that voice is an "aphonic" one. While education includes, as its first step, a "calling to the student: a calling now to his attention, now to his interior life, now to social life" (241); while it includes a response to "the mysterious and much desired call" (360), education cannot take place in a noise that risks losing the child's attention (361). It is for this reason that part of musical education is the recognition of the difference between sound and noise. Similarly, the chapter entitled "How the Teacher Should Teach a Lesson" bears this epigraph from Dante's Inferno, canto 10: "le parole tue sien conte [may your words be counted]." The Montessori teacher is not to be loquacious; she must make her words count. In an effort to demonstrate what would constitute a bad lesson, Montessori offers the following example:

A teacher wanted to show the children the difference between noise and sound. She begins by offering the children a rather lengthy story; at that point a person, with whom she came to a prior arrangement, knocks at the door. The teacher interrupts herself and yells: "What is that? What happened? . . . Oh! I can no longer connect my thoughts, I can no longer continue the story, I no longer remember anything; we will have to let it go. Do you know what happened? Did you hear? Do you understand? It was a *noise*! . . . Oh! I prefer cradling this child (she picks up a mandolin dressed up in a blanket). Dear child, I prefer to play with you! Do you see it? Do you see the child I hold in my arms?" Some of the children say: "That's not a child," others: "That's a mandolin." The teacher: "No, no, this is a child: do you need proof? Oh, quiet, quiet, I think it is crying. . . . " She plucks the strings under the blanket. "Oh! Did you hear? . . . The baby cried. . . . " Some children: "That was the mandolin." "Those are the cords," . . . The teacher: "Quiet, children, listen carefully to what I am doing." She uncovers the mandolin and openly plucks the cord: "It is a sound!" (226–27)

Montessori comments:

To pretend that from such a lesson a child understands the teacher's intention, that is, her desire to make evident the distinction between noise and sound, is impossible. The child will gather that she was making a joke, or that she is a little nuts, because she loses the thread of her story because of a noise and because she mixes up a mandolin with a child. And for certain, what is encamped before the child's consciousness is the figure of the teacher, not the object of the lesson. (227–28)

The lessons, which are individual, never collective, in a Montessori classroom, must elicit the fewest possible words from the teacher; they are to be limited to the act of naming only. Mandolins are not babies, after all. Nomenclature and the exact use of language are central to the teacher's lessons and should be conducted along the lines of Séguin's "three periods": the association of a sensorial perception with its name; the recognition of the object that corresponds to the name; and the memory of the name that corresponds to the object. Thus, once the child has learned the proper use of the cylinder insets, for example, the teacher will sit down with the child, choose the largest and the smallest cylinders, point to them each separately and state: "This is large"; "This is small." In the second part of the exercise, the teacher will ask the child to hand her first the large cylinder, then the small one. Finally, in the third period, she will point to one of the cylinders and ask: "What is this like?" (457). Beyond this act of naming, however, the teacher is to remain silent, and her response to error, as well, must be that of silence and not correction, because error merely signifies that the child is not yet ready to absorb the offered lesson. He or she is not yet ready for the abstraction that language entails: "The lessons of nomenclature must consist very simply in provoking an association between the name and the object, the abstract idea that the name itself represents"(445). Language, as naming, is for Montessori, fundamentally a baptism: "The lesson of the name . . . completes [the child's] spontaneous work. The idea is known; it is alive because of his own work: and now comes the baptism, the name, the consecration" (358n107).

The teacher's language, her act of naming, is thus fundamentally a supplement to the child's "spontaneous work." The teacher must, beyond her baptism of things, remain silent, partly so that the child may hear another voice, the one spoken by things themselves. To some extent, this is the voice of nature—what Montessori refers to as "the moaning voice of needy life" (307)—but more importantly, this voice refers to those objects that exist in the child's prepared environment:

True, the teacher supervises; but it is things of all kinds that "call" to children of various ages. Actually, the shine, the colors, the beauty of cheerful and adorned things are also "voices" that attract the attention of the child and stimulate him to action. Those objects have an eloquence that no teacher could ever attain: take me, they say; keep me intact; put me where I belong. And the action completed according to the thing's invitation gives the child that cheerful satisfaction, that awakening of energy that predisposes him to the most intellectually challenging work of intellectual development. Many times, however, there is more than one voice of the things that call him: the call is made up of a complex order: some important work requires not only one child, but an organized collectivity, as well as an apprenticeship and long preparation. This is the case with setting the table, serving a meal, and clearing the dishes. (276)

The Writing Hand

Montessori's education to freedom, centered as it is on the language of things, functions as an inscription on the body's muscles, and therefore this education is grounded not in speech but in the act of writing. Montessori has little time for Rousseauist, "natural" education where culture constitutes a corruption of man and morals. In this sense, her education must be understood as a supplement in Derrida's sense of the term, that is, as an *inversion* of the relationship between speech and writing (Derrida 1974). Writing as practice and as ontology constitutes the privileged moment of a Montessorian education; it is that which makes speech possible. Hence the need not for a "natural environment" of learning, but for a *prepared* one, an environment structured not by what is but by what is made. The child learns through work, not play, and in that move becomes a man, *homo faber*: "Man passed from the state of nature to an artificial state through agricultural labor: when he discovered the secret of intensifying the products of the earth, he obtained the gift of civilization" (314). Man's "natural" state is that of artifice, to the extent that it makes possible a relationship between man and things.

The prepared environment *is* the Montessori classroom, that space *made* for children and thus capable of becoming the child's new home. All homes require a disposition of the environment, that is, furniture and objects of use. It must allow for the "freedom of the pupils in their spontaneous manifestations" (183), which implies, first and foremost, the abolition of the school desk and its substitution with furniture that has been adapted to the child's size, strength, and physical abilities. There are no toys in such a space, but rather objects that the child can manage and manipulate—small and light tables, chairs, couches, sinks, and closets. There is also, of course, Raphael's *Madonna* and the Montessorian didactic apparatus. Montessorian lore has it that children do not *want* toys, that even when presented with them, they will always choose the didactic materials instead.

Marja Schwegman has noted that the construction of a harmonious environment, one that is furthermore consciously separated from the personal influence of the teacher, constitutes both Montessori's originality and her Italianness. Thus, the prepared environment founds an educational project as an art form that is inspired by a concept of form born with Giotto and that links art (or artifice) to a positive knowledge of the world. Typical of this Italian artistic concept, according to Schwegman, is that art is conceived as a representation of a system of relations (space) in which each thing (object or figure) finds its proper meaning in relation to other things. Montessori's *Case* constitute, in this sense, an artistic representation of society, one that is urban, prepared, worked over. Within such a space, the child has at her disposal didactic objects that allow her to educate herself. The teacher in this space is nothing but the impersonal link between the environment and the child. The child's need for order—her drive, that is, to coordinate the different movements of her body—makes the child form a relationship with the things of the environment. Montessori's method is thus founded and completed when the child enters a relationship with the thing, when she engages her prepared environment (Schwegman 1999, 73–74).

"The most satisfying labor to children is not sowing but harvesting. . . . Harvesting intensifies, so to speak, the interest in sowing" (Montessori 2000, 316). The prepared environment offers the possibility of a harvest, of a picking, and, given the freedom of movement in this environment, this is always a "free choice," guided, as free choice demands, by an *invisible hand*. The nature of this hand, its secret or invisible quality that makes it so different from the hand of the puppeteer is that this hand educates the child, insofar as it makes him reach out with his own hand to pick the object most capable of satisfying his needs. "Here we are in praxis. Here we are in the school. The materials for sensorial development, established as a result of experimental research, are part of the environment" (319). Thus Montessori introduces the subsection entitled "Free Choice" in the chapter "The Nature of Education," a subsection added only with the 1926 edition. "The material is exposed here: he only has to extend his hand in order to pick [*cogliere*] it." What drives the child to choose one object over the other is not imitation, not only because there is only one such object in the environment and the child cannot therefore imitate another child's choice, but also because the child will become so immersed in the object that he will become oblivious to the outside world: "Imitation in fact binds [the subject] to the outside. Here we have exactly the opposite phenomenon: that is, the abstraction from the exterior world, and the extremely close bond with the intimate and secret world operating within the child" (319). The teacher becomes simply irrelevant before this attention, this "revelation of an interior world" (319), and, if she interferes with the child's relationship to the object established by his free choice, she can only harm the child's development.

The child's engagement, his choice of the didactic apparatus, has one fundamental goal—known by the child himself: to educate the senses. The education of the senses has two goals: the *biological* one of aiding the physiological development of the child and the *social* one of preparing the child for his relationship with the environment. For Montessori, the psychophysical development is crucial; it precedes intellectual development and dominates the lives of children until the age of approximately six. Above all, physiological development perfects the organs of the senses and opens the neurological paths of projection and association. Such training is, for Montessori, explicitly modern, as it trains the body for scientific observation, professionalization, and intelligent consumption. It is necessary, she states, to prepare children for an attitude of observation, "made necessary as a modern form of civic life" (431). We must recognize that it is from "observations that are born the discovery of Roetgen's [*sic*] rays, Herzian [*sic*] waves, the vibrations of radium, as we also expect from them the great applications similar to Marconi's discovery of the telegraph" (431). Subjects capable of observation are important in everyday life, as well. Observation makes us smart consumers because it allows us to recognize fresh foods, to understand when we are being cheated by some new product, to read labels, to be better doctors and patients as we become capable of reading the body's signs, and so on. Observation also makes us more discerning consumers of culture, because "aesthetic harmonies of nature and art escape those who have uncouth senses" (431–35).

The Montessorian didactic apparatus is made up of a series of objects that in a graduated manner have the goal of educating the senses:

> The sensorial material consists of a system of objects, grouped according to a determinate physical quality of their bodies—such as color, shape, dimension, sound, roughness, weight, temperature, etc. For example, there is a group of bells that reproduce musical tones, a collection of tablets graduated according to color, a group of solids of identical shape but of graduated dimensions, others, instead, that differ in their geometric shape, things of different weight but of the same size, etc etc.
>
> Each single group represents the same quality, but to different degrees—involved, then, is a gradation whereby the differences between objects vary regu-

larly and, when possible, are mathematically established. . . . Each group of objects . . . has at its extremities a "maximum" and a "minimum" in the series that determine the group's limits. (321–22)

The didactic apparatus thus trains the tactile, thermal, baric, stereognostic, visual, auditory, chromatic, and olfactory senses of the child's body. Two aspects are crucial to such an apparatus. First, it permits the *isolation* of each separate sensorial activity, indeed, it requires it. One might even say that the apparatus prepares the child to a specifically modernist aesthetic, insofar as it teaches the musical quality of music, the painterly quality of painting, a system of representation that has only the act of representing as its object. Isolation makes possible the act of distinguishing: "a tactile impression is clearer when the object does not conduct heat" (323). The object is isolated according to a single sensorial quality, and the subject, as well, is isolated from the world as she or he engages solely and concentratedly with that object. Therefore, the apparatus is precise and makes possible an internal and external analytic work capable of giving order to the infantile mind.

Second, the didactic apparatus controls for error and thereby takes over the job of the teacher. There is only one way to use the materials. The didactic apparatus is like a string of buttons where, if a button is placed in the wrong buttonhole or a button is forgotten, an empty hole will remain at the end of the process. Here, too, the objects speak instead of the teacher: "The objects, from the furniture to the individual materials for development, are denouncers whose admonishing voice cannot be escaped. Light colors and polish denounce dirt; the furniture's lightness denounces moves that are yet imperfect and crude, as they fall or are dragged across the floor. Thus, the whole environment is a strict educator, a sentinel always on the alert, and every child hears its admonishments as if he stood alone before that inanimate master" (324).

The didactic apparatus, therefore, makes self-education possible through the methodic education of the senses. The education of the senses, that is, the concrete notions that may be gathered from the environment through the senses, should not, Montessori insists, be confused with the language that provides a "nomenclature to concrete ideas" (353). Take the pianist, for example, she states: a piano teacher may instruct the pianist in where the notes are on the keyboard; she may indicate their graphic representation on manuscript paper; she may even foretell what the music will sound like when played. She cannot, however, play for the music student, because playing relies on the manual training of the pianist her- or himself. While the pianist is not made by exercise alone, that is, without the "direction" of the teacher, nevertheless, what must take place is "the long, patient application to exercises that serve to give agility to the articulation of the fingers and the tendons, in order to make *automatic* the coordination of specific muscular movements and to reinforce the hand muscles through repeated use of the organ" (353; my emphasis).

We return here to the centrality of the hand and to the possibility that the hand, in its very invisibility as a function of power, is in fact the privileged site of Montessori's sensorial training. In the *Metodo,* as elsewhere, Montessori tells the story of her encounter with Itard's and Séguin's works, an encounter that would prove so crucial to the writing of her own theory of education. "I set out to study the works of Itard and Séguin. I felt the need to meditate upon them. And therefore I did something I had never done before and that few perhaps could repeat: I copied out [*ricopiai*] in Italian, from beginning to end, the writings of these authors, in cursive, almost as if preparing books similar to those of the Benedictine monks before the diffusion of print. I did this in cursive in order to have the time to weigh the meaning of each of their words and to read the spirit of their authors" (126).

The writing hand occupies by far the longest sections of the *Metodo.* The act of writing serves as a foundation for what Montessori calls a "muscular memory" that is established during the child's "physiological period" (566), that is, between the ages of three and six, as the means by which the child enters the world of the symbolic. Writing is in some sense consonant with a process of what she calls the materialization of the abstract: "If we are thus able to 'materialize' an abstract idea by presenting it in a proper form to the child—in other words, as a *palpable object*—will the child's mind be able to appreciate it or be profoundly interested in it? The sensorial material may certainly be considered according to this point of view: as a *materialized abstraction.* The material presents 'color'—'dimension'—'form'—'smell'" (486). And further on: "Just as grammar and stylistics are not possible in spoken language, and it is therefore necessary to fall back on written language, because it keeps before our eyes the discourse to be analyzed, so it is with the word. The analysis of that which flees is not possible. It is necessary to *matterize* [*materiare*] language and make it stable" (601).

The training of the tactile sense begins the education of the senses and grounds the act of writing in the body. One might even venture that Montessori's concern with touch has an obsessive quality, one that comes about as the result of a prohibition. In the restrictions of the taboo, Freud tells us, "touching plays a part similar to the one it plays in 'touching phobias.' . . . Touching is the first step towards obtaining any sort of control over, or attempting to make use of, a person or object" (Freud 1950, 43). Touching phobias originate in the small child's desire to touch himself, in other words, in masturbation (37), and it is not insignificant that Montessori's only mention of a misuse of the hand is when it engages in masturbation (Montessori 2000, 437), though she displaces its origins to a maleficent environment. The conflict between touching and its prohibition may, Freud states, be indeed displaced "if certain actions are performed. Thereafter, these actions *must* be performed: they become compulsive or obsessive acts, and there can be no doubt that they are in the nature of expiation, penance, defensive measures and purification. The commonest of those obsessive acts is washing in water. . . . [The violation against the prohibition of touching] can be made good by a similar 'ceremonial' " (Freud 1950, 36–37).

And so, Montessori's lessons of the tactile sense begin with a bath: "Because in order to exercise the tactile sense it is necessary to touch, bathing the hands in tepid water has the additional advantage of teaching the child a principle of propriety: that of not touching objects, except with clean hands" (Montessori 2000, 368–69). With clean hands, then, Montessori teaches the child how to touch a surface. She takes the child's fingers into her own hand and makes them move delicately across the surface of the proper didactic materials. Of particular importance, and I shall return to this, is that the child do this *with her or his eyes closed* (369–70)—"as the blind do," Montessori had already stated in a 1908 report on her writing method (Montessori 1988, 95). The didactic materials are made up of a variety of tablets covered with smooth paper, variously graded emery boards and sandpaper, as well as differently textured fabrics.

This tactile apparatus is followed by the materials dedicated to the training of "visual-tactile-muscular perception" (Montessori 2000, 394), built around a series of wooden tablets that contain a variety of geometric insets that are furnished, "in order to facilitate their handling" (394), with little brass buttons (see fig. 8.3). "Annexed" to these tablets are a set of white cardboard squares (see fig. 8.4): "on a first series of these is glued a blue geometric shape of paper, in the same color as that of the inset pieces and which repeats in shape and dimension all the geometric figures of the collection. In the *second series* of identical cardboard sur-

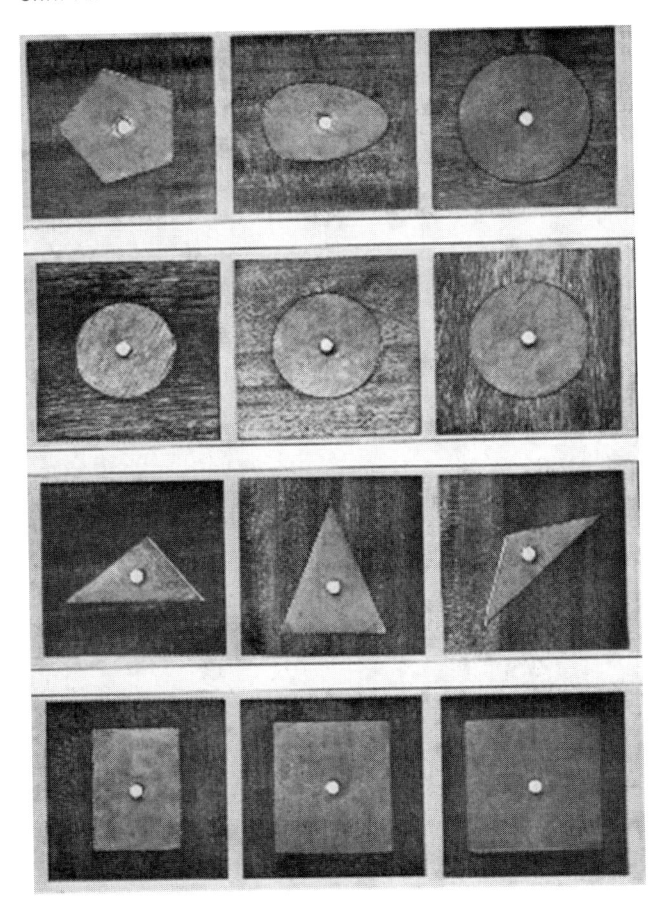

Figure 8.3 "Geometric inset tablets." (From Montessori, *Metodo della pedagogia scientifica.*)

faces is the glued *outline*, also in blue, of the same geometric figures, and the outlines are 1 cm thick. In the *third series* of identical cardboard surfaces are the outlines that reproduce the figures in the same dimensions and shapes, but this time they are *drawn by a black line*" (399).

When the child is first introduced to the inset tablets, he apparently does not immediately *visually* recognize where the correct pieces go. For this reason, Montessori must intervene: "*Recognition* is helped a great deal when one associates the visual sensation with tactile-muscular sensations. I have the child touch the contour of the shape with *the index finger of his right hand* . . . and make sure that this becomes *a habit* to the child. . . . In fact, the child that as yet cannot recognize the shape by *looking at it,* can recognize it, however, when he *touches it*" (401–2).

The association between the tactile-muscular sense and the visual one, indeed, the grounding of the latter in the former, produces bodily, muscular memory: the child accurately places the insets into their proper *holes,* not because he sees their identity but because his body remembers it. And therefore the eye comes into play only at that point when the transition is made from the concrete to the abstract. Once the child has mastered the inset tablets, can literally and metaphorically place the shapes into their corresponding holes *blindfolded,* he can move on to the cardboard series. In the first series, that of the full reproduction of the shapes, it is the eye that controls the exercise: the child must *recognize* the figure and then place the wooden shape perfectly on top of the drawing so as to hide it (see fig. 8.5).

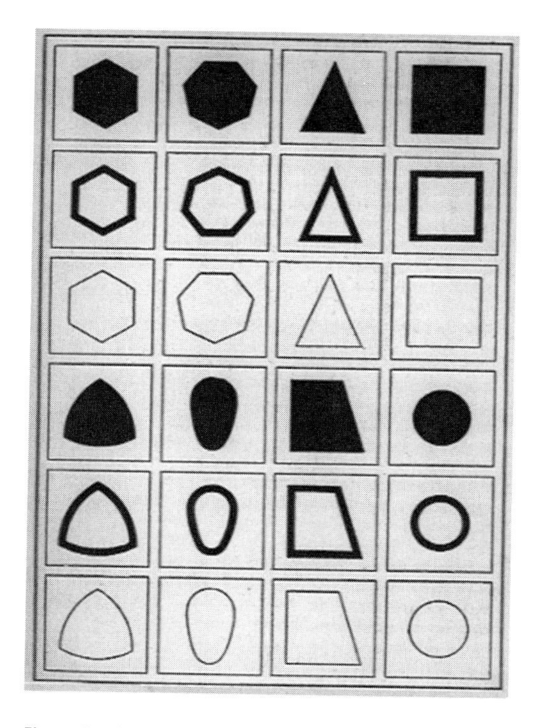

Figure 8.4 "Annexed cards." (From Montessori, *Metodo della pedagogia scientifica.*)

Figure 8.5 "Like the blind do." (From Montessori, *Metodo della pedagogia scientifica.*)

We have thus passed from the hole, from another kind of "*nulla*," to its symbolic representation. In the second series, the child again places the wooden shapes on the equally colored outlines. This is an extraordinarily important step:

> The child is gradually passing from *the concrete to the abstract.* At first he was handling only *solid objects,* then he moved on to a plane figure, that is, to a plane that in itself does not exist; now he is moving on to the *line.* But this line represents for him not the abstract contour of a plane figure; rather it is the *path many times completed by his index finger:* that line constitutes *the trace of a movement.* When passing over again with his finger the contour of the figure on the cardboard in such a manner that the figure disappears there where the finger touches it, the child has the impression of actually leaving a trace. Furthermore, because the trace disappears there where he touches, it is the *eye* that guides his movement. This movement, however, *was already prepared* by the moment when the child touched the solid contours of the wooden pieces. (404–5)

Abstraction is reached when, in the third series, the child encounters the black line. Here, not surprisingly, we finally meet not the finger that touches, but the pencil directed by a hand, one that has made this movement many times before and that therefore completes this movement *automatically.*

One may be tempted to assert that the child has here finally reached the stage of writing. But in fact, the child has always already been writing, doing so when for the first time he reached out and touched. As Montessori puts it rather tersely: "When he touches, he writes" (543). It is entirely legitimate to claim that Montessori is here part of that network that Friedrich Kittler has called the "discourse network of 1900," one that places writing as a physiological act at the center of the classroom (1990, 185). Loyal also, and by the same token, to the basic precepts of Italian positivism, Montessori heralds a "new era of writing, one that has an *anthropological basis*" (2000, 507).[4] The psycho-physiological study of writing entails, analogous to the positivist shift from object to subject, crime to criminal, deed to doer, a similar move: "to examine the *individual* who writes, not *writing*; the *subject*, not the *object*" (506). The study or the observation of the writing subject, the subject qua writing, is immensely productive, for it brings forth, as if "a surprise and a true gift of nature" (507), a new name: "method of spontaneous writing" (507). Such spontaneous writing, closely related to the future "explosion into writing," as well as to the sparseness of a language where words must be counted, leads to a discourse that, as Kittler points out, relies on a *telegraphic style*: "Ever since Nietzsche, the logic of the signifier has become a technique of sparseness and isolation, and minimum signs release maximum energy. Hermeneutic theories, with their notions of context, are inadequate to such a calculus. They are familiar only with organic relationships and with a continuous—that is, psychological or historical—narrative representation of them. The relative value of signifiers, by contrast, is given mathematically; its articulation is called counting" (Kittler 1990, 190). The child's act of writing, as Montessori herself puts it, "in this age achieves the function that is achieved by mathematics in the mind of the adult. It recalls the child's attention with a special intensity because from the composed word an idea results. And the signs with which the child composed it, could, by virtue of the choice and position of the letters, be compared to the data of a problem or to the terms of an equation" (Montessori 1988, 103).

The writing subject requires analysis, that is, the breakdown of the physical act into its separate mechanisms (Montessori 2000, 506), in order to produce the maximum energy with the least possible input. To this end, Montessori distinguishes between two types of movement that constitute the act of writing: one concerned with handling the writing implement, the other with designing the form of each letter of the alphabet. Together, these two activities make up the "motor mechanism" of writing, and they are to be distinguished from the work of intelligence that is also part of the act: "The fact that a machine may allow man to write clarifies how these two things—that is, the mechanics and the higher function of intelligence used by graphic language to express itself—can be separated one from the other" (523). One may not, I believe, glean from this analysis of the writing subject that such a subject is to be distinguished from the writing machine, in other words, the typewriter. On the contrary, the subject comes into being as writing subject by virtue of its prosthetic supplement, in an act that solders the body to the machine: the child's hand or finger cannot be separated from the pencil. We know that the typewriter was invented for the blind, just as Edison, the inventor of the gramophone and one of Montessori's earliest American admirers, was a teacher of the deaf. The media, according to Kittler, "like psycho-physical experiments, begin with a physiological deficiency" (1990, 231). Montessori's method, one inherited from the earliest scientific experiments with deaf-mutes, has this "media effect," that is, the production of a kind of automatic writing, the "syllabic hodgepodge" that constitutes the language of children and the mentally and physically deficient (Kittler 1990, 229). The simultaneously occurring experiments in psychophysics, the isolation of automatic functions that are rigorously separated from the brain's synthetic operations of sense-creation, undermine the distinction between normal and pathological and investigate, instead, the everyday capabilities that are usually deemed superfluous, pathological, or obsolete (215). Children thus learn to write without thinking, to read without understanding. The act of automatic writing uncouples, therefore, writing from reading, the signifier from the signified.

The signifier acts as an inscription on the body in the form of what Nietzsche in *The Genealogy of Morals* calls a *mnemotechnics,* a branding of the body that transforms the passage from nature to culture from that of an educational continuum to one of shock or trauma. If writing is this inscription on the body, this touching or abrasion, then it is no surprise that Montessori's children are writers by virtue of their contact with sandpaper: "Because I had the children touch the contours of the geometric figures of the inset tablets, it obviously followed to have them touch with their fingers also the *figures of the alphabetic letters*" (Montessori 2000, 509). The two components of writing—holding the

Figure 8.6 "Writing is touching." (From Montessori, *Metodo della pedagogia scientifica*.)

instrument and shaping the letter—originate in a mnemotechnics of the body when the child touches, shapes, and traces its lines with his hand. He moves to writing "proper" once he has learned to hold the writing implement and can recognize and reproduce the alphabet with his sensorial apparatus: his hand, his eyes and his ears. Montessori has children trace, with pencil, the wooden inset pieces on a piece of paper, drawing their outlines and then coloring them in with variously colored pencils. From this activity, the children become masters of the writing implement and so "perfect themselves in writing without writing" (534).

The didactic apparatus for the teaching the alphabet comprises letters made of sandpaper and letters cut out of either cardboard or leather (see fig. 8.6). In a first step, the teacher places two letters, for example, *i* and *o*, before the child and says: "This is *i*; this is *o*." She then leads the child's right index finger along the sandpaper letter, "in the sense of writing" (536). And therefore, "'to know how to touch,' and 'to know how not to touch' will consist in *knowing the sense* [*senso*: sense, meaning, direction] according to which one traces a determinate graphic sign" (536). Again, and this is crucial, the child may, indeed should, trace the rough surfaces of the letters with his eyes shut, in order to produce a tactile-muscular memory of the letter: "In the end, the child does not have his hand follow a visual image. Instead, it is the *tactile sensation* that makes the child's hand trace that movement which will then become fixed in muscular memory" (537). As Montessori had emphasized in "Come si insegna a leggere e a scrivere," her method is an *analytic* one that lays bare the separation of functions: "But what most directly leads to the goal and form, one could even say the basis of the method, is the guided preparation of the movement of writing, a movement that in the common [i.e., old] method consisted of a long and arduous effort that *the hand must make in order to imitate that which the eye sees*. And yet between the visual sensation (the letter) and the motor act (writing) there exists no direct central relationship, as, for example, exists by virtue of heredity between auditory language and spoken language" (Montessori 1988, 102). As earlier with the geometric shapes, the child does not recognize a letter by looking at it, but by touching it. Though the child has never in his life written a single letter of the alphabet himself, he has always been writing because he touches. He is also reading because he has made a connection, an association between his tactile and visual memories and the sound of a letter. He will therefore rather quickly progress to composing words himself by using the letters of the didactic apparatus. For example, and this example is hardly fortuitous, the "directress *very* clearly pronounces a word, for example, hand [*mano*]. . . . She repeats the sounds several times. Almost always the child . . . will reach for an *m* and put it on the table" (547).

It is here, then, that a "reasoning mind" (550) is finally formed. Montessori is quite adamant that what the children are doing is a *work founded in the body*, not an externally imposed rote or mechanical memory. The children compose the word *hand* because it exists as memory trace in their own bodies, not because they have memorized it in the traditional way or because the Italian language is merely phonetic: the child, instead "looks intently at the letter box, while *imperceptibly moving his lips*, and one by one he picks the necessary letters, *without committing a single orthographic error*. . . . It was in this manner that I dictated to our children the German names *Darmstadt*, *Petermann*, despite the fact that they obviously had never heard these words pronounced before. They composed them without any sign of surprise or difficulty by translating *all the sounds*, that is, without omitting a single letter that made up the word" (548). By thus analyzing and fixing spoken language to the written order, indeed by fixing the image of the graphic sign as separate from spoken language—hence the nonsense of *Darmstadt* and *Petermann*—the child will turn himself into a writing

Figure 8.7 "Explosion into writing." (From Montessori, *Metodo della pedagogia scientifica*.)

machine and thus continuously take dictation: "It will soon occur that the child, when hearing a word or thinking of a known word, will *see all the necessary letters* that make up the word *line up* in his mind, with a *facility* that is truly surprising" (549).

Writing turns into one continuous dictation in the form of an inner compulsion that—once the child takes a pen into his own hand—can express itself only as an explosion. And so, on one sunny winter day, Montessori is out on the terrace with the children and she hands a small child a piece of chalk so that he may draw: "The child for a moment seemed to explode into some joyous act, and then he screamed: 'I am writing! I am writing!' and he knelt down and on the ground he wrote the word *hand*, and then with enthusiasm he also wrote: *chimney*, then *roof*. . . . [The other children joining him] set out to write a variety of words, too: *mamma, mano*" (555). Supposedly, not one of these children had ever written a single word before, and yet here they were writing entire words, entire sentences all at once, flawlessly and dexterously. It seems a miracle or dream, for revealed here is the fact that graphic language takes place not gradually but only in the form of an explosion (556). And the children begin to write everywhere: on the floors, the walls, the windows, the doors, in an explosive flurry of activity that Montessori has difficulty containing (see fig. 8.7). It is almost as if she had created a monstrous, unnatural mechanism, a Frankenstein that requires some system of brakes:

This impulsive work that I was unable to slow down during the first days made me think of nature's wisdom when it *gradually* develops spoken language and develops it *contemporaneously* with the gradual formation of ideas. If nature acted imprudently like me and had the senses harvest rich and ordered materials; if it allowed the development of an entire patrimony of ideas and thereby completely prepared articulate language, in order to then tell the child who hitherto has been absolutely mute: "Go! Speak," we would witness the phenomenon of a sudden, mad logorrhea. The child would begin to speak nonstop and without brake until his lungs became exhausted and his vocal chords consumed, and he would pronounce the strangest and most difficult words. . . . We must provoke graphic language less suddenly. But even if we make it come into being more gradually, we must nonetheless provoke it as a *spontaneous fact* that exists from the very first time in an almost *perfect* form. (558–59)

As much as *Darmstadt* or *Petermann* or even *tetto* may seem just so much Kittlerian syllabic babble, what the children write, even in their seeming innocence and ignorance, has a double materiality, for this is a materiality that not only evinces the fact that writing is founded in bodily memory, but also one that exists by virtue of its grounding in a historical reality that is concrete and specific. Dictation is taken, and it produces in the children's bodies a memory that is far more effective than the rote recitation of the lives of Risorgimento heroes and heroines. It is a certain, specific dictation, one that is reproduced in all the editions of the *Metodo* (see fig. 8.8). In the writing of babes, the bodies of the king and his consort return as a form of power that exists and is effective by virtue of its writerly quality, that is, because it is no longer externally imposed but brought home, privatized, interiorized.

Taking Dictation

Interiorization, the process that describes the essence of Montessori's educational project, constitutes in her system a kind of nodal point, one that leaves open the nature of those strings that make up this knot, and one that therefore also leaves unanswered the nature of those strings that attach the subject to his prepared, historical environment. What kind of social bond comes into being by virtue of this Montessorian interior; and, in turn, what kind of subjectivity is permitted by the bond that is set into motion by the Montessorian apparatus? What is the relationship, ultimately, between the writing subject who comes into being as a result of a dictation and the teacher who is both pas-

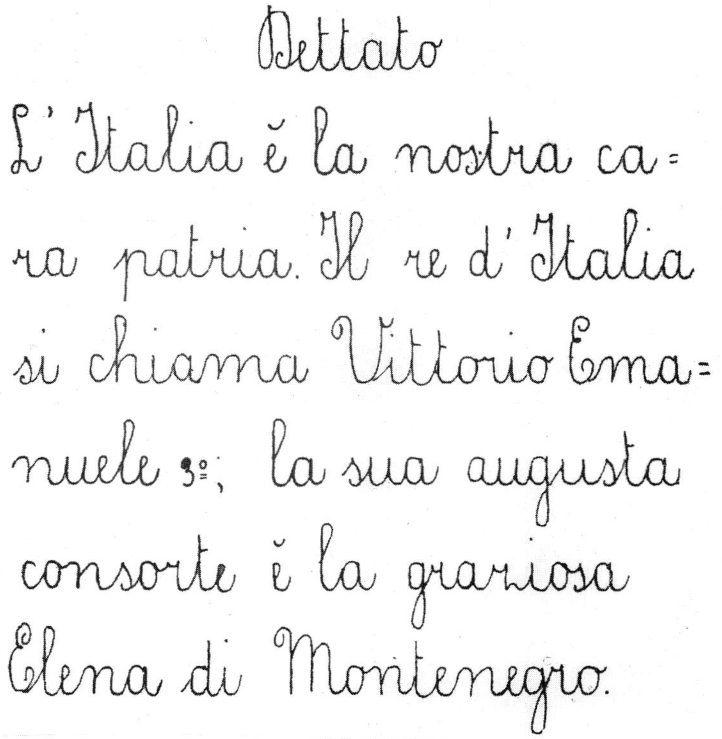

Dettato
L'Italia è la nostra ca=
ra patria. Il re d'Italia
si chiama Vittorio Ema=
nuele 3º; la sua augusta
consorte è la graziosa
Elena di Montenegro.

Figure 8.8 Dictation: "Italy is our beloved fatherland. The King of Italy is Victor Emanuel III; his august consort is the gracious Elena of Montenegro." (From Montessori, *Metodo della pedagogia scientifica*.)

sive or absent, and yet also a dictator? What kind of subject is made in a system that is accused of both excessive freedom and dictatorial tendencies?

In an attempt to answer these questions, my final comments will, after a detour through another of Montessori's texts, take the form of a comparison between a *text*, the dictation about kings and queens I have already mentioned, and another form of dictation, though now in the shape of a photograph taken of a Montessori classroom sometime during the 1930s.

But I will begin with a detour through the address delivered by Montessori to the National Congress of Italian Women in 1908, entitled "The Sexual Morality in Education." Pedagogical anthropology and its subcategory biometrics have made it possible—so Montessori begins—to reconstruct the perfect "average man" according to mathematical laws and in an environment that is devoid of guilt and sin, in accordance with pure nature and with the established proportions that "correspond precisely to those that Greek art had immortalized in its statuary. We could thus become the great artists of the world of the future, the shapers of perfect human beauty, not in marble, but in living flesh" (Montessori 1995c, 154). This new man, this symbol of perfection, this Christ-like figure of the future, gives birth to a new awareness, to a sense of eugenic responsibility toward the species. The new sexual morality that both produces and is produced by the new man will make possible a procreation guided by scientific principles. And yet an odd paradox guides this knowledge, insofar as it is predicated on a strange education, wherein "the teacher disappears, even almost its scientific content disappears, before the birth of a conscience of those who listen. This is so because this conscience leads to a responsibility toward the species . . . and a feeling of horror for the carelessness by which humanity treads on this great responsibility" (154). Montessori's anti-Darwinian, epigenetic, and ultimately vitalist elimination of environmental adaptation partly grounds the elimination of the teacher: "Education can perfect and guide, but it cannot alter the individual once he is created: what kind of education could make an imbecile intelligent, a blind man see, turn the morally insane into a useful and normal man? An individual's personality is essentially determined at conception in that egg cell that is invisible and microscopic but that contains the whole individual." And hence the paradox: education is "truly omnipotent when it acts for those who do not yet exist, when it assumes the position of sovereign and director of the biological future of the species" (154).

How then impart such a lesson, one that seemingly is predicated on the disappearance of a teacher who is nevertheless sovereign, but has as its main object those who are not yet born? In fact, Montessori states, it is only as parable that the lesson of sexual morality can be given: "I chose two parables that I owe to illustrious women who have left us eloquent syntheses that summarize in a simple but profoundly efficient manner this elevated question, especially regarding the maternal work of educating children" (154–55). These parables, parables that in Montessori's examples are to teach male sexual continence and answer the question of where babies come from, work in fact a *reversal* of the traditional handbooks of proper female behavior, wherein it was woman's duty to sacrifice herself for the sexual freedom of her son.

Two parables, then, of exemplary maternal education, and they impart lessons about sovereign presence and absence. The first parable, that of "Madame Héricourt," conveys the message that the mother must teach her son sexual continence, that he must refrain from dishonoring women, that he must sacrifice himself not only to her honor but to her very strength:

> We have great examples of the true mother from antiquity. Veturia, for example, is a mother and a strong woman, who leaves the walls of the city and breaches the enemy's lines in order to confront a powerful son. . . . She confronts her son, this great leader of armies, in order to ask him whether he is a traitor to the fatherland. And this great, victorious leader, faced with his mother's admonishments, will sacrifice his promises and his life. The true mother should today be like this mother; she should leave behind the walls of prejudice and the borders of slavery, to have such dignity as to be capable of stopping her son and telling him: "Son, you will not be a traitor to humanity!" But to teach such heights, the mother must change—she cannot be this omnipotent and great woman if she is like today's mother, who is nothing but the guardian, or as they say, the educator, of the child. She who educates must, as much as possible, make herself like the one she educates. . . . The mother who desires to follow man and be the mother of man, must make herself virile, be like him a fighter in the social environment. (155–56)

The second parable comes from "Nelly" and addresses the problem of creation. The prohibition against women telling the truth about human sexuality, which leads them instead to tell lies about storks and other such fables, is grounded, for Montessori, not only in women's moral slavery to men but also in a "fatal sin," a "fatal confusion" between means and ends: "an original sin due to which man loses the vision of all that which is great. The concept of species may adequately illustrate this idea. The creation of living beings, life eternalized in its wondrous variety, this is greatness, this is the river. Conception, the cell of conception, that insignificant speck, nothingness, that is the means. He who loses sight of the end and fixates on the means, makes himself small and necessarily degrades himself. This original sin is properly a sin of scientific interpretation: it is not a sexual sin" (159). Because of this confusion between means and ends, we are today, Montessori continues, stuck in original sin, a fact which is evidenced in the proliferation of seduction, prostitution, and irresponsible maternity, on the one hand, and, on the other, in the blind and starved obsession over virginity.

The shame, according to Montessori, that surrounds contemporary sexuality today is indeed fully justified, because it points to society's inability to distinguish between its means and its final destination. Therefore, the aim of all sexual education must be to distract the attention of the new men "from the means, in order to refocus it on the greatness of the end; whence to repair and protect individuals from the danger of the fall, to surround the child with the great splendor of that admirable end that leads to creation and eternal life" (159). The mother, as well as the school, to the extent that the school socializes the maternal function, must be the primary agents of such a lesson, a lesson to be given—quite paradoxically—not through lengthy narratives of explication (which would, in a sense, return our attention to the means) but through a sensory contact with the mother's body: "It would be enough for the child to see his pregnant mother. . . . And try to touch with his little hands those new feelings of him who will be his brother." Ultimately, the mother's lesson must simply be that of *being* a mother. This is also a lesson that therefore knows its own limits, for it will be the school to which will be reserved "the important problem of imparting the great lessons of the ends of creation, by method, study, and science" (159). And yet this school, in turn, must itself be modeled on the mother, for the new mother is by definition always already eccentric, that is, defined by a love that can only be by virtue of its relationship to eternity: "Maternal love does not reside in the mother's heart; maternal love is something bigger. It is the form assumed by life in order to protect and conserve itself, a great thing beyond creatures, for it seems to touch its origins in life itself" (161).

These, then, are the lessons conveyed by the two parables: on the one hand, the mother as sovereign queen to whom the son must bow in order to become lover of the nation; and on the other hand, the strange absence of the mother, who because of this absence rectifies original sin at the moment when the child touches her maternity. A virile maternity, therefore, one that structures a dialectics of presence and absence, becomes here the primary transmitter of (sexual) knowledge and the site where the national citizen, the new man, is born. I have insisted that such a subject is, for Montessori, quintessentially textual, the result, that is, of a dictation that inscribes into its textual body the fable of kings and queens. In this sense, the resultant text constitutes a worked-over bodily inscription of the family romance from which the subject is born.

As a point of contrast to this textual inscription/creation of the subject, I would like to introduce, finally, a visual representation of

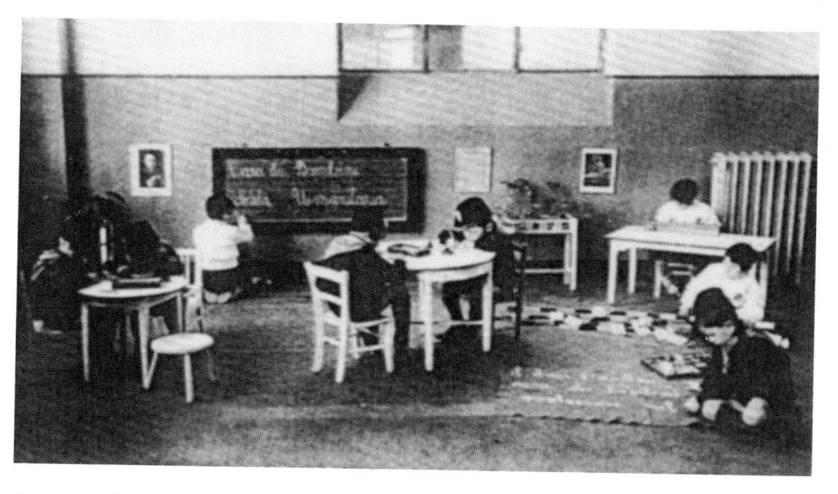

Figure 8.9 Fascism in the classroom. Milan, 1930s. (Società Umanitaria, Milan.)

the Montessori classroom (see fig. 8.9). At a first glance, and as Luisa Lama has noted, this image appears to be that of a typical Montessori classroom: we see children quietly working for themselves; we see the prepared environment replete with didactic apparatus, the proper furniture, and the potted plants (Lama 2002).[5] On closer inspection, however, we begin to notice that the children are dressed in fascist uniforms, those proper to the Balilla and the Piccole Italiane. And then we also notice, as Lama has put it, a "clamorous absence" (310): there is no teacher in this picture, no Montessorian directress, that figure so absolutely crucial to the method, to the extent that it is she who mediates between the child's inner world and the broader social environment. And yet there is indeed an adult present in the classroom—in the shape of a portrait on the wall, hung low enough for it to be at eye-level with the children. It is the image of the dictator Mussolini. Furthermore, one of the children sitting on the floor is taking dictation. He is writing: "il duce è nostro [the Duce is ours]." Perhaps, Lama speculates, the teacher is no longer necessary because she has been replaced by the man who now "directs" all Italians: Benito Mussolini.

It is the nature of this replacement that concerns me here, this substitution of Mussolini for Montessori or the Montessorian teacher. It constitutes indeed, as Lama says, "a problematic knot in the history of Montessorianism" (311), a knot that Lama, however, limits to the relationship between Montessori and the fascist regime. It is as if Lama wanted to put her own parenthesis around both fascism and Montessori, symptomatically, for instance, by dating the photograph "perhaps in the second half of the 1930s, when the doctor is already far from Italy and her schools are no longer her own." But does the literal absence of Montessori constitute a kind of guarantee of purity of method or, for that matter, an essential freedom for the Montessorian child? If the photograph had been taken early in the 1930s (and we do not know this), would the problem not necessarily become more complex? My point here is not to insist on this latter possibility so much as to point to the need to think of Montessorian absence along more differentiated, less literal lines, that is, along lines that take into account Montessori's own writing about writing children, who *always* take dictation in her prepared environment. Thus, I ask, is there some kind of fundamental difference, one that would support other political, cultural, and ideological differences, between children who take dictation about kings and queens from a Montessori teacher and those who take dictation from a portrait of the Duce?

The fascist regime itself operated precisely with a literal understanding of absence when it hoped for a successful application of the method in the shape of a Montessorianism without Montessori, when, in other words, it believed it could lead Italian children to an explosion into writing without the intervention of the Montessori teacher herself. It was in fact this use of her method, this *utilitarian and instrumentalist application*, to which Montessori objected, not only vis-à-vis the fascist understanding of it, but also already two decades earlier in her refusal to allow her method to become Americanized. As she had made clear in the *Metodo*, her educational method certainly involved a technique, but this technique could not function autonomously, lest it thereby defaulted on its educational purpose. The teacher had to be present, but present in the form of a radical absence: she had, in a sense, to make herself into a kind of "*nulla*," into a zero. In other words, she had to be both sovereign and nothing, to hold in tension both parables that circumscribe sexual (and subjectival) creation. In the end, this constitutes the difference between the children's dictation in the fascist classroom and the *text* that makes up the children's writings about kings and queens. While in the first, the photograph, Montessori is literally absent, in the second she is present by virtue of her radical absence. The first allows for a superficial understanding of freedom, one that leans toward abandonment; the second constitutes a free subject qua writing subject. Hence, I would contend, Montessorian freedom arises out of the presence of the dictator who exists because she is absent, because she is unrepresentable to the extent that she has been interiorized as writing. Such a notion had to be unpalatable to Mussolini, who would have objected to the absent part as much as to the "she" part. Montessori opposes her own concept of freedom to other, more literalist understandings of freedom, incorrect notions of freedom either because they are identical to the abandonment of the child to his or her own conflictual desires or because they exist only superficially, instrumentally, as an *attitude*.

In a 1914 essay on the "fundamental principles" of the method, Montessori targets Tolstoy and Dewey as exemplary of such misunderstandings of freedom: "Tolstoy conceives of the free school as based in the work of the *Teacher*, who, having rid himself of curricula and all other ties, may freely understand the needs of the child and thereby fulfill them. Dewey, on the other hand, entrusts the freedom in schools to the children, a freedom that is founded in reciprocal control and thus in the pupils' feelings of responsibility for each other. But these two fundamental approaches lack a grounding of freedom, insofar as this freedom is entrusted to *attitudes* that, in both teacher and pupils, may fail" (Montessori 1995b, 165). Montessori advocates neither complete freedom for the teacher (the leader or dictator) nor for the child, because the first is ultimately authoritarian and the second, American one, introduces a kind of monitorialism and thus places too many burdens on the child. Indeed, Montessori is remarkably close to Freud's own interrogation of the social bond here, one that he would investigate in *Group Psychology and the Analysis of the Ego* (1920) and in *Civilization and Its Discontents* (1930) and that he too, in its democratic version, would posit as founded in the negotiation and working-over of transferential desires vis-à-vis authority (the superego) and of identificatory drives among the members of a social group.[6]

What kind of social bond, then, does Montessori articulate for her educational method? First, I would think, it must be present but fundamentally invisible, and it is this invisibility that grounds her ultimately textual method in science and in modern technology. The teacher must, as I have said earlier, function as an invisible hand. In the programmatic statement Montessori wrote for the first issue of a new journal to be published by the *Opera nazionale Montessori* in 1932, she declared that it was the goal of the journal to "contribute to the real construction of a new civilized world," a construction that had to be understood as a reconstruction, beginning with the education of children and the practical organization of a developmental environment (Montessori 1932, 67). Given this goal, the Montessori movement had to refuse any relationship with "the innumerable relics of the old world"; the movement had to be unilateral and combative but nevertheless recognize its allies. Among such allies, Montessori counts scientific discoveries in biology, nutritional studies, and gymnastics. She also lists (in first place) psychoanalysis. To these she adds, furthermore, cultural organizations such as the Balilla, children's theaters, and the movies. Finally, the journal should also be concerned with all scientific discoveries that were useful for the society of the future, discoveries whose applications might make it possible to utilize nonlocalized energies (the radio, atomic energy) and thus make men and women independent from geographic obstacles (70). This list may very well constitute a summary of the complexities of Montessori's legacy, as it combines fascist youth movements with psychoanalysis, modern science, and technology.

Unquestionably, Montessori had a great interest in promoting and making use of modern technologies that cut the subject loose from the strings that attached him or her to tradition. In this sense, she participated in the construction of a subject who might be thought of as a "wireless subject."[7] Nevertheless, Montessori also refused a kind of technological reductionism, one that would confine the subject to being a product of mere technique. Though Montessori's subject is not the psychoanalytic subject, she does bring into being for this subject an interiority constituted through transferential mechanisms that refuse both the appeals of great dictators and instrumentalist techniques. She shared with Freud the need to construct an interiority of the subject by virtue of his or her capacity to successfully negotiate the transferential relation. Contrary to Freud, however, she named the failure of such a negotiation the original sin of confusing ends and means. She thus realigned her scientific principles, and this not just opportunistically, to Christian, indeed Catholic, principles. What she may have had over Freud, perhaps, was the possibility that her science gave space to a teacher who was a woman.

Conclusion

This book has portrayed the making of a viable and vexed Italian modernity during the first fifty years or so following Unification, a modernity that was in place prior to Italy's entry into the Great War and prior to the rise of fascism. At the same time, it refutes the teleological assumption that would drive Italy inevitably into the hands of a fascist dictatorship. In this sense, it takes issue with Barrington Moore's famous thesis that Italy modernized "from above," as well as with Silvio Lanaro's claim that the Italian post-Unification period was certainly well on its way to becoming a modernized nation but that everything in its development already prefigured a fascist solution (Moore 1993; Lanaro 1980). In my chosen texts, I have here tried to show that these texts' authors were neither blind traditionalists nor protofascists.

Of course, this does not imply that the period preceding the First World War bore no relationship to what was to come. Maria Montessori, as I just showed, flirted with some of fascism's presuppositions, but a commitment to freedom of and through education prevented an ultimate absorption of her method into the regime. Italian positivism, as well, produced an ambivalent legacy. I have argued that a more nuanced reading of Lombroso's work makes it difficult to insert him into some inevitable totalitarian logic, if for no other reason than that a science of police surveillance was not the primary item on his intellectual agenda. Lombroso always remained a socialist, whether as a member of the Italian Socialist Party or not. His disciples fell on either side of the political divide after 1922.

His daughters Paola and Gina and his sons-in-law Guglielmo Ferrero and Paolo Carrara went into exile after Mussolini's rise to power, and they stayed away after the racial laws in 1938. Sighele—who died before World War I—briefly joined the Irredentist movement of his native Trento but left it because he opposed extreme versions of Italian nationalism. Nevertheless, as I mentioned, Sighele had his reservations about parliamentary democracy. Enrico Ferri and Vincenzo Mellusi, on the other hand, became devoted supporters of Mussolini's regime and made important contributions to the articulation of fascist ideology.

Similarly, the parliamentary novel became an important vehicle for both the description but also the critique of the Italian parliamentary system, and though its exemplars over the years became increasingly strident in their demands for "masculine" solutions to the conundrums of democratic effeminacy, such demands were anything but univocal. The conservative and deeply Catholic Antonio Fogazzaro, for instance, advocated a Catholically inspired leadership that harked back more to Gioberti's Neo-Guelphism than forward to Mussolini's fascism. And Serao, I have argued, despite her avowed antifeminism, nevertheless provided an analysis of Italian cultural and political relations to the newly formed government, an analysis that was acutely aware of these relations' grounding in gender politics. Finally, Edmondo De Amicis—always a committed socialist—demonstrated but also participated in the construction of an Italian physical body saturated with pleasure but nonetheless dedicated to the patriotic building of the fatherland.

And yet despite the lack of predetermination in Italy's social and cultural development, Italian fascism was not—as Benedetto Croce so famously put it—a parenthesis in modern Italian history. The sociopolitical, cultural, and scientific landscape I have described most certainly also set the stage for what was to come after the collapse of the liberal state in 1922. I would propose, however, that my own reading of the period between Unification and the fascist regime opens the possibility of a reevaluation of all those sociopolitical, cultural, and scientific forces that together would come to constitute Italian fascism. At the end of the chapter on Sighele, and as an example, I have pointed to one possible site of such a reevaluation. There I proposed that one factor in fascist consent may very well have been shaped *not* by an unlimited suggestive and seductive relationship to the Duce, but instead, quite paradoxically, by the subject's *defense* against such a relation through practices of autosuggestion and self-making. What I am then proposing is that a closer study of the period between 1860 and 1920 may very well shape future understandings of the fascist phenomenon itself. In this context, I would insist that teleology must be replaced by a complicated pattern of continuity and discontinuity.

Another site of continuity is undoubtedly that provided by the Catholic Church, not only and most obviously because of its explicit political alliance with the fascist regime, but more importantly because it was the only institution capable of building—in the post-Unification period—a national-popular movement on the basis of those marginalized by Italy's democratic process. The Vatican's mass following by women and southern peasants was, therefore, from its inception antidemocratic but, as I have argued, not therefore antimodern. The extraordinary holding power of this movement finds proof in the fact that it survived fascism itself. But such holding power also suggests that fascism itself had deep roots in Catholicism.

Strikingly absent from my discussion is the Italian thinker who became both the most trenchant analyst of and successor to the Pinocchio Effect. This thinker is, of course, Antonio Gramsci. If the Pinocchio Effect describes a mode of thought that seeks to negotiate between the anxiety about a potential emptiness regarding Italian national existence and the bond that nonetheless ties that Italian to his or her national existence, between an interrogation of the material, presymbolic form of this subject and his or her ideological, symbolic existence in the world, then the greatest heir to that thought was Gramsci's concept of hegemony. Like De Sanctis, Gramsci thought of hegemony as a schooling.[1] Every relationship of hegemony, Gramsci famously stated, "is necessarily an educational relationship" (Gramsci 2000, 348). And similar to De Sanctis, Gramsci's own engagement with a national pedagogy led him to distinguish between but not oppose "instruction" and "education." And like Montessori, Gramsci refused pure passivity or a mechanical reception of knowledge (Gramsci 2000, 312–13). Finally, like Pinocchio, Gramsci distinguished, within the knowledge that is constitutive of a child's consciousness, between a knowledge that is *certain* and a knowledge that is *true,* which is how he differentiated between a knowledge that is actively acquired and made part of self-making (the certain) and a knowledge that is passively received, imposed from the outside (the true): "The 'certain' of an advanced culture becomes 'true' in the framework of a fossilized and anachronistic culture. There is no unity between school and life, and so there is no automatic unity between instruction and education. In the school, the nexus between instruction and education can only be realized by the living work of the teacher" (Gramsci 2000, 313). If the teacher is unable to provide a link between instruction and education, then school as the site where Italians must be made will become a rhetorical exercise because "the material solidity of what is 'certain' is missing, and what is 'truth' will be a truth only of words: that is to say, precisely, rhetoric" (313).

Gramsci's theory of hegemony has been the subject of a long and extensive debate, especially since the term was adopted as the founding stone of a democratic strategy by European communist parties after 1945. Here, for the purposes of my own argument, I would like to think of the concept of hegemony in relation to Gramsci's pedagogy, one that encompasses a spectrum between the certain and the true. The certain marks not only a successful pedagogy but also a successful because democratic-popular hegemonic relation between the people and the state. Furthermore, it describes not only education but a synthesis between education and instruction: that is, not mere passive obedience but active consent; not mere rote repetition of a past tradition but an activation of the past for the future. Certainty allows for an attachment to the state at the level of the subject's transformative capacities. It describes, as Althusser would have it, that moment when the subject turns toward the law in an act of (self-)mastery. Certainty's opposite is both mere obedience but also—and quite strikingly—truth. This is striking because truth, for Gramsci, comes to be aligned not only to mechanical obedience, to ideology in its worst sense, but also to a fundamental untruth, to what Gramsci also terms fetishism:

> How fetishism can be described. A collective organism is made up of single individuals, who form the organism in that they have given themselves a hierarchy and a determinate leadership which they actively accept. If each of the single components thinks of the collective organism as an entity extraneous to himself, it is evident that this organism no longer exists in reality, but becomes a phantasm of the intellect, a fetish. . . . The relations between the individual and the organism come to be seen as a dualism, and a critical outward attitude arises on the individual's part towards the organism. . . . At any event a fetishistic relation. The individual expects the organism to act, even though he himself does not act and does not consider that, precisely because his attitude is shared by many others, the organism is necessarily inactive. (Gramsci 2000, 243–44)

Truth, insofar as it is a fetishism and refuses its existence in social reality, is a lie. It pertains, as Derrida has remarked, to a purely epistemological domain that refuses its implications with social relations or what Derrida calls a testimonial logic, by which he means *both* the juridical language of bearing witness and the awareness of such a language's grounding in performativity (Derrida 2002). And this returns us to Pinocchio's nose, one that does not represent the opposition between lies and truth—this opposition belongs to the fetishized world that surrounds him—but to certainty: a certain sign, a testimony or symptom to the fact that such a thing as the lie exists. The lie, Derrida states with reference—not coincidentally—to Freud's *Kinderlügen* (children's lies), is a "revealing symptom, the avowal of another truth" (69).

The failure to give up truth, to mourn it in the same way one mourns the past and all that which has been lost, to develop the capacity to distinguish between certainty and truth, may well be not only what produced Italian fascism, but more generally, conceptual attachments to power in Italy that have prohibited an engagement with Italian history beyond the existence of a parenthesis around fascism. Foucault once stated that in "political thought and analysis, we still have not cut off the head of the king" (1978, 88–89). And Roberto Esposito views such a killing as a kind of inevitable introjection: the "reassumption of the head into the political body . . . is the strategic move that allows the old metaphor to survive and even to regenerate itself from its apparent death . . . because the real decapitation should have definitely extinguished its semantic charge. If this does not occur, it is because . . . this head, even before falling, has been incorporated and dissolved into the collective organism of the nation. The latter becomes the new subject of the analogy, now translated from the old body of the king to that of the citizens united into one single people" (Esposito 2003, 140).

The Jewish Triestine poet Umberto Saba wrote in one of his first *Scorciatoie* dated February 1945 and entitled "The History of Italy": "Italians are the only people (I believe) who have, at the origin of their history (or of their legend), a fratricide. And it is only through parricide (the killing of the old) that one can begin a revolution. Italians want to give themselves a father and have from him, in exchange, the permission to kill their brothers" (Saba 2001, 8). In April of that same year, Italians would, of course, execute their primal father and publicly exhibit his body in a public square. Saba, in another entry, titled, significantly, "Totem and Taboo," and written immediately after the event (49), noted that the first symptoms of remorse, if not denial, showed themselves immediately: Italians, "in order to express themselves, sought cross streets, streets that were oblique and covered; words that could be interpreted only by he who has an ear for the language of the unconscious. They said: 'They should have killed along with him, before him, many others' (and what followed were names and last names, all now of people who—relative to him—were young; *brothers* rather than fathers)."

The murder of the father and the decline of the paternal metaphor have the potential to survive, then, as Freud already taught us, through his incorporation, his fetishization as a kind of Villellian skull, and thereby create a new social bond within the body of the nation itself, as a metaphor that is always ever ready to reliteralize itself in the shape of new leaders.

Notes

INTRODUCTION

1. In a recent review of the immensely popular thriller series by the Sicilian Andrea Camilleri, Francesco Erspamer has remarked on the Italian incapacity to create a productive relationship with its own past. Italy still today is unable to historicize, even to mourn its past, and consequently continues to indulge in what Erspamer calls a specifically Italian rhetoric of nostalgia. The critic notes the paradox of this structure: "At the very moment when design impresses its 'made in Italy' on the world as a laboratory of the new and when the country, and not only formally, has entered the European Union and left behind archaic social structures and behaviors, what is being affirmed in a broad array of social sectors is a rhetoric of nostalgia, one that is abstract and consolatory but nonetheless influential in its ability to shape the current self-representation of Italians" (Erspamer 2002, 1).
2. Angelo Mosso, the important physiologist who will appear in later chapters, claimed that Italianness was marked by "Latin effeminacy," a characteristic that he traced back to an Italian penchant for sensuality. Mosso's is not a purely racial argument, however; instead, he places responsibility for the situation at the feet of a "false education," to the extent that Italian men were treated like children even when they became adults. Such an education is for him "German," since the new state blindly imitated its northern neighbors and therefore repressed Italian natural tendencies. Mosso thus straddles an argument between nature and culture, not quite making a racist argument, but nevertheless believing that education must in some sense reflect

inherent national traits. I have not in this book addressed the question of racial theories or the so-called Southern Question in the constitution of an Italian identity. A fine analysis of the latter is provided by Nelson Moe (2002). For Angelo Mosso's discussion of Italian effeminacy, see Mosso 1897a.

3. See in this regard especially the recent study by Judith Surkis (2006).
4. The literature on Italian "backwardness" is immense. Other than the influential study by Asor Rosa (1975), see also Bocca 1990, Bollati 1996, Cerroni 1996, Galli della Loggia 1998, Romano 1996, Rusconi 1993, Schiavone 1998, and Tullio-Altan 1989 and 1995.
5. The vacuous, inessential essence of Italians appears, for instance, in two films that engage two crucial moments in Italian history: the creation of the nation in the 1860s and the founding of the Republic in 1948. In Luchino Visconti's *Senso* (1954), the director's great Risorgimento film, the Austrian officer Franz Mahler, in response to an uprising at the opera house in Venice, has this to say about the Italian nationalists: "This is just the war for Italians. Showers of confetti with mandolin accompaniment." And in Roberto Rossellini's 1945 *Rome Open City,* the German SS officer Bergman tells the Resistance hero before being tortured: "You Italians suffer from the disease of rhetoric." While in both films, these words are spoken by foreigners, indeed foreign oppressors, Visconti's point is to show that such an assessment of *italianità* is accurate, while Rossellini has his hero die a martyr's death to prove the falsity of the claim.
6. The extent to which Marx's work may itself have participated in or responded to the project of formulating a concept of the postliberal subject, as well as the latter's insertion into a Foucauldian notion of disciplinary power, requires further investigation. What I am proposing here is that the Marxian theory of ideology may well have constituted one of the foremost theoretical attempts at such an interrogation.
7. Derrida recently made a similar point in relation to the problem of lying—not an insignificant topic in light of Pinocchio's famous nose. If lying is defined as an intentional act of misrepresentation or falsification, even if we know that intentionality and truth are subject to all kinds of deconstructive practices, it is nevertheless crucial that we keep the idea of the lie for political purposes. The examples Derrida cites are historical revisionism and negationism, which must be unmasked as a lie (Derrida 2002).
8. For the work of Agamben, see in particular Agamben 1998 and 2005; for recent uses of Pauline theology see Badiou 2003 and Žižek 2003.
9. See Stewart 1998 and Žižek 1994b.
10. Esposito's notion of immunity is similar to Derrida's use of the *pharmakon,* that entity that describes both the disease and its cure, a relationship not of opposition but of instrumental support. The *pharmakon* describes a logic where that which opposes itself to its other does not exclude

that other but, on the contrary, includes it and substitutes it in a vicarious manner. See Derrida 1983. Esposito's concept of immunity is also similar to Freud's idea of *Angstbereitschaft,* a measured amount of anxiety geared to avert traumatization. All citations of Italian texts are my own translations, unless otherwise indicated.

11. Though not mentioned by name here, this is Esposito's most direct criticism of Agamben, for whom bare or sacred life comes into being within the folds of sovereign power's "state of exception."
12. De Sanctis's assessment of the nation's investment in opera as foundational for the Italian national character is echoed by Antonio Gramsci: "Verdi's music, or rather the libretti and plots of plays set to music by him, are responsible for the 'artificial' poses in the life of the people, for ways of thinking, for a 'style.' . . . To many common people the baroque and the operatic appear as an extraordinarily fascinating way of feeling and acting, as a means of escaping what they consider low, mean and contemptible in their lives and education in order to enter a more select sphere of great feelings and noble passions. . . . Opera is the most pestiferous because words set to music are more easily recalled, and become matrices in which thought takes shape out of flux" (Gramsci 2000, 373).

CHAPTER ONE

1. Bazzocchi nevertheless provides his own "modest proposal" of investigating the deep connection between the puppet and the Italian national imaginary, a connection that he finds in a shared "adolescent bloc." Alberto Asor Rosa, as well, attributes the book's enormous and enduring success to the possibility that an infantile Italy recognized itself not only in the pranks of the wayward puppet but also in his traumatic encounter with a cruel reality. Italy was thus playing out an anxiety of not "making it" to worthy citizenship and expressed this anxiety in the need for sacrifice. Collodi, according to Asor Rosa, perfectly expressed the psyche of the child and of the Italian people. He described both the pedagogical imperative of the educational process and the pain, its unnatural character, to the extent that it was ethical, i.e., willed and obligatory. Collodi's text is quintessentially Italian because it intuits that post-Unification Italy was living the drama of one who changes from puppet to man and knows that this process is painful. Collodi's is not, therefore, a nostalgia for the old order but, more universally, the nostalgia connected to becoming an adult (Asor Rosa 1975, 926ff).
2. For a representative range of such critical endeavors, see Fondazione nazionale Carlo Collodi 1976 and 1981, as well as Tempesti 1993.
3. For a comprehensive history of puppets, see Nelson 2001.
4. The complex relations between suggestion and love will be the specific focus of my chapter on the psychologist of the masses, Scipio Sighele.

5. Yorick's is one of the first volumes dedicated in Italy to puppets and to popular culture. In this, it contributes to a wider movement to overcome "regional particularities in the name of a burgeoning comprehensive character, the Italian" (Rak 1993, 83).
6. It is possible that Yorick is here referring to Kleist's famous essay on the marionette theater (Kleist 1982).
7. Cited in Segel 1995.
8. Both essays are now in De Sanctis 1972.
9. Turiello 1994, 21. This small volume comprises extracts from Turiello's much larger *Governo e governati in Italia*. All references are to this abridged edition.
10. The complementary opposite of *scioltezza* in discourses of Italian national character traits is *ozio* (indolence), the Italian penchant for a *dolce far niente* that, apparently, describes the Italian. Silvana Patriarca, in a recent review of the term *ozio* in Risorgimento texts, sees the term as essentially feminizing (2005). *Scioltezza*, I would hold, is more masculine and therefore has recuperative potential for Italianness. It is only its tendency toward excess that is dangerous.
11. Mazzini had made a similar claim already in the 1830s. Indeed, the Italian predilection for melody and song found its fullest expression in the Italian operatic tradition, and it was to this tradition that Mazzini assigned nationalist redemptive capacities once Italy had found a composer capable of leading the nation (Mazzini 1906–1943).
12. This distinction informs Mikkel Borch-Jacobsen's analysis of the Freudian ego (1988). Borch-Jacobsen, in coining the neologism "the suggect," insists on the intimate bond that exists between the modern, but also Freudian, subject and the process of suggestion.
13. We might remember that Walt Disney gets rid of the problem altogether by simply eliminating this inconvenient remainder: the puppet in the film becomes the real boy, for inside the wood lies the child.
14. "The kettle was painted on the wall. You can imagine how he felt. His nose, which was already long, grew longer still by at least four inches" (Collodi 1986, 113).
15. Perella (1986) notes that the use of "*marionetta*" here is interesting, for the word used for Pinocchio is generally "*burattino*." In only one other occasion is he referred to as a marionette, namely, in Fire-Eater's theater.
16. A similar moment is repeated shortly before Pinocchio's transformation into a boy: "One morning he said to his father: 'I'm going to the market . . . to buy myself a jacket, a nice cap, and a pair of shoes. When I come back home . . . I'll be so well-dressed that you'll take me for a wealthy gentleman.' And when he was outside he began running in high spirits" (455).
17. I owe this information to Marta Braun (1992, 166ff).
18. See chapter 6 below.

19. This reading is typical, defining most generally the Right and Left positions toward the text. These positions do not necessarily disagree on the structure of the text itself. The debate centers largely on where to put the "real puppet," on the Left, so to speak, or on the Right. Thus, according to the Right, Pinocchio demonstrates the need for an education of a child's subversive tendencies. The Left, on the other hand, claims that Pinocchio's journey marks a forced return to the margins after his attempt at gaining freedom. A middle-of-the-road reading stresses, again, that the novel demonstrates how life must be confronted *seriously,* that is, in a manner that mediates between pleasure and duty. Typical of the latter, and depending on a rather simplified Freudian terminology, is Mark I. West 1986, 112–15.
20. Roberto Esposito has commented on the strong biopolitical connotations of the term *fraternity,* especially when compared to the other two terms of the democratic-revolutionary triad: *liberty* and *equality.* He attributes the latter terms' more enduring political success to their greater capacity for abstraction and universalization. *Fraternity,* on the other hand, has had a less successful history in political theory because from the outset it has "been intensely biopolitical. . . . Because it is too concrete and because it has direct roots in natural *bios.* The fact that it assumes, at the very moment it appears on the political scene, a strong national, indeed nationalist connotation in the form of an appeal to the sacredness of the French nation, already to some extent puts it into conflict with its claim to universalism" (Esposito 2004, 189). Surprisingly, Esposito does not here mention fraternity's other "biopolitical" aspect: its obvious grounding also in gender, which—given its elimination of half of the population—does indeed undermine its claims to universality.
21. For a detailed tracing of Collodi's sources in Christian apocryphal texts and lore, see Pierotti 1981.
22. The metaphor of the queen bee as the embodiment of false—because authoritarian and female—power is one also used by Freud. For an analysis of such a matriarchy in Freud's political-cultural texts, see my own analysis (Stewart 1998).
23. Of course, the proposal of a Pinocchian self-education was not heard by those who were its objects, because they could not read the text. *Pinocchio*'s readers were the children of the bourgeoisie, and therefore the book not only represents the riddle to be solved about how to convert the precapitalist poor into productive salaried laborers, but functions also as a threat to those tempted to backslide from their already attained bourgeois existence.
24. Freud's language is remarkably close here to both Giorgio Agamben's notion of a "bare life" that both exceeds the subject and yet is that which is also the subject's essence and to Roberto Esposito's "immunitary paradigm" wherein "life" must be preserved from itself. See Agamben 1998 and Esposito 2003.

25. I thank Nanette Salomon for this term.
26. Marta Braun makes a similar claim for Marey's legacy. While largely absent after the turn to high modernism among painters and sculptors, "it is still a vital part of the visual language of popular culture. In advertising, videos, illustration, cartoons, and caricatures, Marey's repeated overlapping forms remain the single most important means of representing time, speed and motion" (Braun 1992, 316).

CHAPTER TWO

1. Cited in Clara Gallini 1983, 190–91.
2. Enrico Morselli (1852–1929) was variously director of the mental asylums of Macerata, Genova, and of the clinic attached to the University of Turin. Besides being an eminent teacher of psychiatry, he was also a prolific writer and the participant founder of the *Rivista sperimentale di freniatria,* the *Rivista di filosofia scientifica,* and the *Rivista di patologia nervosa e mentale.* Though an eminent theorist of the positivist movement, Morselli was one of the first and the few to systematically engage the work of Freud, an effort that came to fruition in his 1926 work *La psicoanalisi.* Patrizia Guarnieri has written extensively on Donato and his treatment by Morselli; see esp. Guarnieri 1988 and 1990.
3. For a more detailed analysis of this, see Stewart 1998.
4. For a survey of approaches that seek to move beyond such normative models, see Ascoli and Henneberg 2001.
5. For a review of this literature, see Ellenberger 1970, Gould 1992, and Winter 2000.
6. We will encounter Itard again in the chapters on Maria Montessori, for whom Itard was central to her construction of a new pedagogy.
7. I would disagree here with Iaccarino's own estimation of the Italian situation. She has stressed a Pinelian rejection of the therapeutic relation by Italian medical culture, a rejection based, in her opinion, on "an alliance between the official medical establishment and clerical Catholicism, both of which turn themselves into defenders of the social (the family, the state) against the dangers of those moral disorders provoked by hypnosis, and not, as in Paris, into the representatives of scientific truth and of the individual's right not to be manipulated." Iaccarino attributes the spread of hypnotism, then, not to its rootedness in the medical community, but to its spread in popular culture. In Italy, so she states, hypnotism became the object of vulgarization and commercial spectacularization, in large measure explained by the fact that protohypnotic practices had long before existed in extraliturgical religious forms that for centuries had become institutionalized in the figures of the magician and the soothsayer. As a corollary, hypnotism, for her, finds no support amongst Italian intellectuals or official bourgeois culture (Iaccarino 1996, 172). I will return

to this issue at the end of this chapter and question whether the lines of demarcation between "official" and "popular" culture can be as hermetically sealed off as Iaccarino implies. For immediate purposes, however, and as the works of Morselli and Sighele make clear, at least positivist scientists were very much interested in the medical uses of hypnosis and consequently in the problem of the therapeutic relation, and they did not shy away from discovering their data in the domains of popular culture.

8. The literature on the connection between hypnotism and theater is immense, but see Parssinen 1977, Owen 1990, and King 1997. For a discussion of the Italian context, see especially Patrizia Guarnieri 1988.

9. Lombroso conducted a study of the "Donatizzati" of Turin, and it is from his study that we today know the sociological composition of the group. Lombroso was intent on determining the ill effects of Donatization on individuals. For a more detailed analysis of this, see Gallini 1983, 203ff.

10. The inability to perform a parliamentary speech, "like in dreams," is a dominant trope in the extremely popular parliamentary novels of the period. The hero, usually a novice deputy from the southern provinces, at the crux of the narrative plot, rises to give a great speech in parliament—usually a critique of the parliamentary system itself—and faints in a fit of male hysteria. For a more detailed analysis of this topos, see Caltagirone 1993. For the parliamentary novel as a favored site of the male hysteric, see my following chapter.

11. Jaap van Ginneken's study (1992) is the only one in English that seriously analyzes Sighele's thought. In Italian, few monographs exist, but see Landolfi 1981, Velicogna 1986, Garbari 1988, and Donzelli 1995.

12. This text is the fifth and enlarged edition of a work originally entitled *La folla delinquente.*

13. Morselli claimed, following Donato, that the latter's presence was not required for his subjects to act suggestively.

14. It is no coincidence, I believe, that one of the greatest theorists of ideological consent is another Italian, namely, Antonio Gramsci. In articulating the concept of hegemony, Gramsci sought to theorize the structure of consent as the exercise of power without the direct use of force. A rereading of Gramsci's theory of hegemonic consent in this context would be worthwhile.

15. *Incubus* and *succubus* rely on the idea of two bodily positions in a supine state: *incubare,* to lie on top; and *sucubare,* to lie on the bottom. In Italian, *incube,* a masculine noun, is defined as he who exercises a strong suggestion on others. In medieval demonology, an incubo was an evil spirit of nocturnal oppression, imagined as a demon who either sat on the chest of a male or female sleeper (whence the contemporary standard meaning of nightmare) or descended upon a female sleeper to seek carnal intercourse with her. The most significant characteristic of the term *succube* or *succubo* is its considerable gender trouble. It is a masculine noun, first appearing

in the sixteenth century, but refers to a female spirit who, it was believed, sought sexual intercourse with men by lying under them. She was thus the female counterpart to the incubus. In a second meaning, *succubo* also refers to a weak and will-less man who is subjected to the power of a woman. In its general Italian usage today, it refers to a state of submission to the will of others, due to the person's lack of personality or spirit of revolt. A succubus is thus a seductive, and hence powerful, weakling.

16. The positivist school seems to have had a particular predilection for this passage, as it is also cited repeatedly by Cesare Lombroso, Enrico Ferri, and others. Sighele's insistent use of literary examples to construct his scientific arguments is striking, though it supports my contention that Italian positivism relied for its theories on largely aesthetic categories. It is not fortuitous, in this context, that many members of the positivist school were also active writers of fiction, as well as literary critics. In the case of Sighele, the perhaps most interesting "collaboration" between science and literature was Sighele's interaction with D'Annunzio. There seems to have been, though the actual method of mutual suggestion is somewhat unclear, a rather pronounced "suggestive relationship" between Sighele's composition of *La coppia criminale* and D'Annunzio's novel about infanticide, *L'innocente*. For a discussion of the relationship between nineteenth-century Italian literature and science, see Cavalli Pasini 1982. Barbara Sòrgoni (1998) similarly argues that positivism was less interested in reducing cultural categories to biological ones than in naturalizing cultural discourses in favor of scientific approaches to social problems.
17. The structural difference between an incubal and succubal sphere and mode of existence is somewhat akin to that of the difference between sadism and masochism. As Gilles Deleuze (1991) has argued, though in popular conceptions sadism and masochism are viewed in terms of a complimentary relation, the two phenomena in fact occupy two radically different universes.
18. I thank my student Nayantara Kilachand for pointing out that it is the *maternal* body that ultimately deconstructs the opposition between incubus and succubus. The maternal body can be subsumed neither to the category of the incubus nor to that of the succubus, because she is indeed both. The pregnant woman is an incubus to the extent that she controls the existence of the fetus. On the other hand, she is also a succubus insofar as she tends to the child's existence in the act of predicting his every need and desire.
19. I find it curious, in this context, that Roberto Esposito finds a subversive potential of the immunitary paradigm to be located in the fact of pregnancy and parturition. In the concluding chapter of his *Immunitas,* as well as in his following *Bíos,* the Italian philosopher views the scission opened up by the doubled, pregnant body as one way by which to develop philosophically a notion of community that positively engages the other

as same yet different: "Parturition is not only an offer of life, but the effective site where life becomes two, opens itself to difference in regard to itself, according to a movement that essentially contradicts the immunitary logic of self-conservation. Against any presupposed interiorization, it exposes the body to a division that has always traversed it as the outside of its inside, the external of the internal, the common of the immune. This is true for the individual body as much as for the collective body: the latter thus shows itself as challenged, infiltrated, hybridized by a diversity that is not only external but also internal" (Esposito 2004, 113). I see this aspect of Esposito's work as a symptom of a serious limitation. On the one hand, it points to an undertheorized vitalist tendency in his work. On the other hand, it also—and in the context of an exposition of a biopolitics without gender—returns him to a philosophical and cultural Catholicism that has the image of the Madonna and Child at its center.

20. I assume this describes Sighele's own relationship with his master and teacher, Cesare Lombroso.
21. Freud too was to attempt an analysis of the contours of this new discontent in *Civilization and Its Discontents,* and he too would locate the problem in the rise of a new form of domination, that of the superego. I have analyzed this in more detail in Stewart 1998.
22. Daniel Paul Schreber was another thinker of little creatures that crawled inside man's body and that disrupted not only his thinking but also the proper exercise of legal power (Schreber 1988).
23. For analyses of Freud's "justice in the nursery," see Forrester 1997; Rose 1993; Stewart-Steinberg 2007.
24. For a discussion of the creation of the "social" as the site of intervention into the privacy of the family, see Donzelot 1979. For an extremely interesting discussion of the French debate about child abandonment, see Schafer 1997; for the Italian history of child abandonment, see Kertzer 1993.
25. For a discussion of the concept of fascination in the Mezzogiorno, see the wonderful anthropological study by De Martino 1959. De Martino makes the point that the phenomenon of fascination cannot be reduced to the persistent survival of peasant culture, because fascination also came to be a fundamental part of southern, bourgeois, and enlightened culture through the practice of *iettatura.*
26. Sighele 1893–1894. Sighele gathered his information from an account of the prosecuting magistrate, one professor Silvio Tonnini, and his own text bears all the traces of a serious working-over to achieve the desired rhetorical effects. The "facts" must therefore be taken with a grain of salt, because accounts by the participants themselves do not exist.
27. This is Gallini's reading of the text (Gallini 1983, 289ff).
28. Sighele 1923, ix. The passage is from Sighele's 1909 preface.
29. I do not mean to imply by this that Italian positivism inevitably found

its true expression in and through fascism. The positivist movement in Italy cannot be reduced to either Left or Right, not only because its major proponents who were still alive in the 1920s fell on either side of the political spectrum, but also because the fascist movement's commitment to modernization is extremely complex. Thus, the question whether fascism signified, in the terms of this discussion, a *return* to the incubus or not remains an open one. Sighele himself is known to have flirted with nationalism, mostly in the name of the irredentism of his native Trento, but to have withdrawn from the nationalist movement because of its political radicalism. For a reading of Italian positivism as frequently at odds with its own determinist stipulations, see chapter 6 below.

30. For an interesting discussion of "personality" as the foundation of the self in twentieth-century America, see Susman 1984. Susman links the birth of "character" to Fordism and new mechanized modes of production, a connection also detected by Gramsci.

CHAPTER THREE

1. For the connection between fin-de-siècle aesthetics and Catholicism, see Hanson 1997.
2. See especially chapter 1. See also Briganti 1972 and Madrignani 1980.
3. Alberto Banti has recently argued that the idea of "invented tradition" should be used guardedly, because, at least in the Italian case, the ideological elements that make up this tradition are not invented but recycled from the past and put to new usages. I do not see this caveat to be in fundamental opposition to Hobsbawm's argument, one that would make room for such recycling. See Banti 2000, 149–50.
4. Serao moved to Rome from Naples in 1882 and sought her own "conquest of Rome" in the literary world that was beginning to form in the capital city. According to Anthony Gisolfi, her novel must therefore be read in the autobiographical sense of a southerner who is bent on the conquest of the city for her own purposes. See Gisolfi 1968, 55.
5. I gather Chabod is referring here to the post–World War II referendum on the monarchy and the subsequent rise of Christian Democracy.
6. This energy was clearly absent in 1929, when the monarchy had been sufficiently weakened by fascism in order for the Mussolini government to sign the concordat with the Vatican that had been so bitterly fought up to this point by the liberals.
7. Thus, for instance, at the beginning of the century, Giacomo Leopardi had already set the parameters of a vision that consistently confirmed the Italian tendency toward *scioltezza* and Pinocchian running: "The stroll, spectacles, and Churches are the principal occasion of society for the Italians . . . because Italians do not like domestic life, nor do they enjoy conversation. . . . Therefore they stroll, they go to spectacles and

amusements, to mass and to sermons, to sacred and profane feasts" (Leopardi 1998, 56). De Sanctis in his *Storia,* you will remember, explained the Italian propensity to visuality in terms of the absence of a Reformation and thus reform of the church in Italy. And many observers, as diverse as Gramsci or Luchino Visconti, have linked this national trait to the Italian love for opera and melodrama. For this connection, see Steinberg and Stewart-Steinberg 2006.

8. Bollati 1983. Of particular interest here is the chapter "Il modo di vedere italiano (note su fotografia e storia)" [The Italian way of seeing (Notes on photography and history)].
9. Bollati 1983, 127–28. Bollati's "regressive seeing" may be compared here to Adorno's notion of regressive listening, a process that he links to the fetish character of modern music. See Adorno 1991.
10. "Né copia, né invenzione, ma invito all'arte piemontese [neither copy, nor invention but an invitation to Piedmontese art]," states a recent guide to the castle (Maggio Serra 1985). The impact of D'Andrade's concept was profound and far-reaching, and his novel approach was soon emulated all over Europe, especially at the 1900 Paris Exposition of Vieux Paris. For descriptions of the 1884 Exposition in Turin, see the official catalogue of the exposition: *Torino e l'Esposizione italiana del 1884* (1884); and the essays that appeared in *Illustrazione italiana* during 1884. I also found helpful Maggio Serra 1982.
11. Camillo Boito, in two essays written about the exposition for the *Nuova Antologia* in 1884, insists, approvingly, on the element of fantasy and harmony in the fake village and castle. Indeed, he clearly privileges the harmony of this arrangement that inspires lofty thoughts about literature and the glory of the Italian past over the more banal modern art on show in the other pavilions of the exposition (Boito 1884a and 1884b).
12. Another use of the "family romance" as an analytic tool for a national founding myth is provided by Hunt 1992.
13. Among all the existing biographies of Italy's first queen, the less bedazzled is Casalegno 1956.
14. It is not fortuitous that the parliamentary novel's greatest flourishing coincides with the birth of the social sciences in Italy, of political science (Gaetano Mosca's theory of elites in *Elementi di scienza politica* dates from 1896) and of sociology (Vilfredo Pareto's *Trattato di sociologia generale* was published in 1916, though the basics of his thought had already appeared at the turn of the century). We have already encountered Sighele's mass psychology. All these texts, theoretical and literary, have in common the theorization of the need for either a charismatic leader or a restricted political elite. Another parliamentary novel that demands this leader in an updated version of Catholic leadership is Antonio Fogazzaro's *Daniele Cortis,* the hero of which is a Daniel in the den of lions combined with the anagrammatic "Cristo."

15. Serao 1997, 29. There exists an English translation of the novel in print. I have relied on this translation but made changes as they seemed necessary. For the English, see Matilde Serao 1992.
16. Serao comes close here to Siegfried Kracauer's later description of the mass ornament. The Tiller Girls, a group of militarily trained women who danced in formation, were, according to Kracauer, "no longer individual girls, but indissoluble girl clusters whose movements are demonstrations of mathematics. . . . The ornaments are composed of thousands of bodies. . . . The regularity of their patterns is cheered by the masses, themselves arranged by the stands in tier upon ordered tier. . . . The ornament resembles *aerial photographs* of landscapes and cities in that it does not emerge out of the interior of the given conditions, but rather appears above them" (Kracauer 1995, 76–77). I thank Stephen Marth for reminding me of this comparison.
17. One could argue with Shoshana Felman that this mediating function between structural and historical trauma is the very essence of literature. For more on the relationship between philosophy, history, and literature as different discourses that engage what she calls "madness," see Felman 2003.
18. "What the community has 'lost'—the immanence and the intimacy of a communion—is lost," Nancy states, "only in the sense that such a 'loss' is constitutive of 'community' itself." "Community therefore occupies a singular space; it assumes the impossibility of its own immanence, the impossibility of a communitarian being in the form of a subject. In a certain sense community acknowledges and inscribes—this is its peculiar gesture—the impossibility of community" (Nancy 1991, 12, 15).
19. Henry James repeatedly has the protagonists of his novels engage in nocturnal walks in the Colosseum. In *Daisy Miller,* for instance, the young Winterbourne, as a "lover of the picturesque," decides that the place would be worth a glance under moonlight: "he passed in among the cavernous shadows of the great structure, and emerged upon the clear and silent arena. The place had never seemed to him more impressive. . . . As he stood there he began to murmur Byron's famous lines, out of Manfred; but before he had finished his quotation he remembered that if nocturnal meditations in the Colosseum are recommended by the poets, they are deprecated by the doctors. The historic atmosphere was there, certainly; but the historic atmosphere, scientifically considered, was no better than a villainous miasma" (James 1986, 110). Daisy Miller will, of course, die of the Roman malaria at the end of the novel, and she too has caught the fever through her exposure to Roman ruins. It is interesting that James wrote an essay on Serao in 1901, which lauds Serao's style for its "rare energy" and its "immense *disinvoltura*" and Neapolitan passion, but that ultimately finds James caught in a miasmic, indefinable quality of Italianness from which escape is needed at the hands of "dear old Jane Austen":

"It is at the category of the familiar that vulgarity begins. There may be a cool virtue therefore even for 'art,' and an appreciable distinction even for truth, in the grace of hanging back and the choice of standing off, in that shade of the superficial which we best defend by simply practicing it in season. A feeling revives at last, after a timid intermission, that we may not immediately be quite able, quite assured enough, to name, but which, gradually clearing up, soon defines itself almost as a yearning. We turn round in obedience to it—unmistakably we turn round again to the opposite pole, and there before we know it have positively laid a clinging hand on dear old Jane Austen" (James 1969, 313).

20. According to one such observer, it was "symptomatic that just as the first Italy had the myth of the Great King, Umbertian Italy had to content itself with a kind of matriarch and idolize the figure of the beautiful Lady Queen. . . . The monarchy became personified in the royal Woman; she almost became the nation's destiny, a destiny that, alas, had already for other reasons fallen into similar feminine sentiments" (cited in Casalegno 1956, 154).

CHAPTER FOUR

1. For further treatments of Marey's work, see also Dagognet 1992, Rabinbach 1990, Brain 2002, Frank 1988, Horn 2003, and Doane 2002.
2. In this sense, Marey's is similar to Freud's model of the psychic apparatus. For Freud, as well, the human body in its *psychic* makeup is a constellation of forces that are either freely circulating or bound (or what he calls cathected). The difference between the two is not only that for Freud energy is located in the psyche, as opposed to Marey's location of energy in physiology, but above all, that for Freud the apparatus constitutes the psyche as such, whereas for Marey, the apparatus is a supplement that provides knowledge of the body's functioning.
3. Mary Ann Doane has pointed out that Marey shares his resistance to cinema with Freud. Thus Freud "systematically avoided using cinema and photography as analogies for the psyche in favor of other, optical but nonphotographic technologies" (Doane 2002, 61): the microscope, the telescope, and, of course, the antiquated Mystic Writing Pad. Marey, for his part, criticized cinema for its collaboration with defective senses and its capacity, indeed, its need, to produce illusion. I would add that both Freud and Marey also used and struggled with archaeological metaphors of the human body and psyche whereby the past is viewed to inevitably exist in pictographic forms.
4. See also Williams 1986.
5. Joshua Cole has made a similar point for the case of France. Here, too, nature is denatured, perceived to be unable to take care of itself and thus in need of intervention (Cole 2000).

6. See also Rabinbach 1990 and Esposito 2003, who make a similar argument, both emphasizing an external and invading conception of illness and the consequent derailing of morality as a cause of disease.
7. See also, of course, Foucault 1977 and 1978.
8. For a historical overview of physical education in post-Unification Italy, see Ferraro Bertolotto 1984 and Bonetta 1990a.
9. I use the term *supplement* in a manner analogous to Jacques Derrida's in his reading of the relationship between nature and culture in Rousseau. See Derrida 1974.
10. Baumann's idea of a prosthetic compensatory mechanism is the same one detected by Esposito in a political discourse geared to the simultaneous threats to but also dangers of individualism, dating from the early twentieth century and beyond (especially the works of Helmuth Plessner and Arnold Gehlen), which Esposito views as centered on the idea of *Entlastung*—an exoneration and also a disburdening—of the individual. *Entlastung,* in Gehlen, "is the action on oneself by which 'man transforms the elementary burdens by which he is weighed down into the opportunity to preserve his own life.' Precisely: the means by which man *transforms*—inverts and converts—but does not abolish the instinctual matter by which he is negatively constituted and that he can only reproduce in immunized form" (Esposito 2003, 126).
11. Both gymnastic and cinema, then, operate for Baumann through the effects of an apparatus. See Jean-Louis Baudry's seminal work on this question in Baudry 1986a and 1986b.
12. Mosso's commitment to a Helmholtzian vision of modern labor is made explicit, for instance, in Mosso 1891.
13. As Nietzsche put it in 1888, "Definition of the Teuton: obedience and long legs" (Nietzsche 1967a, 180).
14. Siegfried Kracauer's comments are enlightening: "The bearer of the ornaments is the *mass* and not the people, for whenever the people form figures, the latter do not hover in midair but arise out of a community. . . . The patterns seen in the stadiums and cabarets betray no such origins. They are composed of elements that are mere building blocks and nothing more" (1995, 76).
15. The reference is here, of course, to Daniel Gottlieb Moritz Schreber, the father of Daniel Paul Schreber and the author of the immensely influential *Kallipädie, Ärztliche Zimmergymnastik* and other texts on orthopedics, gymnastics, and physical education, the most important of which had been translated into Italian and were thus familiar to the Italian gymnastics movement.
16. By the end of the century, nearly 90 percent of the Italian teaching body was made up of women. In the novella, the superintendent of schools has this to say about the management of his female employees: "One quickly opens up a hornets' nest. This is quite a charge, you know, that requires

tact and delicacy. . . . It is a question of keeping afloat a family of between two hundred and fifty and three hundred women who are young and old, married and widowed, and who come from all social classes. And along with them, a corps of headmistresses. . . . It would be easier to deal with the thirty princesses of the House of Hohenzollern. Imagine the worries they give me, what with their loves, their illnesses, weddings, honeymoons, exams, maternity leaves, rivalries, conflicts with superiors and with relatives" (De Amicis 1996, 6).

17. This is the reading of *Amore e ginnastica* provided by Daria Valentini. For this critic, Pedani's invasion of the male sphere, the character's virility, constitutes a sexual and social threat whose denouement can only be the co-optation of her sexuality into the safe haven of heteronormativity. Indeed, Valentini goes so far as to argue that Pedani is a precursor to the ideal fascist woman, as she will become both a wife and mother for the fatherland, as well as a model for a warrior nation that celebrates physical fitness and strength (Valentini 1990).
18. De Amicis wrote *Amore e ginnastica* during the early part of 1891. The lecture was given in August. It is worth pointing out that De Amicis lifted entire passages from the novella and reused them in the lecture.
19. "I too am an enemy of exaggeration," De Amicis has one of the characters say in *Amore e ginnastica* (De Amicis 1996, 31). The speaker, another of the inhabitants in Celzani's apartment building, comes probably closest to De Amicis's own voice.
20. It is possible to see a parallel here between Mosso's and De Amicis's critique of the gymnastics movement and Marey's reservations about Muybridge's cinematographic practices.
21. Anita Gramigna has pointed out that what De Amicis seeks to show in many of his pedagogical texts is not simply an ideal betrayed by praxis but, more fundamentally, the violence of the relationship between pedagogical discourses and social plot upon which the former discourses are nevertheless woven (Gramigna 1996, 204).
22. This De Amicis in fact did repeatedly. His *Romanzo di un maestro,* as well as *La maestrina degli operai* both take on the comico-tragic vicissitudes of the teaching profession in the wake of the educational reforms.
23. Ferraro Bertolotto has pointed out that the failure of state-sponsored physical education and the simultaneous success of private initiatives may have not been fortuitous. Thus, she states: "Sport associationism was born with multiple intentions, among which emerges the one of imparting to the young a kind of para-military instruction. It ended up coinciding with the principles of liberalism that upheld private initiative in order to manage such initiative according to the perspective of those principles that came to be defined as *interests of the fatherland*" (Ferraro Bertolotto 1984, 134). As a consequence, the government could count on a whole series of institutions that were loyal to the official ideology

of free initiative, while also reaching those workers who were unreachable through the schools. One might add that such "associationism" also provided the grounds for the later, fascist corporate organization of leisure time. On this, see De Grazia 1981.

24. George Mosse has made a similar observation about the German and Austrian socialist "new man": "it was the socialist ideal of a 'new man' that provided a counterpoint to many of the qualities of normative manhood: a masculinity based upon solidarity, the renunciation of all force, and the rejection of nationalism as an ideal that would serve to purify modern man" (Mosse 1996, 119).
25. In his discussion of Boccaccio's representations of sexual fascination, Giuseppe Mazzotta quotes Andreas Capellanus's *The Art of Courtly Love:* "Love gets its name (*amor*) from the word for hook (*amus*), which means 'to capture' or 'to be captured,' for he who is in love is captured in the chains of desire and wishes to capture someone else with his hook. Just as a skillful fisherman tries to attract fishes by his bait and to capture them on his crooked hook, so the man who is captive of love tries to attract another person by his allurements and exerts all his efforts to unite two different hearts with an intangible bond, or if they are already united he tries to keep them forever" (Mazzotta 1986, 121). I thank Daniel Tonozzi for pointing out this reference.

CHAPTER FIVE

1. We have encountered an example of such expert, extralegal intervention in Sighele's text dealing with the events at Mezzojuso.
2. Esposito's work is important for providing us with a nuanced understanding of biopolitics. Nevertheless, his lack of engagement with the question of gender is surprising and disturbing. It is the use of women and mothers—at least as I trace it here for the Italian case—that made possible an incursion of a biopolitical logic into the domain of law.
3. For a general overview of European and American infanticide legislation, see Jackson 2002 and Wrightson 1982. For Germany, see Hull 1996 and Schulte 1984; for France, Fuchs 1992; for the Russian case, Engelstein 1992; and for the British one, Rose 1986 and Higginbotham 1992.
4. The Rocco criminal code of 1930 repeated and even extended this definition. Under fascist law, infanticide became a separate crime, distinct from other forms of homicide, and it gained its specificity on the basis of the question of honor. The honor criterion was eliminated from the Italian criminal code only in 1981 and was replaced by a "state of dereliction, loneliness, marginalization, the lack of socioeconomic means and relations beyond affective ones."
5. The 1865 Civil Code prohibited the search for paternity (article 180) and the search for maternity (article 376). However, article 190 allowed a child

the right to search for his or her mother. In fact, it was only the prohibition against the search for the father that was consistently respected in practice, because by the end of the nineteenth century, practices of identification in relation to mothers were instituted via administrative measures.

6. In fact, many members of the Lombroso school were enthusiastic, if not brilliant, novelists, reflecting the school's tendency to "insert itself in concrete ways into the tissue of reality in order to change it and to create an *engagée* literature; in order to search for a welding of theory and practice that places the intellectual of this period, both in science and in literature, into close contact with society and its needs. This contact would be completely severed by the idealist reaction" (Cavalli Pasini 1982, 59).
7. Christine Krueger offers an alternative tradition of literary representations of infanticidal mothers, a tradition that leads not to the public staging of the woman's crimes but to the idea of a woman's privacy: "literary treatments of infanticide contributed to this effort to protect women from the state by elaborating a representation of infanticide that insisted on its private character—a strategy which remains successful, if limiting, in securing reproductive rights today" (Krueger 1997, 271). Because Krueger is discussing literary representations of infanticide in the British context, where concealment was illegal, the right to privacy played a very different role when compared to the Italian context, where concealment was a duty. One may also wonder whether the theatrical quality of Catholic culture is not also a significant criterion of difference here.
8. Of the thirty-one cases of infanticide tried in the Bologna courts between 1880 and 1913 studied by Selmini, twenty-four were committed in the countryside by women belonging to the class of day laborers, a fact that pointed to the increasing capitalization of agriculture and impoverishment of the Italian peasantry. Very few of the women tried appeared to have actively hidden their (illegitimate) pregnancy. Few demonstrated maternal sentiments toward the child, a fact that would become crucial for the investigating magistrates and doctors. The absence of maternal feelings, indeed, often an unawareness by the women of having even committed a crime, led the authorities to conclude that these women lacked socialization, either because they were mentally infirm or because they were not properly morally educated.
9. In a later text, Ferriani proposed more concrete *institutional* solutions to the problem of dishonest women. These included permanent committees composed of salaried officials with the duty of tracking down degenerate parents, as well as houses for degenerate mothers that would gather in one place those women condemned for violence against their children. These houses would put into place a simple but rigorous pedagogical program geared to instilling the gentle sentiments of motherhood into the resident women. Crucial to such a program was work, which, Ferriani believed,

had the capacity to reconstruct maternal feelings on the basis of expiation and emulation (Ferriani 1893).

10. Heroism is, quite paradoxically, Ferri's argument against the effectivity of punishment more generally. Early Christians went to their deaths and confronted all sorts of torture because convinced of the justice of their cause; similarly, the socialist movement and the Russian Nihilists faced imprisonment and death because they viewed themselves as the carriers of justice. In all these cases, the threat of punishment was completely ineffectual (Ferri 1885, 18).
11. According to Esposito, the site of conjunction between the sphere of the individual and that of the species is in and through the modern immunitary paradigm. Here, the two spheres are unified through the management of the body. Biopolitics is realized in the material bodies of individuals constituted as population: "it is as if the metaphor of the body finally itself took on a body" (Esposito 2003, 163–64).
12. Silvia Schafer has remarked, in speaking about the French context, on an obsession with two conflicting tendencies in the political and administrative attitudes toward the family: on the one hand, the propagation of the ideal of the moral, self-governing family, and on the other hand, a growing fear about a domestic moral crisis that required governmental intervention (Schafer 1997, 22).
13. The perpetual shortage of milk in the foundling homes led them increasingly, during the last quarter of the century, to require that the mother of an illegitimate child "do service" (often up to a year) as a wet nurse for the foundling home as a method of payment for having her own child accepted. Up until the late nineteenth-century reforms, however, she was forbidden to nurse her own infant. It was only with efforts to control syphilitic contagion that arguments about her maternal sentiments and their social productiveness began to be made.

CHAPTER SIX

1. The most recent such reading may be found in Gibson 2002. Renzo Villa has insisted that Lombroso's criminal anthropology was not developed from his defense of the state and that in fact he broadened his anthropological scope in proportion to its shrinking application at the level of the state. Furthermore, Lombroso's so-called followers took very little from Lombroso, while he in turn depended on them for putting some order into his thought. For example, Salvatore Ottolenghi, the inventor of Italian police science, relied more on Adolphe Bertillon's scientific apparatus than on Lombroso's scientific findings (Villa 1985, 208ff).
2. Lombroso himself may have felt hurt by these attacks, but he had no compunction in simply placing his detractors on another of his lists, that of the so-called mysoneists. The mysoneists were all those who hated or

feared the new and revolutionary brought to the world by rebels, geniuses, prophets, deviants, and the insane: in other words, people like himself.

3. A representative example of the portrayal of Lombroso as a kind of good-natured and bumbling failure may be found in Luigi Guarnieri 2000. Guarnieri reads Lombroso as dominated by a kind of Quixotic drive to self-destruction, by an "autolesionism" that compelled him not only to search in those territories defined by Umbertian Italy as beyond the norm, but also to a "gigantic, torrential investigation into crime and deviance, thus ending up diligently working for his own discredit and ruin." Lombroso's was a "real and true crusade conducted with enormous and unheard of waste of energy and intelligence, of physical and psychic resources, with the only result of having procured for himself a frightful posthumous fame" (15). For Guarnieri, this is all the more paradoxical, insofar as Lombroso was widely read throughout the world; he constituted, along with Gabriele D'Annunzio, Enrico Caruso, and Guglielmo Marconi, one of Italy's greatest intellectual exports.
4. The term *mattoide* is untranslatable. It is the equivalent in the field of the insane of *criminaloid* in the world of crime.
5. This is, however, exactly what Lombroso will do: make breathing patterns into a style, to the extent that the subject will be grounded no longer in free choice, but in the idea of a pattern.
6. See also Hacking 1982 and Kern 2004.
7. For discussions of Morelli's work, other than that of Ginzburg, see Preziosi 1989 and Wollheim 1973.
8. The story was originally published in *Strand Magazine* in 1893, the same year that the journal carried an article on the human ear as a source for detecting individuality.
9. Freud in *The Ego and the Id* makes a similar point; in fact, famously, he calls the ego a *bodily* ego (1960, 20).
10. This is of course the story narrated by Michel Foucault in his *Discipline and Punish* (Foucault 1977).
11. The resemblance to the "savage writing" described by Claude Lévi-Strauss in *Tristes Tropiques* is quite striking (Lévi-Strauss 1981).
12. Nietzsche states: "perhaps indeed there was nothing more fearful and uncanny in the whole prehistory of man than his *mnemotechnics*. 'If something is to stay in the memory it must be burned in: only that which never ceases to *hurt* stays in the memory'—this is a main clause of the oldest . . . psychology on earth. . . . Man could never do without blood, torture and sacrifices when he felt the need to create a memory for himself; the most dreadful of sacrifices and pledges . . . , the most repulsive of mutilations . . . , the cruelest rites of religious cults . . . —all this has its origin in the instinct that realized that pain is the most powerful aid to mnemonics" (Nietzsche 1967b, 61).
13. Lombrosan criminal anthropology, Villa states, is an upside-down

anthropology, an anthropology of the negative or of the margin, within which the "normal"—a besieged species—encloses and protects itself (Villa 1985, 8).

14. Dante Alighieri 1996.

CHAPTER SEVEN

1. For other analyses of this myth, see Agnew 1997, Asor Rosa 1975, and Ascoli and Henneberg 2001.
2. The reference is here to Croce's famous remark that fascism constituted a mere parenthesis in Italy's onward march toward liberty and progress and that once this parenthesis had been closed, the country would return to its more authentic character as embodied in the liberalism of the pre–World War I Giolitti era (Croce 2004).
3. Silvana Patriarca (1998) has, however, pointed out that the decline of the number of so-called active women in the workforce and the rise of the number of housewives at the end of the nineteenth century may be connected more to changes in modern census-taking techniques than to actual changes in the normal workforce.
4. See also Schafer 1997, Zelizer 1994, and Bravo 2001.
5. Together with the good, self-sacrificing mother who models her life along lines similar to the lives of saints, another dominant trope of nineteenth-century Italian literature is the school mistress. The motif of the beleaguered innocence of the "*maestrina,*" her destiny entirely circumscribed by suffering, her slow but inevitable death caused by tuberculosis, poverty, and hunger, and her closeness to the dangers of seduction, these are literary tropes repeated obsessively by Edmondo De Amicis, Matilde Serao, Vittorio Imbriani, and others. For an analysis of this literature, see Bini 1991.
6. The English translation of Montessori's most important text is highly unreliable. It is published as *The Montessori Method* (Montessori 1964). I have preferred to rely on the Italian edition of the *Metodo* and provided my own translations.
7. Trabalzini is correct in stressing this shift in Montessori's method. I would differ from her analysis, however, over how to interpret Montessori's "Catholicism." I understand Trabalzini to see the relationship between religion and science to be one of straightforward supersession, whereas I would insist that the two elements coexist in complicated forms in Montessori's work. Not insignificantly, Montessorianism has held to this day great appeal for so-called Catho-communists because of the movement's combined commitment to both progress and Catholic values. Catho-communism was, of course, the cultural offspring of Enrico Berlinguer's political strategy in the 1970s of a "historic compromise" between the Communist Party and Christian Democracy.
8. The use of quotes in Standing's book requires some clarification. He

repeatedly attributes words to Montessori that were never published. Instead, they function as part of the Montessori lore and legend, an oral tradition that Montessori did her best to promote. It is from Standing that key events in Montessori's life derive. These events are frequently retroactive constructions that give the narrative the teleological force of predestination or prefiguration. Here, for instance, we learn that Montessori "already" in her own childhood was concerned with the well-being of children.

9. Standing places the "prophetic incident" later, at a time when Montessori was contemplating leaving medical school. "She passed a shabbily dressed woman accompanied by a child of some two years of age. The woman was dishevelled and dirty. . . . It was not the woman, however, but the child who was destined to alter the course of her life. Whilst the mother tuned up her professional whine, the little child, quite unconcerned, continued to sit on the ground playing with a small piece of coloured paper. There was something in the child's expression—so serenely happy in the possession of that worthless scrap of coloured paper, observing it with the full absorption of its little soul—that, suddenly . . . she turned round, and went straight back to the dissecting room" (Standing 1957, 25–26).
10. This is inaccurate. The first woman was in fact Ernestina Paper, who graduated from the University of Florence in 1877.
11. For a thorough description of Montessori's early years up to the creation of the Case dei bambini, see Babini and Lama 2000. I am much indebted to Babini and Lama for their information about Montessori's involvement with the Italian feminist movement.
12. Sante De Sanctis (1862–1935) was one of the first in Italy to develop experimental approaches to physiological psychology. An institutional reformer and prolific writer on a broad number of themes, he was noted above all for his book on dreams, a text cited also by Freud as one of the most important treatises on dreams before the birth of psychoanalysis. De Sanctis, in turn, was familiar with Freud's work, and there exists a correspondence between the two physicians.
13. "The Organization of Evil that takes the form of a Good Imposed by the environment on all of Humanity through Suggestion" (Montessori 1972). Few commentators have noted these pages. The exceptions are Scocchera 1990 and Schwegman 1999.
14. See Buttafuoco 1988 and Bravo 2001. Tellingly, in her own interventions at the 1896 Congress in Berlin and again at the 1899 London Congress, Montessori stressed women's political and social rights over and against their particular political party affiliations. A truly scientific and feminist approach to the women's question was thus early on marked, for her, as one that stood above party politics (Montessori 1995a and 1995d). The emphasis put by practical feminism on questions of (sexual) morality is supported by Montessori's intervention at the First National Congress

of Italian Women in Rome in 1908, where she delivered a paper on education and sexual morality (Montessori 1995c).

15. See also Scaraffia 1990, Turi 1987, and Accati 1983.
16. The apparitions at Lourdes were the most spectacular example of the use of these new politics and technologies. See Harris 1999.
17. Such subsumption was not necessarily smooth or without conflict. Lucia Scaraffia has shown how Catholic women's organizations often "got out of hand," becoming radicalized in ways that the Church was not able fully to control (Scaraffia 1999).
18. The claim that Italian women are "naturally" untouched by either perverse erotic desires or prudery was a common trope during the period. Italian women, unlike their European and American counterparts, engaged in healthy, reproductive sex only and were impervious to refined, modern displays of their charms. See here, especially, Michels 1912. For a more detailed analysis of this trope, see De Giorgio 1987.
19. Giuseppe Montesano (1868–1951) obtained his medical degree from the University of Rome and became deeply involved with the reform of the treatment of handicapped children. Montesano was one of the signatories of Croce's antifascist manifesto in 1925.
20. The silence on this point may be interpreted, of course, in terms of the "indecency" of Montessori's illegitimate child. However, and this may be more pertinent in the end, the silence about Montesano may also relate to a possible "theft of ideas" or at least competitiveness between Montessori and Montesano. In any case, the fact that Montesano was actively engaged in pedagogical experiments with mentally handicapped children disturbs the myth about Montessori having gone it all alone.
21. Giuseppe Sergi (1841–1936) was professor of anthropology in Bologna, then in Rome. He was the founder in 1906 of the *Rivista di antropologia* and the inventor of the so-called *carta biografica,* a biographical chart that could follow the medical history of mental patients over a period of time. As I discussed in an earlier chapter, this biographical chart was a crucial tool in creating the welfare mother. Sergi's researches in experimental psychology focused on the possibility of referring psychic phenomena back to a biological substratum.
22. The passage allows, however, for an alternative reading, one that would be founded in what D. W. Winnicott terms "transitional objects." Transitional objects are objects used by the infant to create the capacity to think or symbolize the interior world of the child as distinct from the outside world (Winnicott 1971, 1–12).
23. In the privatized environment of American Montessori schools today, the ritual meal has remained untouched, though some of its ritualized qualities have been displaced to the command that parents provide "wholesome" meals for their Montessorian children.

24. Other Italian delegates, in fact, protested Montessori's presence at the congress, because she had not been sent by any of the women's organizations. Montessori also did not particularly endear herself to other Italian delegates when she stated in her "Saluto delle donne italiane" that it was not so much Italian laws or Italian men that were holding back the emancipation of women, but women themselves (Montessori 1995a, 140).
25. See also Brennan 2004. Montessori herself appears to have been particularly gifted in this regard. Friends and acquaintances of Montessori have repeatedly stressed her ability to read unconscious desires and wishes, as well as the wider cultural environment.
26. The *Metodo* was translated into English in 1913 as *The Montessori Method*. The book was an overnight success in the United States and was of particular interest to progressive intellectuals, who saw in education a tool of social redemption and Americanization for the flood of new immigrants that had arrived on American soil. Thus, what above all interested American audiences was the possibility of leading immigrant children to quick results in speech, reading, and writing. In the United States, Montessori was received by Margaret Wilson, the daughter of the president; Alexander Graham Bell, the inventor of the telephone and teacher of deaf-mutes; Thomas Edison, the inventor of the gramophone and also teacher of the deaf; and Helen Keller. Montessori returned to the United States in 1915 for the Panama-Pacific International Exhibition in San Francisco, where "her children" were exhibited in a glass pavilion set up as a Montessori classroom. The audience was able to watch the children there "explode into writing and reading." Negotiations for the ultimate Americanization of the Montessori system failed, however, largely over the question of teacher training. Montessori refused to allow anyone but herself to train teachers, and she thereby kept control over the movement in her own hands. Interest in Montessori subsided in the United States rather quickly, largely due to John Dewey's criticisms, and would only resurface after World War II. For the best description of Montessori's American connections, see Kramer 1988.
27. Rosa (1866–1951) and Carolina (1870–1945) Agazzi were the founders of a "Casa dei bambini" in Mompiano (Brescia), a nursery school where children lived communally and where a "natural" and "spontaneous" environment was held to foster the emotional growth of children. The Agazzi method was largely a reworking of the pedagogical principles of Froebel.
28. See also Bonetta 1990b.
29. I owe much of the information on the fate of Montessori in fascist Italy to Kramer 1988, Trabalzini 2003, and Lama 2002.
30. For Gentile, the positive aspects of the Montessori method were located principally in the absence of passivity and uniformity, that is, in the

emphasis on self-education proposed by the method. He was critical, however, of its individualistic aspects, as well as of its lack of cultural content in the higher grades. For these reasons, he supported the educational experiment, but only for the first and second grades (Trabalzini 2000, lxi).

31. Economic policy toward Rome was largely dictated by a fear of the Paris Commune; it thus sought to avoid turning the city into a large, industrial metropolis similar to Paris, where the working class lived in concentrated areas and was therefore easier to organize politically.
32. Pius X's encyclical against Catholic modernism, *Pascendi dominici gregis,* dates from the same year.
33. For an attempt at answering this question, see Cafagna 1986.
34. The political and cultural avant-garde in Rome was made up of a tightly knit circle, one described by Montessori herself in "La questione femminile e il Congresso di Londra," published in the Milan journal *Italia femminile,* which from 1899 to 1902 was under the direction of Sibilla Aleramo. In 1902 Aleramo moved to Rome, where she lived with Giovanni Cena. Montessori, along with Luigi Pirandello (whom she already knew as a colleague at the Magistero femminile), Gaetano Salvemini, and the sculptor Leonardo Bistolfi, were frequent visitors at Aleramo's and Cena's home. The Nathan administration actively supported the *Comitato per le scuole dei contadini,* an organization dedicated to establishing schools in the *Agro romano* and whose members included Angelo and Anna Celli, Giovanni Cena, and Aleramo. Participants, including Montessori, of the First National Congress of Italian Women in 1908 visited the schools, and subsequently *Case dei bambini* were opened in the *Agro romano* with Nathan's support. For the circle around Aleramo, see the introduction to Aleramo 1982; for schools in the *Agro romano,* Bonetta 1989.
35. The San Lorenzo project was dedicated to creating hygienic citizens, as much as to hygienic housing. Thus, signs were affixed in the courtyards of the tenements, proclaiming, for instance, that "A hygienic home is the health of children" or "He who takes care of his home, takes care of himself."
36. Typical of such a position is Francesco de Bartolomeis's criticism that the Montessorian method is overly "psychological": "if we look at Montessori's work as it developed from the period of the first *Case* to its final manifestations, we may notice a general deficiency in that area that seemed to have inspired Montessori to accept Talamo's invitation: an interest in social questions. We mean to say that if we want to engage her social interests . . . at the level of education, methods, didactic organization, or the choice of materials etc., they did not penetrate into Montessori's scientific convictions, but remained something external" (de Bartolomeis 1953, 26).

CHAPTER EIGHT

1. For an excellent survey and comparison of the different editions, see Trabalzini 2003. Trabalzini is also one of the editors of the new critical edition of the *Metodo* published by the Opera Nazionale Montessori.
2. Francesco Randone (1864–1935) founded the "Scuola di arte educatrice," a school that had the support of ministers of education Ruggero Bonghi and Guido Baccelli and that still exists in Rome to this day. He was also a known figure in the art world of fin-de-siècle Rome. A painter and famed ceramicist (Randone rediscovered the ancient Etruscan formula for making the black clay that was so distinctive of Etruscan pottery), he earned his notoriety foremost because he lived with his numerous family inside that part of the old Roman walls that today run at the top of Via Veneto. His restoration project of the Roman city walls placed him in contact with the archeological community and also earned him the name of "Maestro delle Mura." Randone and his family created a distinct form of pottery that he called *"estrinsecazione"*—that is, the representation of the essence or soul of his subject—by the use of the Etruscan methods. He also gathered around him a broad array of Roman artists, musicians, and intellectuals in meetings or soirees that were made up of a mixture of lectures, exhibits, concerts, and even spiritualist séances. The Roman symbolist movement, the futurists Balla and Marinetti, reformist intellectuals, scientists—Randone was also a noted draftsman for scientific tracts—were all visitors to the Roman walls. Montessori was unquestionably a frequent guest, as her 1907 essay on Randone makes clear. Montessori's contacts with Rome's avant-garde artists would then belie any criticism that she had no understanding of modern culture. Paola Trabalzini, in a private communication, hypothesizes that Randone's eccentricity and known connections to progressive, democratic circles may have inspired Montessori to drop the chapter on manual labor and pottery from the 1926 edition of the *Metodo*. For background information on Randone, see de Feo 2000; on Montessori's association with Randone, see Montessori 1907 and Alatri 2000.
3. The theme of original sin, sexual morality, and the centrality of the zero as constitutive absence are the central coordinates of Montessori's "'Sexual Morality in Education,'" an essay to which I shall return at the end of the chapter.
4. Significantly, this phrase is struck from the text of the 1926 edition, that is, when Montessori was seeking to tone down her intellectual background in the positivist movement.
5. I owe my knowledge of this photograph to Lama, but she does not reproduce it in her essay (see Lama 2002).
6. Like Montessori, Freud viewed both the failure to interiorize authority and

the unchecked proliferation of identification as threats to a democratic polity. For further analyses of Freud's theory of politics, see Forrester 1997, Borch-Jacobsen 1988, and Stewart 1998.

7. I owe this term to Timothy Campbell.

CONCLUSION

1. Gramsci was not only a careful reader of De Sanctis, but also guaranteed his survival after 1945, as Communist Party intellectuals, following in Gramsci's footsteps, recuperated De Sanctis as a major thinker of Italian modernity.

Works Cited

Accati, Luisa. 1983. Il furto del desiderio: Relazioni sociali nell'Europa cattolica del XVII secolo: alcune ipotesi. *Memoria* 7:7–16.

Adorno, Theodor. 1991. On the Fetish Character in Music and the Regression of Listening. In *The Culture Industry: Selected Essays on Mass Culture.* Ed. and intro. by J. M. Bernstein, 29–60. London: Routledge.

Agamben, Giorgio. 1998. *Homo Sacer: Sovereign Power and Bare Life.* Trans. Daniel Heller-Roazen. Stanford, CA: Stanford University Press.

———. 2005. *State of Exception.* Trans. Kevin Attell. Chicago: University of Chicago Press.

Agnew, J. 1997. The Myth of Backward Italy in Modern Europe. In *Revisioning Italy: National Identity and Global Culture,* ed. Beverly Allen and M. Russo, 23–42. Minneapolis: University of Minnesota Press.

Alatri, Giovanna. 2000. Maria Montessori e l'arte vasaia. *Vita dell'infanzia,* 49, no. 8 (October): 12–14.

Aleramo, Sibilla. 1982. *Amo dunque sono.* Milan: Mondadori.

Alighieri, Dante. 1996. *Inferno.* Trans. and ed. Robert M. Durling and Ronald M. Martinez. New York: Oxford University Press.

———. 2003. *Purgatory.* Trans. and ed. Robert M. Durling and Ronald M. Martinez. New York: Oxford University Press.

Althusser, Louis. 1994. Ideology and the Ideological State Apparatuses. In *Mapping Ideology,* ed. Slavoj Žižek, 100–140. London: Verso Books.

Apostolidès, Jean-Marie. 1988. Pinocchio, or a Masculine Upbringing. *Merveilles et Contes* 2, no. 2 (December): 75–85.

Arcoleo, Giorgio. 1972. Pulcinella dentro e fuori di teatro. In *L'arte, la scienza e la vita,* by Francesca De Sanctis, 499–508. Turin: Einaudi Editore.

Ascoli, Albert R., and Krystyna Henneberg, eds. 2001. *Making and Remaking Italy: The Cultivation of National Identity around the Risorgimento.* New York: Berg.

Asor Rosa, Alberto. 1975. *La cultura (Storia d'Italia: Dall'Unità a oggi).* Turin: Einaudi Editore.

Babini, Valeria Paola. 1986. L'infanticida tra letteratura medica e letteratura giuridica. In *L'età del positivismo,* ed. Paolo Rossi, 453–74. Bologna: Il Mulino.

———. 1996. *La questione dei frenastenici: Alle origini della psicologia scientifica in Italia.* Milan: Franco Angeli.

Babini, Valeria Paola, and Luisa Lama. 2000. *Una "Donna Nuova": Il femminismo scientifico di Maria Montessori.* Milan: Franco Angeli.

Badiou, Alain. 2003. *Saint Paul: The Foundation of Universalism.* Trans. Ray Brassier. Stanford, CA: Stanford University Press.

Baima Bollone, Pier Luigi. 1992. *Cesare Lombroso, ovvero il principio dell'irresponsabilità.* Turin: Società Editrice Internazionale.

Ballestrini, Rafaello. 1888. *Aborto, infanticidio e esposizione d'infante.* Turin: Fratelli Bocca Editore.

Banti, Alberto. 2000. *La nazione del Risorgimento: Parentela, santità e onore alle origini dell'Italia unita.* Turin: Einaudi Editore.

Baudry, Jean-Louis. 1986a. The Apparatus: Metapsychological Approaches to the Impression of Reality in Cinema. In *Narrative, Apparatus, Ideology: A Film Theory Reader,* ed. Philip Rosen, 299–318. New York: Columbia University Press.

———. 1986b. Ideological Effects of the Basic Cinematographic Apparatus. In *Narrative, Apparatus, Ideology: A Film Theory Reader,* ed. Philip Rosen, 286–98. New York: Columbia University Press.

Baumann, Emilio. 1882. *Meccanica umana.* Bologna: Editore-Propretario F. G. Valle.

———. 1900. *Psico-Cinesia, ovvero l'arte di formare il carattere.* Rome: self-published.

Bazzocchi, Marco. 1992. I territori di Pinocchio. *Verri,* ser. 9, no. 1–2 (March–June): 147–50.

Beccaria, Cesare. 1986. *On Crimes and Punishment.* Indianapolis: Hackett Publishing.

Belardinelli, Mario. 1986. I cattolici nella vita politica romana. In *Roma nell'età giolittiana: L'amministrazione Nathan: Atti del Convegno di Studio (Roma, 28–30 maggio 1984),* curated by the Istituto per la Storia del Risorgimento italiano, 1–36. Rome: Edizioni dell'Ateneo.

Benjamin, Walter. 1969. *Illuminations.* New York: Schocken Books.

Berry, Laura. 1999. *The Child, the State, and the Victorian Novel.* Charlottesville: University Press of Virginia.

Bertoni Jovine, Dina. 1965. *Storia dell'educazione popolare in Italia.* Bari: Editori Laterza.

Bini, Giorgio. 1991. La maestra nella letterature: Uno specchio della realtà. In *L'educazione delle donne: Scuole e modelli di vita femminile nell'Italia dell'Ottocento,* ed. Simonetta Soldani, 331–62. Milan: Franco Angeli.

Bizzozero, Giulio. 1898. Il cittadino e l'igiene pubblica. *Nuova Antologia,* April 16, 615–35.

Bocca, Giorgio. 1990. *La disunità degli italiani.* Milan: Garzanti.

Boero, Pino. 1984. Amore, socialismo e ginnastica. In *Non si sgomentino le signore . . . ,* by Edmondo De Amicis, ed. Pino Boero et al., 21–57. Genova: Tilgher-Genova.

Boito, Camillo. 1884a. Il castello medioevale all'Esposizione di Torino. *La Nuova Antologia* 19:250–70.

———. 1884b. Il bello nella esposizione di Torino. *La Nuova Antologia* 19:25–45.

Bollati, Giulio. 1996. *L'italiano: Il carattere nazionale come storia e come invenzione.* Turin: Einaudi Editore.

Bonetta, Gaetano. 1989. *Scuola e socializzazione fra '800 e '900.* Milan: Franco Angeli.

———. 1990a. *Corpo e nazione: L'educazione ginnastica, igienica e sessuale nell'Italia liberale.* Milan: Franco Angeli.

———. 1990b. La scuola dell'infanzia. In *La scuola italiana dall'Unità ai nostri giorni,* ed. Giacomo Cives, 1–53. Florence: La Nuova Italia.

Borch-Jacobsen, Mikkel. 1988. *The Freudian Subject.* Trans. Catherine Porter. Stanford, CA: Stanford University Press.

Brain, Robert M. 2002. Representation on the Line: Graphic Recording Instruments and Scientific Modernism. In *From Energy to Information: Representation in Science and Technology, Art, and Literature,* ed. Bruce Clarke and Linda Dalrymple Henderson, 155–77. Stanford, CA: Stanford University Press.

Brambilla, Alberto. 1992. *De Amicis: Paragrafi eterodossi.* Modena: Murchi Editore.

Braun, Marta. 1992. *Picturing Time: The Work of Etienne-Jules Marey.* Chicago: University of Chicago Press.

Bravo, Anna. 2001. Madri fra oppressione ed emancipazione. In *Storia sociale delle donne nell'Italia contemporanea,* ed. Anna Bravo, Margherita Pelaja, Alessandra Pescarola, and Lucetta Scaraffia, 77–125. Bari: Laterza.

Brennan, Teresa. 2004. *The Transmission of Affect.* Ithaca, NY: Cornell University Press.

Briganti, Alessandra. 1972. *Il parlamento nel romanzo italiano del secondo Ottocento.* Florence: Le Monnier.

Bulferetti, Luigi. 1975. *Lombroso.* Turin: UTET.

Butler, Judith. 1997. *The Psychic Life of Power: Theories in Subjection.* Stanford, CA: Stanford University Press.

Buttafuoco, Annarita. 1988. La filantropia come politica: Esperienze dell' emancipazzionismo italiano nel Novecento. In *Ragnatele di rapporti:*

Patronage e reti di relazione nella storia delle donne, ed. Lucia Ferrante, Maura Palazzi, and Gianna Pomata, 166–87. Turin: Rosenberg & Sellier.

Caesar, Ann. 1992. Introduction to *The Conquest of Rome,* by Matilde Serao. New York: New York University Press: v–xxii.

Cafagna, Luciano. 1986. Il blocco laico del 1907 fra realtà nazionale e realtà romana. In *Roma nell'età giolittiana: L'amministrazione Nathan: Atti del Convegno di Studio (Roma, 28–30 maggio 1984),* curated by the Istituto per la Storia del Risorgimento italiano, 37–52. Rome: Edizioni dell'Ateneo.

Caltagirone, Giovanna. 1993. *Dietroscena: L'Italia post-unitaria nei romanzi di ambiente parlamentare.* Roma: Bulzoni Editore.

Calvino, Italo. 1996. Nota introduttiva. In *Amore e ginnastica,* by Edmondo De Amicis, vii–xi. Milan: Mondadori.

Canfield Fisher, Dorothy. 1912. *A Montessori Mother.* New York: Henry Holt.

Caplan, Jane. 1997. "Speaking Scars": The Tattoo in Popular Practice and Medico-Legal Debate in Nineteenth-Century Europe. *History Workshop Journal* 44:107–42.

———. 2000. "National Tattooing": Traditions of Tattooing in Nineteenth-Century Europe. In *Written on the Body: The Tattoo in European and American History,* ed. Jane Caplan, 156–73. Princeton, NJ: Princeton University Press.

Caracciolo, Alberto. 1956. *Roma capitale: Dal Risorgimento alla crisi dello stato liberale.* Rome: Editori Riuniti.

Carducci, Giosuè. 1935. L'eterno femminino regale. In *Edizione nazionale delle opere.* Vol. 24, *Confessioni e battaglie,* 321–43. Bologna: Nicola Zanichelli Editore.

Carpi, Leone. 1878. *L'Italia vivente: Studi sociali.* Milan: Vallardi.

Carrara, Francesco. 1912. *Programma del corso di diritto criminale: Parte speciale, ossia esposizione dei delitti in specie.* 9th ed. Florence: Casa editrice Fratelli Cammelli.

Caruth, Cathy. 1996. *Unclaimed Experience: Trauma, Narrative, and History.* Baltimore: Johns Hopkins University Press.

Casalegno, Carlo. 1956. *La regina Margherita.* Turin: Einaudi Editore.

Catarsi, Enzo. 1995. *La giovane Montessori.* Ferrara: Corso Editore.

Cavalli Pasini, Annamaria. 1982. *La scienza del romanzo: Romanzo e cultura scientifica tra Otto e Novecento.* Bologna: Patron Editore.

Cerroni, Umberto. 1996. *L'identità civile degli italiani.* Lecce: Piero Manni.

Chabod, Federico. 1996. *Italian Foreign Policy: The Statecraft of the Founders.* Trans. William McCuaig. Princeton, NJ: Princeton University Press.

Chatman, Seymour. 1979. The Styles of Narrative Codes. In *The Concept of Style,* ed. Berel Lang, 230–44. Ithaca, NY: Cornell University Press.

Ciampi, Gabriella. 1986. L'amministrazione Nathan: I servizi. In *Roma nell'età giolittiana: L'amministrazione Nathan: Atti del Convegno di Studio (Roma,*

28–30 maggio 1984), curated by the Istituto per la Storia del Risorgimento italiano, 154–97. Rome: Edizioni dell'Ateneo.

Coates, Paul. 1973. *Photographing the Invisible.* New York: Arno.

Cole, Joshua. 2000. *The Power of Large Numbers: Population, Politics, and Gender in Nineteenth-Century France.* Ithaca, NY: Cornell University Press.

Collodi, Carlo. 1948. Pane e libri. In *Tutto Collodi per i piccoli e per i grandi,* ed. Pietro Pancrazi, 278–82. Florence: Felice Le Monnier.

———. 1986. *The Adventures of Pinocchio.* Bilingual ed., trans. Nicolas J. Perella. Berkeley: University of California Press.

———. 1995. Ragazzi di strada. In *Opere,* 179–88. Milan: Mondadori.

Colombo, Giorgio. 2000. Lombroso, ancora. In *La scienza infelice: Il Museo di antropologia criminale di Cesare Lombroso,* ed. Giorgio Colombo, 221–48. Turin: Bollati Boringhieri.

Copjec, Joan. 1994. *Read My Desire: Lacan against the Historicists.* Cambridge, MA: MIT Press.

Covington Packard, Rosa. 1972. *The Hidden Hinge.* Notre Dame, IN: Fides Publishers.

Croce, Benedetto. 1946. *La critica e la storia delle arti figurative.* Bari: Laterza.

———. 2004. *Storia d'Italia: Dal 1871 al 1915.* Naples: Bibliopolis.

Dagognet, François. 1992. *Etienne-Jules Marey: A Passion for the Trace.* Trans. Robert Galeta with Jeanine Herman. New York: Zone Books.

David, Michel. 1966. *La psicoanalisi nella cultura italiana.* Turin: Bollati Boringhieri.

Davies, Ivor. 1979. New Reflections on the *Large Glass:* The Most Logical Sources for Marcel Duchamp's Irrational Sources. *Art History* 2:1.

De Amicis, Edmondo. 1984. *Non si sgomentino le signore. . . .* Ed. Pino Boero et al. Genova: Tilgher-Genova.

———. 1990. *Nel giardino della follia.* Pisa: ETS.

———. 1995. *Cinematografo celebrale.* Rome: Salerno Editrice.

———. 1996. *Amore e ginnastica.* Milan: Mondadori.

de Bartolomeis, Francesco. 1953. *Maria Montessori e la pedagogia scientifica.* Florence: La Nuova Italia Editrice.

de Feo, Giovanna Caterina. 2000. *Francesco Randone: Il Maestro delle Mura.* Rome: Associazione Amici di Villa Strohl-Fern.

De Giorgio, Michela. 1987. Italiane fin de siècle. *Rivista di storia contemporanea* 2:212–39.

De Grazia, Victoria. 1981. *The Culture of Consent: Mass Organization of Leisure in Fascist Italy.* New York: Cambridge University Press.

Deleuze, Gilles. 1991. Coldness and Cruelty. In *Masochism,* trans. J. Macneil. Cambridge, MA: Zone Books.

———. 1993. *The Fold: Leibniz and the Baroque.* Trans. Tom Conley. Minneapolis: University of Minnesota Press.

De Martino, Ernesto. 1959. *Sud e magia.* Milan: Feltrinelli Editore.

Derrida, Jacques. 1974. *On Grammatology.* Trans. Gayatri Chakravorty Spivak. Baltimore: Johns Hopkins University Press.

———. 1983. *Dissemination.* Trans. Barbara Johnson. Chicago: University of Chicago Press.

———. 2002. *Without Alibi.* Ed., trans., and intro. by Peggy Kamuf. Stanford, CA: Stanford University Press.

De Sanctis, Francesco. 1970a. Il limite. In *I partiti e l'educazione della nuova Italia,* 170–73. Turin: Einaudi Editore.

———. 1970b. Il realismo moderno. In *I partiti e l'educazione della nuova Italia,* 154–58. Turin: Einaudi Editore.

———. 1970c. La coltura politica. In *I partiti e l'educazione della nuova Italia,* 101–4. Turin: Einaudi Editore.

———. 1970d. La democrazia in Italia. In *I partiti e l'educazione della nuova Italia,* 136–40. Turin: Einaudi Editore.

———. 1970e. La maggioranza. In *I partiti e l'educazione della nuova Italia,* 159–62. Turin: Einaudi Editore.

———. 1970f. La misura dell'ideale. In *I partiti e l'educazione della nuova Italia,* 163–65. Turin: Einaudi Editore.

———. 1970g. Le forze dirigenti. In *I partiti e l'educazione della nuova Italia,* 174–78. Turin: Einaudi Editore.

———. 1970h. L'insegnamento della ginnastica nelle scuole secondarie, normali e magistrali. In *I partiti e l'educazione della nuova Italia,* 249–67. Turin: Einaudi Editore.

———. 1972. La scuola. In *L'arte, la scienza e la vita,* 305–15. Turin: Einaudi Editore.

———. 1996. *Storia della letteratura italiana.* Turin: Einaudi.

Di Bello, Giulia, and Patrizia Meringolo. 1997. *Il rifiuto della maternità: L'infanticidio in Italia dall'Ottocento ai nostri giorni.* Pisa: Edizioni ETS.

Doane, Mary Ann. 2002. *The Emergence of Cinematic Time: Modernity, Contingency, the Archive.* Cambridge, MA: Harvard University Press.

Dolar, Mladen. 1993. Beyond Interpellation. *Qui Parle: Literature, Philosophy, Visual Arts, History* 6, no. 2: 75–96.

Donzelli, Maria. 1995. Psicologia delle folle e scienza politica in Italia a fine 800. In *Folla e politica: Cultura filosofica, ideologia, scienze sociali in Italia e Francia a fine ottocento,* ed. Maria Donzelli, 9–21. Naples: Liguori Editore.

Donzelot, Jacques. 1979. *The Policing of Families.* New York: Pantheon Books.

Doyle, Arthur Conan. 2001. *The Adventures and Memoirs of Sherlock Holmes.* New York: Random House.

Ellenberger, Henri. 1970. *The Discovery of the Unconscious.* New York: Basic Books.

Engelstein, Laura. 1992. *The Keys to Happiness: Sex and the Search for Modernity in Fin-de-Siècle Russia.* Ithaca, NY: Cornell University Press.

Erspamer, Francesco. 2002. I colori della nostalgia. *La rivista dei libri/New York*

Review of Books, http://www.larivistadei.libri.it/2002/02/erspamer.html, 1–10.

Esposito, Roberto. 2003. *Immunitas: Protezione e negazione della vita*. Turin: Einaudi Editore.

———. 2004. *Bíos: Biopolitica e filosofia*. Turin: Einaudi Editore.

Fattorini, Emma. 1999a. *Il culto mariano fra Ottocento e Novecento: Simboli e devozione. Ipotesi e prospettive di ricerca*. Milan: Franco Angeli.

———. 1999b. A Voyage to the Madonna. In *Women and Faith: Catholic Religious Life in Italy from Late Antiquity to the Present*, ed. Lucetta Scaraffia and Gabriella Zarri, 281–95. Cambridge, MA: Harvard University Press.

Felman, Shoshana. 2003. Foucault/Derrida: The Madness of the Thinking/Speaking Subject. In *Writing and Madness (Literature/Philosophy Psychoanalysis)*, 35–55. Stanford, CA: Stanford University Press.

Ferraro Bertolotto, Maria Cristina. 1984. Prospettiva storica dell'educazione fisica. In *Non si sgomentino le signore . . .* , by Edmondo De Amicis, ed. Pino Boero, 91–135. Genova: Tilgher-Genova.

Ferri, Enrico. 1885. *La scuola criminale positiva: Conferenza del Prof. Enrico Ferri nella Università di Napoli*. Naples: Enrico Detken Libraio-Editore.

Ferriani, Lino. 1889. *L'infanticida nel codice penale e nella vita sociale: Considerazioni*. Milan: Dumolard.

———. 1893. *Madri snaturate: Studio psichico giuridico*. Milan: Casa editrice Galli di C. Chiesa e F. Giundani.

Flugel, J. C. 1950. *The Psychology of Clothes*. London: Hogarth Press.

Fondazione nazionale Carlo Collodi. 1976. *Studi collodiani*. Pescia: Fondazione nazionale Carlo Collodi.

———. 1981. *C'era una volta un pezzo di legno: La simbologia di Pinocchio*. Atti del Convegno organizzato dalla Fondazione Carlo Collodi. Milan: Emme Edizioni.

Forrester, John. 1997. Justice, Envy, and Psychoanalysis. In *Dispatches from the Freud War*. Cambridge, MA: Harvard University Press.

Foucault, Michel. 1977. *Discipline and Punish*. New York: Vintage Books.

———. 1978. *The History of Sexuality: An Introduction*. New York: Pantheon Books.

———. 2000a. About the Concept of the Dangerous Individual. In *Power*, by Michel Foucault. Ed. James D. Faubion. New York: New Press: 176–200.

———. 2000b. The Birth of Social Medicine. In *Power*, by Michel Foucault. Ed. James D. Faubion. New York: New Press: 134–56.

———. 2000c. Truth and Juridical Forms. In *Power*, by Michel Foucault. Ed. James D. Faubion, 1–89. New York: New Press.

Frank, Robert G. 1988. The Telltale Heart: Physiological Instruments, Graphic Methods, and Clinical Hopes, 1854–1914. In *The Investigative Enterprise: Experimental Physiology in Nineteenth-Century Medicine*, ed. William

Coleman and Frederic L. Holmes, 211–90. Berkeley: University of California Press.

Freud, Sigmund. 1950. *Totem and Taboo.* New York: W. W. Norton.

———. 1959a. Family Romances. In *The Standard Edition of the Complete Psychological Works,* trans. James Strachey, vol. 9, 235–41. London: Hogarth Press.

———. 1959b. *Group Psychology and the Analysis of the Ego.* New York: Norton.

———. 1959c. The Moses of Michelangelo. *Standard Edition,* vol. 13, 211–38. London: Hogarth Press.

———. 1960. *The Ego and the Id.* New York: Norton.

———. 1961. *Beyond the Pleasure Principle.* New York: Norton.

———. 1965. *The Interpretation of Dreams.* New York: Avon.

Frigessi, Delia. 2003. *Cesare Lombroso.* Turin: Einaudi.

Fuchs, Rachel. 1992. *Poor and Pregnant in Paris: Strategies for Survival in the Nineteenth Century.* New Brunswick, NJ: Rutgers University Press.

Gabriele, Mino. 1981. Il burattino e lo specchio. In *C'era una volta un pezzo di legno. La simbologia di Pinocchio,* 43–46. Milan: Atti del Convegno organizzato dalla Fondazione Carlo Collodi.

Gagliardi, Antonio. 1980. *Il burattino e il labirinto: Una lettura di Pinocchio.* Turin: Tirrenia-Stampatori.

Galli della Loggia, Ernesto. 1998. *L'identità italiana.* Bologna: il Mulino.

Gallini, Clara. 1983. *La sonnambula meravigliosa: magnetismo e ipnotismo nell'Ottocento italiano.* Milan: Feltrinell Editore.

Garbari, Maria. 1988. *Società ed istituzioni in Italia nelle opere sociologiche di Scipio Sighele.* Trento: Società di studi trentini di scienze storiche.

Gasparini, Giovanni. 1997. *La corsa di Pinocchio.* Milan: Vita e Pensiero.

Giacanelli, Ferruccio. 2000. Introduction to *La scienza infelice: Il museo di antropologia criminale di Cesare Lombroso,* by Giorgio Colombo, 7–32. Turin: Bollati Boringhieri.

Gibson, Mary. 1999. *Prostitution and the State in Italy, 1860–1915.* Columbus: Ohio State University Press.

———. 2002. *Born to Crime: Cesare Lombroso and the Origins of Biological Criminology.* Westport, CT: Praeger Press.

Gigliozzi, Giovanni. 1997. *Le regine d'Italia: La bella Rosina regina senza corona, margherita l'ammaliatrice, Elena la casalinga, Maria José la regina di maggio.* Rome: Newton & Compton Editori.

Ginzburg, Carlo. 1989. *Clues, Myths, and the Historical Method.* Trans. John Tedeschi and Anne Tedeschi. Baltimore: Johns Hopkins University Press.

Gisolfi, Anthony M. 1968. *The Essential Matilde Serao.* New York: Las Americas.

Givone, Sergio. 1981. Figure della tradizione ebraico-cristiana in *Pinocchio.* In *C'era una volta un pezzo di legno: La simbologia di Pinocchio,* 59–92. Atti del Convegno organizzato dalla Fondazione nazionale Carlo Collodi di Pescia. Milan: Emme Edizioni.

Gombrich, Ernst H. 1963. *Meditations on a Hobby Horse, and Other Essays on the Theory of Art.* London: Phaidon.

Gould, Alan. 1992. *A History of Hypnotism.* Cambridge: Cambridge University Press.

Gramigna, Anita. 1996. *"Il romanzo di un maestro" di Edmondo De Amicis.* Florence: La Nuova Italia.

Gramsci, Antonio. 1975. *Quaderni del carcere.* Turin: Einaudi Editore.

———. 1977. Manzoni e gli umili. In *Letteratura e vita nazionale.* Rome: Editori Riuniti.

———. 2000. *The Gramsci Reader.* Ed. David Forgacs. New York: New York University Press.

Guarnieri, Luigi. 2000. *L'atlante criminale: Vita scriteriata di Cesare Lombroso.* Milan: Mondadori.

Guarnieri, Patrizia. 1988. Theatre and Laboratory: Medical Attitudes to Animal Magnetism in Late-Nineteenth-Century Italy. In *Studies in the History of Alternative Medicine,* ed. Roger Cooter, 118–39. Oxford: Macmillan Press.

———. 1990. *The Psyche in Trance: Inquiries into Hypnotism.* Badia Fiesolana, Florence: European University Institute.

Gunning, Tom. 1995. Phantom Images and Modern Manifestations: Spirit Photography, Magic Theater, Trick Films, and Photography's Uncanny. In *Fugitive Images: From Photography to Video,* ed. Patrice Petro, 42–71. Bloomington: Indiana University Press.

Hacking, Ian. 1982. Biopower and the Avalanche of Numbers. *Humanities in Society* 5, nos. 3–4: 279–95.

———. 1990. *The Taming of Chance.* Cambridge: Cambridge University Press.

———. 1996. Automatisme Ambulatoire: Fugue, Hysteria, and Gender at the Turn of the Century. *Modernism/Modernity* 3, no. 2: 31–43.

Hanson, Ellis. 1997. *Decadence and Catholicism.* Cambridge, MA: Harvard University Press.

Harris, Ruth. 1989. *Murders and Madness: Medicine, Law, and Society in the Fin de Siècle.* Oxford: Clarendon Press.

———. 1999. *Lourdes: Body and Spirit in the Secular Age.* Harmondsworth: Penguin.

Higginbotham, Ann R. 1992. "Sin of the Age": Infanticide and Illegitimacy in Victorian London. In *Victorian Scandals: Representations of Gender and Class,* ed. Kristine Ottesen Garrigan, 257–88. Athens: Ohio University Press.

Hobsbawm, Eric, and Terence Ranger, eds. 1992. *The Invention of Tradition.* Cambridge: Cambridge University Press.

Horn, David. 2003. *The Criminal Body: Lombroso and the Anatomy of Difference.* New York: Routledge.

Hull, Isabel. 1996. *Sexuality, State, and Civil Society in Germany, 1700–1815.* Ithaca, NY: Cornell University Press.

Hunt, Lynn. 1992. *The Family Romance of the French Revolution.* Berkeley: University of California Press.

Iaccarino, Bianca. 1996. Il rapporto uomo-donna nell'ipotismo di fine Ottocento: Attrazione, seduzione, amore. In *La presenza dimenticata: Il femminile nell'Italia moderna fra storia, letteratura, filosofia,* ed. Graziella Pagliano, 163–85. Milan: Franco Angeli.

Jackson, Mark. 2002. The Trial of Harriet Vooght: Continuity and Change in the History of Infanticide. In *Infanticide: Historical Perspectives on Child Murder and Concealment, 1500–2000,* ed. Mark Jackson, 1–17. Aldershot, Hauts, UK: Ashgate.

James, Henry. 1969. Matilde Serao. In *Notes on Novelists, with Some Other Notes,* 294–313. New York: Biblo & Tannen.

———. 1986. *Daisy Miller.* London: Penguin Books.

Kafka, Franz. 1970. *Sämtliche Erzählungen.* Frankfurt: Fischer Verlag.

Kern, Stephen. 2004. *A Cultural History of Causality: Science, Murder Novels, and Systems of Thought.* Princeton, NJ: Princeton University Press.

Kertzer, David I. 1993. *Sacrificed for Honor: Italian Infant Abandonment and the Politics of Reproductive Control.* Boston: Beacon Press.

King, W. D. 1997. "Shadow of a Mesmerizer": The Female Body on the "Dark" Stage. *Theatre Journal* 49:189–206.

Kittler, Friedrich. 1990. *Discourse Networks 1800/1900.* Trans. Michael Metteer and Chris Cullens. Stanford: Stanford University Press.

Kleist, Heinrich von. 1982. On the Marionette Theater. Trans. Christian-Albrecht Gollub. In *German Romantic Criticism,* ed. A. Leslie Willson. German Library, vol. 21, 238–44. New York: Continuum.

Kracauer, Siegfried. 1995. *The Mass Ornament: Weimar Essays.* Trans. ed., and intro. Thomas Y. Levin. Cambridge, MA: Harvard University Press.

Kramer, Rita. 1988. *Maria Montessori: A Biography.* Cambridge, MA: Perseus Publishing.

Krauss, Rosalind. 1978. Tracing Nadar. *October* 5:29–47.

Krueger, Christine L. 1997. Literary Defenses and Medical Prosecutions: Representing Infanticide in Nineteenth-Century Britain. *Victorian Studies* 40, no. 2: 271–94.

Labriola, Antonio. 1970. *Scritti politici.* Bari: Laterza.

Lacan, Jacques. 1992. *The Ethics of Psychoanalysis: The Seminar of Jacques Lacan, Book VII.* Trans. Dennis Porter. New York: W. W. Norton.

LaCapra, Dominick. 1989. *Soundings in Critical Theory.* Ithaca, NY: Cornell University Press.

———. 1994. *Representing the Holocaust: History, Theory, Trauma.* Ithaca, NY: Cornell University Press.

———. 2001. Trauma, Absence, Loss. In *Writing History, Writing Trauma,* 43–85. Baltimore: Johns Hopkins University Press.

Lama, Luisa. 2002. Maria Montessori nell'Italia fascista: Un compromesso fallito. *Il Risorgimento: Rivista di storia del Risorgimento e di storia contemporanea* 54, no. 2: 309–41.

Lanaro, Silvio. 1980. *Nazione e lavoro: Saggio sulla cultura borghese in Italia 1870–1925.* 2nd ed. Venice: Marsilio Editori.

Landolfi, Elena. 1981. *Scipio Sighele: un giobertiano fra democrazia nazionale e socialismo tricolore.* Rome: G. Volpe.

Lang, Berel. 1978. Style as Instrument, Style as Person. *Critical Inquiry* 4, no. 4: 715–39.

———. 1979.Looking for the Styleme. In *The Concept of Style,* ed. Berel Lang, 174–82. Ithaca, NY: Cornell University Press.

Leopardi, Giacomo. 1998. *Discorso sopra lo stato presente dei costumi degl'italiani.* Milan: Biblioteca Universale Rizzoli.

Leschiutta, Pierpaolo. 1996. *"Palimsesti del carcere": Cesare Lombroso e le scritture proibite.* Naples: Liguori Editore.

Lévi-Strauss, Claude. 1981. *Tristes Tropiques.* New York: Atheneum.

Lombroso, Cesare. 1895. *Grafologia.* Milan: Ulrico Hoepli.

———. 1896. The Savage Origin of Tattooing. *Popular Science Monthly,* April, 793–803.

———. 1899. Il delinquente ed il pazzo nel dramma e nel romanzo moderno. *Nuova Antologia* 79:665–81.

———. 1902. *Nuovi studi sul genio.* Palermo-Naples: Sandron.

———. 1932. Osservazioni sul mondo esterno e sull'io: Diario giovanile di Cesare Lombroso (1854–1857). *Archivio di antropologia criminale, psichiatria e medicina legale,* March 20, 3–39.

———. 1988. *After Death—What? Researches in Hypnotic and Spiritualistic Phenomena.* Trans. William Sloane Kennedy. Wellingborough, Northhamptonshire, UK: Aquarian Press.

———. 1996. *Palimsesti del carcere: Storie, messaggi, iscrizioni, graffiti dei detenuti delle carceri alla fine dell'Ottocento.* Florence: Ponte alle Grazie.

———. 1998. *Gli anarchici: Psicopatologia criminale d'un ideale politico.* Milan: Claudio Gallone Editore.

———. 2000a. Claustrofobia e claustrofilia. In *Delitto, genio, follia: Scritti scelti,* ed. Delia Frigessi, Ferruccio Giacanelli, and Luisa Mangoni. Torino: Bollati Bolinghieri.

———. 2000b. *Delitto, genio, follia: Scritti scelti.* Ed. Delia Frigessi, Ferruccio Giacanelli, and Luisa Mangoni. Turin: Bollato Boringhieri.

———. 2004.Criminal Anthropology: Its Origins and Application. In *The Criminal Anthropological Writings of Cesare Lombroso Published in the English Language Periodical Literature during the Late 19th and Early 20th Centuries,* ed. David M. Horton and Katherine E. Rich, 63–82. Lewiston, NY: Edwin Mellen Press.

Lombroso, Cesare, and Guglielmo Ferrero. 1923. *La donna delinquente: La prostituta e la donna normale.* 4th ed. Turin: Fratelli Bocca.

Lombroso, Cesare, Enrico Ferri, Raffaele Garofalo, and Giulio Fioretti. 1886. *Polemica in difesa della scuola positiva.* Bologna: Zanichelli.

Lombroso-Ferrero, Gina. 1915. *Cesare Lombroso: Storia della vita e delle opere narrata dalla figlia*. Turin: Bocca.

Loos, Adolf. 1998. *Ornament and Crime: Selected Essays*. Riverside, CA: Ariadne Press.

Madrignani, Carlo Alberto. 1980. *Rosso e nero a Montecitorio: Il romanzo parlamentare della nuova Italia (1861–1901)*. Florence: Vallecchi.

Maggio Serra, Rosanna. 1982. Il borgo del Valentino: Repertorio del gotico piemontese. Preface to *Borgo e castello medioevali in Turino,* by Adolfo Frizzi, ix–xv. Turin: Bottega D'Erasmo.

Maggio Serra, Rosanna, ed. 1985. *Torino 1884: Perchè un castello medioevale? Precisazioni e guida*. Turin: Musei civici.

Marey, Etienne-Jules. 1876. Lectures on the Graphic Method in the Experimental Sciences, and on Its Special Application to Medicine, Delivered at the Medical Congress in Brussels, September 21st, 1875. *British Medical Journal,* January 15, 65–66.

Mazzini, Giuseppe. 1906–1943. La filosofia della musica. In *Scritti editi ed inediti,* vol. 8, 119–65. Imola: Cooperativa tipografico-editrice Paolo Galeati.

Mazzoni, Cristina. 1997. Parturition, Parting, and Paradox in Turn-of-the-Century Italian Literature (D'Annunzio, Aleramo, Neera). *Forum Italicum* 31, no. 2:343–66.

Mazzotta, Giuseppe. 1986. *The World at Play in Boccaccio's Decameron*. Princeton, NJ: Princeton University Press.

Mellusi, Vincenzo. 1937. *Madri doloranti: L'incosciente nella dinamica del delitto*. Naples: Alberto Morano Editore.

Meyer, Leonard B. 1979. Towards a Theory of Style. In *The Concept of Style,* ed. Berel Lang, 21–71. Ithaca, NY: Cornell University Press.

Michels, Robert. 1912. *I limiti della morale sessuale*. Turin: Fratelli Bocca.

Miller, Alice. 1981. *The Drama of the Gifted Child: How Narcissistic Parents Form and Deform the Emotional Lives of Their Talented Children*. New York: Basic Books.

Miller, Pavla. 1998. *Transformations of Patriarchy in the West, 1500–1900*. Bloomington: Indiana University Press.

Moe, Nelson. 2002. *The View from Vesuvius: Italian Culture and the Southern Question*. Berkeley: University of California Press.

Montessori, Maria. 1904. L'influenza delle condizioni di famiglia sul livello intellettuale degli scolari: Ricerche d'igiene a antropologia pedagogiche in rapporto all'educazione. *Rivista di filosofia e scienze affini* 2:3–4.

———. 1907. Arte educativa. *La Vita,* August 6.

———. 1910. *Antropologia pedagogica*. Milan: Valardi.

———. 1932. Programma. *Montessori: Rivista bimestrale dell'Opera Montessori* 1, no. 2: 67–70.

———. 1964. *The Montessori Method*. New York: Schocken Books.

———. 1972. *Formazione dell'uomo*. Milan: Garzanti.

———. 1988. Come si insegna a leggere e a scrivere nelle "Case dei Bambini" a Roma. *Il Quaderno Montessori* 5, no. 17 (Spring): 94–103.

———. 1995a. Il saluto delle donne italiane. In *La giovane Montessori,* ed. Enzo Catarsi. Ferrara: Corso Editore.

———. 1995b. I principi fondamentali del metodo, 1914. In *La giovane Montessori,* ed. Catarsi.

———. 1995c. La morale sessuale nell'educazione. In *La giovane Montessori,* ed. Catarsi.

———. 1995d. La questione femminile e il Congresso di Londra. In *La giovane Montessori,* ed. Catarsi.

———. 1995e. La via e l'orizzonte del femminismo. In *La giovane Montessori,* ed. Catarsi.

———. 1995f. L'educazione dei piccoli degenerati. In *La giovane Montessori,* ed. Catarsi.

———. 1995g. Miserie sociali e novi ritrovati della scienza. In *La giovane Montessori,* ed. Catarsi.

———. 2000. *Il metodo della Pedagogia Scientifica applicato all'educazione infantile nelle Case dei bambini.* Critical ed. Rome: Edizioni Opera Nazionale Montessori.

Moore, Barrington. 1993. *The Social Origins of Dictatorship and Democracy: Lord and Peasant in the Making of the Modern World.* New York: Beacon Press.

Morelli, Giovanni. 1995. *Italian Painters: Critical Studies of Their Works.* Excerpted in *Art History and Its Methods,* ed. Eric Fernie, 106–15. New York: Phaidon Press.

Morselli, Enrico. 1886. *Il magnetismo animale: la fascinazione egli stati ipnotici.* Turin: Roux e Favale.

Mosse, George. 1996. *The Image of Man: The Creation of Modern Masculinity.* New York: Oxford University Press.

Mosso, Angelo. 1891. La fatica e la legge dell'esaurimento. *Nuova Antologia* 33:262–80.

———. 1892. La riforma della ginnastica. *Nuova Antologia* 121:237–67.

———. 1894. *L'educazione fisica della gioventù.* Milan: Treves.

———. 1897a. Le cagioni della effeminatezza Latina. *Nuova Antologia* 72:249–65.

———. 1897b. L'esaurimento nervoso. *Nuova Antologia* 127:201–18.

———. 1903. *Mens sana in corpore sano.* Milan: Treves.

Nancy, Jean-Luc. 1991. *The Inoperative Community.* Trans. Peter Connor, Lisa Garbus, Michael Holland, and Simona Sawhney. Minneapolis: University of Minnesota Press.

Nathan, Ernesto. 1998. *Scritti politici.,* ed. A. M. Isastia. Foggia: Bastogi.

Nelson, Victoria. 2001. *The Secret Life of Puppets.* Cambridge, MA: Harvard University Press.

Nietzsche, Friedrich. 1967a. *The Case of Wagner.* New York: Vintage Books.

———. 1967b *On the Genealogy of Morals.* Trans. Walter Kaufmann. New York: Vintage Books.

Noakes, Richard. 2002. "Instruments to Lay Hold of Spirits": Technologizing the Bodies of Victorian Spiritualism. In *Bodies/Machines,* ed. Iwan Rhys Morus, 125–63. New York: Berg.

Owen, Alex. 1990. *The Darkened Room: Women, Power and Spiritualism in Late Victorian England.* Philadelphia: University of Pennsylvania Press.

Pacifici, Vincenzo. 1986. L'amministrazione Nathan: Il problema edilizio. In *Roma nell'età giolittiana: L'amministrazione Nathan: Atti del Convegno di Studio (Roma, 28–30 maggio 1984),* curated by the Istituto per la Storia del Risorgimento italiano, 198–252. Rome: Edizioni dell'Ateneo.

Pagliani, Luigi. 1876. *Sopra alcuni fattori dello sviluppo umano: Ricerche antropometriche.* Turin: Stamperia reale di Torino.

———. 1913. *Trattato di igiene e di sanità pubblica colle applicazioni alla ingegneria e alla vigilanza.* 2 vols. Milan: Casa Editrice Francesco Vallardi.

Parssinen, Terry. 1977. Mesmeric Performers. *Victorian Studies* 21:87–104.

Patriarca, Silvana. 1998. Gender Trouble: Women and the Making of Italy's "Active Population," 1861–1936. *Journal of Modern Italian Studies* 3, no. 2: 144–63.

———. 2003. *Numbers and Nationhood: Writing Statistics in Nineteenth-Century Italy.* Cambridge: Cambridge University Press.

———. 2005. Indolence and Regeneration: Tropes and Tensions of Risorgimento Patriotism. *American Historical Review* 110, no. 2: 380–408.

Pazzi, Muzio. 1913a. *Disordini psichici della donna in rapporto con le funzioni sessuali normali e patologiche.* Bologna: Gamberini & Parmeggiani.

———. 1913b. *Il Sanatorio materno: Progetto schematico.* Bologna: Gamberini & Parmeggiani.

———. 1913c. La personalità psichica muliebre in rapporto ai reati di infanticidio o di procurato aborto. *Gazzetta italiana delle levatrici,* 9.

———. 1913d. Per la profilassi dell'aborto criminoso e dell'infanticidio. *Lucina,* 2–3. Bologna: Stabilimento poligrafico emiliano.

Pelaja, Maria. 1981. Istinto di vita e amore materno. *Memoria* 1:46–52.

Perella, Nicolas. 1986. An Essay on *Pinocchio. Italica* 63, no. 1: 1–47.

Perone-Capano, Raffaele. 1889. *L'infanticidio e l'esposizione d'infante nel loro significato onto-filogenetico.* Naples: Tipografia Cav. Aurelio Tocco.

Pierotti, G. L. 1981. Ecce Puer (Il libro senza frontispizio e senza indice). In *C'era una volta un pezzo di legno: La simbologia di Pinocchio,* 5–41. Milan: Emme Edizioni.

Pogliano, Claudio. 1984. L'utopia igienica (1870–1920). In *Malattia e medicina,* ed. F. Della Peruta. *Storia d'Italia, Annali 7.* Turin: Einaudi Editore.

Pomata, Gianna. 1980. Madri illegitime tra ottocento e novecento: storie cliniche e storie di vita. *Quaderni storici* 44:497–542.

Poovey, Mary. 1988. *Uneven Developments: The Ideological Work of Gender in Mid-Victorian England.* Chicago: University of Chicago Press.

Porciani, Ilaria. 1991. Il Plutarco femminile. In *L'educazione delle donne: Scuole e modelli di vita femminile nell'Italia dell'Ottocento,* ed. Simonetta Soldani, 297–317. Milan: Franco Angeli.

———. 1993. Stato e nazione: L'immagine debole dell'Italia. In *Fare gli ital-iani: scuola e cultura nell'Italia contemporanea,* ed. Simonetta Soldani and Gabriele Turi. Vol. 1: *La nascita dello stato nazionale,* 385–428. Milan: Il Mulino.

———. 1997. *La festa della nazione: Rappresentazione dello stato e spazi sociali nell'Italia unita.* Bologna: Il Mulino.

Preziosi, Donald. 1989. *Rethinking Art History: Meditations on a Coy Science.* New Haven, CT: Yale University Press.

Prezioso, Biagio. 1995. Introduction to *Cinematografo celebrale,* by Edmondo De Amicis, 7–24. Rome: Salerno Editrice.

Rabinbach, Anson. 1990. *The Human Motor: Energy, Fatigue, and the Origins of Modernity.* Berkeley: University of California Press.

Rak, Maria Giovanna. 1993. Documenti per la storia dei burattini nel secolo XIX. In *Pinocchio fra i burattini,* ed. Fernando Tempesti, 79–99. Florence: La Nuova Italia.

Rausky, Franklin. 1980. *Mesmer o la rivoluzione terapeutica.* Milan: Feltrinelli.

Ricci, Giovanni. 1984. Per una lettura del pensiero educativo di De Amicis. In *Non si sgomentino le signore . . . ,* by Edmondo De Amicis, ed. Pino Boero et al., 59–90. Genova: Tilgher-Genova.

Rodari, Gianni. 1976. Pinocchio nella letteratura per l'infanzia. In *Studi collodiani,* ed. Fondazione Nazionale "Carlo Collodi," 37–57. Pescia: Cassa di Risparmio di Pistoia e Pescia.

Romanelli, Raffaele. 1988. *Il commando impossibile: Stato e società nell'Italia liberale.* Bologna: Il Mulino.

Romano, Sergio. 1996. *Le Italie parallele: Perchè l'Italia non riesce a diventare un paese moderno.* Milan: Longanesi.

Rose, Jacqueline. 1993. *Why War?—Psychoanalysis, Politics, and the Return to Melanie Klein.* Oxford: Blackwell.

Rose, Lionel. 1986. *The Massacre of the Innocents: Infanticide in Britain 1800–1939.* London: Routledge & Kegan Paul.

Rusconi, Gian Enrico. 1993. *Se cessiamo di essere una nazione.* Bologna: Il Mulino.

Saba, Umberto. 2001. Scorciatoie. In *Tutte le prose.* Milan: Mondadori.

Sacher-Masoch, Leopold. 1991. Venus in Furs. In *Masochism,* trans. J. McNeil. Cambridge, MA: Zone Books.

Santner, Eric. 1996. *My Own Private Germany: Daniel Paul Schreber's Secret History of Modernity.* Princeton, NJ: Princeton University Press.

Scaraffia, Lucetta. 1990. *La santa degli impossibili: Vicende e significati della devozione a Santa Rita.* Turin: Rosenberg & Sellier.

———. 1999. "Christianity Has Liberated Her and Placed Her alongside Man in the Family": From 1850 to 1988 (Mulieris Dignitatem). In *Women and Faith: Catholic Religious Life in Italy from Late Antiquity to the Present,* ed.

Lucetta Scaraffia and Gabriella Zarri, 249–80. Cambridge, MA: Harvard University Press.

Scaraffia, Lucetta, and Gabriella Zarri, eds. 1999. *Women and Faith: Catholic Religious Life in Italy from Late Antiquity to the Present.* Cambridge, MA: Harvard University Press.

Schafer, Silvia. 1997. *Children in Moral Danger and the Problem of Government in Third Republic France.* Princeton, NJ: Princeton University Press.

Schiavone, Aldo. 1998. *Italiani senza Italia: Storia e identità.* Turin: Einaudi.

Schreber, Daniel Paul. 1988. *Memoirs of My Nervous Illness.* Cambridge, MA: Harvard University Press.

Schulte, Regina. 1984. Infanticide in Rural Bavaria in the Nineteenth Century. In *Interest and Emotion: Essays on the Study of Family and Kinship,* ed. Hans Medick and David W. Sabean, 300–316. Cambridge: Cambridge University Press.

Schwegman, Marja. 1999. *Maria Montessori.* Bologna: Il Mulino.

Scocchera, Augusto. 1990. *Maria Montessori: Quasi un ritratto inedito.* Scandicci (Florence): La Nuova Italia Editrice.

Segel, H. B. 1995. *Pinocchio's Progeny.* Baltimore: Johns Hopkins University Press.

Sekula, Allan. 1986. The Body and the Archive. *October,* Winter, 3–64.

Selmini, Rossella. 1987. *Profili di uno studio storico sull'infanticidio: Esame di 31 processi per infanticidio giudicati dalla corte d'assise di Bologna dal 1880 al 1913.* Milan: Dott. A. Giuffrè Editore.

Serao, Matilde. 1992. *The Conquest of Rome.* Ed. Ann Caesar. New York: New York University Press.

———. 1997. *La conquista di Roma.* Rome: Bulzoni Editore.

———. 2002. *Il ventre di Napoli.* Cava de' Tirreni: Avagliano Editore.

Sergi, Giuseppe. 1914. Alcune idee sull'educazione. *La Nuova Antologia* 49, March 1, 65–69.

Sighele, Scipio. 1889. Sull'infanticidio. *Archivio giuridico* 42:177–209.

———. 1893. *La coppia criminale: Studio di psicologia morbosa.* Turin: Fratelli Bocca.

———. 1893–1894. Il dramma di Mezzojuso. In *Il mondo criminale italiano,* ed. Augusto G. Bianchi, Guglielmo Ferrero, and Scipio Sighele. 3 vols., 13–57. Milan: L. Omodei Zorini Editore.

———. 1913. *Morale privata e morale politica.* Milan: Fratelli Treves.

———. 1923. *I delitti della folla studiati secondo la Psicologia, il Diritto e la Giurisprudenza.* 5th, enlarged ed. Turin: Fratelli Bocca.

Smirnoff, Victor. 1995. The Masochistic Contract. In *Essential Papers on Masochism,* ed. M. A. F. Hanly, 62–73. New York: New York University Press.

Sòrgoni, Barbara. 1998. *Parole e corpi: antropologia, discorso giuridico e politiche sessuali interrazziali nella colonia Eritrea (1890–1941).* Naples: Liguori Editore.

Standing, Edwin M. 1957. *Maria Montessori: Her Life and Work*. New York: Penguin Books.

Steedman, Carolyn. 1985. Prisonhouses. *Feminist Review* 20:7–21.

Steinberg, Michael, and Suzanne Stewart-Steinberg. 2006. Fascism and the Operatic Unconscious. In *Opera and Society in Italy and France from Monteverdi to Bordieu*, ed. Victoria Johnson, Jane Fulcher, and Thomas Ertman, 267–88. Cambridge: Cambridge University Press.

Stewart, Suzanne R. 1998. *Sublime Surrender: Male Masochism at the Fin-de-Siècle*. Ithaca, NY: Cornell University Press.

Stewart-Steinberg, Suzanne. 2007. Girls Will Be Boys: Envy, Gender and the Freudian Social Contract. *differences* 18, no. 2.

Stone, Jennifer. 1994. Pinocchio and Pinocchiology. *American Imago* 51, no. 3: 329–42.

Stoppato, Alessandro. 1887. *Infanticidio e procurato aborto*. Verona: Drucker & Tedeschi.

Studlar, Gaylin. 1980. *In the Realm of Pleasure: Von Sternberg, Dietrich and the Masochistic Aesthetic*. New York: Columbia University Press.

Surkis, Judith. 2006. *Sexing the Citizen: Morality and Masculinity in France, 1870–1920*. Ithaca, NY: Cornell University Press.

Susman, Warren I. 1984. *Culture as History: The Transformation of American Society in the 20th Century*. New York: Pantheon Books.

Tausk, Victor. 1991. On the Origin of the "Influencing Machine" in Schizophrenia. In *Sexuality, War and Schizophrenia: Collected Psychoanalytic Papers*, ed. Paul Roazen, 185–219. New Brunswick, NJ: Transaction Publishers.

Tempesti, Fernando, ed. 1993. *Pinocchio fra i burattini*. Atti del convegno del 27–28 marzo, 1987. Florence: La Nuova Italia.

Toesca, Pietro. 1997. La filosofia di Pinocchio, ovvero l'Odissea di un ragazzo per bene con la memoria di burattino. *Forum Italicum* 31, no. 2: 459–86.

Torino e l'Esposizione italiana del 1884. Cronaca illustrata della esposizione nazionale-industriale ed artistica del 1884. Turin-Milan: Roux e Favale & Treves, 1884.

Trabalzini, Paola. 2000. *Il Metodo della pedagogia scientifica: Genesi e sviluppi*. In *Il metodo della Pedagogia Scientifica applicato all'educazione infantile nelle Case dei bambini*, by Maria Montessori, xlv–lxix. Rome: Edizioni Opera Nazionale Montessori.

———. 2003. *Maria Montessori: Da* Il metodo *a* La scoperta del bambino. Rome: Aracne Editrice.

Tullio-Altan, Carlo. 1989. *Populismo e trasformismo: Saggio sulle ideologie politiche italiane*. Milan: Feltrinelli.

———. 1995. *Italia: Una nazione senza religione civile*. Udine: Istituto Editoriale Veneto Friuliano.

Turi, Monica. 1987. La costruzione di un nuovo modello di comportamento femminile: Maria Goretti tra cronaca nera e agiografia. *Movimento operaio e socialista* 3:223–36.

Turiello, Pasquale. 1994. *Sul carattere degli italiani.* Rome: Calice Editore.

Valentini, Daria. 1990. Amore e ginnastica. *Annali d'italianistica* 16:103–19.

van Ginneken, Jaap. 1992. *Crowds, Psychology, and Politics, 1871–1899.* Cambridge: Cambridge University Press.

Velicogna, Nella. 1986. *Scipio Sighele: dalla criminologia alla sociologia del diritto e della politica.* Milano: A. Giuffrè.

Villa, Renzo. 1985. *Il deviante e i suoi segni: Lombroso e la nascita dell'antropologia criminale.* Milan: Franco Angeli.

Violi, Alessandra. 2005. Storie di fantasmi per adulti: Lombroso e le tecnologie dello spettrale. In *Locus Solus: Lombroso e la fotografia,* ed. Silvana Turzio, Renzo Villa and Alessandra Violi, 43–69. Milan: Bruno Mondadori.

Ward, Tony. 2002. Legislating for Human Nature: Legal Responses to Infanticide, 1860–1938. In *Infanticide: Historical Perspectives on Child Murder and Concealment, 1500–2000,* ed. Mark Jackson, 249–69. Aldershot, Hauts, UK: Ashgate.

West, Mark I. 1986. From the Pleasure Principle to the Reality Principle: Pinocchio's Psychological Journey. In *Proceedings of the Thirteenth Annual Conference of the Children's Literature Association,* ed. S. R. Gannon and R. A. Thompson, 112–15. Kansas City: University of Missouri–Kansas City:

Williams, Linda. 1986. Film Body: An Implementation of Perversions. In *Narrative, Apparatus, Ideology: A Film Theory Reader,* ed. Philip Rosen, 507–34. New York: Columbia University Press.

Winnicott, Donald W. 1971. *Playing and Reality.* London: Routledge.

Winter, Alison. 2000. *Mesmerized: Powers of Mind in Victorian Britain.* Chicago: University of Chicago Press.

Wollheim, Richard. 1973. Giovanni Morelli and the Origins of Scientific Connoisseurship. In *On Art and the Mind: Essays and Lectures,* 177–201. Cambridge, MA: Harvard University Press.

Wrightson, Keith. 1982. Infanticide in European History. *Criminal Justice History* 3, no. 1:1–20.

Yorick Figlio di Yorick [P. C. Ferrigni]. 1884. *La storia dei burattini.* Florence: Tipografia Editrice Fieromosca.

Zaccaria, Giuseppe. 1996. Introduction to *Palimsesti del carcere,* by Cesare Lombroso, 9–29. Florence: Ponte alle Grazie.

Zanichelli, Domenico. 1889. *Monarchia e papato in Italia.* Bologna: N. Zanichelli.

Zelizer, Viviana A. 1994. *Pricing the Priceless Child: The Changing Social Value of Children.* Princeton, NJ: Princeton University Press.

Žižek, Slavoj. 1989. *The Sublime Object of Ideology.* London: Verso Books.

———. 1992. *Enjoy Your Symptom! Jacques Lacan in Hollywood and Out.* New York: Routledge.

———. 1994a. The Spectre of Ideology. In *Mapping Ideology,* ed. Slavoj Žižek, 1–33. London: Verso Books.

———. 1994b. "The Wound Is Healed Only by the Spear That Smote You": The Operatic Subject and Its Vicissitudes. In *Opera through Other Eyes,* ed. David J. Levin, 177–214. Stanford, CA: Stanford University Press.
———. 2002. *Welcome to the Desert of the Real.* London: Verso.
———. 2003. *The Puppet and the Dwarf: The Perverse Core of Christianity.* Boston: MIT Press.

Index